YEATS

YEATS

HAROLD BLOOM

OXFORD UNIVERSITY PRESS
LONDON   OXFORD   NEW YORK

OXFORD UNIVERSITY PRESS

London   Oxford   New York
Glasgow   Toronto   Melbourne   Wellington
Cape Town   Ibadan   Nairobi   Dar es Salaam   Lusaka   Addis Ababa
Delhi   Bombay   Calcutta   Madras   Karachi   Lahore   Dacca
Kuala Lumpur   Singapore   Hong Kong   Tokyo

The generous permission of Senator Michael Yeats, A. P. Watt & Son, and The Macmillan Company for quotations from the following writings of W. B. Yeats, and of Miss Holly Stevens and Alfred A. Knopf, Inc. for quotations from the following writings of Wallace Stevens, is gratefully acknowledged:

The Variorum Edition of the Poems of W. B. Yeats, edited by Peter Allt and Russell K. Alspach, copyright 1903, 1906, 1907, 1912, 1916, 1918, 1919, 1924, 1928, 1931, 1933, 1934, 1935, 1940, 1944, 1945, 1946, 1950, 1956, 1957 by The Macmillan Company. Copyright 1940 by Georgie Yeats. Copyright © 1968 by Bertha Georgie Yeats and Anne Yeats.

Essays and Introductions, by W. B. Yeats, copyright © 1961 by Mrs. W. B. Yeats.

The Letters of W. B. Yeats, edited by Allan Wade, copyright © 1953, 1954 by Anne Butler Yeats.

Mythologies, by W. B. Yeats, copyright © 1959 by Mrs. W. B. Yeats.

A Vision, by W. B. Yeats, copyright 1937 by The Macmillan Company, renewed 1965 by Bertha Georgie Yeats and Anne Butler Yeats.

W. B. Yeats' Explorations, selected by Mrs. W. B. Yeats, copyright © 1962 by Mrs. W. B. Yeats.

Tea at the Palaz of Hoon and passages from *The Collected Poems of Wallace Stevens,* copyright 1923, 1931, 1954 by Wallace Stevens.

The Necessary Angel, copyright 1951 by Wallace Stevens.

Opus Posthumous, copyright © 1957 by Elsie Stevens and Holly Stevens.

Preface

Yeats was a poet very much in the line of vision; his ancestors in English poetic tradition were primarily Blake and Shelley, and his achievement will at last be judged against theirs. One of the purposes of this book is to initiate such a judgment, though no pretence is made toward completing it.

Yeats, Hardy, and Wallace Stevens seem to me the poets writing in English in our century whose work most merits sustained comparison with the major poets of the nineteenth century. I am aware that such an opinion will seem extreme to scholars and admirers of Eliot, Pound, Williams, Frost, Graves, Auden, and others, but the phenomenon of high contemporary reputations dying away permanently has occurred before, and will again. Donne and Shelley vanish for generations and are then revived, but Eliot and Pound may prove to be the Cowley and Cleveland of this age, and a puzzle therefore to future historians of our sensibilities. Though this book sets itself against the prevalent critical idolatry of Yeats, I do not believe that Yeats (or Stevens) will vanish as Eliot and Pound will, and I do not desire to deny the undoubted stature of Yeats's achievement. But I do want to set that achievement in a historical perspective, and to examine its quite genuine limitations more fully than I have seen them examined. It may be that Yeats is as good a poet as a bad time for the imagination could produce, but we will hardly learn the imaginative limitations of our own age if we inflate Yeats's value beyond all reasonable measure. One distinguished modern critic, R. P. Blackmur, asserted that Yeats was the most considerable lyric poet in the language since the seventeenth century, a judgment that is astonishing, but which has gone uncontroverted except by the equally distinguished critic Yvor Winters, who sensibly condemned Yeats as a talented but confused Romantic poet. I say "sensibly" because Yeats, as Winters accurately observed, was a Romantic poet who grew only more Romantic despite all his attempts to modify his tradition, and if you are as massively anti-Romantic a critic as Winters was, then you are as sensible to condemn Yeats as you are to discard Blake, Wordsworth or the later Wallace Stevens. What is not very sensible, but is still prevalent, is to praise Yeats for being what he was not, a poet of the Metaphysical kind.

Yeats's ideas, according to Winters, were contemptible; to the leading Yeats scholars, from Richard Ellmann to Thomas Whitaker, they were not, and if we have a common reader of poetry in our time, they do not appear so to him either. There is, I think, much nonsense in Yeats's ideas, and much that is necessarily pernicious from a humanistic (or even merely humane) point of view, but there is more wisdom than nonsense, and a humanistic perspective is not in itself wholly relevant to the mature Yeats, who deliberately went beyond it to a more drastic position, as Lawrence did also. Wallace Stevens is the representative humanistic poet of our time, and I think that he speaks directly to and for our condition as Yeats and Lawrence do not, but poets who present private apocalypses are representative of much that is central in this century also, and they have the special value of being thorough rebels against our culture. Yeats's rebellion was an equivocal one, but it was intense enough, and scholars who attempt to perpetuate humanistic tradition, whether of a secular or religious variety, ought to be a little warier of a play like *Purgatory* than they appear to be.

I have tried, in this book, to study the major relations of Yeats's work to English poetic tradition, rather than to any of the esoteric traditions that Yeats clearly invokes. Whitaker in particular among Yeats's critics has made a strong case for the relevance of certain esoteric traditions to Yeats's work, but the greater relevance of poetic tradition to a poet seems to me inescapable. Yeats attempted to be a spiritual alchemist, but he became a visionary poet, though an inconstant one.

As this is a prolegomenon to a larger study of poetic influence, in addition to being a critical reading of Yeats, I have attempted the experiment of beginning the book with approaches to Yeats down several nearly parallel paths. Full discussion of Yeats's work does not commence until part way through Chapter 6. The first five chapters are meant to give mutually supportive views of distinct problems of influence; for instance, Shelley's *Alastor,* its tradition and effect upon Yeats, is discussed in three separate but related contexts in Chapters 1, 4, and 6, and receives later consideration in Chapters 9 and 13. Blake's influence is studied throughout, as well as Shelley's, and to a lesser extent Pater's. The two other important literary influences upon Yeats, Nietzsche's and Balzac's, should be studied separately, as they present critical problems of another kind. Those influences that came to Yeats from the Spirit of our Age are described in Richard Ellmann's *Eminent Domain.* The equally belated influence of eighteenth-century Anglo-Irish prose writers has been discussed by many scholars, but also is omitted here because there is something factitious about it. Unlike the Romantic tradition, it did not find Yeats; he tried to impose it upon himself, with dubious results.

The discussion of Yeats's work in this book is arranged in a rough chronology, except for the placement of the chapters on *A Vision,* which are inserted at about the point of the first full formulation of Yeats's "system," rather than at the time of the actual composition and publication of either version that Yeats completed. I have grouped my discussions of the plays, which has disturbed chronology also, in a few places.

My debts to the scholarly criticism devoted to Yeats are abundant, and I hope recorded throughout this book. I am grateful to the John Simon Guggenheim Memorial Foundation and its President, Gordon N. Ray, for a Fellowship during the academic year 1962–3 that enabled me to write the first draft of this book. I am grateful also to the Society for the Humanities, Cornell University, and its director, Max Black, for a Fellowship during the academic year 1968–9, which permitted me to complete the final draft, and to continue my study of poetic influence.

For Richard Ellmann and Martin Price

Contents

x

YEATS

I looked and saw between us and the sun
A building on an island; such a one
As age to age might add, for uses vile,
A windowless, deformed and dreary pile;
And on the top an open tower, where hung
A bell, which in the radiance swayed and swung.

        · · ·

"And such,"—he cried, "is our mortality,
And this must be the emblem and the sign
Of what should be eternal and divine!—
And like that dark and dreary bell, the soul,
Hung in a heaven-illumined tower, must toll
Our thoughts and our desires to meet below
Round the rent heart and pray—as madmen do
For what? they know not,—till the night of death
As sunset that strange vision, severeth
Our memory from itself, and us from all
We sought and yet were baffled."

            Shelley, *Julian and Maddalo*, 98–103, 120–30

What in the midst lay but the Tower itself?
  The round squat turret, blind as the fool's heart,
  Built of brown stone, without a counterpart
In the whole world. The tempest's mocking elf
Points to the shipman thus the unseen shelf
  He strikes on, only when the timbers start.

  Browning, *Childe Roland to the Dark Tower Came*

  I shall find the dark grow luminous, the void
fruitful when I understand I have nothing, that the
ringers in the tower have appointed for the hymen
of the soul a passing bell.

            Yeats, *Per Amica Silentia Lunae*

1: Introduction

Dr. Johnson, despite his profound understanding of the relations between poets, was too involved in his own relation to Milton to understand fully that particular case of poetic influence. Except for the Founder, Freud, we do not expect any doctor of the mind to analyze his own case, or even necessarily to see that he constitutes a case. Even so, when a poet is also a gifted critic, we rightly do not expect him to know or describe accurately what his relation to his precursors is. We need to be warier than we have been in contemplating such a poet-critic's portraits of his precursors, for the portraits necessarily show us not what the precursors were, but what the poet-critic needed them to have been.

The most remarkable such portrait in poetic history that I know is the cosmic one rendered of Milton by Blake throughout his work, but particularly in the "brief epic" called *Milton*. Blake's Milton is the Poet proper, the heroic Bard whose inspiration is absolute, and whose achievement stands as a second Scripture, all but as sacred as Scripture itself. Blake, in *The Marriage of Heaven and Hell,* entered upon a massive re-interpretation of Milton that almost every modern scholar has judged to be a misinterpretation. So I suppose it is, as all significant reading of one creator by another must be. Poets, or at least strong poets, do not read one another even as the strongest of critics read poetry. Poetic influence is a labyrinth that our criticism scarcely begins to explore. Borges, the scholar of labyrinths, has given us the first principle for the investigation of poetic influence:

> In the critics' vocabulary, the word "precursor" is indispensable, but it should be cleansed of all connotation of polemics or rivalry. The fact is that every writer *creates* his own precursors. His work modifies our conception of the past, as it will modify the future. In this correlation the identity or plurality of the men involved is unimportant.[1]

Though the theory of poetic influence I pursue swerves sharply from Borges, it accepts the poet's *creation* of his precursors as starting point. But the relation of ephebe or new poet to his precursors cannot be cleansed of polemics or rivalry, noble as the aesthetic idealism of Borges is, because the relation is not clean. Poetic influence, to many critics, is just something that happens, a transmission of ideas and images, and whether or not influence causes anxiety in the later poet is regarded as a problem of temperament or circumstance. But the ephebe cannot be Adam early in the morning. There have been too many Adams, and they have named everything. The burden of unnaming prompts the true wars fought under the banner of poetic influence, wars waged by the perversity of the spirit against the wealth accumulated by the spirit, the wealth of tradition. This chapter intends first to suggest some aspects of these wars, and next to trace a particular line of poetic influencing that moves from Milton to Wordsworth to Shelley and then on to Browning and Yeats. Chapter 4 will tell the story of the early influence of Shelley on Yeats, and the whole body of this book will tell the continuous story of the lifelong influence of Shelley, Blake, and Romantic tradition in general upon Yeats, but these stories, to be coherent, must rely upon some understanding of the problem of poetic influence, and of the particular kind of Romantic tradition within which Yeats was influenced. Most specifically, Yeats's immediate tradition could be described as the internalization of quest romance, and Yeats's most characteristic kind of poem could be called the dramatic lyric of internalized quest, the genre of *Sailing to Byzantium, Vacillation,* and many of the *Supernatural Songs,* and indeed of most of Yeats's major works.

Poetic influence, as I conceive it, is a variety of melancholy or an anxiety-principle. It concerns the poet's sense of his precursors, and of his own achievement in relation to theirs. Have they left him room enough, or has their priority cost him his art? More crucially, where did they go wrong, so as to make it possible for him to go right? In this revisionary sense, in which the poet creates his own precursors by necessarily misinterpreting them, poetic influence forms and malforms new poets, and aids their art at the cost of increasing, finally, their already acute sense of isolation. Critics of a Platonizing kind (in the broad sense, which would include such splendid critics as Borges, Frye, Wilson Knight) refuse to see poetic influence as anxiety because they believe in different versions of what Frye calls the Myth of Concern: "We belong to something before we are anything, nor does growing in being diminish the link of belonging." So, a poet's reputation and influence, that is, what others think he is, is his real self. Milton is what he creates and gives. I urge the contrary view, for the melancholy only the strongest of poets overcome is that they too must belong to something before they are anything, and the link is never diminished. As scholars we can accept what grieves us as isolate egos, but poets do not exist to accept griefs. Freud thought all men unconsciously wished to beget themselves, to be their own fathers in place of their phallic fathers, and so "rescue" their mothers from erotic degradation. It may not be true of all men, but it seems to be definitive of poets *as poets*. The poet, if he could, would be his own precursor, and so rescue the Muse from her degradation. In this sense, poetic influence is analogous to Romantic love; both processes are illuminated by Patmore's egregious remark: "What a Lover sees in the Beloved is the projected shadow of his own potential beauty in the eyes of God." This is certainly what the ephebe or potential poet sees in his precursor, and is akin to Valéry's observations: "One only reads well when one reads with some quite personal goal in mind. It may be to acquire some power. It can be out of hatred for the author."

Reading well, for a strong or potentially strong poet, is necessarily to read as a revisionist. This is particularly true in a tradition like the Romantic, where the poet becomes so haunted by himself, that he begins to present himself as the unique problem. As strength increases, the poet can read only himself, for he contains his own antagonist, a blocking agent or element in his creativity that has gone over to restriction and hardness. Several Romantic poets have named this blocking figure, Blake most notably when he called it the Covering Cherub. Before the Fall (which for Blake is before the Creation, the two events being one) the Covering Cherub was the pastoral figure Blake named Tharmas, a unifying process making for undivided consciousness—the innocence, pre-reflective, of a state without subjects and objects, yet in no danger of solipsism, for it lacked also a consciousness of self. Tharmas is a poet's (or any man's) power of realization, even as the Covering Cherub is the power that blocks realization.

In later chapters of this book, on Blake and Yeats and on *A Vision,* I shall explore Yeats's interpretation of the Covering Cherub, his view of that figure as he found it in Blake. Blake took the Covering Cherub from Ezekiel, who denounces the figure as a former protector of Eden now become an enemy of the truth, a guardian keeping man from Eden. In a passage of Blake's *Milton* that profoundly affected Yeats, a whole catalog of imaginative error is recited, and its dwelling-place named:

> All these are seen in Miltons Shadow who is the Covering Cherub
> The Spectre of Albion in which the Spectre of Luvah inhabits.
> In the Newtonian voids between the Substances of Creation.[2]

Milton's Shadow here partly means his influence upon later poets, for his Shadow, in being identified with the Covering Cherub, becomes one with everything in the fallen world that blocks imaginative redemption. Milton too is a guardian of the truth who has become, in spite of himself, an anxiety-principle or demonic agent. In this book, I follow in the tradition of Blake and Yeats by employing the Covering Cherub as the emblem of the negative or stifling aspect of poetic influence. As such, this figure of creative anxiety is akin to the Sphinx, emblem of sexual anxiety, who came dangerously close to becoming Yeats's Muse. Though the Sphinx appears more explicitly than the Covering Cherub in Yeats's poetry, the Cherub manifests itself in many forms, tending to appear whenever Yeats invokes his precursors in his poetry.

Before passing to a consideration of the specific line of poetic influence that led to Yeats, one point raised often in this book requires early clarification. The revisionary readings of precursors that are involved in Yeats's poems and essays are not being condemned by me, in anything that follows. They are taken instead as a series of swerves away from the precursors, swerves intended to uncover the Cherub, to free Yeats from creative anxieties. Sometimes, for shorthand, I will call them by the Lucretian term *clinamen,* taking Blake's and Jarry's different uses of this principle of swerving as my precedents. These examples of the *clinamen* can help us understand Yeats's poems, or the poems of any poet when we read those poems in relation to their ancestors. One purpose of the analyses of Yeats's poems and plays offered by this volume is to suggest a newer kind of practical criticism, one which results directly from an awareness of each poet's own relation to his precursors. It is perhaps inevitable that Yeats, the conscious heir of the Romantics, compels us to a new kind of critical study of Romantic influence.

From this necessarily fragmented account of a working theory of poetic influence, I pass to the history of a particular element in the Romantic line of poetic influence. Where did Yeats's characteristic kind of poem come from? Yeats's most typical poem is a dramatic lyric that behaves as though it were a fragment in a mythological romance, as though the poet himself as quest-hero undertook continually an odyssey of the spirit. There is a tendency throughout later Romantic poetry for this pattern to establish itself. Among poets of our century, Stevens, Lawrence, Hart Crane and others, as well as Yeats, show it in their very different ways. Poets of the middle Romantic generations—Shelley, Keats, Whitman, Browning—developed this pattern, directly or indirectly, through encounter with its Wordsworthian original, the Solitary of *The Excursion.* But we need to go further back, to Milton, to understand the origins of Wordsworth's Solitary, who may be called the first *antithetical* quester, in Yeats's difficult sense of *antithetical*.

Except for *Paradise Lost,* Milton's most influential poems were the two matching or contrary octosyllabics, *L'Allegro* and *Il Penseroso*. This truism of literary history rewards continuous pondering, for why did these two poems in particular engender so extraordinary and long-lasting a progeny, from Parnell's *A Hymn to Contentment* in 1714 through Thomson, Dyer, Collins, Gray, the Wartons, Smart (to mention only the principal figures) on to Keats's *Fancy,* Clare's *Solitude* and Shelley's wonderful *To Jane: The Invitation* in 1822? All these are only overt imitations; more important is the profound kind of influence exerted by the *Allegro-Penseroso* pairing on the general structure of the eighteenth-century sublime ode, on Blake and on Wordsworth. Foster Damon usefully surmised that the archetype for Blake's idea of matching, contrary *Songs of Innocence and Experience* is Milton's pairing, and the suggestion for Blake may have been a prolonged one, as the Miltonic poems continue to inform the vision of the contrary states of being, Beulah and Generation, in Blake's major poems. The influence on Wordsworth of the octosyllabics is the most important of all these, for subsequent poetic history. There is no direct influence whatsoever of Milton or Wordsworth upon Yeats, but the single poem that most affected his life and art (and Browning's as well) is Shelley's *Alastor,* and the line leading to *Alastor* and its remorseless version of Romantic quest goes from *Il Penseroso* through Wordsworth's *Excursion*.

Both *L'Allegro* and *Il Penseroso* emerge from the mode of pastoral romance, and become, as Geoffrey Hartman says, a new kind of romance in their creation of a *persona* or presiding consciousness:

> Who is the speaker here if not a magus, dismissing some spirits and invoking others? . . . With Milton the Spirit of Romance begins to simplify itself. It becomes the creative spirit. . . . *L'Allegro* and *Il Penseroso* are . . . romantic monologues. They show a mind moving from one position to another and projecting an image of its freedom against a darker, daemonic ground.[3]

These illuminating observations clarify the origins of a great sub-tradition, of the Romantic magus or quester who pursues the image of his mind's freedom only to subside at last into the context of the darker, daemonic ground. This is a sub-tradition that Yeats ended in himself, though we may read its satyr-play in Stevens's *The Comedian as the Letter C*. What moved most the imagination of the young Yeats was a vision that begins in *Il Penseroso*:

> But first, and chiefest, with thee bring,
> Him that yon soars on golden wing,
> Guiding the fiery-wheeled throne,
> The Cherub Contemplation,
> And the mute Silence hist along,
> 'Less *Philomel* will daign a Song,
>
> . . . .
>
> I woo to hear thy Eeven-Song;
> And missing thee, I walk unseen
> On the dry smooth-shaven Green,
> To behold the wandring Moon,
> Riding neer her highest noon,
> Like one that had bin led astray
> Through the Heav'ns wide pathles way;
>
> . . . .
>
> Or let my Lamp at midnight hour,
> Be seen in som high lonely Towr,
> Where I may oft out-watch the *Bear*,
> With thrice great *Hermes*, or unsphear
> The spirit of Plato to unfold
> What Worlds, or what vast Regions hold
> The immortal mind that hath forsook
> Her mansion in this fleshly nook:
> And of those *Daemons* that are found
> In fire, air, flood, or under ground,
> Whose power hath a true consent
> With Planet, or with Element.

This is "the lonely light that Samuel Palmer engraved,/ An image of mysterious wisdom won by toil," associated by Yeats also with Shelley's visionary Prince Athanase. Such light purifies and purges the mind's anxieties, its fear that it is only the passive receiver of external influences, and its lack of confidence in possessing a reciprocal power over the world of outward sense. Milton's solitary brooder, purged of these anxieties, attains a purified consciousness in which, after being dissolved "into extasies" he goes past experience into the organized innocence of "somthing like Prophetic strain." Later questers following after him were not to end so well.

Milton's purgatorial poem, *Paradise Regained,* prompted Blake's purgatorial *Milton,* another work of Jobean trial. The *Purgatorio* of Wordsworth is *The Excursion,* the poorest incontrovertibly major poem in Romantic tradition. Like Wordsworth's first important poem, *The Vale of Esthwaite, The Excursion* stems more from *Il Penseroso* than from *Paradise Regained,* or any other English poem. I refer not only to the elements of influence pointed out by Hartman—"the ambulatory scheme, as well as the compression of time"—but to a deeper level of influence also.[4] Milton's wandering solitary is the finished man of whom Wordsworth's Solitary is the demonic parody. Where Milton's brooder purifies his self-consciousness, and purges a dangerous violence from within away from the mind, Wordsworth's Solitary personifies that violence, that part of the poetic mind that is destructive of imagination. Milton's magus has uncovered the Cherub, and welcomes the Cherub's unfallen form, Ezekiel's and Revelation's guider of "the fiery-wheeled throne," or "the Cherub Contemplation" as Milton calls him. Wordsworth's Solitary is a failed magus, tormented by an excessive self-consciousness that will never be purged into a possible ecstasy. The Solitary's despair cannot be overcome because it is both a despair at being oneself and at having failed to be oneself, a double sense of reduced imagination and of diseased imagination. Wordsworth gives us a man who has lost family, revolutionary hope, and the capacity for affective joy, but who suffers the endless torment of not being able to lose his imaginative power, which now lacks all objects save himself. This is the state of being Blake named Ulro, the hell of the selfhood-communer. The Solitary is in negative quest, in vain flight away from his own creative potential. As such, he is a surrogate for Wordsworth himself, as Wordsworth presumably could not consciously know. But as readers, poets encountering Wordsworth's Solitary could not fail to recognize in him the central form of that despair that comes only to the most imaginative men.

Byron and Keats and Clare were among those readers, but for later poets like Browning and Yeats and Hardy, the important reader was Shelley, whose *clinamen* away from *The Excursion* created a new kind of poem, and almost a new kind of poetry.

A. C. Bradley first noted the relation between Shelley's *Alastor* and *The Excursion:*

> *The Excursion* is concerned in part with the danger of inactive and unsympathetic solitude; and this, treated of course in Shelley's own way, is the subject of *Alastor*. . . .[5]

The relation between the poems is more involved and extensive than Bradley realized, as later scholarship has shown. *Alastor* is Shelley's first important poem, and it begins his seven-year wrestling match with Wordsworth as Covering Cherub that still goes on in his last poem, the unfinished *The Triumph of Life*. What Milton was to Blake and to Wordsworth, Wordsworth was to Shelley, as Shelley was in turn to Browning and Yeats, an influence so appealing to the earlier self that the earlier self had to be modified, indeed almost abolished. One of the modes of change, as all these were strong poets, necessarily was the persuasive misinterpretation of the precursor, a process carried on not only in commentaries but in each poet's sequence of major poems. *Alastor* takes its theme from *The Excursion*'s Solitary, for an imaginatively inescapable reason, best expressed as the necessity to state the contrary to the views set forth by the Wanderer, Wordsworth's surrogate. Here is the vision Shelley rejected, and Yeats after him, for in Yeatsian terms this is *primary* wisdom, a nineteenth-century *objectivity* Yeats longed to overthrow:

> to relinquish all
> We have, or hope, of happiness and joy,
> And stand in freedom loosened from this world,
> I deem not arduous; but must needs confess
> That 'tis a thing impossible to frame
> Conceptions equal to the soul's desires;
> And the most difficult of tasks to *keep*
> Heights which the soul is competent to gain.
>
> . . . .

> Oh! no, the innocent Sufferer often sees
> Too clearly; feels too vividly; and longs
> To realize the vision, with intense
> And over-constant yearning;—there—there lies
> The excess, by which the balance is destroyed.
> Too, too contracted are these walls of flesh,
> This vital warmth too cold, these visual orbs,
> Though inconceivably endowed, too dim
> For any passion of the soul that leads
> To ecstasy; and all the crooked paths
> Of time and change disdaining, takes its course
> Along the line of limitless desires.

Book IV, "Despondency Corrected," 132–9, 174–85

This is not only the Wanderer's reproof and warning to the Solitary, and thus of one part of Wordsworth's imagination to the other, more dangerous part, but it already states a Shelleyan and Yeatsian dialectic of soul and self, mind and heart, contending in the *antithetical* man, as Yeats was to call him. The Wanderer is the *primary*, "objective" man of *A Vision*, while the Solitary is the quester who is doomed to carry subjectivity to its limit, in the search for a possible ecstasy, away from a possible wisdom. Wordsworth was too honest a poet to show us the self or heart converted by the soul, and the Solitary does not recant in *The Excursion*. But he does not develop either, though Wordsworth scattered many hints for his development, hints gathered together by Shelley in *Alastor*.[6] The Solitary speaks of the necessary isolation of the *antithetical* quester:

> To friendship let him turn
> For succour; but perhaps he sits alone
> On stormy waters, tossed in a little boat
> That holds but him, and can contain no more!

IV, 1085–8

Here is the central image of *Alastor*, and of much else in Shelley's poetry. Also quarried from the Solitary's state are two other central images—of *Alastor*, Shelley's career, and Yeats's poetry also—the star of infinite desire and the fountain, pool or well of generative life in which that star is reflected. More important than these three symbolic images—crucial as they were to Shelley and to Yeats after him, who assumed characteristically that Shelley had them from esoteric sources—is the whole context of Wordsworthian nature that *Alastor* appropriated from *The Excursion,* and from elsewhere in Wordsworth, Coleridge, and Southey. For the antagonist of the *antithetical* quest in *Alastor* is nature itself, which cannot contain the imagination's furious drive after finalities. *Alastor,* and Shelley's fundamental stance as a poet, result from a profound and divided reaction against Wordsworthian natural religion, a reaction that combined in Yeats with Blake's parallel reaction to create a new kind of Romantic magus, very different from Milton's ambulatory sage.

Yeats, in a note he appended to Lady Gregory's *Cuchulain of Muirthemne* (1903), spoke of a "traditional and symbolical element in literature" that preceded humanism, or any sense of man's importance. This element, highly un-Blakean, is deeply consonant with the *antithetical* quest of *Alastor,* and accounts (as Yeats realized) for much of the remorseless intensity and power of the poem. Our quests are for similitudes, in Yeats's notion of this primordial element in romance. *Alastor*'s descriptions are like those Yeats posits, when "nobody described anything as we understand description," but only went from one similitude to another: "One was always losing oneself in the unknown, and rushing to the limits of the world." [7] That sentence is the perfect account of the consciousness whose monument is *Alastor,* and Yeats's poems in that mode after it.

I give a critical analysis of *Alastor* in Chapter 6, but a few of its difficulties and peculiar features must be noted now for an understanding of Yeats's poetic genesis. *Alastor* is a strangely balanced poem, as a few critics have understood, but as no poet deeply drawn to the poem has felt. The most accurate summary is by F. A. Pottle, in his study of Shelley and Browning:

> The influence of Shelley is apparent in the very subject matter of *Pauline.* In *Alastor,* Shelley had done something very similar to what Browning attempted in *Pauline.* The theme of *Alastor* is usually misunderstood. It really depicts, just as *Pauline* does, the ruin

of a self-centered nature; here through solitude, as in *Pauline* through introspection. . . .[8]

Yet the poet-hero of *Alastor* (as of *Pauline*, or *The Wanderings of Oisin* and *The Shadowy Waters*) has a particular kind of self-centered nature, just as the Solitary did. The force centering on the self is the imagination, and so the theme of *Alastor* is the destructive power of the imagination. Shelley's poem balances dangerously on the narrow edge of the poet's extravagance; the imagination is at once "inflamed and purified," as the poem's "Preface' says. And the "Preface," though it never moved Yeats as the poem did, precisely states the Yeatsian view of the imagination. In Yeats as in Shelley, the imagination normally functions in a manner that Blake regarded as a disaster. Twice in Blake, in *The Four Zoas* and in *Jerusalem*, the same great passage is employed to evidence the sorrow of Man when he falls into worship of his own Shadow:

> Then Man ascended mourning into the splendors of his palace
> Above him rose a Shadow from his wearied intellect
> Of living gold, pure, perfect, holy; in white linen pure he hover'd
> A sweet entrancing self delusion, a watry vision of Man
> Soft exulting in existence all the Man absorbing.[9]

Blake says this shows Man "Idolatrous to his own Shadow," which is probably the definitive Blakean comment upon Yeats. If he read *Alastor*, Blake might have said the same, but been only half right. Shelley's heroine Cythna, in a passage of *The Revolt of Islam* that Yeats frequently recalls, warns against "the dark idolatry of self" which condemns us to the labyrinth of remorse, and this admonition is certainly part of *Alastor*'s overt meaning also. Yet Shelley's notion of the tendencies of the isolated imagination is clearly a mixed one, and he is more attracted than repelled by its potential for destruction, at least in *Alastor*. Even the "Preface" shows his characteristic division between head and heart, at once intellectually disapproving but emotionally sympathizing with his poet-hero's solipsism:

> The Poet's self-centered seclusion was avenged by the furies of an irresistible passion pursuing him to speedy ruin. But that Power which strikes the luminaries of the world with sudden darkness

and extinction, by awakening them to too exquisite a perception of its influences, dooms to a slow and poisonous decay those meaner spirits that dare to adjure its dominion. . . . Among those who attempt to exist without human sympathy, the pure and tender-hearted perish through the intensity and passion of their search after its communities, when the vacancy of their spirit suddenly makes itself felt. . . .[10]

"That Power" is the imagination, and the luminaries are young poets, even as "those meaner spirits" are Wordsworth, Coleridge, Southey, who by 1815 might be regarded as having abjured the imagination's dominion, and joined the world of objective, *primary* men, to read the "Preface" as Yeats would have read it. Shelley's mixed sympathies are shown in his poem's title, *Alastor, or The Spirit of Solitude. Alastor* is an afterthought, suggested to Shelley by Thomas Love Peacock as a name, *not* for the hero, called "the Poet" all through the poem, but for his dark double, his evil genius or avenging *daimon*, the Shadow or selfhood that stalks him until he wastes in death. Shelley is too subtle to objectify the *alastor* at any point in the poem, and Yeats (perhaps indeliberately, but I doubt this) therefore made the "mistake" of calling the Poet himself Alastor when he wrote about Shelley. This revelatory "mistake" is of the same imaginative order as that made by the common reader (and viewer) in calling Victor Frankenstein's creature Frankenstein, when considering Mary Shelley's novel, which has profound affinities with her husband's poem, and explores a similar problem in the Romantic mythology of the self. Victor Frankenstein is haunted by his *daimon* as Shelley's Poet by his *alastor,* for both inventors have failed to love outside the solipsistic circle of the self. Narcissus-like, the Poet and Dr. Frankenstein might well cry out:" my image no longer deceives me" and "I both kindle the flames and endure them." [11]

In the fragment of *Prince Athanase,* written late in 1817, Shelley returned to the theme of Yeats's *antithetical* quester, but in the more Yeatsian form of having eliminated doubts about the validity of solitary quest. Athanase, though a youth "grown quite weak and gray before his time," is racked by pity for man's estate, rather than by his own solipsistic quest for a soul out of his soul that is only a narcist version of his own soul. Further from Yeats's own state of existence than the Poet of *Alastor* was, he is also closer to Yeats's ideal of the magus:

> His soul had wedded Wisdom, and her dower
> Is love and justice, clothed in which he sate
> Apart from men, as in a lonely tower,
>
> Pitying the tumult of their dark estate.

Few passages in poetry can have meant more to the young Yeats than this, in which the division between heart and mind, or Yeats's self and soul, is set forth to perfection. To the solitary youth Yeats was (like Browning before him), here was a full portrait of the pride and agony of his own poetic self:

> Though his life, day after day,
> Was failing like an unreplenished stream,
> Though in his eyes a cloud and burden lay,
>
> Through which his soul, like Vesper's serene beam
> Piercing the chasms of ever rising clouds,
> Shone, softly burning; though his lips did seem
>
> Like reeds which quiver in impetuous floods;
> And through his sleep, and o'er each waking hour,
> Thoughts after thoughts, unresting multitudes,
>
> Were driven within him by some secret power,
> Which bade them blaze, and live, and roll afar,
> Like light and sounds, from haunted tower to tower
>
> . . . .
>
> For all who knew and loved him then perceived
> That there was drawn an adamantine veil
>
> Between his heart and mind—both unrelieved
> Wrought in his brain and bosom separate strife.
> Some said that he was mad, others believed
>
> That memories of an antenatal life
> Made this, where now he dwelt, a penal hell;
> And others said that such mysterious grief

From God's displeasure, like a darkness, fell
On souls like his, which owned no higher law
Than love. . . .[12]

Yeats was to affirm that Shelley was among the religion-mak-
ers, a judgment that would be stranger had Browning and other
Shelleyans not made it also. The portrait of Athanase is one of
Shelley's weakest; the poem is only a fragment, and needed revision. But the curious universalism of Shelley redeems it, and helps
explain the unique nature of Shelley's influence in the later nineteenth and earlier twentieth century. Because Shelley has been
handled so grossly by modern criticism, we have forgotten or simply failed to see how extensive his influence was, and how diverse
his disciples were. Shelley's influence was first manifested in Beddoes and Thomas Wade, and then in the Cambridge circle of
Hallam and Tennyson, and independently in the young Browning. In the early Victorian period there are also G. H. Lewes, Dis-
raeli, Kingsley, J. S. Mill, and later the major Shelleyans after
Browning—Swinburne, Yeats, Shaw, Hardy, and minor figures
like Francis Thompson and James Thomson.[13] Still later, there is
a deep influence of Shelley on Forster and Virginia Woolf, whose
The Waves may be the last Shelleyan work in the language. If we
take the five principal Shelleyans, principal in terms of their own
literary power and the intensity of Shelley's influence, then we
have the very odd grouping of Browning, Swinburne, Yeats, Shaw,
and Hardy, who may be judged to have nothing in common *except* Shelley-as-precursor. To have helped engender so astonishingly varied a progeny would be a striking phenomenon in a poet
more versatile than Shelley; that Shelley, a great poet certainly
but primarily a lyrist and always an imaginative extremist, had so
strong an effect is so unusual a part of literary history as to de-
serve further study, which I cannot give it here. But the portrait
of Athanase gives us a hint for understanding the phenomenon of
Shelley's influence; he provided developing imaginations with a
paradigm for the torments of their own processes of incarnating
the poetical character in themselves.[14] He became, as Yeats says
often, the type of the poet, the poet proper, but in a wholly different sense as compared to representative poets of the past. Mill,

writing in 1833, pointed to Shelley as "perhaps the most striking example ever known of the poetic temperament," a view close to Hallam's notion that Shelley was a supreme poet of sensation as opposed to reflection. With Browning, the next major poet in Shelley's tradition, the view of Shelley becomes wholly one of temperament, and we are given a useful case of poetic influence to serve as a parallel with Yeats's conception of Shelley-as-precursor.

Shelley's *Alastor* joined Wordsworth's *The Excursion* as *antithetical* influences upon Keats's *Endymion,* the largest single instance of the new mode of internalized quest-romance that culminated in *The Wanderings of Oisin* and *The Shadowy Waters.* Unlike *Pauline* and *Oisin, Endymion* is a reaction against *Alastor,* and its relative failure may have made Shelley's remorseless pattern all the more inevitable for later nineteenth-century poetry. Endymion's quest is ostensibly fulfilled, and in opposition to the Poet of *Alastor* he is permitted to find a natural love made identical with the ideal he has pursued. But this is a desperate, even a mechanical resolution, and is clearly the weakest element in the poem, as Keats realized himself. The pattern of the great odes and *The Fall of Hyperion* is much closer to the dark tradition of the *antithetical* quester who must fail, in the natural world, and whose only victories are in the realm of an integral vision.

Browning is not often brought into discussions of Yeats; scholars sometimes cite Yeats's dismissal of Browning in the brief, beautiful essay, "The Autumn of the Body," in 1898, where Goethe, Wordsworth, and Browning are grouped together as the modern poets responsible for the decline of poetry. Because of them "poetry gave up the right to consider all things in the world as a dictionary of types and symbols and began to call itself a critic of life and an interpreter of things as they are." [15] The disdain for Goethe and Wordsworth, however unmerited on these grounds, was consistent, but Yeats's attitude toward Browning was always a little nervous, as though he feared and wished to avoid Browning's influence. Writing just after Browning's death, he noted that "thought and speculation were to Browning means of dramatic expression much more than aims in themselves," but he did not say that psychology was only a means for Browning also, and clearly psychologizing was what he disliked and feared, even in *The Ring and the Book*.[16] As early as 1887, he acknowledged that Browning, as opposed to the Pre-Raphaelite poets, could create heroines with a life of their own, and this Pre-Raphaelite failing was to remain always a central characteristic of his own plays.[17] The characteristic Browning dramatic lyric or dramatic monologue had come, as Yeats knew, out of Browning's struggle with Shelley's influence. Yeats, undergoing precisely the same struggle as Browning, not with the aspects of Shelley that touched Shaw and Hardy, but with the *antithetical* quester of *Alastor* and *Prince Athanase,* was menaced also by Browning's *clinamen* away from Shelley. A poem like *The Gift of Harun Al-Rashid* of 1923 shows how dangerous Browning's influence was for Yeats at one of those rare times when Yeats allowed it to approach him.[18] Monologues of the mythical self were to be Yeats's own *clinamen* away from the Shelleyan dialogical lyric or mythicizing romance, and the Browningesque psychologizing would have balked Yeats's deepest energies.

In 1931, Yeats wrote to Mrs. Shakespear that in his twenties, and younger: "I wanted to feel that any poet I cared for—Shelley let us say—saw more than he told of, had in some sense seen into the mystery." [19] Yeats was still echoing Browning's "Essay on Shelley" of 1852, which profoundly affected his own essay on Shelley, and much else in his earlier criticism. Compare Browning on Shelley:

> We may learn from the biography whether his spirit invariably saw and spoke from the last height to which it had attained. An absolute vision is not for this world, but we are permitted a continual approximation to it, every degree of which in the individual, provided it exceed the attainment of the masses, must procure him a clear advantage. Did the poet ever attain to a higher platform than where he rested and exhibited a result? Did he know more than he spoke of? [20]

In Yeats, more of a consistent visionary, the question is altered to "saw more than he told of," but the question is still Browning's, and as much an autobiographical one for both Browning and Yeats as it was an enquiry into Shelley. Both poets started as passionate emulators of Athanase and the Poet of *Alastor*. Criticism has attended to the obvious differences between the mature work of Browning or Yeats and the earlier, palpably Shelleyan work, but criticism must turn to the more profound similarities if the reading of Browning or Yeats is to progress past our current banalities. *Childe Roland to the Dark Tower Came* and *The Tower* are not less Shelleyan poems than *Pauline* and *Oisin;* they are more Shelleyan because they undertake more strenuously the burden of uncovering the Cherub, of finding the true continuity between each poet's earlier and later selves, or else seeing that the continuity cannot be found, and that a terrible loss therefore must be confronted. As this book is a study of Yeats and not of Browning, I shall give only a single instance of the parallel problem the two poets met, confining myself to the Shelleyan image of the tower, and to only one example of it.

When Browning, in *Pauline,* the rhapsodic quest-poem that begins his canon, attempted to state his relation to Shelley, he chose the terms of betrayal. This invocation of Shelley assigns to Browning the role of the Poet shadowed by the *alastor,* as contrasted to Shelley who is free:

> And if thou livest—if thou lovest, spirit!
> Remember me, who set this final seal
> To wandering thought—that one so pure as thou
> Could never die. Remember me, who flung
> All honor from my soul—yet paused and said,
> "There is one spark of love remaining yet,
> For I have nought in common with him—shapes
> Which followed him avoid me, and foul forms
> Seek me, which ne'er could fasten on his mind;"

Mrs. Miller, in her biography of Browning, makes clear how central this passage is in his life and work. Her general summary of Browning's subsequent relation to Shelley is definitive. The "ashes and sparks" of Shelley's prophecy had ignited a conflagration in Browning's soul:

This conflagration was to die down; it was to be smothered; it was to be forcibly quenched; but one thing remained; Browning had recognised in the fearless spiritual independence of Shelley a principle of conduct whereby to measure, in the years to come, not only the sum of his own poetic achievement, but the very nature of human integrity itself.[21]

The value of Mrs. Miller's insight is demonstrated when she applies it to *Childe Roland to the Dark Tower Came*, one of the culminations of the tradition of Romantic quest. In Mrs. Miller's reading, the poem's implicit burden, for Browning, is "the retribution appropriate to his own sin" in abandoning his spiritual independence (his early Shelleyanism) to his mother's Evangelical faith. What results is the "corruption and sterility" of Childe Roland, the failed quester, and Browning thus defines his own refusal to see and speak from the last height to which his soul had attained.[22] Though this is part of a valid reading of the poem, I believe we must go further with it if the poem's richness is not to be obscured. *Antithetical* for Yeats does not mean "contrasting" or "opposite" but "anti-natural" (not "unnatural"); and certainly in this sense would have been accepted by Wordsworth as a descriptive adjective for his Solitary. In *Alastor,* the Poet's quest is again clearly set against the context of nature, for nothing natural can ever fulfill him. But in Browning and in Yeats the quester finds nature not so much an antagonist as an irrelevance. Childe Roland, a kind of perverse phenomenologist, reads reality not in genuine appearances, but in a willed phantasmagoria; and mere natural appearances, of any kind, bored Yeats always. Shelley, in *Alastor,* is a poet of controlled phantasmagoria; in *Childe Roland to the Dark Tower Came* and *Byzantium* the phantasmagoria takes control.

Yeats, in his chief essay on Shelley, remembered that: "Maddalo, in *Julian and Maddalo,* says that the soul is powerless, and can only, like a 'dreary bell hung in a heaven-illumined tower, toll our thoughts and our desires to meet below round the rent heart and pray.' " [23] Yeats rightly adds Julian's (Shelley's) reply to Maddalo's (Byron's) mordant observation:

> Where is the love, beauty, and truth we seek
> But in our mind? and if we were not weak
> Should we be less in deed than in desire?

These are the rhetorical questions to which Childe Roland at last learns an answer, the answer of his own trumpet of a prophecy, of passing a Last Judgment upon himself. To learn it he confronts Maddalo's tower, "a windowless, deformed and dreary pile;/ And on the top an open tower," in the shape of "the Tower itself/ The round squat turret, blind as the fool's heart." With the names "of all the lost adventurers my peers,"—the failed *antithetical* questers, the ruined poets, tolling like a bell all around him, Childe Roland attains, for just the moment before destruction, the Condition of Fire. "In a sheet of flame/ I saw them and I knew them all." For the first time in his life, since he set out on the quest, the knight (and poet) can call himself "dauntless," but at a terrible price. For that moment, Childe Roland finds the dark grow luminous, the void fruitful, for he too understands that he has and had nothing. The ringers in the tower toll a passing bell, and he is content that this be the hymen of his soul.

But Yeats, though I am employing his language, was never content with this perpetual tragedy of the *antithetical* quest, the self suffering its own loneliness as a finality. His tower too is half-dead at the top, but he had no sense of personal betrayal, for he never left behind him the self of his first poethood. The creative mind shown us in *The Circus Animals' Desertion* is driven to enumerate old themes, all of them *antithetical,* and in that recall finds its way back to the heart or self of the quester, the swordsman's personality as opposed to the saint's character or soul. Between Browning and Yeats there intervened the Neo-Romantic revival of the Pre-Raphaelites and Pater, and they altered the direction of Yeats's swerve away from Shelley. I postpone then an account of Yeats's early relation to his major precursor until my fourth chapter, and turn now to consider Yeats first in his immediate heritage, and then in the context of his own generation, which he named "Tragic."

2: Late Victorian Poetry and Pater

Walter Pater, in the "conclusion" (dated 1868) to his book on the Renaissance, made the highest claim for poetry that his generation brought forth:

> . . . we have an interval, and then our place knows us no more. Some spend this interval in listlessness, some in high passions, the wisest, at least among "the children of this world," in art and song. For our one chance lies in expanding that interval, in getting as many pulsations as possible into the given time. Great passions may give us this quickened sense of life, ecstasy and sorrow of love, the various forms of enthusiastic activity, disinterested or otherwise, which come naturally to many of us. Only be sure it is passion—that it does yield you this fruit of a quickened, multiplied consciousness. Of this wisdom, the poetic passion, the desire of beauty, the love of art for art's sake, has most; for art comes to you professing frankly to give nothing but the highest quality to your moments as they pass, and simply for those moments' sake.

Pater, like so many other major critics and poets of the nineteenth century, is still out of fashion, having been dismissed by

T. S. Eliot to the large Limbo inhabited by those who did not keep literature in its proper relation to Christian belief. The passage from Pater just given is a central one in Romantic tradition, its affiliations being on the one side with the Keats of the great odes and *The Fall of Hyperion,* and on the other with the Wallace Stevens of *The Auroras of Autumn* and the casually titled but powerful and climactic essay, *Two or Three Ideas.* Yeats, who began as a disciple of Pater (through the catalyst of Lionel Johnson) ended very much in Pater's doctrine, proclaiming the "profane perfection of mankind," the lonely ecstasy of creative joy.

Recent critics who attempt responsible examinations of Pater, partly in reaction against Eliot, tend to be unnecessarily apologetic, and to misrepresent the passionate aesthetic humanism that gives Pater's vision its individual quality. That Yeats himself came to misrepresent Pater has provided part of our difficulty in seeing Pater plain, for Yeats is perhaps the most eloquent misrepresenter in the language. Wherever Yeats's debts were largest, he learned subtly to find fault. He rarely judged Blake to be other than "incoherent," while Shelley became his favorite instance of poetic genius defeated for lack of "the Vision of Evil." So also Pater was judged to have caused the disaster of the Tragic Generation, to have taught Johnson, Dowson, Wilde, and Yeats himself "to walk upon a rope, tightly stretched through serene air" until "we were left to keep our feet upon a swaying rope in a storm." [1]

The severest danger of Pater's aesthetic vision, as the "Conclusion" to *The Renaissance* makes clear, is that you need to be a poet of genius and a moral titan fully to sustain it. The possible hero of Pater's passage, though Pater might not have believed this, is Keats or Blake. By the high standard of that passage, no poet of Pater's time could be judged absolutely to "give us the quickened sense of life," and to yield us incontrovertibly the "fruit of a quickened, multiplied consciousness." In his "Introduction" to *The Oxford Book of Modern Verse* (1936), Yeats identifies himself as having been a member of the "new generation" in revolt against Victorianism, the generation of the Rhymers' Club, setting themselves to oppose "irrelevant descriptions of nature, the scientific and moral discursiveness of *In Memoriam* . . . the political eloquence of Swinburne, the psychological curi-

osity of Browning, and the poetical diction of everybody." [2] The
Rhymers' Club, and its lasting effect upon Yeats, will be examined later. Yeats's attitude toward the greater Victorian poets, and
the Paterian basis for that attitude, is a useful start into Yeats's
long and self-contradictory (but very productive) evolution from
one kind of Romanticism to another.

Yeats said of himself that he began "in all things Pre-Raphaelite" and his attitude toward Tennyson was an intensification of
the Pre-Raphaelite resurgence of Victorian Romanticism. Broadly
speaking, Tennyson and Arnold stem as poets from Keats and
Wordsworth while Browning clearly received his initial impetus
from Shelley, as Yeats did after him. But there was an overt movement against the misunderstood aesthetic humanism of Keats in
Arnold and Tennyson, and a quasi-religious reaction against
Shelley in Browning. These matters have all been studied brilliantly elsewhere, and are cited here to suggest that the revolt of
Yeats's Tragic Generation was a carry-over from the Pre-Raphaelites, though with the powerful example of Baudelaire providing
a personal and self-destructive difference from the role of the poet
as Rossetti and Morris had conceived it.

Yeats's first characteristic poetry began to be written about
1885 and climaxed in the long poem, *The Wanderings of Oisin*,
in 1889. It is instructive to consider Yeats's early poetry in its contemporary context, in conjunction that is with the best English
poetry of the year just before the highly individual and much-
studied decade of the Nineties. In 1889, *The Wanderings of Oisin
and Other Poems* was issued in London. The principal volumes
of poetry brought out that year were Browning's last, *Asolando:
Fancies and Facts;* Tennyson's last but one, *Demeter, and Other
Poems;* and Swinburne's *Poems and Ballads* (Third Series). There
is no reason to believe, from Yeats's letters and other records,
that he looked into any of these volumes with much concern,
or with much interest, and he is not likely to have been much
impressed by any of them. From our very distant perspective,
they are impressive books, and show Victorian poetry departing
in the glow of a good sunset. The Swinburne volume includes
To a Seamew, Neap-Tide, and some fine attempts at Border
Ballads, while the Tennyson has *Demeter and Persephone,*

The Progress of Spring, and *Merlin and the Gleam.* Browning's *Asolando* is as remarkable an old man's volume as Yeats's posthumous *Last Poems and Plays* was to be, and indeed is in some ways clearly parallel to the *Last Poems,* particularly in its frustrate lust and its imaginative protest against failing nature. What rises from both last volumes is a powerful, almost pre-ternatural exultation. Though Yeats never mentions it, he might as an old man have read the "Prologue" to *Asolando* with acute recognition of its theme:

> And now? The lambent flame is—where?
>   Lost from the naked world: earth, sky
> Hill, vale, tree, flower,—Italia's rare
>   O'er-running beauty crowds the eye—
> But flame? The Bush is bare.

The theme is that of Wordsworth's *Intimations* Ode, the shuddering loss of primal vision, to be followed by the saving gain of the compensatory imagination, the "sober coloring" given by the mature mind that has kept watch over human mortality. Since Wordsworth, this has been a major theme in poetry, and is omnipresent in our own time, most remarkably in Wallace Stevens's *The Auroras of Autumn* and *The Rock,* and in the entire progression of Yeats's work. In the moment poised before the full onset of Yeats's Tragic Generation, it received definitive presentation by Browning, and by Ruskin in *Praeterita* and by Pater in all his autumnal cadences, for it is the underlying dialectic of Pater's analysis of aesthetic existence. Yet its more partial and unsatisfactory expressions, by the aged Tennyson and the prematurely aging Swinburne, can explain better the abortive poetic revolt of the Tragic Generation, with its climax in the creative impasse that faced the young Yeats about the turn of the century. Browning, for whom Yeats kept a wary respect, is too strong in *Asolando* to yield to anything short of the Christian God who transcends, but Swinburne and Tennyson movingly lack the outrageous toughness of sensibility that allowed Browning to scoff at the notion that a transcendental godhead had faded.

Swinburne's *Neap-Tide,* as the title indicates, is a poem of low tide, not just the lowest of a month but of a life-time:

Far off is the sea, and the land is afar.
  The low banks reach at the sky,
  Seen hence, and are heavenward high;
Though light for the leap of a boy they are,
  And the far sea late was nigh.

The fair wild fields and the circling downs,
  The bright sweet marshes and meads,
  All glorious with flowerlike weeds,
The great gray churches, the sea-washed towns,
  Recede as a dream recedes.

The glory and the freshness of a dream have departed; "the world's light wanes . . . and the gleams overhead change." For Swinburne, at least, there is no recompense, no sober coloring that is still a coloring, and "now no light is in heaven." Tennyson, in *Merlin and the Gleam,* at "the land's last limit," escapes the Swinburnean despair only by the desperate resource of denying that the gleam was ever of the sunlight, moonlight, or starlight. Yeats, in his marvelous essay on "The Philosophy of Shelley's Poetry," affirmed in effect that Blake would have assigned the gleam to sunlight, Keats to moonlight, and Shelley to starlight. *Merlin and the Gleam* has its own vigor as a poem, but it evades where Wordsworth and Coleridge engage crucial difficulties, and where Blake, Keats, and Shelley in their separate ways found fresh answers to the Wordsworthian crisis of imagination.

For Pater, and for Lionel Johnson and the young Yeats after him, no evasion and no explicit answer would suffice when brought into the presence of a fading inspiration, a softening of the hard flame. If ecstasy could not be maintained, then life had failed. So the Paterian tight-rope, swaying in a storm, that Yeats blamed for his generation's tragedy:

While all melts under our feet, we may well grasp at any exquisite passion, or any contribution to knowledge that seems by a lifted horizon to set the spirit free for a moment, or any stirring of the senses, strange dyes, strange colours, and curious odours, or work of the artist's hands, or the face of one's friend. Not to discriminate every moment some passionate attitude in those about us, and in the very brilliancy of their gifts some tragic dividing of forces on their ways, is, on this short day of frost and sun, to sleep before evening.

Of the major Victorian poets known to Yeats, only Rossetti had something of this intensity, and only Morris in his earlier phase had something of this spirit. But by 1889, Rossetti had been dead seven years, and Morris had long ceased to be a Pre-Raphaelite poet, and was an active Socialist pamphleteer. The future, in 1889, ought to have been with the poets of Yeats's own generation; with Arthur Symons, exactly Yeats's age, with Lionel Johnson and Ernest Dowson, both two years younger, and with Yeats himself. Symons was to outlive even Yeats, but Johnson was dead at thirty-five and Dowson at thirty-three, and none of the three was to make a style, or to mature a vision. Yet they started substantially as Yeats started, and their influence upon him as examples, rather than as accomplishments, was to remain constant. There are more echoes of their poetry in the middle and later Yeats than are generally realized, but their principal effect upon him was in the style of their lives, and their stance as poets, rather than in their actual work.

Yeats was to remark, in chronicling his generation, that Rossetti was a subconscious influence, perhaps the most powerful of all, upon them, though they looked consciously to Pater for their "philosophy." [3] Yet it is difficult now to find as much relevance to us, as Yeats's readers, in Rossetti as in Pater, and the inadequacy may be in Rossetti's poetry itself. What Rossetti's poetry lacks is neither reason nor passion, and it would be absurd to fault it on formal considerations, its workmanship being excellent. Its range of sensibility is too narrow; where Pater's essays at their best touch the universal, Rossetti's poems rarely do, though both writers present us with instances of an almost purely aesthetic consciousness.

Yeats had a particular admiration for Rossetti's *The Stream's Secret,* and maintained this regard throughout his life. It is a difficult poem for most readers now—hard to like, obscure to the understanding, but it is a strong work, and Yeats's ability to respond to it is a mark of the difference between the poet and most of his current admirers. To comprehend *The Stream's Secret* is both to know Yeats better, and to be reminded that he was born more than a century ago. *The Stream's Secret* is an audacious lyric because of its length; nothing *happens* in its 234 lines. Rossetti is concerned to sustain an intensity, yet the intensity is of baffled passion, and the stream's secret, which is, presumably, whether and when parted lovers will be re-united, remains untold:

> O soul-sequestered face
>   Far off,—O were that night but now!
> So even beside that stream even I and thou
>   Through thirsting lips should draw Love's grace,
> And in the zone of that supreme embrace
>   Bind aching breast and brow.
>
>   O water whispering
>   Still through the dark into mine ears,—
> As with mine eyes, is it not now with hers?—
>   Mine eyes that add to thy cold spring,
> Wan water, wandering water weltering,
>   This hidden tide of tears.

The poem quests for the lost hour, in a pattern natural to the young Yeats himself, for it is the pattern common to post-Romantic love poetry. The lover's mind cannot bear to believe that it passes a fiction upon itself, yet it knows only the pain of recollection, and has no hope. What is left is the intensity of the consciousness of loss, but also Rossetti's insistence on a freedom from the spirit of place, though not from time: "And they that drink know nought of sky or land/ But only love alone." The lover's night is not now, and the poem ends, not in a lover's faith, but in his agnosticism: "As with mine eyes, is it not now with hers?" Yeats must have believed that Rossetti's imagination had not gone far enough, could not accept the necessity of escaping time's tyranny by the greater audacity of believing in a fiction that willingly dismissed the relevance of experience.

Rossetti moves toward the "privileged moment" of Walter Pater, but he does not allow himself to arrive at it. The poets with whom Yeats first identified himself—Johnson, Dowson, Symons—attempt the quest for the privileged moment, even as their younger contemporary Joyce was to seek his early epiphanies, again under Pater's influence. The school of Lionel Johnson and Yeats was founded upon what they took to be an anti-Words-worthian, anti-Tennysonian thesis: against recollection. Yeats was fond of quoting Verlaine on *In Memoriam:* "When he should have been broken-hearted, he had many reminiscences." [4] Verlaine, with Catullus and Baudelaire, meant pure poetry for Johnson and his friends, according to Yeats. The continuously high pitch of emotion maintained by Rossetti in *The Stream's Secret* makes it pure poetry in this curious sense.

Yeats did Pater a notorious disservice when he began *The Ox-ford Book of Modern Verse* by printing in *vers libre* the famous purple passage on the Mona Lisa. As the passage reverberates in so much of Yeats, including his visions of annunciation, it is worth examination at least as an influence upon him, but it is more than that, being one of Yeats's "sacred texts," both as an ex-ample of pure poetry and as imaginative doctrine:

> She is older than the rocks among which she sits;
> Like the Vampire
> She has been dead many times,
> And learned the secrets of the grave;
> And has been a diver in deep seas,
> And keeps their fallen day about her;
> And trafficked for strange webs with Eastern merchants;
> And, as Leda,
> Was the mother of Helen of Troy,
> And, as St. Anne,
> Was the mother of Mary;
> And all this has been to her but as the sound of lyres and flutes,
> And lives
> Only in the delicacy
> With which it has moulded the changing lineaments,
> And tinged the eyelids and the hands.

To Yeats, this was a vision of flux, where the individual was nothing, a foreshadowing of the *Cantos* of Pound (as Yeats read those poems) and of Yeats's own *Last Poems and Plays*. This seems a paradoxical reading of Pater, who was interested in the assertion of personality against the flux of sensations, and who exalted the aesthetic moment in which a radiance dazzles us amidst the flux. Pater's Mona Lisa is an eternal type, Leda or St. Anne, not the mother of a civilization or of a god, but a more remote ancestress, one generation before the climax. Her unconcern is like the disinterestedness of Pater's Marius, and stems from a refusal to surrender consciousness to any event or belief, and so from a disdain of renunciation, very like Yeats's own. Yet there is wisdom in Yeats's reading of the passage; its undersong, like the implications of the greater passages in the "Conclusion" to Pater's *Renaissance,* suggests the triumph of flux over art, over the privilege of the visionary moment. Yeats reads the Mona Lisa description as Blake would have read it; this is the archetype of Rahab the Whore, mother of the indefinite, queen of the abyss of objects without contour, lines without clear outline. On such a reading, or over-reading, the poem that Yeats has made out of Pater's prose has its quasi-Blakean greatness. Yeats is giving us an instance of genuine poetic influence, of the poet creating his precursor. This Mona Lisa is the ancestress of one aspect of the Female in many of Yeats's poems and plays: the Muse as Destroyer, the dancer with the poet's severed head. To Yeats, as a student of Blake, the "strange webs" of Pater's vision recalled the work of Enitharmon, Queen of Heaven:

> Weaving to Dreams the Sexual Strife
> And weeping over the Web of Life.

She weeps over it, but she has woven it, and it is woman's triumph, the courtly love code of deceit. Yeats would have remembered also Enitharmon in Blake's *Europe,* to whom all of history is a dream, even as it is here to Pater's woman. For Pater's equivocal ideal is a kind of Sphinx, and his pursuit of the privileged moment or epiphany is a Romantic quest only in the deliberately self-defeating tradition of Shelley's *Alastor.* Pater does not offer any resolution to the post-Romantic or post-Wordsworthian dilemma; he offers rather a clear vision of it. The defeat of Yeats's generation of poets was not due to their adoption of Pater's vision, but of their inability to bear it, to live with it as he did.

Pater's "privileged moment" is as much an implicit attack upon recollection as Blake's "pulsation of an artery" is. The school of Wordsworth, down to Arnold and even the Tennyson of *In Memoriam,* emphasized continuity as a human and even poetic virtue, and saw all ecstasy as being brief and painful, as in the lost "aching joys" and "dizzy raptures" of *Tintern Abbey.* Pater had no myth of memory; he knew too well that we always lived in a place not our own, and much more not ourselves, that we have only an interval, and then our place knows us no more. Even our longings are not immortal, and the after-images left behind by experience are less vivid than the after-images of unfulfilled desire. Pater's emphasis upon intensity of experience is both inevitable and potentially ennobling, however dangerous the emphasis proved to his disciples, including Wilde, Beardsley, Dowson, and Johnson. The moral analogue to Pater's aesthetic impressionism is relativism; the movement of sensations is matched by the flux of contending beliefs and actions, no one of which can be more final than another. Pater kept his difficult balance by an Epicurean detachment, but such a stance could produce only the lyricism of a Landor (or the middle Yeats) and not the more generous art of the younger Yeats or of Lionel Johnson. Pater did not press for finalities, in life or in art; his doctrine implies that all finalities are disasters. Though this has been judged the wisdom of a Trimmer, or of a ritualist, it is something else in Pater, without ceasing to be wisdom. For Pater had his own Vision of Evil (to use Yeats's later phrase) but believed that the apprehension of art could set it aside, and could save an aesthetic man from entering too directly or too fully into his own self-destructiveness. The "Conclusion" to *The Renaissance* is certainly morally equivocal, and allows itself to be so read as to produce a Dorian Gray, but it need not be read so grossly; Pater himself was not a vulgarizer. Wilde, an extraordinarily accurate critic when he chose to be, had the unhappy tendency to reduce Pater to literalism whenever he read him, and Yeats's earlier readings of Pater seem at least touched by Wilde's example (or Johnson's).

Since Pater haunts Yeats's poetry and thought, as do Blake,

Shelley, Balzac, Nietzsche, but no others to that extent, so far as I can surmise, it is of some importance to this study to determine Pater's position in Romantic tradition. Different as they are, Blake, Shelley, Balzac, and Nietzsche have an apocalyptic vitalism more or less in common, but Pater seems oddly placed in this group of really crucial literary influences upon Yeats. His Romanticism seems less central than theirs, if only because he represents the Romantic tradition in its apparent decadence or decline. But this is not to see Pater plain, as Yeats in his depths learned to see him. Pater, though he would never have intended this, is the central link between nineteenth and twentieth-century Romanticism in Britain and America, the figure who stands mid-way between Wordsworth and his followers, and such major modernists as Yeats, Joyce, Pound, and Wallace Stevens. Pater's criticism, still so little read or valued in our time, explains (the more powerfully for doing it implicitly) why all post-Romantic poetry resolves itself into another aspect of Romanticism, despite its frequently overt anti-Romanticism, as in Pound, Eliot, and their school.

Pater has played this role not only because of his real strength, which is an aesthetic example and in his highly individual mode of impressionistic "appreciation" (his own word), but also because of his excursions into historicism, which are as curious and fascinating as Yeats's own, Yeats's indeed being derived from them, to a surprising extent, as Whitaker and Engelberg have demonstrated. Perhaps historicism is the clue as to what unites the major influences upon Yeats, since Blake, Balzac, and Nietzsche all formulated patterns of history, as Pater and Yeats did also, and Shelley, despite his hatred of history, knew too well that the strength of his apocalyptic desires was not sufficient to cancel even his own sense of historical necessity, of the great and inevitable cycles of creation and destruction. Figures as diverse as Plato and Spengler, in value as in their concerns, were of interest to Yeats primarily because of their historical speculations, to which one can add as odd a duo in Vico and Emerson.

Pater's vision of history is itself a Vision of Evil, in Yeats's sense, because it too sees opposites as living each other's death, dying each other's life. Wilde, with an acuteness anticipating

Yeats's, chose to convert Pater's vision into a theory of masks, blandly insisting that Plato and Hegel made sense to the aesthetic or ideal man only when their metaphysics could be phrased in the still more dialectical language of criticism. Pater, in his deceptive way, was as bewilderingly dialectical as any man, and would not have been surprised by the mask-seeking quests of the later Yeats. Pater might even have seen Yeats as another Plato, in the tradition of Shelley's interpretation of Plato as a skeptical poet (an interpretation stemming from Montaigne). The hero of Pater's remarkable study, *Plato and Platonism*, is a poet for whom the center could not hold, for whom things fell apart, but who could not abide in aesthetic reverie, as Pater would have done. Perhaps Pater's Plato, like his Marius, is a pre-Renaissance Renaissance man, a precursor of Romanticism's wisdom of the heart, the freedom of the imagination. Pater's Plato is remarkably like Yeats's Blake; both are figures in the peculiar history of Poetic Influence, which has little to do with history as such. Yeats's Shelley, as will be shown, is the very archetype of a figure of Poetic Influence, for Yeats's Shelley is a grand naïf who incarnates what Nietzsche and Pater prophesied as a transformation of the dance of contraries into an agony of trance, the poetic dream of apocalypse.

For Pater, the truest art of the nineteenth century was necessarily a renaissance of the Renaissance, which perhaps was the program of English Romanticism. But Pater's Renaissance is as historical a vision as Yeats's Byzantium (or Eliot's Age of the Metaphysicals). In Botticelli Pater found again what he was to find in so many incongruous figures, the refusal to choose a single form of the spiritual life, a refusal that culminates in the hero of *Marius the Epicurean*. To accept a single system of belief would be to reject the others, and to accept Christianity would call for some measure of renunciation of the imagination's possibilities. Those possibilities lay in the flux of sensations, to be experienced during our brief day of frost and sun, and to be saved, if saved at all, only through the exercise of the arts.

This may be why Pater dreamed of so radical a fusion of form and content in the arts, an unrealizable dream from Baudelaire to the most extreme of our modernists, but which has been revived in recent years, under the influence of Action painters and mixed-media theorists. Pater's statement of his aesthetic ideal is notorious, yet we may have failed to notice how wistful it is:

All art constantly aspires towards the condition of music. For while in all other kinds of art it is possible to distinguish the matter from the form, and the understanding can always make this distinction, yet it is the constant effort of art to obliterate it. That the mere matter of a poem, for instance, its subject, namely, its given incidents or situation—that the mere matter of a picture, the actual circumstances of an event, the actual topography of a landscape—should be nothing without the form, the spirit, of the handling, that this form, this mode of handling, should become an end in itself, should penetrate every part of the matter: this is what all art constantly strives after, and achieves in different degrees. . . .

This is not a Renaissance but a Romantic dream. In Keats it stems from the hope for poetry as a more disinterested mode than any other available to men, but even in Keats the hope proved illusory, and poetry has a design upon us again in the purgatorial dream of *The Fall of Hyperion*. In Wallace Stevens the Paterian ambition is absorbed and then turned upon itself for:

> Poetry
> Exceeding music must take the place
> Of empty heaven and its hymns.

What Pater bequeathed then to the poetic generation of Johnson, Dowson, Symons, and Yeats was first, an impossible aesthetic ideal; second, a stance against belief and against recollective spiritual nostalgia, whether personal or societal; third, a desperate trust in the flux of experience itself; but fourth, the final conviction that the fruit of experience is an intense consciousness or passion that cannot accommodate itself to experience again, that must seek its fulfillment in a dream that knows itself to be only a dream. In Yeats, as in Stevens after him, this legacy was the valid starting point for a poetic career, but Yeats and Stevens were outrageously tough spirits, men of powerful intellect and cunning imaginations, like the major Romantics long before them. But for the poets of the Tragic Generation, who were very gifted but not strong men, Pater was a dangerous teacher, a personally reserved and hermetically withdrawn master whose art had no relation to his life, and who opened the way, not to the purgatory or middle-realm of an achieved art, but to self-destruction. That there was nothing inevitable in this can be seen by the following:

> One has to pierce through the dithyrambic impressions that talk of the gods makes to the reality of what is being said. What is being said must be true and the truth of it must be seen. But the truth about the poet in a time of disbelief is not that he must turn evangelist. After all, he shares the disbelief of his time. He does not turn to Paris or Rome for relief from the monotony of reality. He turns to himself and he denies that reality was ever monotonous except in comparison. He asserts that the source of comparison having been eliminated, reality is returned, as if a shadow had passed and drawn after it and taken away whatever coating had concealed what lay beneath it. Yet the revelation of reality is not a part peculiar to a time of disbelief or, if it is, it is so in a sense singular to that time. Perhaps, the revelation of reality takes on a special meaning, without effort or consciousness on the part of the poet, at such a time. Why should a poem not change in sense when there is a fluctuation of the whole of appearance? Or why should it not change when we realize that the indifferent experience of life is the unique experience, the item of ecstasy which we have been isolating and reserving for another time and place, loftier and more secluded.[5]

This is Pater assimilated to a still more elaborate skepticism, and to a harsher reality, but even its ending point is not far from Pater's. To Stevens, this unacknowledged ancestor was "that dreadful Walter Pater," whose books might lie somewhere in the attic, but the cultural debt remains an evident one. The flower of Paterian poetry is *Harmonium* rather than the early Yeats, who had a number of mythologies to purge before he made his own, and thus found his way out of Pater's impressionistic skepticism. Stevens mocks the Paterian sensibility, and some critics have read him as a thoroughgoing ironist toward his own aesthetic *personae,* but these readings become increasingly suspect as a reader learns how massively *Harmonium* anticipates *The Whole of Harmonium,* as Stevens wished to call his *Collected Poems.* Here is the central poem of the Paterian vision, Stevens's *Tea at the Palaz of Hoon:*

> Not less because in purple I descended
> The western day through what you called
> The loneliest air, not less was I myself.
>
> What was the ointment sprinkled on my beard?
> What were the hymns that buzzed beside my ears?
> What was the sea whose tide swept through me there?
>
> Out of my mind the golden ointment rained,
> And my ears made the blowing hymns they heard.
> I was myself the compass of that sea:
>
> I was the world in which I walked, and what I saw
> Or heard or felt came not but from myself;
> And there I found myself more truly and more strange.

This is Stevens's version of the incarnation of the Poetical Character, or the re-birth of the poet as Apollo. The triumphant final tercet, with its fine anticipation of *The Idea of Order at Key West,* is the declaration of the mind knowing its own autonomy, declaring that outward sense is wholly the servant of its will. Hoon becomes the Romantic Imagination in celebration of itself, and his final line recalls Pater's definition of the Romantic spirit as adding strangeness to beauty. But the poem is Paterian throughout; its ironies are entirely in the second tercet, and these are not so much spoken by Hoon, as taken up by him in answer to what Blake called the Idiot Questioner, this poem's anti-Romantic. What the poem affirms is not a deliberate solipsism, but a triumph in which exuberant self-recognition overcomes the dread of solipsism, and proclaims a self so expanded and confident that all external regions are merely filled with "the escapades of death," as the climactic phrase of a similar epiphany was to call the universe of death in Stevens's later masterpiece, *Notes Toward a Supreme Fiction.* The vision of Pater has prolonged its life well beyond the term set by Eliot and his school, but only in the work of poets as formidable as Stevens and the later Yeats.

3: The Tragic Generation

Arthur Symons, writing a "Memoir" of Ernest Dowson in 1900, said of his recently deceased friend: "He was unhappy, and he dared not think," and went on to observe that Dowson had "the face of a demoralized Keats." Yeats catches the same moment of acknowledged defeat when he mordantly says: "Then in 1900 everybody got down off his stilts; henceforth nobody drank absinthe with his black coffee; nobody went mad; nobody committed suicide; nobody joined the Catholic church; or if they did I have forgotten." [1] With so little affirmed of the Tragic Generation by its two most eminent survivors, it is scarcely surprising that the group has so low or even non-existent a poetic reputation today.

A fresh look at Dowson and Johnson reveals that they are austere poets, and despite the coloring of Verlaine in them they find their natural company with two earlier English generations of *poètes maudits*, The Age of Sensibility of Gray and Collins, among others, and the post-Shelleyan school of Darley and Thomas Wade, Beddoes, and the earlier Clare. Between these two groups came the greatness of the six or seven major Romantic poets, just as between the generation of Darley and that of Johnson there had come the four or five major Victorians. Perhaps now, with the handful of major Modernist poets dead, we are in the midst of another twilight time in which extraordinary talents are fated to defeat by the spirit of the age, and we will learn to be more cautious in appreciating minor but inevitable poets.

In Yeats's vision of Lionel Johnson's spiritual form, his friend had "renounced the joy of the world without accepting the joy of God," a curious reversal of the stance of Pater's Marius, who somehow had accepted both, though with the appropriate reservations. Yeats's Dowson "sought from religion . . . something of that which the angels find who move perpetually, as Swedenborg has said, towards 'the dayspring of their youth.' " [2] In the second, definitive version of his "public philosophy," *A Vision,* Yeats classified Dowson as a man of Phase Thirteen, The Sensuous Man, with Baudelaire and Beardsley, and said of this Phase: "Self-hatred now reaches its height, and through this hatred comes the slow liberation of intellectual love." [3] For both poets, Yeats intuited a specifically religious failure, a hesitation or immaturity that kept them from the peace of the Church they both sought. His choice of their poems in *The Oxford Book of Modern Verse* is shrewdly and well done, and magnifies them by presenting their deepest and most controlled yearnings for what they knew they could not hold to steadily or fully.

The Dowson presented by Yeats is first of all the desperate expender of self, who sighs convincingly: "Yet is day over long," and chants, rather less convincingly:

> Unto us they belong,
>   Us the bitter and gay,
> Wine and woman and song.

This is the passion of Dowson's most notorious poem, the splendidly dreadful *Non sum qualis eram bonae sub regno Cynarae:*

> I cried for madder music and for stronger wine,
> But when the feast is finished and the lamps expire,
> Then falls thy shadow, Cynara! the night is thine;

> And I am desolate and sick of an old passion,
>> Yea hungry for the lips of my desire:
> I have been faithful to thee, Cynara! in my fashion.

There is nothing quite like that in the early Yeats, and we might wish that there had been. Even the earliest love poems of Yeats are too cunning, too ironically frustrate, for him to reach an expression of exultation. His intensities, from the start, are ghostly, and rise from the antithetical side of natural passion, from the Romantic and Paterian knowledge that all imaginative expectation is in excess of experiential possibility. It is in this spirit that Yeats chooses his other poems from Dowson, poems of the dream, most notably *Flos Lunae* and *To One in Bedlam*. Love's defeat and poetic madness, in these lyrics, prepare for the last poem in Yeats's arrangement, *Extreme Unction*, a pathetic and moving revelation of Dowson's reach toward faith:

> Upon the eyes, the lips, the feet,
>> On all the passages of sense,
> The atoning oil is spread with sweet
>> Renewal of lost innocence.
>
> The feet, that lately ran so fast
>> To meet desire, are soothly sealed;
> The eyes, that were so often cast
>> On vanity, are touched and healed.
>
> From troublous sights and sounds set free;
>> In such a twilight hour of breath,
> Shall one retrace his life, or see,
>> Through shadows, the true face of death?
>
> Vials of mercy! Sacring oils!
>> I know not where nor when I come,
> Nor through what wanderings and toils,
>> To crave of you Viaticum.
>
> Yet, when the walls of flesh grow weak,
>> In such an hour, it well may be,
> Through mist and darkness, light will break,
>> And each anointed sense will see.

This is a subtler and better lyric than the more conventional *Nuns of the Perpetual Adoration,* in which Dowson yearns for a cloistered rest that seems in itself assured, much in the manner of Hopkins's *Heaven-Haven.* Dowson is most impressive when he can admit how remote he is from the desired context of the spiritual. Only the first two stanzas of *Extreme Unction* are at peace, and even they stop short of assent. The third stanza is an open question, and the fourth is desperately agnostic, even bewildered, as to Dowson's own experience, as though he scarcely can have consciousness of culpability when indeed he has no consciousness of literal events. Despite the "yet" opening the final stanza, Dowson ends on a "will see" heavily qualified by the earlier "it well may be." How are the senses to be redeemed when the poet cannot even recollect a reality that they have encountered? It is Dowson's peculiar poetic strength, and spiritual weakness, that he knows fully neither the present moment nor the past. He had learned from Pater not to study the nostalgias in any personal sense, but only as a longing for ritual, almost in its own right. But he could not learn the other term of Pater's dialectic, which is the exaltation of the privileged moment, from which recollection need not fall away, so strong is that moment.

Yeats was closer, personally and poetically, to Lionel Johnson than to Dowson, and Johnson's now seems a larger achievement than Dowson's, or that of Wilde and Symons, if they be considered as poets only. It is impossible, after Yeats, to see Johnson plain, for the portrait of Johnson in Yeats's *The Trembling of the Veil* is extraordinarily vivid, and has an imaginative energy that Johnson himself displays only in a literal handful of poems: *Mystic and Cavalier, The Precept of Silence, To Morfydd, By the Statue of King Charles at Charing Cross,* and, above all, *The Dark Angel.* Yeats anthologized the last three of these, but preferred to the first two another group: *The Age of a Dream, The Church of a Dream,* and *Te Martyrum Candidatus.*

Johnson, to Yeats, was the contemporary of the antithetical man, living *contra naturam* in his library:

That room was always a pleasure to me, with its curtains of grey corduroy over door and window and book-case, and its walls covered with brown paper, a fashion invented, I think, by Horne, that was soon to spread. There was a portrait of Cardinal Newman, looking a little like Johnson himself, some religious picture by Simeon Solomon, and works upon theology in Greek and Latin and a general air of neatness and severity; and talking there by candlelight it never seemed very difficult to murmur Villiers de l'Isle-Adam's proud words, "As for living, our servants will do that for us." [4]

But Yeats follows this by observing that Johnson lived a phantasmagoria in compensation for his withdrawal from life, a phantasmagoria that ended in acute alcoholism. Despite this end, Yeats emphasizes the sternness of Johnson's moral character, and the pride of his acute intellect. The center of Johnson's personal myth is to be found in the poet's conscious realization of his responsibility for his own degradation, and in his consequent necessity of making a fiction to surmount that degradation. But Johnson, unlike Arnold, did not make the saving fiction, perhaps because he knew his own disaster to be more personal than societal or cultural, perhaps (as Yeats surmised) because of his immediate adherence to an aesthetic tradition that separated overt morality from poetic concern. In his elegy for Lady Gregory's son, Yeats made his famous characterization of Johnson as "much falling," remembering Johnson's judgment upon himself in *Mystic and Cavalier*:

> Go from me: I am one of those, who fall.
> What! hath no cold wind swept your heart at all,
> In my sad company? Before the end,
>   Go from me, dear my friend!

Though the poem is addressed to Horne, it might as well have been to Yeats. Like *A Cornish Night,* which Johnson did dedicate to Yeats, the poem is a vision of a spiritual reality from which the poet is not wholly excluded, but in which he is isolated, so that he cannot participate even in the mutuality of a sanctified death. His is *The Precept of Silence:*

> I know you: solitary griefs,
> Desolate passions, aching hours!

> I know you: tremulous beliefs,
> Agonized hopes, and ashen flowers!
>
> The winds are sometimes sad to me;
> The starry spaces, full of fear:
> Mine is the sorrow on the sea,
> And mine the sigh of places drear.

The Biblical "sorrow on the sea" is the universal sadness of all Johnson's verse, epitomized by "the saddest of all kings," the martyred Cavalier, Charles, who has joined the White Horsemen of *Te Martyrum Candidatus,* and whose statue gives the poet a prophecy of his own fate:

> Although his whole heart yearn
> In passionate tragedy:
> Never was face so stern
> With sweet austerity.
>
> Vanquished in life, his death
> By beauty made amends:
> The passing of his breath
> Won his defeated ends.

Johnson's defeated ends have the dignity of all self-renunciations. They include the extraordinary passion of *To Morfydd,* a love lyric Yeats judged "incomparable," and which Blake and Shelley would have admired as the fit song of the Spectre or *alastor,* the daimon desiring, not his opposite, but only his mirrored self, with the solipsistic refrain of *Mine are your eyes.* But even a spectral love lyric is a strain for Johnson; more congenial are the dream poems that always lingered in Yeats's memory, the two sonnets in which Johnson longed for his spiritual home, *The Age of a Dream* and *The Church of a Dream.* The first climaxes in an image endemic in modern poetry: "Now from the broken tower, what solemn bell still tolls,/ Mourning what piteous death?" Though Johnson calls for an answer, he offers none, unless it be implicit in *The Church of a Dream,* also written in 1890, a year before the poet's conversion:

> Sadly the dead leaves rustle in the whistling wind,
> Around the weather-worn, gray church, low down the vale:

The saints in golden vesture shake before the gale;
The glorious windows shake, where still they dwell enshrined;
Old saints by long dead, shrivelled hands, long since designed:
There still, although the world autumnal be, and pale,
Still in their golden vesture the old saints prevail;
Alone with Christ, desolate else, left by mankind.

Only one ancient Priest offers the Sacrifice,
Murmuring holy Latin immemorial:
Swaying with tremulous hands the old censer full of spice,
In gray, sweet incense clouds; blue, sweet clouds mystical:
To him, in place of men, for he is old, suffice
Melancholy remembrances and vesperal.

Whitaker has demonstrated the influence of this poem upon
The Black Tower, the last poem that Yeats wrote, left unrevised
at his death.[5] However faded Johnson's poem is for us, something
permanent and vivid in Yeats's consciousness found satisfaction in
it. It came to represent, one can surmise, the Christianity that
Yeats neither accepted nor rejected, as Pater before him never
quite rejected traditional belief. The gale, in Johnson's poem, is
derived from the autumnal wind of Shelley, the nineteenth century's emblem of revolutionary change. But this wind of creation
and destruction scarcely blows through the natural world here;
the nature of Shelley's dead leaves is set aside after the first two
lines. Johnson's concern is with tradition; his "Saints in golden
vesture" anticipate Yeats's sages in *Sailing to Byzantium,* who also
are invoked as golden beings, alone with the Divine. But Johnson's also is the Church of a dream; no more is it an actuality
than Yeats's Byzantine vision. Between Johnson and Christian
reality there falls the shadow of the Hinderer or Interceptor, the
Dark Angel who is invoked in Johnson's masterpiece:

Dark Angel, with thine aching lust
To rid the world of penitence:
Malicious Angel, who still dost
My soul such subtile violence!

Because of thee, no thought, no thing,
Abides for me undesecrate:

Dark Angel, ever on the wing,
Who never reachest me too late!

When music sounds, then changest thou
Its silvery to a sultry fire:
Nor will thine envious heart allow
Delight untortured by desire.

Through thee, the gracious Muses turn
To Furies, O mine Enemy!
And all the things of beauty burn
With flames of evil ecstasy.

Because of thee, the land of dreams
Becomes a gathering place of fears:
Until tormented slumber seems
One vehemence of useless tears.

When sunlight glows upon the flowers,
Or ripples down the dancing sea:
Thou, with thy troop of passionate powers,
Beleaguerest, bewilderest, me.

Within the breath of autumn woods,
Within the winter silences:
Thy venomous spirit stirs and broods,
O Master of impieties!

The ardour of red flame is thine,
And thine the steely soul of ice:
Thou poisonest the fair design
Of nature, with unfair device.

Apple of ashes, golden bright;
Waters of bitterness, how sweet!
O banquet of a foul delight,
Prepared by thee, dark Paraclete!

Thou art the whisper in the gloom,
The hinting tone, the haunting laugh:
Thou art the adorner of my tomb,
The minstrel of mine epitaph.

I fight thee, in the Holy Name!
Yet, what thou dost, is what God saith:

Tempter! should I escape thy flame,
Thou wilt have helped my soul from Death:

The second Death, that never dies,
That cannot die, when time is dead:
Live Death, wherein the lost soul cries,
Eternally uncomforted.

Dark Angel, with thine aching lust!
Of two defeats, of two despairs:
Less dread, a change to drifting dust,
Than thine eternity of cares.

Do what thou wilt, thou shalt not so,
Dark Angel! triumph over me:
Lonely, unto the Lone I go;
Divine, to the Divinity.

It is the representative poem of its decade, and much the best
poem written in English during the Nineties. It is also, just now,
easy to undervalue, or to characterize as a period piece only. Ian
Fletcher notes that the Dark Angel is both Satan and Johnson's
own shadow self, which to Blake would be an identity anyway.[6]
Johnson was a fanatically learned man, but his learning was narrow and orthodox, unlike the curious learning of Yeats. Johnson
tends always to control his allusions; Fletcher points out the
echoes in this poem of Bridges and of Crashaw, and the direct allusion to Plotinus in the italicized concluding lines.[7] But to a
reader like Yeats, schooled by Blake and Shelley as well as by esoteric texts, *The Dark Angel* must have read as a poem about the
Shadow, or rather an address to the unanswering Shadow. What
matters then in the poem would have been the status of the Dark
Angel as Spectre or *alastor,* and not as Satan. The Dark Angel for
Yeats was primarily cultural history; for the more desperate and
solitary Johnson, trapped in his homosexuality, the Dark Angel
was a purely personal history. The companion to Johnson's great
lyric of anguished self-recognition is nowhere to be found in
Yeats, but perhaps can be located in Hart Crane's *The Broken
Tower* or in D. H. Lawrence's *Shadows,* both of them death-
poems or final utterances.

To Yeats, who was always a kind of Gnostic, salvation from

the start lay in the encounter with the Other, or *daimon* as Yeats named him. In Johnson's poem, though God sanctions the Accuser, redemption can come only by a triumph over the *daimon,* for Johnson was (or strove to be) eminently orthodox. *The Dark Angel,* with a simple twist, could have become a great esoteric lyric, and meant more to readers from Yeats onward than it has done. But Johnson's dilemma was the one that Yeats would have confronted if he had followed his friends of the Tragic Generation into the nostalgia of orthodox belief:

> Though I cannot explain what brought others of my generation to such misfortune, I think that (falling backward upon my parable of the moon) I can explain some part of Dowson's and Johnson's dissipation:—

>> What portion in the world can the artist have
>> Who has awakened from the common dream
>> But dissipation and despair? [8]

Brooding further on Dowson and Johnson, Yeats reached his ultimate judgment upon their relation to faith:

> The typical men of the classical age (I think of Commodus, with his half-animal beauty, his cruelty, and his caprice) lived public lives, pursuing curiosities of appetite, and so found in Christianity, with its Thebaid and its Mareotic Sea, the needed curb. But what can the Christian confessor say to those who more and more must make all out of the privacy of their thought, calling up perpetual images of desire, for he cannot say, "Cease to be artist, cease to be poet," where the whole life is art and poetry, nor can he bid men leave the world, who suffer from the terrors that pass before shut eyes. Coleridge, and Rossetti, though his dull brother did once persuade him that he was an agnostic, were devout Christians, and Stenbock and Beardsley were so towards their lives' end, and Dowson and Johnson always, and yet I think it but deepened despair and multiplied temptation. [9]

In following this passage by quoting the first four stanzas of *The Dark Angel* Yeats was stating both his generation's temptation for him, and his refusal to yield to it, despite his recognition that Johnson in particular represented the apparently legitimate and fated end of a tradition that Yeats traced back to Spenser:

> When Edmund Spenser described the island of Phaedria and of Acrasia he aroused the indignation of Lord Burleigh, that "rugged forehead," and Lord Burleigh was in the right if morality were our only object.
>
> In those islands certain qualities of beauty, certain forms of sensuous loveliness were separated from all the general purposes of life, as they had not been hitherto in European literature—and would not be again, for even the historical process has its ebb and flow, till Keats wrote his *Endymion*. I think that the movement of our thought has more and more so separated certain images and regions of the mind, and that these images grow in beauty as they grow in sterility. . . . Had not Matthew Arnold his faith in what he described as the best thought of his generation, Browning his psychological curiosity, Tennyson, as before him Shelley and Wordsworth, moral values that were not aesthetic values? But Coleridge of the *Ancient Mariner,* and *Kubla Khan,* and Rossetti in all his writings, made what Arnold has called that "morbid effort," that search for "perfection of thought and feeling, and to unite this to perfection of form," sought this new, pure beauty, and suffered in their lives because of it.[10]

It is against these observations that we can now read *The Dark Angel* and see the full extent of its insight, for one of Yeats's finest gifts is his sense of context, or of poetic influence, his critical awareness of the effect of poets upon one another. Johnson's Dark Angel, on the most reductive of levels, is Johnson's own inverted sexual desire, but this "aching lust" is a subtler and larger desire also, the High Romantic desire, destructive of Christianity, "to rid the world of penitence." The Dark Angel sets himself against remorse even as Blake writes *The Human Abstract* against pity or Shelley's Cythna preaches against contrition in *The Revolt of Islam*. To Blake and Shelley, of course, "pity" and "remorse" were the hypocritical virtues of a corrupted and institutionalized faith, but there is no reason ever to believe that they meant less than what they said. For Johnson, as a Last Romantic, Shelley as man and poet was almost a type of Christ, but *The Dark Angel* is a Romantic poem attacking Romanticism, in prophecy of much

Modernist poetry, and it can be understood specifically as an anti-Shelleyan and even anti-Yeatsian poem.

Writing in 1900, two years before Johnson's death, Yeats equivocally summed up his friend's achievement as being peripheral, yet almost a heterocosm, for "he has made a world full of altar lights and golden vestures, and murmured Latin and incense clouds, and Autumn winds and dead leaves, where one wanders remembering martyrdoms that the world has forgotten." [11] The eloquence of the Paterian style here (as a prose master Yeats never left Pater's school) makes an elaborate tribute to Johnson, and as elaborately withdraws from that tribute. Finely as Yeats characterizes Johnson here, *The Dark Angel* tends to refute him, since it clearly is a palinode. Though the poem takes its flight from the world of Wilde's Dorian Gray, it is from that world rather than of it. The problem is one of degrees of profundity, of the adequacy and scope of Johnson's Vision of Evil as against that of his fellows of the Beardsley Period. Pater, as before, is both the source and the problem. Detached and skeptical, he preached by implication the subtle doctrine that moral dualism and aesthetic wholeness had to co-exist, impossible as it was to maintain a pragmatic balance between them. Wilde's novel and some of Beardsley's best works maintain something like a balance, but most of the work of the Nineties does not, or turns to ironies in evasion of the theme of the *doppelgänger*. Johnson does not evade any of his dilemmas in *The Dark Angel,* but he engages the theme of the daimonic self so directly only by overthrowing the Paterian aesthetic vision and following instead, at least this once, the very antithesis of it, the unmixed spirituality of Newman. Still, *The Dark Angel* would be no poem at all if it did not do full justice, as it does, to Johnson's own deepest sensibility, of which "a craving that made every atom of his body cry out" formed an essential part. The undersong of *The Dark Angel* is that the ferocity of Johnson's intellectual passion for the Holy Name is yet insufficient to defeat the Angel; Johnson's struggle is to keep his adversary from triumphing over him, in an endless and bewildered match. Pater's insistence upon aesthetic ruthlessness, on the indifferent item of ecstasy, the notorious gem-like flame, is not refuted but enhanced by Johnson's desperate orthodoxy:

> Through thee, the gracious Muses turn
> To Furies, O mine Enemy!
> And all the things of beauty burn
> With flames of evil ecstasy.

The "evil" is Johnson's own self-judgment, and would have made Pater rather uncomfortable. Deeply in thrall, yet holding on to the eternal freedom of the Holy Name, Johnson attains the single full triumph of his poetry in the poem's last four stanzas. The Dark Angel is, despite all, part of God's purposes, like the accusing Satan of the Book of Job. Johnson chooses, convincingly, the better "of two defeats, of two despairs." His final voyage is not the heroic and knowingly unknowing flight of the visionary skeptic, Shelley, at the close of *Adonais*, but the trusting Neoplatonic (and Christian) movement to an assured reality:

> This, therefore, is the life of the Gods, and of divine and happy men, a liberation from all terrene concerns, a life unaccompanied with human pleasures, and a flight of the alone to the alone.[12]

Yeats lived to speak the last word on Johnson and Dowson, Wilde and Beardsley and the others of their generation, a last word the more definitive for its careful, implicit separation of Yeats himself from the fate of his friends, and from Johnson in particular, whom in some sense he had loved:

> Why are these strange souls born everywhere to-day, with hearts that Christianity, as shaped by history, cannot satisfy? Our love-letters wear out our love; no school of painting outlasts its founders, every stroke of the brush exhausts the impulse, Pre-Raphaelitism had some twenty years; Impressionism thirty perhaps. Why should we believe that religion can never bring round its antithesis? Is it true that our air is disturbed, as Mallarmé said, by "the trembling of the veil of the Temple," or that "our whole age is seeking to bring forth a sacred book"? Some of us thought that book near towards the end of last century, but the tide sank again.[13]

In *A Vision* Yeats phrased the matter less rhetorically, but with greater precision, in defining the phase of Beardsley and Dowson:

Self-hatred now reaches its height, and through this hatred comes the slow liberation of intellectual love. There are moments of triumph and moments of defeat, each in its extreme form, for the subjective intellect knows nothing of moderation.[14]

What Yeats learned, not so much from the experience of his own generation, as from his heightening myth of its disaster, was what Pater taught well or badly, depending upon the imaginative strength of his disciples. Unity of Being, which Yeats never ceased to seek, was the goal of the Paterian quest, and perhaps of all questing in the Romantic tradition. The poets of the Tragic Generation did not fail for seeking the wrong goal, but because they lacked the human strength to put their faith in art alone, as Pater, Yeats, and Stevens did. The last irony of the Nineties is that its poets, except for Yeats, could not follow their art for art's sake alone.

4: Shelley and Yeats

Yeats says that he had a relatively late sexual awakening, when nearly seventeen, and that his first sexual reveries took their images from Shelley's poems *Alastor* and *Prince Athanase,* and from Byron's *Manfred*—all to be expected from a boy who was seventeen in 1882.[1] Yeats's first poetry was an attempt at a Spenserian epic on the story of Roland, which was abandoned for the Spenserian and Shelleyan blend that was to develop into Yeats's first published poetry, not to be found in his *Collected Poems,* but printed in the *Dublin University Review* when Yeats was twenty, and now available in the appendices to the "Variorum" edition of his poetry.

The longest and most ambitious of these works is an allegorical verse-drama, *The Island of Statues,* subtitled by Yeats *An Arcadian Faery Tale—in Two Acts,* which I shall briefly summarize. Two Arcadian shepherds, timid but clamorous creatures, love a proud shepherdess who scorns them for their lack of courage. A hunter, to win her love, goes forth on a quest to the enchanted Island of Statues, seeking a mysterious flower, which is guarded by a dread enchantress. The choice of the wrong flower on this Island has turned many a quester into stone, and the hunter suffers a similar fate. He is then sought to turn by his shepherdess, who pauses long enough in her wanderings to provoke her two timid pastoral suitors into a mutually destructive duel for the favors she does not intend to grant. Reaching the enchanted Island of Statues in the disguise of a boy, she entices the enchantress into falling in love with her, and so gains the enchanted flower, with which she restores the statues into breathing flesh, and thus destroys the poor enchantress, as earlier she had destroyed her shepherd-suitors. This frightening little Arcadian drama ends with the shepherdess, her hunter-lover, and the other restored statues resolving to remain forever on the Island. The closing touch, befitting the play's theme, is that the rising moon casts the shadows of the hunter and the other restored creatures far across the grass, but the destructively successful quester, the shepherdess, stands shadowless in the moonlight, symbolizing the loss of her soul. Yeats, in later life, writing about Shelley, said that a man's mind at twenty contains everything of importance it will ever possess. Whatever we think of this as a general principle, it does seem relevant to Yeats himself. *The Island of Statues* takes its Circe-like enchantress from Spenser, and most of its verse-texture from Shelley, yet its decadent and savage theme is curiously Yeats's own, holding in embryo much that is to come. The shepherdess's desire to convert her Arcadian lovers into murderous men-of-action; the equivocal enchantress longing for the embrace of ordinary flesh; the frozen sculpture that ensues from a defeated naturalistic quest; the mocking and embittering moonlight that exposes an occult victory as a human defeat—all these, despite their Pre-Raphaelite colorings, are emblems that Yeats was never to abandon. But the verse-drama, and most of its companion-pieces written up through 1885, he certainly did abandon. One of these pieces, a dramatic poem called *The Seeker,* introduces an Old Knight who has devoted sixty years to a dream-led wandering in search of his beloved enchantress. Her vision had made him a coward on the field of battle; now at last he has found her and craves a single glance at her face before he dies. A sudden light bursts over her, and he sees her as what she is—a bearded witch, called Infamy by men. The witch raises a mirror, in which the Knight sees his own shadowed face and form, and he dies. This grim fantasy is rather clearly blended out of Shelley's *Alastor* and Fradubio's discovery in *The Faerie Queene* that his beloved is the Whore of Infamy, Duessa; but Yeats's allegory is characteristically more savage and more destructively self-directed. The quest that reduces a man-of-action to a coward is truly only a lust after infamy, and ends with a mirrored image of the faded self. Though Yeats rejected *The Seeker* as he had *The Island of Statues,* he chose long afterward to open his *Collected Poems* with a Song originally printed as an Epilogue to both *The Island of Statues* and *The Seeker*. A satyr enters, carrying a sea-shell, emblem of poetic prophecy in Wordsworth and in Shelley. He chants:

> The woods of Arcady are dead,
> And over is their antique joy,
> Of old the world on dreaming fed—
> Grey truth is now her painted toy—
> But O, sick children of the world,
> Of all the many changing things
> In dreary dancing past us whirled,
> To the old cracked tune that Chronos sings,
> Words alone are certain good.

The chant goes on to offer the hypothesis that our world may be only a sudden flaming word, soon to be silenced. The reader is therefore urged not to seek action or truth, but only whatever story a murmuring sea-shell will give to him, after which the satyr closes by insisting on the value of mere dreaming as its own end. As an epilogue to works that have given us a vision of the dream as self-destruction this is very curious, and even the young poet's faith in a verbal universe is rather disconcertingly allied to the Shelleyan image of a self-consuming flame. What Yeats had attained to in 1885 was precisely that dead-end of vision that Shelley had come to in *Alastor* some seventy years before, and moreover at about the same age at which Shelley also had come to the crossways of life and art. That this parallel between the two poets was altogether deliberate on Yeats's part, one has not the slightest doubt. His Arcadian plays were followed in 1886 by the dramatic poem *Mosada* and the much more powerful *The Two Titans,* both of them overwhelmingly Shelleyan poems. In *Mosada* a Moorish maiden is martyred by the Inquisition because she practices magic in order to recover a vision of her lost Christian lover, who by a characteristic Yeatsian touch enters the poem as his own anti-self, no less than the Grand Inquisitor. *The Two Titans* is rather misleadingly subtitled *A Political Poem* and therefore has been read subtly but reductively by Richard Ellmann as an allegory of Ireland's bondage to England.[2] Yet here, though with a rhetoric so Shelleyan as to be scarcely his own at all, Yeats wrote the most imaginatively impressive poem of his youth before *The Wanderings of Oisin,* though it perhaps has its preposterous aspects if it is read as political allegory alone. Gerard Manley Hopkins, resident in Dublin during 1886, read *The Two Titans,* called its allegory "strained and unworkable" yet found the poem to contain fine lines and vivid imagery. *The Two Titans* is a mixture of the archetypal situations presented by Shelley in two very different poems, the baffled quest-romance *Alastor,* and the darkly triumphant lyrical drama, *Prometheus Unbound.* One of Yeats's Titans is "a grey-haired youth" like the doomed poet in Shelley's *Alastor;* like Prometheus he is imprisoned on a rock, but this is a wave-beaten promontory, where he is chained to a fiercely dreaming Sibyl of a Titaness. The poem is thus either an anticipation of Blake's influence on Yeats, as it reproduces the situation most powerfully set forth by Blake at the opening of his ballad, *The Mental Traveller,* or more likely, it is the first of the many times that the influences of Blake and Shelley will mingle in Yeats's poetry, until their confluence will help produce such masterpieces as *The Second Coming* and the Byzantium poems. All that happens in Yeats's *The Two Titans* is that the enchained poet makes yet another heroic attempt to get free of the Titaness and fails, receiving as his reward a sadistic kiss from his tyrannical captor, who is yet as bound as he is. On the Shelleyan and Blakean analogues, the poem has a clear and impressive meaning—the poet, if he relies on a naturalistic Muse, participates in the bondage of nature, and is devoured by his own Muse, destroyed by the cyclic rhythms of a running-down natural world. With *The Two Titans* we come to the end of Yeats's first poetic period—he now is twenty-one years old: a considerable poet rather desperately struggling with an overwhelming influence, Shelley's, that he must somehow modify if he is to achieve his own individuality, and just beginning to undergo a kindred influence of Blake—more liberating for being free of the very personal elements in Yeats's early Shelley-obsession.

Some poets, as we know, never recover from the immortal wound of the poetry they first come to love, though they learn to mask their relationship to their own earlier selves. In 1914, when he was nearly fifty, Yeats wrote the very beautiful section of his *Autobiographies* entitled *Reveries over Childhood and Youth.* He was past the mid-point of his poetic career, and already well into that middle style in which he is furthest from Romantic tradition, the style of the volumes *The Green Helmet* and *Responsibilities,* a bitter, restrained style, relying on the themes of self-correction, disillusionment, a new control. His poetic models for a time will be Landor and Donne and what he has to say in 1914 of his own earlier feelings for Shelley is therefore not likely to be colored by a strong positive emotion, and is all the more valuable for our present purpose, which is to trace how a poetic influence can apparently be repudiated, and yet go underground, like Coleridge's Sacred River, until it emerges finally with a turbulence of creation and destruction, in a form more powerful than before.

The seventeen-year-old Yeats, experiencing the awakening of sexuality, slept out among the rocks in the wilds around Howth Castle, where later he would walk with Maud Gonne in that most desperately unsuccessful and yet poetically fruitful of courtships. "As I climbed along the narrow ledge," he reminisced, "I was now Manfred on his glacier, and now Prince Athanase with his solitary lamp, but I soon chose Alastor for my chief of men and longed to share his melancholy, and maybe at last to disappear from everybody's sight as he disappeared, drifting in a boat along some slow-moving river between great trees. When I thought of women they were modelled on those in my favorite poets and loved in brief tragedy, or like the girl in *The Revolt of Islam,* accompanied their lovers through all manner of wild places, lawless women without homes and without children." [3]

The avenging *daimon* or *alastor* in Shelley's poem is the dark double of the melancholy poet, the spirit of solitude that will haunt him and drive him on to destruction. As such he is probably Yeats's first literary encounter with the notion of an anti-self, to be so richly developed later in Yeats's writing. Prince Athanase, the young magus in his lonely tower, we will meet many times again in Yeats's work, while the lawless heroine Cythna, of Shelley's *Revolt of Islam,* will inform Yeats's heroic conception of Maud Gonne as a rebel against all established order.

The *antithetical* solitude of the young Shelley, with his gentleness and humanitarian character, who yet creates as the heroes of his early poetry the isolated figures of sage, magician, violent revolutionary, and proudly solitary noble and poet, is very clearly the ultimate origin of Yeats's later theories of the mask and the antithetical self. The young Yeats elaborated a not very convincing autobiographical parallel between himself and the young Shelley —since Shelley was persecuted at Eton as "Shelley the atheist" so Yeats was made miserable at school in London as "the Mad Irishman." John Butler Yeats, the poet's father, occupies the role of Shelley's Dr. Lind, nursing the imagination of the young poet. Yeats noted also the adolescent Shelley's interest in the occult, though he either ignored or condemned the mature Shelley's dismissal of such interests.

Later in the *Reveries over Childhood and Youth* Yeats tells us that he made Shelley's *Prometheus Unbound* the first of his sacred books or poetic scriptures. In *Four Years,* the next of his *Autobiographies,* the influence of Shelley is cited as having given him his two prime images. "In later years," he writes, "my mind gave itself to gregarious Shelley's dream of a young man, his hair blanched with sorrow, studying philosophy in some lonely tower, or of his old man, master of all human knowledge, hidden from human sight in some shell-strewn cavern on the Mediterranean shore." [4] The young man is Prince Athanase:

> His soul had wedded Wisdom, and her dower
> Is love and justice, clothed in which he sate
> Apart from men, as in a lonely tower,
>
> Pitying the tumult of their dark estate.

The image of the old man was to haunt Yeats's poetry even more decisively. In *Four Years* he calls it the passage of poetry that "above all ran perpetually in my ears." It is the dialogue from *Hellas* concerning the sage Ahasuerus, the Wandering Jew who will become the Old Rocky Face of *The Gyres,* that *daimonic* intelligence we must urge to look out at our world from his secret home, "where he swells in a sea-cavern/ 'Mid the Demonesi," less accessible than the Sultan or God:

> Some feign that he is Enoch; others dream
> He was pre-Adamite, and has survived
> Cycles of generation and of ruin.[5]

These two images are the *personae* of Yeats in the first and in the final phases of his career as a poet—the prematurely old young man seeking the secret wisdom, and the ageless old magus who has conquered age by long possessing such wisdom. Between is the bitter phase of the middle Yeats, anti-Romantic against his own grain, lamenting that traditional sanctity and loveliness have vanished, and that Romantic Ireland is dead and gone.

Both these images, as Yeats himself said, are always opposite to the natural self or the natural world, an insight as to the poetic role arrived at by Shelley and by Blake alike. We can see Yeats demonstrating an astonishing critical power as he ascertains this truth in the magnificent essay on Shelley written by him in 1900, and curiously mis-entitled *The Philosophy of Shelley's Poetry,* for it is a study of Shelley's imagery, and even more of the emotional dialectic of Shelley's poetry, and finally one of the earliest studies of poetry as myth-making that we have. For Yeats it was more than just an essay on Shelley—the erstwhile disciple was now thirty-five, at the mid-point of his life, and consciously determined to throw off the embroidered coat of his earlier poetry—to demonstrate, for a while, that there's more enterprise in walking naked. In that coat there were prominently displayed what Yeats called the reds and yellows that Shelley had gathered in Italy. The poet of *The Rose* and *The Wind Among the Reeds,* now sought what his father had called "unity of being"—to write in perfect tune with the tension of his own lyre. At least one aim of Yeats's essay on Shelley is to demonstrate that the poet of *Prometheus Unbound* lacked this Unity of Being, and so could not realize his full gifts as a poet.

The clue to Yeats's dissatisfaction with Shelley is given by Yeats throughout this otherwise model essay. Shelley—we know—was the most heroic of agnostics, humanistically convinced that "the deep truth is imageless," as Demogorgon puts it in *Prometheus Unbound*. But Yeats, who hungered after belief, could not accept this. He in effect blames Shelley for not being Yeats—for not seeking the support of a popular mythology, or of magic and occult tradition—indeed he closes his essay by denouncing Shelley for having been "content merely to write verses," when he possessed and should have realized the religion-making faculty. He cannot then forgive Shelley for not having founded a new faith, and he contrasts Shelley to Blake, for he believes that this is precisely what Blake attempted to do. Critically speaking, this is both fascinatingly perverse and yet of the utmost importance. Yeats has read Shelley with great accuracy and insight, but will not abide in that reading, for if Shelley's way as a poet is right, then indeed Yeats's developing way is wrong. In compensation, Yeats has read Blake with great inaccuracy and deliberately befuddled insight, so as to produce an antithetical poetic father to take Shelley's place.

Before moving on to Blake and Yeats, a closer inspection of Yeats's first essay on Shelley should serve to test these generalizations. Yeats begins by stating his early belief about the relation between poetry and philosophy. "I thought," he writes, "that whatever of philosophy has been made poetry is alone permanent, and that one should begin to arrange it in some regular order, rejecting nothing as the make-believe of the poets." [6] From this early principle he goes on to state his mature belief at thirty-five: "I am now certain" he affirms, "that the imagination has some way of lighting on the truth that the reason has not," and he offers as evidence for his certainty that he has just re-read *Prometheus Unbound,* and it seems to him to have an even more certain place than he had thought among the sacred books of the world. He then proceeds to show that Shelley's *Prometheus* is an apocalyptic work, and he brilliantly parallels Shelley and Blake by way of Shelley's most Blakean poem, *The Witch of Atlas*. It is the calculating faculty or reason which creates ugliness, and the freed faculty of imagination that alone creates the exuberance that is beauty, and so becomes the supreme agency of what a poet can consider as moral good. In the poet's infinite desire to break through natural barriers and so uncover an altogether human universe Yeats magnificently locates the common ground held by Blake and by Shelley. As Yeats quotes and describes passage after passage from Shelley to support his characterization of that great Promethean as the poet of infinite desire, he reveals also to the student of his own later poetry just those passages that will be transformed into crucial moments in such poems as *Leda and the Swan, Nineteen Hundred and Nineteen, The Second Coming, Sailing to Byzantium,* and *Byzantium, Two Songs from a Play, The Gyres,* and the death-poem, *Under Ben Bulben.* All these poems have quite direct verbal echoes of or allusions to the Shelleyan passages that Yeats quotes. Yet this is of only secondary importance in a consideration of Yeats's Romanticism, or even in seeking to understand the complexity of Shelley's abiding influence on Yeats's poetry. More vital is the argument that Yeats proceeds to conduct with Shelley, once he has demonstrated the religious intensity of Shelley's unappeasable and apocalyptic desires, those infinite aspirations toward a world where subject and object, thought and passion, lover and beloved, shall be joined in perfect wholeness.

Inevitably Yeats concentrates on Shelley's speculations upon death and survival, for the single great theme uniting all of Yeats's poetry from the very start, as he himself proclaimed, is a passion against old age, and the insistence that man has somehow invented death. Shelley died at twenty-nine and Blake was too great a humanist to regard the fear of death as more than a failure of the imagination, but Yeats lived into his seventy-fourth year, and surrendered his imaginative humanism to a rage for survival in some form, however desperately unimaginative. The seeds of this surrender can be found in the most astonishing moment in Yeats's first Shelley essay, when he suddenly passes from quoting the nobly agnostic quatrains that conclude *The Sensitive Plant* to the incredible deduction that those quatrains show Shelley's belief in the *anima mundi* or Great Memory in which all our smaller selves survive. It is an intellectual comedy of dismal intensity to first read Shelley's quatrain and then Yeats's comment upon it. Here is Shelley:

For love, and beauty, and delight
There is no death nor change; their might
Exceeds our organs, which endure
No light, being themselves obscure.

What these lines clearly say is that our senses are inadequate to the full humanity of our desire; Blake says much the same in *The Marriage of Heaven and Hell* when he proclaims that "if the doors of perception were cleansed everything would appear to man as it is, infinite. For man has closed himself up, till he sees all things thro' narrow chinks of his cavern." But in Yeats's reading Shelley's lines are a reference to a palpable spirit-world, a universe of squeaking phantasms that can be invoked by a Soho medium or a self-induced trance. Having so misread, Yeats goes on to condemn Shelley for having no roots in Irish folklore, Hindu theosophy, and cabalistic magic. It is Shelley's freedom from this witch's cauldron, we are asked to believe, that gives some of his poetry that air of rootless fantasy the anti-Shelleyans breathe and condemn. Shelley, Yeats goes on to say, had reawakened in himself the age of faith, but failed to understand that the content of such faith now rested in peasant superstitions and the arcane doctrines of the Rosicrucians.

Remarkable as it is, *The Philosophy of Shelley's Poetry* thus trails off in uncertainty, for Yeats was unable in 1900 to resolve his conflicting attitudes toward Shelley. From 1900 to 1917, there are few allusions to Shelley in Yeats's prose or verse. In this difficult middle period, Yeats turned elsewhere, as I will show in Chapter 11 by a reading of his poems from the turn of the century down to the Great War. From 1917, Yeats's overt concern with Shelley returned, but in a new version, one that receives its full development in the portrait of Shelley in *A Vision,* a portrait analyzed in Chapter 14 of this book. Essentially this is the myth of Shelley as an incipient Yeats who failed to become Yeats because he could not attain to a Vision of Evil. This is a baffling myth, as a reading of the two poets side-by-side would hardly convince a disinterested critic that Yeats recognized as evil most things that are to be abhorred, including violence and prejudice, while Shelley is afflicted by an all-but-excessive consciousness of the prevalence of evil. What Yeats appears to have meant by the Vision of Evil is the conception of the world as a continual conflict.

That Yeats knew better about Shelley we know from his earlier essay on that poet, where he correctly understands the great myth of Demogorgon in *Prometheus Unbound* as the principle of continual conflict that turns over the cycle in the universe from Jupiter to Prometheus, and that threatens destruction again in a world that cannot by its nature be finally redeemed. But Yeats *needed* his myth of Shelley as an embryonic Yeats who had fallen short of the Vision of Evil. Hence the late essay on *Prometheus* of 1932, in which Demogorgon is reinterpreted as being uninterpretable, as making the whole poem incoherent, for now Yeats must see him as the most monstrous of all Shelley's nightmare images of the negation of desire. Yet even here, in an essay clearly intended as a critical palinode, as an anti-Shelleyan document, the full force of Shelley's power upon Yeats breaks through. He has attacked Shelley for not being a mystic, unlike Yeats himself and Blake. The attack is weak—none of the three poets was in fact anything of a mystic—but Yeats throws the strength of his considerable rhetoric into the attack: Shelley's "system of thought"—he says —"was constructed by his logical faculty to satisfy desire, not a symbolical revelation received after the suspension of all desire." In the zeal of his rejecting passion Yeats makes his strongest indictment of Shelley, asserting: "He was the tyrant of his own being." After all that, one would expect a declaration of Yeatsian freedom from this mistaken being, but what follows is one of those moments of total self-revelation in which the paradoxical greatness of the mask-seeking Yeats consists. I quote it in full, so as to preserve its weight and complexity:

> When I was in my early twenties Shelley was much talked about. London had its important "Shelley Society," *The Cenci* had been performed and forbidden, provincial sketching clubs displayed pictures by young women of the burning of Shelley's body. The orthodox religion, as our mothers had taught it, was no longer credible; those who could not substitute connoisseurship, or some humanitarian or scientific pursuit, found a substitute in Shelley. He had shared our curiosities, our political problems, our conviction that, despite all experience to the contrary, love is enough, and unlike

Blake, isolated by an arbitrary symbolism, he seemed to sum up all that was metaphysical in English poetry. When in middle life I looked back I found that he and not Blake, whom I had studied more and with more approval, had shaped my life, and when I thought of the tumultuous and often tragic lives of friends or acquaintance, I attributed to his direct or indirect influence their Jacobin frenzies, their brown demons.[7]

When Yeats wrote this passage, it was more than fifty years since his father had begun to read aloud to him from Shelley, emphasizing such passionate speeches as those at the opening of *Prometheus Unbound* "but never the ecstatic lyricism of that famous fourth act." [8] Much that follows in this book will trace the continuous effect of Shelley upon individual poems and plays of Yeats, but some general estimate of this multiform influence is necessary here. Yeats, despite himself, remained always a poet of autobiographical self-recognition, in the solitary tradition that Shelley had founded upon Wordsworth. Yeats's subject, again despite his own will, tended to be his relation as poet to his own vision, in Shelley's mode rather than Blake's, for Blake largely centered on the content of the poetic vision itself. Shelley provided Yeats with a lyric model even as the Noh drama finally provided him with a model that made possible his plays for dancers; the idea of the Yeatsian lyric is Shelley's idea, powerfully modified, but still recognizable.

5: Blake and Yeats

As an old man, past seventy, Yeats looked back at his own work and found its first principle: "A poet writes always of his personal life, in his finest work out of its tragedy, whatever it be, remorse, lost love, or mere loneliness; he never speaks directly as to someone at the breakfast table, there is always a phantasmagoria." [1] A man sits down to breakfast, but a poet is a passion, redeemed out of nature into coherence. Because of this redemption, all men are richer in creative power. For this world is too poor, as Blake said, to bring forth a single seed. In his plenitude, Yeats was what he claimed to be, Blake's disciple, and the motto of the *Collected Poems* might have been: "Where man is not, nature is barren." [2]

But, if this was his declared first principle, Yeats sought strangely for his subject matter, when he "spoke or tried to speak out of a people to a people." [3] Not many now read Yeats, on the several continents where he is read, because he went from cottage to cottage with Lady Gregory and helped her to gather the visions and beliefs of the cottagers.

Some writers on Yeats, sharing his belief in the paradoxical universalism that frequently attends a fierce nationalism, have found nothing strange in his choice of subject matter. Insofar as he made of his nationalism a kind of phantasmagoria, Yeats was true to his deepest poetic principles, and the Irish element in his vision is rarely an imaginative impediment, as the occult element often is. The strangeness I speak of is not the national aspect of Yeats's subject matter but rather the folk aspect, the emphasis upon communal wisdom. Yeats sought allies everywhere for his struggle against what he called "a new naturalism that leaves man helpless before the contents of his own mind." [4] The voice of the folk, he felt, might help replace the lost, lamented "romantic movement with its turbulent heroism, its self-assertion." In Irish popular religion, particularly in the stories recorded by Lady Gregory, Yeats found sanction, as he thought, for his own version of Christianity, the extraordinary faith of the hermit Ribh in *Supernatural Songs*. If Blake had identified Christ with Los, the Imaginative Man of the epic *Jerusalem*, then Yeats might identify Christ also with the "Self" of the Upanishads, and insist that the identification was "a legitimate deduction from the Creed of St. Patrick." [5] In some sense, "legitimate," in this context, means sanctioned by analogues in popular tradition, or what Yeats took to be analogues. It remains difficult to think of *A Vision* as a religious book, or of Yeats as a religious poet. Heterodoxy is not the difficulty; one thinks of D. H. Lawrence and Hart Crane as religious poets, even as Blake and Shelley were religious poets, but Yeats is finally quite apart from these, and the religion he thought came from the folk is something other than religion in the Christian sense. Yeats, like his hypothesized people, delighted in active men, and responded to gesture and exuberance. His religion, as he was fond of saying, was that of Homer and the beggar-man, a *pietas* of hearth and blood-kindred, a feeling for the unity of life, and an acceptance of life as tragedy. It is true that there is, as Cleanth Brooks has suggested, a residual sense of another kind of religion in Yeats, an apprehension that the Godhead lay beyond all of the antinomies that the poet could create or encounter. Yet this Godhead Yeats neither craves nor fears. At stroke of midnight the hidden God may win, and make nonsense of the poet's deepest convictions as to this world and the next, but the possibility of such an intervention is not allowed to alter the poet's convictions in his actual poems. It is a little redundant to argue this matter in any case, as Yeats did not suffer from any lack of credulity. Blake asserted that anything possible to be believed was an image of truth. Yeats bettered him in finding it possible to believe anything whatsoever, if it were sufficiently marvelous, and made enough of a gap in nature. This generosity of spirit is unmatched among modern poets, and perhaps unmatched in tradition since the days of Sir Thomas Browne. The redemptive aspect of Yeats's occultism is to be located in this area of humane receptivity. What is irksome about *A Vision* is not its "wildness," in the Emersonian sense of its creative freedom, but rather that it is not wild enough. Yeatsian exuberance, throughout the book, is too much curbed by what the poet himself called a "harsh geometry." Yeats was remembering, perhaps, his frequent characterizations of Blake's mythology as being "harsh and difficult," though veteran readers of Blake tend not to find this harshness any longer.

Yeats's vibrant advantage over every other modern poet—Rilke, Valéry, Stevens, to name only the greatest—is the constant impression that he is rendering the thing itself, the passionate moment in all of its immediacy. It is a quality (or a magician's trick) that Yeats shares with Browning, and indeed may have learned from Browning. Yeats confessed that Browning's influence was a dangerous one for him. I take this to mean that Browning's concentration on the "good moment" has a way of draining the tragic element out of life. Childe Roland dies a Kafkan death—"like a dog," Kafka might have remarked of this death also—yet the Childe dies exultantly, dauntlessly sounding the trumpet of an individual existence. This is not a Yeatsian death, for it is died in dread of death, not in contempt of death, and yet it is died with a courage more relevant to us than the Yeatsian heroism is. Childe Roland dies death our death; Cuchulain dies the mysterious death of the hero, who by the irony of the Yeatsian dialectic must live the life-in-death of the convicted coward. What seems to have tempted Yeats in Browning is Browning's greatest glory, the self-consuming and solitary passion of the individual, the Protestant who has betrayed his inner light, yet who knows how to die for and by the inner light. Yeats believed in that light, but he believed in the shadow also that he cast when he moved in that light, and he honored that shadow as Browning did not.

Men decay with the years, in reality, in Yeats, in Browning, but bodily decrepitude, which is folly in reality, becomes wisdom in Yeats, and is scarcely acknowledged in the prodigiously hale Browning. Blake acknowledges it, but refuses to see any relation for it to wisdom, and knows the reality of the "foolish body," and the inconsequence of that reality; becoming "stronger and stronger" in "Spirit & Life," and in "The Real Man The Imagination which Liveth for Ever" even as "this Foolish Body decays." [6] For Blake, the body is flux to the imagination's force; the imagination's movement disdains the circular eddy that is the body's cycle. There is then no wisdom of the body, and if no natural wisdom is possible, then natural religion is pernicious error. Here is one of the fundamental points at which Blake and Yeats diverge, with important consequences.

Force and flux are not contraries, in the Blakean sense, for their interaction does not make for progression, even in Yeats's view. Nor does Yeats welcome them equally, except when they merge into an identity for him. The love of process is always a curious love for Yeats. Love itself is process for Yeats; we are always in love, we love what vanishes, and it does not vanish more or less quickly because we love it.

Yeats was not one of those rare visionaries who love the future, and he was most certainly a man who, in Stevens's phrase, had studied the nostalgias, who loved a number of pasts, most of them historically quite non-existent. The Urbino and the eighteenth-century Dublin of Yeats's nostalgias are mere idealizations, and they are to some extent the idealizations of preciousness and snobbery. Byzantium would be a pernicious myth if Yeats had made the mistake of insisting too categorically on its historical adequacy; it moves us because it is out of space and out of time.

Many critics have written of how the fire of experience transformed itself, for Yeats, into the light of what he called "tragic joy." One can worry that the transformation takes place too quickly, that Yeats, unlike Blake's Enion, does not know a total answer to the great question: "What is the price of experience?" [7] "Why should we honor those that die upon the field of battle;

man may show as reckless a courage in entering into the abyss of himself." [8] The nostalgia for the courage of action never left Yeats, but the Romantic polemic in praise of the subjective quest necessarily prevented him from studying that nostalgia. More than any poet in his tradition since Blake, Yeats excelled in audacity, and he followed Blake in the dialectical audacity of transvaluing the ancient quarrel between the objective and the subjective man, the Angel and the Devil in Blake's terms. Readers of *A Vision* are met by a vocabulary in which the objective is the sentimental, the Victorian materialist and the Christian idealist being equated, while the subjective is the antithesis of sentimentality, being the vision of reality that is art. Yeats's dialectic here, though ultimately it stems from Blake, is not very much in Blake's spirit, and rather clearly shadows some of Nietszche's attitudes. Closest, as usual, to Yeats is his immediate master, Pater, for the Yeatsian subjectivity operates, in poems, by means of Pater's secularized epiphanies, in which a peculiar hardness and clarity of vision, momentary but just within the circumference of the natural, is the final reward granted to the *antithetical* quester.

Stevens, though he so deliberately avoids drama, is the overt dramatist of a process that exactly reverses Yeats's:

> It is the old man standing on a tower
> Who reads no book. His ruddy ancientness
> Absorbs the ruddy summer and is appeased,
> By an understanding that fulfils his age,
> By a feeling capable of nothing more.[9]

This image of natural harmony as imaginative completion is in the Wordsworth-Keats line of Romanticism even as Yeats's contrary image of the poet in the tower is in the alternative Romantic convention of Shelley, and in some sense of Blake, with his "Tower of Los." [10] As I have traced the course of Shelley's earlier influence upon Yeats in the previous chapter, I turn now to examine the allied influence of Blake, second only to Shelley's, throughout Yeats's lifetime. I have discussed the earliest traces of Blake's influence in *The Two Titans*. As with Shelley, so with Blake; we must look to J. B. Yeats for the early history of a significant poetic influence upon his son. J. B. Yeats, as a young painter, associated himself with a minor Pre-Raphaelite group, including Edwin J. Ellis, a strong personality, poor painter, worse poet, and rather inadequate man-of-letters and Blake critic. This group, the Brotherhood, followed the Pre-Raphaelites in aiming at a union of painting and poetry, taking Blake and D. G. Rossetti as their masters. To J. B. Yeats, "Blake was a mighty poet," and one he associated with Shelley as late as 1916, when he wrote to his son: "With a single line Blake or Shelley can fill my vision with a wealth of fine things." [11] Despite this association, W. B. Yeats first learned from his father to think of Blake in connection with Rossetti rather than with Shelley, Nietzsche, and other moral rebels, as he did later. "When I was fifteen or sixteen my father had told me about Rossetti and Blake and given me their poetry to read." [12] It was fitting then that Yeats undertook his pioneering if misguided work on Blake in collaboration with his father's friend Ellis, whose passion for Blake had been "picked up in Pre-Raphaelite studios." [13] The portrait of Ellis in *Four Years* is deliberately fantastic, but is close enough to the real Ellis to be convincing.

The Ellis-Yeats edition of Blake has received little analysis, and the melancholy account that follows is partly intended to remedy this largely deserved neglect. [14] The mid-century Blake revival, definitively studied by Deborah Dorfman, had left the text of Blake in dreadful condition, a condition that Ellis and Yeats worsened unbelievably. As interpreters of many specific works, Ellis and Yeats are almost invariably inferior to Swinburne, sometimes grossly so, as on *The Marriage of Heaven and Hell* or *America*. As Miss Dorfman rightly remarks, the Ellis-Yeats edition has two redeeming areas, Yeats's general essay, "The Necessity of Symbolism," and the grasp throughout of Blake's dialectic of Nature and Imagination, which evaded Swinburne. [15] Unhappily, there is much, much else in the Ellis-Yeats edition, which is a monument to the arrogance and ignorance of Ellis, and to Yeats's second great struggle with the Covering Cherub of Poetic Influence, a struggle productive in this edition of some gorgeous nonsense and much more plain nonsense, and productive also, decades later, of *A Vision* and many of its allied poems and plays.

The Works of William Blake, Poetic, Symbolic, and Critical, in three volumes, was published in 1893, after four years' work by Ellis and Yeats. The title page bears, as alarming motto, Hamlet's "Bring me to the test/ And I the matter will re-word, which mad-ness/ Would gambol from." Volume One is "The System," and the second half of the volume is "The Symbolic System," of which the greater part is Yeats's own writing. "The Symbolic System" begins with "The Necessity of Symbolism," Yeats's defence of Blake's supposed mysticism. Yeats says that: "The chief difference between the metaphors of poetry and the symbols of mysticism is that the latter are woven together into a complete system." [16] "Mysticism" here, and throughout Yeats on Blake, seems to mean occultism and more precisely theosophy, of Madame Blavatsky's variety. On Yeats's account, poetic metaphors are the blocks for building theosophical mansions, and poetry is a gnosis that has yet to go the whole way. Invoking Swedenborg, Yeats distin-guishes between "three different degrees" he finds absolutely sepa-rated in Blake: natural, intellectual, and emotional. Natural things have spatial form; so do intellectual things, but their space is mental. Emotional things have "neither form nor substance—dwelling not in space but in time only." [17] This distinction is Yeats's and will reappear, much modified, in the late "Seven Propositions" of what Yeats insisted upon terming his "private philosophy" as contrasted to his "public philosophy" of A Vision.[18] But the distinction is simply not Blake's, and comes, as Yeats says, from the triads of Swedenborg and the theosophists. Nevertheless, Yeats promises that "in Blake we will discover it under many names, and trace the histories of the many symbolic rulers who govern its various subdivisions." [19] "Emotional" is not one of Blake's terms, unlike "natural" and "intellectual," which Blake always opposes to one another, as Yeats says. It is difficult to recall a place in Blake's work where "natural" is used positively or "intellectual" negatively. Blake generally speaks of "intellec-tual vision" as Shelley does of "intellectual beauty"; in each poet, "intellectual" means "beyond the senses," or "more than natural." "Natural" in Blake is almost a synonym for "selfish." But Yeats's notion of Blake's third order, of "emotional" things, is a Yeatsian invention, and initially a puzzling one. The first question must be, why did Yeats use the word "emotional" in this context? There is not a single occurrence of the word anywhere in Blake's verse or prose. Blake speaks of "feelings" or "passions," never of "emotions"; Yeats himself uses "emotion" only twice in all his poetry. The clue is in the Paterian word, almost a concept, "moods," for "The Necessity of Symbolism" employs "moods" not only as a near-synonym for "emotions," but centers its entire argument upon "moods." In 1893, the year in which the Ellis-Yeats edition was published, Yeats printed also the lovely brief lyric, *The Moods,* later to appear in *The Wind Among the Reeds.* Two years later, in a brief essay also called *The Moods,* he returned to his difficult version of the Paterian flux of impressions, the hard, gem-like flame. The lyric contrasts the "fire-born moods," which do not fall away, to time's decay, even of mountains and woods. In the essay, this enigmatic contrast is explained. Imaginative literature differs from all other writing "in being wrought about a mood, or a community of moods." These moods are from the Divinity and all "argument, theory, erudition, observation" must serve the moods. The artist's function is to "discover immortal moods in mortal desires." [20] Yeats derives here from his own father, who despite his unbelief considered personality, and hence poetry, to be divine.[21] We are close to the center of Yeats's vision when we struggle with this concept of "mood," for it encompasses not only his interpretation of Blake, and much of his own earlier poetry, but it is one of the two clearest links between his earlier and later work, the other being the flowering of the Rose into the image of the Mask. Jeffares points to the connection of the lyric and essay, *The Moods,* with *Per Amica Silentia Lunae,* the precursor to *A Vision.*[22] The "condition of fire," a synthesis of Blake, Shelley, and Pater, is contrasted there to "the terrestrial condition," which possesses the strife of good and evil, "but in the condition of fire is all music and all rest." [23] Yeats quotes the lyric, *The Moods,* there, to illustrate this state of achieved consciousness, of peace through art. In *Mosada, The Wanderings of Oisin,* and *The Rose* lyrics, lovers suffer many "moods" that they may approach the peace beyond mood that comes only through these divine messengers. In "The Necessity of Symbolism" Yeats

finds in the moods Blake's deepest meanings, and makes of Blake
something of a Paterian, but more of Yeats himself, the Pre-Raphaelite poet of *The Wanderings of Oisin*.

Blake in fact associated the condition of fire with intellectual
and not with emotional things, and Yeats's misunderstanding is so
fundamental that it scarcely can be mere misunderstanding, but
must be deliberate, an example of that *clinamen* or creative
swerve away from the precursor discussed in my first chapter.
Emotional things and natural things, two absolutely different degrees of reality in Yeats's interpretation of Blake, are actually the
same reality in Blake, belonging to Luvah, the Zoa or regent who
governs natural man and his passionate life. Yeats's misinterpretation is thus double; he associates the freedom of art in Blake
with the emotional rather than the intellectual life, and he removes emotional things from the natural context in which Blake
saw them as trapped. All that he does see accurately (or allow
himself to see) is that Blake firmly rejects nature. In establishing
this much, Yeats made a considerable advance upon Swinburne,
whose Blake was an uneasy blend of Rousseau and De Sade, at
once somehow an heroic naturalist and an erotic rebel straining
against even the limits of nature in his vitalism. Yeats at least
sensed the direction in which Blake's dialectics move, though he
went on to misrepresent the outline of Blake's vision almost totally.

Yeats's arbitrariness is never clearer than when he tells us
Blake's "poetic genius" is "the emotional life," and that "the history of moods is the history of the universe," since "the universal
mood we name God." [24] Something of Yeats's almost obsessive
drive to change Blake's terms is revealed when the figure of Los,
the prophetic principle, is introduced as "the great emotional or
inspired principle." [25] Blake's "energy" in *The Marriage of
Heaven and Hell* is translated by Yeats as "emotion or affection."
Again, Blake's central tenet is spoken of as "this poetic genius or
central mood in all things" or "a mood that goes through all the
moods." Quite suddenly, Yeats arrives at the embryo of his vision
of gyres, and his late struggle of man against God, in another
swerve away from Blake:

The mind or imagination or consciousness of man may be said to have two poles, the personal and impersonal, or, as Blake preferred to call them, the limit of contraction and the unlimited expansion. When we act from the personal we tend to bind our consciousness down as to a fiery centre. When, on the other hand, we allow our imagination to expand away from the egoistic mood, we become vehicles for the universal thought and merge in the universal mood. Thus a reaction of God against man and man against God . . . goes on continually. The "genius" within us is impatient and law-breaking, and only becomes peaceful and free when it grows one with "the poetic genius"—the universal mood.[26]

The translation of Blakean terms here is bold enough to make the entire passage Yeats rather than Blake. Blake's Limit of Contraction is Adam or natural man, the point beyond which we will not fall; it is possible to call this "the personal," if you want to, but hardly possible to call Blake's Prolific "the unlimited expansion," since there always is an outward boundary to energy, even in Blake. Blake's states of being are called moods by Yeats, and Blake's Imagination, which is not a state but the human existence itself, Yeats calls the universal mood or God, agreeing with Blake in this last. But there is no agreement between Blake and Yeats on states of being, for Yeats identifies art with the threefold state Blake called Beulah, and Blake identifies it with a further state, Eden. Beulah, the earthly paradise, world of fulfilled sexuality, is truly a realm of moods, and Blake would not abide in it. Yeats sets his quest toward it because his dialectic is simpler, moving only between a solipsistic self-absorption and the merging of that self in the universal mood. Prophesying *A Vision* and later works, Yeats allows even the poet very little free will: "No man can see or think of anything that has not affinity with his mood or 'state', as Blake preferred to call it." [27] This passive man suits Beulah, a state of being most marked by receptivity, but this is hardly Blake's kind of poet.

Something more of the temperamental and intellectual difference between the two poets can be seen if we apply Yeats's reading to Blake and try to decide how much of Blake's work is rendered irrelevant by it. The principal development in Blake's canon takes place in *The Four Zoas,* which Blake first conceived as a fuller-scale version of the story he had worked out in his minor poems, in the *Songs, America, Europe, The Book of Urizen.* But the poem (as Yeats did not realize) underwent a tremendous metamorphosis during its composition, as the two very different drafts of "Night VII" show. Blake had never been a seer of the emotional life, had never believed that an improvement of sensual enjoyment was more than the start (though the necessary start) of the process of imaginative redemption. Yet he had, in his minor poems, emphasized the necessity of revolution, while implying the insufficiency of revolution alone. The contest in Blake's minor poems is between Orc (fallen form of Luvah) and Urizen, and Blake seems to have known, from the start, that this contest was circular, the endless cycle depicted in *The Mental Traveller.* Blake, unlike Yeats, took no joy in the Wheel, and though Yeats went beyond Swinburne in seeing this, Yeats as an interpreter withdrew from his own insight. Orc ages into Urizen, for Urizen, to use Yeats's terms, has to do with emotional and not with intellectual things.

Yeats's Blake then is a Pre-Raphaelite and Paterian Blake, but while this was a distortion, it did not in itself transform Blake out of all recognition. That happened when Yeats ended "The Necessity of Symbolism" and went on to "The Three Persons and the Mirror," for here and in subsequent sections Yeats's Blake becomes a Gnostic, with profound results for Yeats's own "system" and poetry. Blake was vehemently set against all dualisms, Pauline or Cartesian, let alone the extreme Gnostic modification of Pauline dualism. But Yeats, even before he read arcane literature and became a Rosicrucian adept, was a natural Gnostic. He shared always the Gnostic sense of longing acutely for the soul's fortunate destiny after the body's death, a longing that is the negation of Blake's apocalyptic desires. And he shared also the Gnostics' obsession to learn the names of the demons through whose realms the soul must ascend. From the Gnostics ultimately, Yeats took his deep belief that evil ruled in his own epoch, but that something more congenial would come in the next. For Yeats, like the Gnostics, is profoundly pessimistic, even as Blake, despite all horrors, is humanly hopeful, as Shelley is until his last phase.

Gnosticism derives from the ancient Persian dualism, and its exaltation of the Shadow exactly suited Yeats's temperament, for Yeats was always painfully aware of his own divided consciousness, as against his father's natural unity of being, and so was disposed to welcome any doctrine that sanctified division in the self.

Yeats, from Blake's point of view, is a selfhood-communer in Ulro, a solipsist trapped forever in the realm of mirror-image, like the youth in *The Crystal Cabinet,* whose highest moment of vision yields a momentary stay in an illusive Beulah-world of sexual shadows. Yeats's vision begins, as Whitaker so enthusiastically shows, with the solipsistic reverie upon which all Gnosticism is founded.[28] The Gnostic Divinity beholds himself in the watery abyss, and part of him remains in that reflection, thus making a fallen world. That image in the abyss is the Shadow, and the quest of the Gnostic adept must be to enter the Shadow, for only the Shadow permits a path to redemption. In "The Three Persons and the Mirror" Yeats arbitrarily takes Blake's bitter name for "the vegetable glass of Nature" or "Enitharmon's looking-glass" and assumes that Blake shares the Gnostic confidence in the saving use of that glass. Yeats gives a theosophical Table of Correspondences in which the mirror is called Divine Imagination, precisely the reverse of what Blake found it to be.[29]

After its first two sections, there is little coherence in "The Symbolic System," and I will not assume the tendentious burden of analysis for each section. Yeats's prose in the Ellis-Yeats edition is remarkably uninteresting, particularly when we recall that Yeats is one of the prose masters in the language. There is so much obscurantism, and so much plain mental bewilderment, that we might as well be reading Madame Blavatsky. In what follows I will ignore all parts of Yeats's presentation that do not issue in some important element of his own thought.

In my Chapter 14, *"A Vision:* The Great Wheel," I trace the direct derivation of Yeats's systematic mythology from his own account of Blake, and so I omit here Yeats's curious description of the four Zoas or Giant Forms of Blake's mythology. As curious is Yeats's description of Beulah, which is a little nervous, very abrupt, and surprisingly cursory, considering how full Blake's account of that problematic state of being is. Yeats skips by the ambiguities of

Beulah, noting only "its evil aspect" as being the possibility that we may be "enslaved by the egoistic emotion of the false centre," and he omits the role of Beulah in the Fall.[30] His unhappiness is instructive, and is another indication that he was well aware of the revisionary aspect of his ostensibly exegetical labor.

In Section VI, "The Rotation of Luvah and Urizen," Yeats is very close to his later account of the Great Wheel in *A Vision;* the diagrams are clearly the direct ancestors of *A Vision*'s barren geometries. The very confused summary of Blake's Spectre and Emanation is notable chiefly because Yeats does not link these conceptual images to Shelley's *alastor* and epipsyche, his own more direct source for the quest of shadow after *daimon*. Though Yeats was to owe to a misinterpretation of Blake his savage notion that sexual love is founded upon spiritual hatred, it seems clear that he tended to take his erotic vision from Shelley rather than from Blake.

The most important part of "The Symbolic System" for the student of Yeats's own symbolism is Section IX, "The Covering Cherub." Yeats defines Blake's Covering Cherub as the "mask of created form in which the uncreated spirit makes itself visible." This is an early and obscure formulation of Yeats's theory of the Mask, but has little to do with Blake's Covering Cherub. Yeats notes the origin of the Cherub in Ezekiel, but not how Ezekiel uses the figure, and his account of how Blake regards the Cherub is mistaken:

> He praises or denounces this Covering Cherub according to whether he considers it as a means whereby things, too far above us to be seen as they are, can be made visible in symbol and representative form, or as a satanic hindrance keeping our eager wills away from the freedom and truth of the Divine world. It has both aspects for every man.[31]

Blake never praises the Covering Cherub; Yeats misunderstands, probably genuinely, the passage he cites in support of his assertion, for in the passage Los does not create the subdivisions of the Cherub, but exposes them as error by forcing their manifestation in time and space. To Blake, the Covering Cherub is primarily the fallen form of Tharmas or the instinctual life, the child's power of actualizing its desires. The Cherub manifests himself therefore primarily as a particular kind of anxiety, creative anxiety or the fear of one's own blocked potential. Between ourselves and our desires lies the whole fallen body of nature, the coiling serpent of time and space, and so the Cherub takes on the body of outward nature. Yeats is accurate when he says that "it is the whole bulk of outer things when taken in its widest significance, and upon it Blake pours out his most vehement hatred," but not, as Yeats goes on to add, "his most tender love," for Blake loves the world only when it can be seen as the re-creation of Los, as at the close of Book I of *Milton*.

Yeats's modification of the Covering Cherub, his insistence upon its duality, comes about because he identifies it with love, of which he says "it is the lower part, the mask and cloak of the higher." [32] In this identification, Yeats performs the true work of the poet, and is found by his *clinamen*, his own movement out of and away from Blake. Blake, as I noted in the opening chapter, identified Milton's shadow with the Covering Cherub. Yeats identifies the Cherub with Blake's shadow, which is to say that Yeats found in Blake a theory of sexual love that Yeats wanted to find, though it was barely there to be found. This was not necessary, except for Yeats's highly individual needs, but it has affected the interpretation of Blake until this day. Borges genially insists that we cannot avoid reading precursors differently, once we know their descendants, and literary experience tends to confirm him. We read Milton differently after reading Blake, and Blake differently when we know Yeats.

The Cherub, in Ezekiel, is a guardian of Eden who has fallen into the role of Satanic hinderer. Poetic influence and Romantic love, to return to a surmise of this book's opening chapter, may be the same process; at the least they are similitudes verging toward an identity. Milton's shadow, for Blake, is to some degree Milton's influence; Blake's shadow, for Yeats, is largely a dark vision or obsession that sees sexual love as demonic. For in regard to love, Yeats is a thoroughgoing Gnostic. Love belongs to the other world and can be made manifest in our fallen one only through the Covering Cherub, the shadow the quester enters. In this view, love is a descent, though a necessary one, into the watery abyss of multiplicity and illusive forms. Scholars agree that Gnosticism is necessarily pessimistic but not necessarily ascetic in its sexual aspects, and Yeats again is very much a Gnostic in his modification of Blake. With Blake's image of the emanation Yeats compounds always the Great Mother of the Gnostics, Helena, whom Simon Magus took as his bride in the shape of a harlot he found at Tyre. Yeats has more in common with Simon Magus than with Blake, for Yeats sought the Romantic Muse as his Gnostic Helena, and would have found her in Maud Gonne had the lady permitted it.

It is in the next step of his systemizing of Blake, still in the section on the Covering Cherub, that Yeats allows us to find his center of vision. Blake did not make a specific association between the Covering Cherub and history, though the association is implicit in him. Yeats makes it explicit, for in the Covering Cherub the embryo of *A Vision*'s dialectics of history is formed. The blindness of our love must be woven, for Yeats, by the terrible network of the stars. Yeats could have chosen a dozen different entrances to Blake's twenty-seven phases or Churches of history (the twenty-eighth being the apocalyptic one); he chose to enter through the shadow that is the Cherub. The student of Yeats, particularly of Yeats's relation to his Romantic precursors, must ask why, for the choice is arbitrary in terms of Blake but reflects deep self-knowledge, true imaginative inwardness, on Yeats's part. The movement is from the sorrow of love to the pity beyond all telling hid in the heart of that sorrow:

> The Cherub is divided into twenty-seven heavens or churches, that is to say, into twenty-seven passive states through which man travels, and these heavens or churches are typified by twenty-seven great personages from Adam to Luther . . . one era closes, another commences. . . . In these twenty-seven . . . Blake found . . . the whole story of man's life. . . .[33]

This is a precise enough account of the phases of the moon in *A Vision* but inaccurate for Blake on two points; to Blake these Churches are not necessarily passive, and in them he certainly did not find the whole story of our life. The emphasis on human passivity, and on an astrological completeness, reinforces Yeats's

preference for Beulah as a finality, and his revision of Blake's intellectual warfare into the unification of emotional moods. Yeats
is too anxious to reach the Gnostic conclusion that "the Cherub is
the body of every man," for that is far from Blake's judgment of
the body.[34] Yeats goes on to draw a "spiral diagram" that is his
first gyre, his "Chart of the Descending & Ascending Reason,"
which traces the supposed path through history of Urizen in his
role of Spectre of Albion, the baffled residue that survives the Primal Man's loss of everything he has created and loved.

After this, Yeats's exposition of "The Symbolic System" becomes haphazard, a disordered cataloging of symbolic colors,
dualities, names, stories, images, and body parts. Under the influence of the Christian Cabala, Yeats even collapses into the analysis of symbolic *sounds*. As there is still a tendency among literary
scholars to take Yeats with the utmost seriousness as a critic of
Blake, without enduring the travail of reading through the Ellis-
Yeats edition, I give a few samples of Yeats as Cabalist:

> In *Br*omion the *br* is made evident. They belong to dark anger.
> . . . But in this latter name [Ololon] the *l* is not a letter of dark-
> ness, and it alternates with the o as Ololon (who contained multi-
> tudes of both sexes) alternates her moods till she manifests as a
> virgin at last, just as her name closes with the letter of night.
>   The last two syllables of Palamabron, read backwards from the
> end, mean feminine region (*on*) and masculine fury (*br*). Then
> come three times the letter *a,* a letter of light, as in Ololon came
> three times the letter *o*. Between the vowels are found the maternal
> letter *m* and the liquid *l*,—for Palamabron is doomed to sorrow,
> like Theotormon, but is not so dark as he. The letter *p* is rare
> among Blake's names, and its significance can only be guessed.[35]

There is a lot more of this kind of thing, and it is fun, but
that will suffice. I will not go on to Volume Two, "The Meaning," of the Ellis-Yeats edition, because thankfully the writing
there is by Ellis, though he worked up earlier drafts by Yeats.
Ellis had a tendency to go into trances (literal ones, I mean)
when he read Blake, and so we could not expect him to have read
through to the end of any of the long poems. Yeats somehow contrived to transcribe (more or less) *The Four Zoas,* without read-

ing the poem through either, but then he was much given to reverie, though not so frequently lost in actual trances. My judgment
that neither had read through the long poems is charitable, and
has nothing to do with disputing their interpretations. They
make so many scores of mistakes in recounting the narratives that
any literate student with a little patience could do better.

Yeats, in later years, was uneasy about the Ellis-Yeats edition,
and declined either to endorse it or absolutely to repudiate it. His
two essays on Blake, "William Blake and the Imagination" and
"Blake's Illustrations to Dante," both written four years later, in
1897, and his description of Blake in the account of Phase 16 of *A
Vision* are fairer grounds for judging his mature relationship to
Blake. The brilliant portrait of Blake in *A Vision* will be considered later, in its proper context. "William Blake and the Imagination" salutes the prophet "who loved the future like a mistress," but emphasizes that he "spoke confusedly and obscurely."
Yeats's Blake is still a Pre-Raphaelite poet who "announced the
religion of art" and fought against "bad taste and vulgarity." [36]
In *A Vision* Yeats will know better, when he will associate Blake
with Rabelais and Aretino, in the best critical insight he ever
achieved concerning Blake, who after all insisted that "Exuberance is Beauty." [37]

In the midst of this essay, which presents Blake as a kind of incoherent precursor of Oscar Wilde, Yeats redeems himself by observing that to Blake "the imaginative arts were therefore the
greatest of Divine revelations, and that the sympathy with all living things, sinful and righteous alike, which the imaginative arts
awaken, is that forgiveness of sins commanded by Christ." [38]
With this one observation, Yeats transcends not alone the elaborate nonsense of the Ellis-Yeats edition, but indeed all previous
criticism of Blake. Unfortunately, the remainder of the essay falls
away from this splendid recognition. Instead of developing this
central insight, Yeats returns to absurdity, telling us that Blake
was "content to express every beautiful feeling that came into his
head without troubling about its utility." From this it is an easy
step to the famous and wrong judgment that Blake "was a man
crying out for a mythology, and trying to make one because he
could not find one to his hand." [39] If the imaginative arts are the

greatest of Divine revelations, why should Blake be enslaved by any other man's system? He made his mythology because he conceived such making to be the artist's proper work. Yeats is the man crying out for a mythology, still hoping in 1897 that he will find it among the sacred mountains of Ireland, but fated to realize later that he must make his own.

"William Blake and His Illustrations to the *Divine Comedy*" is a much better essay, praising those qualities "which made Blake the one perfectly fit illustrator for the *Inferno* and the *Purgatorio*" while seeing that he could have no sympathy for Dante's Paradise. Between the two essays of 1897, Blake has progressed from a Pre-Raphaelite to a Symbolist poet. By doing so, he clarifies Yeats's difficult thoughts on the problem of poetic influence. Blake's idea that art renews the vision of the precursor is described as "purifying one's mind, as with a flame, in study of the works of the great masters, who were great because they had been granted by divine favour a vision of the unfallen world from which others are kept apart by the flaming sword that turns every way." [40] Blake, in a passage of *The Marriage of Heaven and Hell* frequently cited by Yeats, had prophesied that when the Cherub with his flaming sword has left the Tree of Life, "the whole creation will be consumed, and appear infinite, and holy whereas it now appears finite & corrupt." [41] Uncovering the Cherub, as Yeats momentarily sees, can be accomplished by the act of becoming one with the redemptive imagination of the precursor. But, once again, Yeats withdraws from Blake's vision, with the famous observation that Blake was "a too literal realist of imagination, as others are of nature." [42]

Yeats's wariness in regard to Blake is strongly evident when he sets forth Blake's quarrel with Dante. In this complex quarrel, Yeats will not take sides, thus anticipating *A Vision*'s assignment of phases, where Yeats joins Shelley and Dante in the *daimonic* Phase 17, while Blake is apart in the "positive" Phase 16. Something of this distinction will be clarified in my chapters on *A Vision;* here it must suffice to see at just what point Yeats again parts from Blake. Blake breaks from history in *Europe* by judging the Christian centuries to be Enitharmon's dream, the troubled sleep that nevertheless will end in historical salvation. But Yeats cannot share even Blake's personal vision of a possible Christianity, the apocalyptic humanism that finds in Jesus a valid augury of organized Innocence. Always a sincere Gnostic, Yeats cannot conceive of salvation as an historical event, nor can he rid his personal religion of the sacramental element so strong in all Gnostics. Blake's casting-out of every aspect of sacramentalism is alien to Yeats's temperament, and in the orthodox symbolism of Dante, with its powerful and coherent abstract correlatives, he finds a pattern to encourage his own quest for abstractions.

To understand Yeats's development, with regard to Blake's influence as to other influences, it is necessary now to go back, from 1897 to 1889 and *The Wanderings of Oisin,* where the Romantic tradition of quest and vision met the current of a national mythology, and mastered it.

6: Anglo-Irish Poetry and *The Wanderings of Oisin*

A representative anthology of English poetry written by the Irish generally emphasizes twentieth-century work, as not much Anglo-Irish poetry before Yeats has received critical attention or approbation. Swift, Goldsmith, Thomas Moore, and George Darley are not particularly Irish in their main achievement, and the principal Victorian Anglo-Irish poets—Allingham, DeVere, Mangan, Ferguson, and Davis—are relatively minor figures when placed in the larger context of Victorian poetry. Yeats's true context is English Romantic tradition from Spenser through Pater and the Tragic Generation, but he saw himself as one of the Anglo-Irish line also ("Nor may I less be counted one/ With Davis, Mangan, Ferguson"). It seems clear that part of Yeats's exoticism, for English as for American and other English-speaking readers, is due to his deliberate Anglo-Irish coloring. The Anglo-Irish poetic tradition is not easily defined or described, but seems nevertheless an authentic one. Its inventors would appear to be Moore, in only one aspect of his work, and J. J. Callanan, like Moore a Romantic disciple of Byron. Callanan's original lyrics are most derived from Byron and Moore, but his versions from the Gaelic introduce a

different kind of effect into English poetry, as in the very fine
Dirge of O'Sullivan Bear. But the effect is not without its hazards,
and an unkind critic might guess that splendid dirge to be a satire
by Peacock, in some of its stanzas:

> Had he died calmly,
>   I would not deplore him,
> Or if the wild strife
>   Of the sea-war closed o'er him;
> But with ropes round his white limbs,
>   Through ocean to trail him,
> Like a fish after slaughter!—
>   'Tis therefore I wail him.

The problem is one of a certain unrestrained exuberance of
rhetoric, of the kind that English Romantic poetry has been
blamed for, but with small reason. Yet American and Irish Romanticism does suffer from it, as in the astonishing Chivers and
much of Poe, and very much in Callanan, Mangan, and Davis,
the principal practitioners of the Gaelic mode in English poetry
before Yeats and his contemporaries. Mangan, whom Lionel
Johnson admired almost excessively, seems to me the most satisfying of Irish poets before Yeats, and is in some respects a purer
poet than Yeats, and certainly a more genuine visionary. Of
course, this is not to assert that Mangan is necessarily a good poet,
but only that he had qualities that Yeats, even as a very great
poet, contrived to lack. Mangan meant little to Yeats, as one can
see by his anthology *A Book of Irish Verse,* which favors the more
conventional (and English) Ferguson and Allingham. To get at
Yeats's true opinions on Anglo-Irish poets, we have to set aside his
statements during the Nineties, when he knowingly overrated
them for political as well as personal reasons, and seek instead his
mature judgment at the age of forty, in a letter to John Quinn, of
15 February 1905:

> Irish national literature, though it has produced many fine
> ballads and many novels written in the objective spirit of a ballad,
> has never produced an artistic personality in the modern sense of
> the word. Tom Moore was merely an incarnate social ambition.

And Clarence Mangan differed merely from the impersonal ballad writers about him in being miserable. He was not a personality as Edgar Poe was. He had not thought out or felt out a way of looking at the world peculiar to himself. We will have a hard fight in Ireland before we get the right for every man to see the world in his own way admitted.[1]

True as this was, Mangan was perhaps a better poet than Poe, though mindless when compared to Poe, and not an artistic personality in Yeats's sense. Mangan is well worth study in his own right, but needs brief consideration here as another instance, like that of Johnson and Dowson, of a way that Yeats chose not to follow. Yeats was a very remarkable literary critic, when he wanted to be, as in his earlier essay on Shelley, but he undervalued Mangan as he did any other poet whose achievement might have helped block his own. Mangan was not so much an Irish Poe as he was a kind of Irish and lesser Nerval, a desperately haunted man with an absolute gift for vision that frequently declined into hallucination, as in poems like *Shapes and Signs, A Vision of Connaught,* and the self-pitying *The Nameless One.* But in at least a few poems—*Ichabod! Thy Glory has Departed,* the Clare-like *And Then No More,* and the famous *Dark Rosaleen*—Mangan frees his vision both from egregious fantasy and from pathos, and writes a kind of poetry that is distinctive and curiously national in its mixture of personal and political apocalypticism. The diffuse figure of the beloved merges perfectly here with the image of the oppressed nation:

> I could scale the blue air,
>   I could plough the high hills,
> Oh, I could kneel all night in prayer,
>   To heal your many ills!
> And one . . . beamy smile from you
>   Would float like light between
> My toils and me, my own, my true,
>   My Dark Rosaleen!
>   My fond Rosaleen!
> Would give me life and soul anew,
> A second life, a soul anew

> My Dark Rosaleen!
> O! the Erne shall run red
>   With redundance of blood,
> The earth shall rock beneath our tread,
>   And flames wrap hill and wood,
> And gun-peal, and slogan cry,
>   Wake many a glen serene,
> Ere you shall fade, ere you shall die,
>   My Dark Rosaleen!
>   My own Rosaleen!

Yeats's frenzies, from the start, were to be more studied, and always highly qualified, as in the final sections of *Meditations in Time of Civil War* and *Nineteen Hundred and Nineteen.* Though Yeats once judged his poems on Irish themes as being in the tradition of Allingham (in a letter to the poet's widow, requesting permission to edit a selected volume of Allingham), it is difficult to hear Allingham in them, as Allingham was very much a Tennysonian poet, whose work always seems rather less Irish in flavor than Tennyson's own *The Voyage of Maeldune*.[2] And Sir Samuel Ferguson, though nowhere near so dull as he is reputed to be, has only his Irish subject matter to evidence that he is a national poet. Ferguson provided Yeats with a general example; his long heroic poems prepare the way for *The Wanderings of Oisin,* but Ferguson's style and manner are less exotic and individual than Allingham's, and to Yeats he seemed at last just what he was, another minor Victorian poet.

Yeats's problem as an Anglo-Irish poet was therefore, in part, having to commence *ab ovo,* but as though an actual achievement lay behind him, when in fact the only really good national poet before him, Mangan, made him uneasy. This uneasiness is central to Yeats; he feared rhetoric, yet Anglo-Irish poetry is rhetorical if it is to be itself. The best Anglo-Irish poets after Yeats—Kavanagh, Clarke, Rodgers—are highly rhetorical, and overstatement is a prevalent (and successful) mode in Synge and O'Casey. Though the most famous lines against rhetoric since Rimbaud's are by Yeats, his vision of reality increasingly demanded a more flamboyant rhetorical procedure than his own statements could have sanctioned. This is not unique in Yeats; the most wearisome critical statements, from Wordsworth to the present day, are those against poetical diction and in favor of the rhythms of supposedly common speech. These statements, whether in Wordsworth, Pound, Eliot, or in the host of little poundlings or elioticians, invariably turn out to have no relation whatsoever to any good poet's actual performance. Whatever the rhythms of Yeats became, they never were conversational. If one wants that, one can go, I suppose, to Auden, Betjeman or Larkin, but not to the High Romantic, Anglo-Irish Yeats.

The Wanderings of Oisin is Yeats's principal, overt attempt at Anglo-Irish mythological poetry. It is probably Yeats's most underrated major poem, in proportion to its high merits, and it is certainly a very rhetorical performance. But it is more than that, for the whole of Yeats is already in it, as he himself always knew. And it is a much better poem than a number of late, famous poems by Yeats that have been consistently over-valued by Yeats's critics; I would much rather reread it than rehearse again, to myself or others, the mere complication of *Among School Children* or the blatancy of *Under Ben Bulben* and *The Gyres*.

The matter of *Oisin* is Irish, based largely upon an eighteenth-century poem by Michael Comyn that Yeats found translated in the *Transactions of the Ossianic Society*. At a later time, Yeats perhaps received his material a bit more directly from the folk, through Lady Gregory, if we are to believe him in this regard. But, with *Oisin,* the reader must begin by remembering how far the poet actually is from his supposed sources; he sits in the British Museum, himself knowing no Gaelic (he never bothered to learn any) and he reads a version of a version. He is so far from mythology, and indeed in every sense so far from Ireland, that we need not be surprised to discover that his poem, despite its Celtic colorings, is in the center of English Romantic tradition, and indeed in one particular current of that tradition, which I have called the internalization of quest-romance.

Spenser is the great ancestor-poet of this tradition, as Yeats shows, not so much in the surprisingly weak essay on Spenser with which he prefaced a volume of selections, as in his choice and arrangement of poems and passages in that book. Our studies of poetic influence, as a critical subject, are still so primitive in theory and pedantic in procedure that we really know very little about the relation of English Romantic poetry to its ancestors in the English Renaissance, or for that matter the relation between Romantic and modern poetry. Yet the poetic line leading to *The Wanderings of Oisin* is clear enough. It goes from Spenser through Milton and on to Blake and Wordsworth. There the tradition splits, the Blake influence coming to Yeats's *Oisin* direct (though with the aid of Balzac, and of some esoteric writers) but the Wordsworthian internalization of the quest reaching Yeats rather through Shelley and Keats and their followers than through Yeats's direct reading of Wordsworth, whom he always tended to dislike and ignore. Nevertheless, it is a genuine peculiarity of literary history that Yeats's *Oisin,* his true starting point as a poet, owes a great deal to a poem Yeats probably never read in full and was repelled by when he looked at, the frigid but all-important Wordsworthian anti-climax, *The Excursion.* It is from the figure of the Solitary in *The Excursion* that the heroes of *Alastor, Endymion,* and *Childe Harold III* derive, and from these questers and their followers in Browning's *Pauline, Paracelsus,* and *Sordello,* and throughout early Tennyson, that Yeats takes his *Oisin.* After Yeats, the tradition appears to end, though it has its satyr-epilogue in the ferocious parody of Stevens's *The Comedian as the Letter C,* where the Paterian quester subsides into a domesticated scholar of the quotidian, his centuries-old journey after the Ideal having led him past so many charmers only at last to leave him in the refuge of "daughters with curls."

The main tradition of the Romantic quest is not one in which the imagination is ravaged by the strength of despair. The great questers, and their creators, suffer from their own proper strength; they are destroyed by the power of hope, by the imagination itself. Blake is the exception; his Spectre of Urthona counsels despair, but Blake was almost unique in literary tradition since the Hebrew prophets. Even the apocalyptic Shelley, who wore a ring saying "The good time will come," suffers as Wordsworth saw the poet suffering, as one who:

> often sees
> Too clearly; feels too vividly; and longs

> To realize the vision, with intense
> And ever-constant yearning;—there—there lies
> The excess, by which the balance is destroyed.

The Solitary is Death-in-Life, a man who can no longer live in nature. He is prophesied earlier in Wordsworth by the driven wanderers of *Guilt and Sorrow* and by the complexly disturbed Marmaduke of *The Borderers*. More directly, he is a phase of Wordsworth himself in *The Prelude,* in its crisis passages, and in the perplexed man who stands at the center of the crisis lyrics, the great trilogy of *Tintern Abbey, Resolution and Independence,* and the *Intimations* Ode. This man—whether it be Wordsworth himself or that abyss in him the Solitary represents—suffers a sadness that is not hopelessness but balked imagination, or rather hope in excess of natural expectation. In Book IV of *The Excursion* Wordsworth gave the motto for the line of romances that goes from *Alastor* to *Oisin:* ". . . 'tis a thing impossible to frame/ conceptions equal to the soul's desires." The actual motto to *Alastor* is from Book I of *The Excursion,* slightly modified by Shelley:

> The good die first,
> And those whose hearts are dry as summer dust,
> Burn to the socket!

Wordsworth's Solitary is Purgatorial Man, perhaps ultimately to be traced back to the Red Cross Knight in Book I of *The Faerie Queene*. It is only an immediate paradox that in the High Romantic period this Man wanders mostly not the wastes of the world but its bowers. For the Romantic versions of the earthly paradise are all purgatorial; the trial is by sex, by repose, by the waters of regressiveness. Yeats's Oisin will meet dancing, victories, and sleep, and these are the stones of the fire. Almost the last straightforward representative of Romantic quest literature we have is the extraordinary prose romance, *A Voyage to Arcturus* by David Lindsay (first published in 1920), in which every antagonist to a Promethean quest is presented as being another form of pleasure. The goal of the quest from the Solitary through Oisin is sublimity, but it is a sublimity impossible to distinguish from an absolute solipsism. It is the sublimity not of conceptions, but only of a hoped-for-potential, one that turns upon infinitude. Words-worth, in *The Prelude,* records his great moments as coming to him in solitude, and he names the greatness carefully as "possible sublimity." If it is a sense, then it is of "something evermore about to be." *The Excursion*'s Solitary suffers not so much the loss of this possibility but the fact that once he felt it as possibility, and his despair is that he wishes vainly to change not what he is but what he was. To forget that once one hoped for the sublime is not possible; to remember it is the anguish of solitude.

This is the matrix of Shelley's *Alastor,* the first mature trial of his imagination, and a successful purgatorial poem for its maker, and for the readers it helped make into poets from Browning to Yeats. The quester of *Alastor* is seeking the spiritual form of his total desire, and the poem grimly traces the extraordinary remorse-lessness of this search. Not merely the origins of much that was permanent in the Yeatsian vision, but its teleology as well, is es-tablished in *Alastor,* and established in a way congenial to Yeats, as an *antithetical* rebellion against Wordsworthian naturalism.

Shelley's Poet has suffered vision, in the shape of a woman who is his emanation or epipsyche, the total form of his imagina-tion. This vision of her is destructive, and *Alastor* is primarily a poem about the destructive power of the imagination, of self-con-sciousness that divides the spirit, and separates it off both from others and itself. The theme of *Alastor* is stated by Yeats, in the ac-cent of Pater, in 1900, all the more effectively for being intended as a general summary of Shelley's myth, rather than a direct read-ing of the poem. Yeats has a vision of Shelley as a man of ancient times who "would have wandered, lost in a ceaseless reverie, in some chapel of the Star of infinite desire." There follows a superb reverie, as central to Yeats as to Shelley:

> I think too that as he knelt before an altar where a thin flame burnt in a lamp made of green agate, a single vision would have come to him again and again, a vision of a boat drifting down a broad river between high hills where there were caves and towers, and following the light of one Star; and that voices would have told him how there is for every man some one scene, some one adventure, some one picture that is the image of his secret life,

for wisdom first speaks in images, and that this one image, if he would but brood over it his life long, would lead his soul, disentangled from unmeaning circumstance and the ebb and flow of the world, into that far household where the undying gods await all whose souls have become simple as flame, whose bodies have become quiet as an agate lamp.[3]

This passage, and much else in *The Philosophy of Shelley's Poetry*, is a prefigurement of Yeats's most beautiful prose work, *Per Amica Silentia Lunae*, itself a prelude to *A Vision*. Yet this beautiful passage seems to me more important than that; Yeats is too bewilderingly complex for any one passage to hold his essence, and still this comes closer than any other I know. What Yeats wanted, as a poet, was to reach at last what, following Blake and Shelley, he called the Condition of Fire, and the immense variety of his art longed always not for a multitude of voices, but to be "struck dumb in the simplicity of fire." The flame here is the hard gem-like flame of Pater, and also the diamond glow of Shelley's *The Witch of Atlas*, and the diamond jubilance beyond the fire of Blake's Eden. The one image, the one adventure, is Shelley's, but also, in Yeats's view, it is Yeats's own, or Dante's, for it belongs to the *daimonic* man, the poet of Phase 17 for whom Unity of Being is most possible, yet whose experiential agony will be "enforced self-realization," which is the agony of self-consciousness of Wordsworth's Solitary and his descendants.

Shelley's quester spurns every natural solace, in the name of his imagination, and thwarted nature takes its revenge by stalking the Poet even as he pursues his vision. The Spirit of Solitude or *alastor* is a shadow, a baffled residue of the natural selfhood the Poet has repudiated. For all this world's beauty, this world belongs to the *alastor*, and the Poet must die unfulfilled, his vision still evanescent. To Keats, the poem *Alastor* was a vital provocation, and the quest-romance *Endymion* is a reaction against both *Alastor* and *The Excursion*. Keats's hero, like Shelley's Poet, is determined (by his creator) to escape the fate of Wordsworth's Solitary. The Solitary lives on, but as death-in-life; the Poet dies, because his passion would not accept the possibility of death-in-life;

Endymion seeks a natural love, a human sympathy, that will yet satisfy the imagination. Keats is greatly confused in his quest-romance (I mean also that there is greatness in his confusion), and Endymion finds both kinds of love, natural and imaginative, and loses both, and at last by Keats's desperation rather mechanically is found to possess both in one. Everything about his poem, but most of all its theme, made Keats uneasy, and its critics still are as uneasy as defenders of *The Excursion. Alastor,* a poem perfectly consistent with itself, is simply the best poem of the three, and its drastic solution *contra naturam* founded a tradition that Wordsworth and Keats could not themselves foster. I venture that the advanced students of poetic influence, when they rise among us, will find *Alastor* to be the true ancestor of an astonishing number of post-Shelleyan poets and poems, including many who presented themselves as overtly anti-Shelleyan. Eliot's *Alastor*-phase, for one example, goes from the early, suppressed (and very fine) *The Death of St. Narcissus* through *The Waste Land,* where nature, society, and history together cannot contain or satisfy the self-destructive imagination. Eliot's apocalypse, even before it became orthodox, is a highly fastidious one, but what raises the fastidiousness to a passion rather than a triviality, or merely a personal pathology, is the Shelleyan shadow or avenging *daimon,* our deep sense as readers that the poet himself is being stalked by his own nature, and must be victimized by its revenge.

The direct history of the *alastor* theme would take us through a relatively uncharted sea of nineteenth-century poetry before reaching Yeats's *The Wanderings of Oisin* and *The Shadowy Waters,* and the matter is too extensive for description here. Darley's fine *Nepenthe,* Thomas Stoddart's extravagant *The Death-Wake,* and much of early Tennyson are a part of the story; so are aspects of the Spasmodic poets and of Swinburne. Browning is more directly relevant to a consideration of Yeats, though, as I have said, the influence of Browning on Yeats is a very difficult one to assess. Yeats himself worried about it, as I have noted, and at least one major effort by Yeats, *The Gift of Harun Al-Rashid* (1923), is an amazing act of ventriloquism, in which Browning speaks again. This is not a work of the novice Yeats, but a long, major poem by

an assured artist of fifty-eight, allegorically presenting the autobiographical genesis of *A Vision,* a book permeated by Blake and
Shelley, but which has a strong flavor of Browning as well. As late
as 1929, Yeats again confesses that Browning is "to me a dangerous influence," and a deep comparative reading of Browning and
Yeats would show why. But a more historical reason for the dangerous affinity can be traced in the legacy of internalized quest
left to both poets by Shelley. Browning's *Oisin* and *Shadowy Waters* are *Pauline* and *Paracelsus,* his first major (and altogether
Shelleyan) poems. Though *Paracelsus* had a direct influence
upon Yeats, the true link here between the two poets seems to be
Browning's powerful essay on Shelley, which is Browning's only
critical testament in prose. Like Hallam's essay on Tennyson,
Browning's Shelley essay had a strong effect on the poetic aesthetic of Yeats during the decade 1893–1903, and both essays are
dominant influences in Yeats's best work as a literary critic, done
from 1896 to 1903 and gathered together as the volume *Ideas of
Good And Evil,* in 1903. The presence of Browning's essay is felt
here most strongly where it would be expected, in the essay on
Shelley, but it can be found also in essays on William Morris and
on Blake.

Browning's essay is, among many other things, an act of exor-
cism. From having been a direct, confessional poet in the mode
that Shelley never wholly abandoned, Browning had recoiled into
the apparently dramatic mode of his major achievements, but at a
hidden personal cost, involving the guilt of having failed the first
fully authentic thrust of his own imagination. Throughout his
life, Browning was to associate the autonomy of his own imagination with the exemplary figure of Shelley, while the claims of an
extra-imaginative authority were personified for him by his
mother and his wife. *Andrea Del Sarto* and *Childe Roland to the
Dark Tower Came* are the best of the highly problematic monologues in which Browning deals with his own imaginative guilt.
Writing in Paris, in December 1851, at the threshold of his full
maturity as a poet, Browning confronts his earlier self in Shelley,
whom he could not cease to love. The essay makes a distinction,
dubious but fascinating, between the "objective" (what Browning

thinks he has become) and the "subjective" poet, of whom Shelley is the great example. The objective poet fashions what "will of necessity be substantive, projected from himself and distinct." The subjective poet is a seer, not a fashioner, and what he sees is the highest reality:

> He, gifted like the objective poet with the fuller perception of nature and man, is impelled to embody the thing he perceives, not so much with reference to the many below as to the One above him, the supreme Intelligence which apprehends all things in their absolute truth,—an ultimate view ever aspired to, if but partially attained, by the poet's own soul. Not what man sees, but what God sees—the *Ideas* of Plato, seeds of creation lying burningly on the Divine Hand—it is toward these that he struggles.[4]

Yeats, as Whitaker notes, echoes this passage twice.[5] Describing Morris, Yeats sees the limitation of the absolutely subjective poet as being also his strength:

> His poetry often wearies us, as the unbroken green of July wearies us, for there is something in us, some bitterness because of the Fall, it may be, that takes a little from the sweetness of Eve's apple after the first mouthful; but he who did all things gladly and easily, who never knew the curse of labour, found it always as sweet as it was in Eve's mouth. All kinds of associations have gathered about the pleasant things of the world and half taken the pleasure out of them for the greater number of men, but he saw them as when they came from the Divine Hand.[6]

Earlier, writing on Blake and the imagination, Yeats recalled Browning more overtly in a highly Paterian defence of "the religion of art," of which Blake had been the prophet:

> We write of great writers, even of writers whose beauty would once have seemed an unholy beauty, with rapt sentences like those our fathers kept for the beatitudes and mysteries of the Church; and no matter what we believe with our lips, we believe with our hearts that beautiful things, as Browning said in his one prose essay that was not in verse, have "lain burningly on the Divine hand," and that when time has begun to wither, the Divine hand will fall

heavily on bad taste and vulgarity. When no man believed these things William Blake believed them. . . .[7]

This use of Browning is illuminated further on in Yeats's essay when Blake's relative good fortune at writing in a bad time is contrasted to poets who worked in a more receptive imaginative context:

> Sometimes one feels, even when one is reading poets of a better time—Tennyson or Wordsworth, let us say—that they have troubled the energy and simplicity of their imaginative passions by asking whether they were for the helping or for the hindrance of the world, instead of believing that all beautiful things have "lain burningly on the Divine hand." But when one reads Blake, it is as though the spray of an inexhaustible fountain of beauty was blown into our faces. . . .[8]

Browning's "subjective poet" has undergone a transformation, here and in the description of Morris. For Browning, Shelley was the supreme subjective poet because of "his noblest and predominating characteristic," caught by Browning with great subtlety in a difficult summary:

> This I call his simultaneous perception of Power and Love in the absolute, and of Beauty and Good in the concrete, while he throws, from his poet's station between both, swifter, subtler, and more numerous films for the connexion of each with each, than have been thrown by any modern artificer of whom I have knowledge. . . .[9]

The films are Shelley's symbolic images, upon which Yeats wrote what is still the best commentary, but it may be that Yeats's *The Philosophy of Shelley's Poetry* is only an expansion of Browning's summary. Browning emphasizes the subjective poet's direct encounter with spiritual realities, while Yeats, whether dealing with Blake, Morris, or Shelley, emphasizes the dialectic of subjectivity, as indeed those poets did before him (though this applies more to the Morris of the prose romances than of the verse). For Browning, the subjective poet is not quite a man, but a kind of angel; for Yeats he is a man who has subsumed experiential evil, while continuing an unobscured gaze at the Condition of Fire, at the simplicities that lie burning on the hand of God. Yeats sees the conflict of subjectivity (as Shelley acutely did) while Browning assumes too readily that the objective poet handles the theme of self-division more thoroughly, even more naturally. This difference in emphasis between Browning and Yeats is a profound one, and there is a great deal to be said for both positions, though the weight of recent opinion inclines to Yeats. Shelley is, as I think time will show, a subtler and finer poet, a more lucid and *intelligent* poet, than Browning or Yeats or most of his subjective progeny. Fashion of course holds otherwise, and Shelley is so genuinely difficult a poet that he may never be in full fashion, but here at least Browning and Yeats alike were better critics than we are; they struggled with Shelley because they recognized his unique excellence in the subjective mode they had to develop (in Browning's case despite himself). *The Wanderings of Oisin* descends into the Shelleyan vortex because it must, but Yeats descends into subjectivity more freely than Browning could allow himself to do. Even in *Paracelsus,* which Browning saw as his first true poem, after rejecting the purely confessional *Pauline,* the subjective burden is given to Aprile, the Shelley-like poet, and not to Paracelsus-Browning. In *Oisin,* Yeats takes no more care to distance himself from his hero than Shelley does in *Alastor.*

Direct commentary on *Oisin* best begins with Yeats himself, writing in 1932, and linking his early long poem with two of his greatest, *A Dialogue of Self and Soul* and *Vacillation:*

> My first denunciation of old age I made in *The Wanderings of Usheen* (end of part I) before I was twenty and the same denunciation comes in the last pages of the book. The swordsman throughout repudiates the saint, but not without vacillation. Is that perhaps the sole theme—Usheen and Patrick—"so get you gone Von Hügel though with blessings on your head"? [10]

The denunciation of old age was also a denunciation of the pragmatic inadequacy of the poet in his youth, desperately starved for the Shelleyan ideal of *Alastor.* Though fulfillment is never found again in nature by Shelley's Poet, the one visitation of the beloved is clearly sexual in its nature. In *The Circus Ani-*

mals' Desertion, one of the best of his final poems, Yeats appeared to reduce *Oisin* to his sexual bitterness in the days of its composition:

> What can I but enumerate old themes?
> First that sea-rider Oisin led by the nose
> Through three enchanted islands, allegorical dreams,
> Vain gaiety, vain battle, vain repose,
> Themes of the embittered heart, or so it seems;
> That might adorn old songs or courtly shows;
> But what cared I that set him on to ride,
> I, starved for the bosom of his faery bride?

Oisin is Yeats's longest poem, by far, and it is so mythologically dense that only *Endymion* rivals it in that regard among the English descendants of *The Faerie Queene.* Before the poem can be understood in its full, triple context—Romantic tradition, Anglo-Irish story, and Yeats's thematic development—it must be seen as a total structure. Though it is as fated and driven a work as *Alastor,* it lacks the powerful simplicity, the really astonishing unity of Shelley's poem. What it offers instead, particularly in its definitive, thoroughly revised version of the mid-Nineties, is a completeness of mythic structure, even as *Endymion* does.

The poem opens with a dialogue between Christianity and poetic myth, St. Patrick and Oisin, in which the representative of purely poetic myth is in the sadness of outrageous old age. As Oisin tells his story to Patrick, he is captured again by its spell, and his would-be converter is reduced to lamenting: "You are still wrecked among heathen dreams." The heathen dream of Oisin's first voyage takes him to a land of youth, poetry, and love, where death appears to be unknown. But, to get there, Oisin "rode out from the human lands" with his temptress Niamh, whose name, to Yeats, meant "brightness or beauty." As the lovers ride out, they see images "of the immortal desires of immortals," images of unfulfilled and unfulfillable desire.

In the land of youthful dancers and lovers to which Oisin came, the song of human joy is heard by immortals as a sadness, an opposition possibly suggested to Yeats by the opening stanzas of Blake's *The Mental Traveller.* The songs of immortal joy are antinomian, and in that unholy passion Oisin lives for a hundred years, until he is recalled to human matters by a part of a warrior's broken lance, washed ashore on the island of Immortals. With a magnificent chant of the Immortals, prophesying in Tennysonian accent the exhausted age that must come to a returned Oisin, the first Book ends. The birds who murmur at the injustice of mutability, the mouse whose speed is only a weariness as the race into time destroys, the kingfisher turning into a ball of dust; these are the emblems of merely natural fulfillment, and these await Oisin. But the Immortals will abide in their youthful love until a Shelleyan apocalypse, when the stars will drop, and a pale rose of the moon will wither away. Primary decay awaits Oisin, but the destruction of the Immortals can come only when the forms of nature dissolve. The warning is the stronger for its dark paradox; to choose nature is to be survived by nature, for the human cannot outlast the natural, but to choose the inhuman is to transcend nature, and yet to live as long as nature lives.

In Book II this dilemma becomes more intense. The emblems of ungratified desire, "youth and lady and the deer and the hound," come by again, and Oisin and Niamh take up their journey, until they reach an island temple modeled on similar structures in Shelley and in Keats. This temple is demon-haunted, and the dusky demon is himself a protean singer, celebrant of a sad revelry, for his eyes are like the wings of kingfishers, emblems of the dust that is nature's. In the fight with Oisin, the demon assumes varied natural shapes, and appears to die at sunset. But he rises on the fourth morn, beginning a new natural cycle, and fights Oisin until he is overcome at another sunset. This rhythm of recurrence goes on for a hundred years, with three days of feasting alternating with one of fighting. What Oisin fights, slays, and yet must face perpetually again is his own double, the natural man or soul in him that will not finally die, but that also cannot finally overcome him. A beech-bough is borne to Oisin, emblematic of his last days, and the Island of Victories must be abandoned as the Island of Dancing was. Oisin leaves a cyclic world, in which a frustrate victory yet induced no frustration, in order to get back toward a cyclic world in which no victories over nature are to be won, and yet a perennial frustration is induced.

In Book III the quest leads to the Island of Sleepers, as it must, for the flight from nature and toward a perpetual gratification of desire dooms the searcher to identify sleep and poetry, without any of Keats's saving complexity in associating the two terms. As the lovers journey again, the familiar *tableaux* of "those that fled, and that followed" pass them, but now Oisin and Niamh recognize, with a sigh, the meaning of the visions. As the second stanza of Book III makes clear, the quest is now haunted by nostalgia for the human world, and an end to illusion (and to love, and poetry) approaches. It comes in the darkness of an Island inhabited by "a monstrous slumbering fold," titans who have put aside their arms and their trophies, titans who are both men and birds, unnatural representatives of an ironic naturalization of the human which is yet a poetry. The bell-branch, "sleep's forebear," appears again, an emblem now of "unhuman sleep" that has come to these monsters, who, however, are more beautiful than men. Oisin makes one heroic effort to rouse the sleepers, but his effort leads only to his own yielding to the bell-branch, and he and Niamh sleep for a century, while he dreams of the human life he abandoned in his quest for a poet's world.

Awakened by the fall of a starling, and so startled by nature out of his profound, unnatural slumber, Oisin feels again "the ancient sadness of man" and abandons Niamh. Warned by her against even one touch of the earth (like the one that nearly kills Keats's Endymion on his return to earth), Oisin nevertheless returns to the human and the natural, and to time's revenges. For he returns to a Christianized Ireland, to humans bowed down by a consciousness of natural sin and defect, and he falls, weak and exhausted, into the world of St. Patrick. Though the poem ends with Oisin's defiant vow to descend to Hell for the company of his brothers, it ends also in passionate defeat, for the quest has been self-destructive. What Oisin has failed to learn is the lesson that Keats and Shelley, the latter in particular, had taught the young Yeats: a quest to thwart nature's limitations must seek out an object that itself shatters nature's value as well as context; the young Oisin had sought in a super-nature what only the imagination can give, and even then only with equivocation.

Yet Oisin is a hero, and his failed quest is Yeats's own, a quest carried on through a century of poetry from Shelley and Keats through to Pater and the Tragic Generation. In their judgments of *Oisin,* scholars as diverse as Henn and Ellmann condemn it for inadequacies of style, but the poem has the style it needs for its themes and actions. Though the poem is so varied, it is more at one with itself than much of the later Yeats is. When he wrote his Introduction to his play *The Resurrection,* Yeats thought back to *Oisin* and achieved the most illuminating of his many insights into his own poem:

> For years I have been preoccupied with a certain myth that was itself a reply to a myth. I do not mean a fiction, but one of those statements our nature is compelled to make and employ as a truth though there cannot be sufficient evidence. When I was a boy everybody talked about progress, and rebellion against my elders took the form of aversion to that myth. I took satisfaction in certain public disasters, felt a sort of ecstasy at the contemplation of ruin, and then I came upon the story of Oisin in Tir na ňOg and reshaped it into my *Wanderings of Oisin.* He rides across the sea with a spirit, he passes phantoms, a boy following a girl, a hound chasing a hare, emblematical of eternal pursuit, he comes to an island of choral dancing, leaves that after many years, passes the phantoms once again, comes to an island of endless battle for an object never achieved, leaves that after many years, passes the phantoms once again, comes to an island of sleep, leaves that and comes to Ireland, to Saint Patrick and old age. I did not pick these images because of any theory, but because I found them impressive, yet all the while abstractions haunted me. I remember rejecting, because it spoilt the simplicity, an elaborate metaphor of a breaking wave intended to prove that all life rose and fell as in my poem. How hard it was to refrain from pointing out that Oisin after old age, its illumination half accepted, half rejected, would pass in death over another sea to another island.[11]

The historical elements in *Oisin*'s myth are analyzed by Whitaker, and the possible autobiographical allegory is sketched by Ellmann.[12] There is another cyclic element in the poem, and Yeats hints at it here. The elaborate rejected metaphor Yeats mentions is in fact Shelley's (in *Adonais* XXXII) and is prefigured throughout *Alastor.* On a giant scale the whole cycle of

Shelley's poetry, from *Alastor* through *The Triumph of Life,* approximates that metaphor. It is the life-cycle of the imagination when the imaginative man cannot be separated from the natural man. In Blake the cycle is displayed on an epic scale in *The Four Zoas,* more briefly in *The Book of Urizen* and, with amazing concentration, in the one hundred lines of the ballad, *The Mental Traveller.* The cycle might be called "the failure of Promethean quest," and Yeats did not repeat it so overtly again after his long quest-poem. He repeated it more subtly, many times, in a series of major lyrics, and he attempted, with mixed success, to regularize the cycle in *A Vision.*

The song of the dancers in Book I of *Oisin* is a direct presentation of the Promethean defiance:

> You stars,
> Across your wandering ruby cars
> Shake the loose reins: you slaves of God,
> He rules you with an iron rod,
> He holds you with an iron bond,
> Each one woven to the other,
> Each one woven to his brother
> Like bubbles in a frozen pond;
> But we in a lonely land abide
> Unchainable as the dim tide,
> With hearts that know nor law nor rule,
> And hands that hold no wearisome tool,
> Folded in love that fears no morrow,
> Nor the grey wandering osprey Sorrow.

The conceptual imagery here is Blake's; the God is Urizen or Shelley's Jupiter; the appeal to revolt is qualified however by the antinomian but equivocal "unchainable as the dim tide," for the tide, whether of ocean or blood-dimmed, is itself in the iron bond of natural cycle, as are the "hearts that know nor law nor rule," but nevertheless obey the cyclic impulses of nature.

This central image expands, in Book II, into the struggle with Manannan, god of the dim tide, "that demon dull and unsubduable." A hundred years of victories are won over the sea, and yet the tide cannot lose:

> I hear my soul drop down into decay,
> And Manannan's dark tower, stone after stone,
> Gather sea-slime and fall the seaward way,
> And the moon goad the waters night and day,
> That all be overthrown.
>
> But till the moon has taken all, I wage
> War on the mightiest men under the skies,
> And they have fallen or fled, age after age,
> Light is man's love, and lighter is man's rage;
> His purpose drifts and dies.

The image is subtler when it is most crucial, at the moment in Book III when the third hundred years, those of dreaming, reach their end:

> I awake: the strange horse without summons out of the distance ran,
> Thrusting his nose to my shoulder; he knew in his bosom deep
> That once more moved in my bosom the ancient sadness of man,
> And that I would leave the Immortals, their dimness, their dews
>   dropping sleep.

The sea's deep bosom is everywhere, the ancient movement of tide passing through the herald, and Oisin, and the dreaming dimness of the Immortals, immortal only as the sea is immortal, heavy with the waters of nature. The sorrow on the sea is the hopelessness of loosening the woven chains that bind even the stars. Yeats ends the poem, not with Shelley's impressively cold farewell to nature, as in *Alastor,* but by going past nature to a choice between finalities: swordsman and saint, Oisin and Patrick, the stones of the fire and the glance of the saved. Oisin, after death, will "dwell in the house of the Fenians, be they in flames or at feast."

In the Anglo-Irish myths of the hero, Yeats had chosen to find a model for what he hoped would be a new kind of *antithetical* quester, closer to the communal experience than Shelley's Poet, Keats's shepherd-prince or Browning's Paracelsus. Where Browning recoiled from the Shelleyan subjectivity, the internalization of the quest, Yeats entered it, embracing the quester's natural defeat as a victory, not of Prometheus or Blake's rebel Orc, but of a man

divided against himself, natural against imaginative, neither capable of final victory over the other. Whether this led, at last, to a
genuinely tragic or otherwise valid vision, is a matter to be
argued still, though almost all of Yeats's critics seem certain that
it did.

7: Early Lyrics and Plays

In 1895, Yeats first used the title *Crossways* for the earlier lyrics he wished to preserve, lyrics composed mostly between 1885 and 1889. Also in 1895, he named a later group of lyrics (1889–1892) *The Rose*. In his definitive ordering of his poetry, these remained the first two groups. The present chapter is a study of these two sets of lyrics, with a glance at Yeats's two plays of the Nineties, *The Countess Cathleen* (1892) and *The Land of Heart's Desire* (1894).

In *A Vision,* Yeats says of the poets of his own Phase 17, *daimonic* men, that they take their Mask or image of desire from the opposite Phase 3, seeking thus an essential "Simplification through intensity," but finding often the false Mask of "Dispersal." [1] He was thinking of his own early poetry, and of Shelley's, and of that general tendency in Romantic tradition for poets to emulate their great precursors by beginning in some variation upon pastoral. *A Vision*'s description of Phase 3 is also necessarily a backward glance at the lyrics of *Crossways*. The man of *Crossways,* as seen by lyrical poets of "the fantastic Phase 17," is "an Image where simplicity and intensity are united." This

Image moves in the visionary landscape of Palmer and Calvert, "among yellowing corn or under overhanging grapes." This Image, Yeats says, "gave to Landor his shepherds and hama- dryads" and "to Shelley his wandering lovers and sages," the Poet of *Alastor,* Athanase, Ahasuerus.[2] It is of course afterthought to find the *antithetical* quester in the shepherds, Indians, lovers, mad kings, faeries, fishermen, and fox-hunters of *Crossways,* but it is Yeats's own afterthought, and would make of these lyrics his own *Songs of Innocence,* and presumably of *The Rose* poems, his own contrary *Songs of Experience.*

Frye remarks that Yeats was a poet who underwent develop- ment, but who sought to make that process appear rather as an unfolding.[3] Keats could be cited as an example of a poet of devel- opment, Blake as one who unfolded, but I think that Yeats, like Shelley, was of both kinds, as much one as the other. All of Shel- ley is in *Alastor,* all of Yeats in *The Wanderings of Oisin,* but both poets sought to break out of their cyclic sorrows into a more generous story of a larger human concern (very differently ori- ented in the two, since Shelley was as much of the extreme Left as Yeats of the extreme Right). In the furthest reach of Shelley, *Pro- metheus Unbound* and *Epipsychidion,* and of Yeats, *The Tower* and *The Winding Stair,* a long journey has been made from *Alas- tor* and *Oisin,* but *Adonais, The Triumph of Life,* and *Last Poems and Plays* take us back to origins again. The frustration of the hero in late Yeats, the fury of the poet at a world unable to sustain heroic virtues, and the bitter reduction of heroism to lust and rage, are a richer return to the realms of the wandering Oisin. Even so, the despair and dialectic of late Shelley are more comprehensive versions of the remorseless Poet who burns through every natural context in *Alastor.* One might venture this formula: Shelley and Yeats were poets of the unfolding rhythm who strove heroically to develop and succeeded, but discovered their authenticity despite such striving, rather than because of it. In Yeats, who lived forty-five years longer and had a cunning tem- perament, the formula is obscured by the revisionist in the poet, who longed to see himself as a Blake rather than a Shelley. Conse- quently, he labored unnecessarily to disguise his own develop- ment, refusing to see that he had been anyway more of an unfolder than he knew. At the end, in his letters and in a poem like *The Circus Animals' Desertion,* he sees the truth, and sets *The Wanderings of Oisin,* rather than *Crossways,* as his point of origin, leading off the definitive arrangement of his poems.

Current criticism has been unfair to the early Yeats, too kind to the middle Yeats, and mostly uncritically worshipful of the later Yeats. I find a remarkable number of lasting poems in both *Crossways* and *The Rose,* both in their original and their revised versions. *Crossways* includes lyrics as powerful as *The Madness of King Goll* and as universal as *The Stolen Child,* while *The Rose* contains so many fine poems that clearly the three years after 1889 must be considered a creative advance even upon *The Wanderings of Oisin.* No poem in *The Rose* is altogether a failure, and several are inevitable expressions of themes central to Yeats's imagination: *Fergus and the Druid, The Sorrow of Love, Who Goes with Fergus?, The Two Trees,* and two altogether neglected poems of extraordinary balance and fullness, *The Man Who Dreamed of Faeryland* and the *Dedication* to a volume of selections Yeats had made from Irish novelists.

In *Crossways,* the poet moves through the equivocal natural world of *Alastor* and *Endymion,* in the Promethean phase of Romantic quest, but with the fierce urgency of the High Romantics modulated into the overtly baffled longing of their Pre-Raphaelite disciples, Rossetti and Morris. Where Shelley and Keats, under Wordsworth's influence, attempt to overcome the dumbfounding abyss between ourselves and the object, the Pre-Raphaelites are curiously willing dualists. Yeats inherits from Rossetti and Morris their doomed attempt to render phantasmagoria as though it were nature, finding realistic detail in imaginary contexts. This accounts for an element of redundancy present in the poetry of *Crossways,* but less prevalent in *The Rose,* where Yeats is more content to surrender the natural as part of the cost the occult fulfillment exacts. Though diction and syntax in early Yeats owe more, I think, to Rossetti than to Shelley, let alone to Blake, the imaginative pattern of *Crossways* and *The Rose* is essentially Shelleyan, with an admixture of Blake in a few poems, most notably *The Two Trees.* The occasional influence of poetic idea from Rossetti is quarried largely from one poem, *The Stream's Secret,* already glanced at in this study. Yeats met Maud Gonne in 1889, and first proposed marriage to her in 1891. From 1891 on, *The Stream's Secret* must have had a particular appeal for him, aside from the general attraction the poem's theme would have created.

In Yeats's essay of 1902 on Morris, beautifully called *The Happiest of the Poets,* he associates Rossetti with Shelley, very convincingly. The genius of both poets "can hardly stir but to the rejection of Nature," for they desire intensity rather than profusion, and so follow "the Star of the Magi," Shelley's Morning and Evening Star, "the mother of impossible hope." Against Rossetti and Shelley, Yeats sets Morris, one of "the worshippers of natural abundance," despite his affinities with Rossetti. Yeats's relation to Morris is a very complex one, but I shall reserve a further account of it until I discuss *At the Hawk's Well,* where the influence is crucial. What matters for the study of *Crossways* and *The Rose* is that Yeats, in those lyrics, is much closer to Rossetti than to Morris, among the Pre-Raphaelites. Swinburne he always resented and disliked, if only for rivalry. They competed as Blake critics, Swinburne being much the better of the two, and as poets, Swinburne again being much the better at the time of his death. Anyone who scoffs at such a judgment is invited to compare *The Lake of Gaube,* written by Swinburne in 1899, to any of Yeats's poems written in or before that year. Anyone who chooses Yeats over Swinburne as a Blake critic is invited to compare them on *The Marriage of Heaven and Hell,* despite Swinburne's curious attempt to assimilate Blake to the Divine Marquis.

By 1902, Yeats was struggling into his middle phase, and necessarily preferred Morris to Rossetti. One of the functions of the essay on Morris is to help in this transition, a smaller-scale repetition of the 1900 essay on Shelley, where Yeats is saying a highly conscious farewell to his own earlier work. So the Morris essay concludes as it begins, with a comparison between Rossetti and Morris, in which we are told that Rossetti, "drunken with natural beauty, saw the supernatural beauty, the impossible beauty, in his frenzy" while Morris "would show us a beauty that would wither if it did not set us at peace with natural things." [4] The distinction is accurate and important, and casts backward illumination upon *Crossways* and *The Rose,* where Yeats is hardly at peace with natural things, but also is rather uneasy with seeing the impossible beauty alone.

As I have emphasized in my introductory chapter, the study of Yeats has suffered from the prejudice against, and ignorance of, the entire tradition of Romantic poetry, without which both early and late Yeats are inconceivable. The middle Yeats, the poet of *Responsibilities*, a Landorian or Jonsonian studier of simpler nostalgias, is highly consonant with the critical presuppositions of most Yeats scholars, but the earlier work they tend to undervalue, and the later poetry they misrepresent, perhaps necessarily. One of the earliest books on Yeats, by the poet Louis MacNeice, is still representative in its prejudices, and one notes the recent foreword by Ellmann, in which we are told that "MacNeice's book on Yeats is still as good an introduction to that poet as we have." [5] To MacNeice, Romanticism is a poetic disease of which Yeats cured himself. MacNeice, in his book, assures us that Pater, the champion of style, is guilty of "a crude use of language," and that "Yeats must have seen that Shelley was a careless craftsman, verbose and facile, sometimes vulgar in both diction and rhythm," an absurdity MacNeice had learned from Auden, who had it from Eliot, who had contrived to invent it for himself. In fairness to MacNeice (and to his continued admirer, Ellmann) I give a rather full quotation from MacNeice's views on early Yeats and the Romantic tradition:

> Yeats's early poems are in the Victorian tradition which itself was a development from the Romantic Revival. Tennyson would not have come into being without Keats. Rossetti would not have come into being without Tennyson. Yeats would not have come into being without Rossetti. One of the chief characteristics of this line of poets—in their better poems—is an autumnal, almost a morbid, languor. The Isle of the Lotus Eaters. Keats, Tennyson, Rossetti, each of them had a remarkable eye and an ear for verbal music, but they looked at the world through glasses coloured with self-pity and their music is sultry, overcharged with the emotions accumulated during the summer and waiting for some thunderstorm to freshen them or clear them away. Rossetti is a decadent poet but the seeds of his decadence are to be found in Tennyson and, before that, in Keats. [6]

It was still possible, in 1967, for the foremost Yeats scholar to commend this. Only the genealogy here is accurate, and that merely in part. Spenser, the ancestor of this line, and the Beulah imagery of Blake, and much Shelley and Morris are other parts of this complex in Yeats, for what MacNeice obscurely saw and failed to describe is a central aspect of Romantic tradition, the vision of the fascination and the dangers of the Lower Paradise. The historians of poetic influence, when that subject is further developed, will map for us the great labyrinth of Lower Paradise that winds from Spenser's Gardens of Adonis through Drayton's Elizium, Milton's Eden, Blake's Beulah, the enchanted bowers of Collins, Coleridge, Wordsworth, and Keats, the ambiguous gardens of Shelley, Tennyson, Rossetti, and Morris, to trail at last into the islands of Yeats's repose and the Florida of Stevens's fantasy. Where there is self-pity anywhere in this labyrinth it is the controlled, thematic, necessary self-pity demanded for the presentation of why this is *Lower* Paradise, and where there is languor, the sense of the autumn of the body, there is always a suggestion of danger and limitation, particularly to the imagination. For this is the state of being created and inhabited by the Romantic Eros, this is the world conceived as an erotic illusion; not the world as gratified desire, but the world as blocked desire, the world presided over by Sphinx and Covering Cherub.

This is the world of *Crossways* and *The Rose,* where we wander as "sick children of the world" seeking "some twisted, echo-harbouring shell," but finding always that "the sea swept on and cried her old cry still." In the first poem of *Crossways, The Madness of King Goll,* Yeats gives the only answer he knows to the sea's cry. Goll is the precursor of Fergus in the *Rose* poems, and of all the later questers in Yeats who will not find peace by abandoning nature for occult satisfactions. The poem goes back to 1884, and is much revised, being (as Parkinson observes) practically a new poem after 1895.[7] I prefer the earlier versions, though I agree that certain poems in *Crossways* were much improved in revision. Goll is a kind of Shelleyan Athanase, "a wise young king," praised for bringing back the age of gold, who in the midst of battle yields to the madness of vision, breaks his spear, and rushes off to become a wandering poet in the woods. He finds a "songless" harp, and sings to it; his singing "sang me fever-free," but now "my singing fades, the strings are torn." He is left, in one early version, to "wail beside the sea," now neither poet nor king, but madman oppressed by the natural. All through the poem beats the refrain: *They will not hush, the leaves a-flutter around me, the beech-leaves old.* This long line, in all the poem's versions, has uncanny force, for the line's meaning changes subtly as it is repeated. Remarkable as Yeats's later mastery of the refrain was, he rarely did more with it than here. At first, the refrain seems to indicate only Goll's madness, the pathetic fallacy run wild, but as the lyric goes on we come to understand better that the fluttering of the leaves is itself a kind of natural supernatural-ism, a force that Goll vainly sought to master, first through king-ship and then through poetry. In any of its versions, *King Goll* is a culmination of the Pre-Raphaelite lyric, almost an epitome of the essential thematic pattern of the Pre-Raphaelite poem. Goll's phantasmagoria fails because it must yield to nature, and his kingship failed because it yielded to vision. Only the poetic fail-ure, at this point, mattered to Yeats, as the Fergus poems in *The Rose* continued to demonstrate.

These poems, *Fergus and the Druid* and Joyce's favorite, *Who Goes with Fergus?* (a lyric in the second scene of *The Countess Cathleen,* and to be considered again in that context later in this chapter) are crucial to an understanding of early Yeats. Parkin-son observes that, in revision, Yeats made Fergus more conscious of his Druid interlocutor.[8] Though Parkinson finds this an im-provement, because it clarifies Yeats's intentions, I prefer the ear-lier version precisely because Fergus is more appropriately solip-sistic in it, as unheeding of the Druid as Self is of Soul in the later *Dialogue.* Yeats's Fergus pursues the shape-changing Druid, but only that he may find himself more truly and more strange. The Druid is the opposite to Fergus as the cowards are to Cuchulain in the late, magnificent *Cuchulain Comforted,* but the cowards in that poem, like Cuchulain, are in the life after death, or as Yeats preferred, the death between lives, and they know their necessity to Cuchulain as the Druid cannot know his to Fergus. What the Druid does know is what it pained Yeats to know for very long, that his "dreaming wisdom' is not what Fergus seeks. When Fergus, disregarding the Druid, takes "this small slate-coloured bag of dreams" he takes on a knowledge purchased by the loss of power, and what he gains is no release from the burden of royal consciousness he sought to shed. He sees a vision of his past metamorphoses—water, light, tree, slave, but also a king, and he apprehends that each change was wonderful in itself, but that to have this new consciousness of all the changes at once is sorrow. "But now I have grown nothing, being all" (revised to "knowing all"); this is a reduction, from which no fresh starts flow. One thinks of the contrasting reduction to wintry vision in Stevens's *The Snow Man,* where the poet learns to behold nothing that is not there, and the nothing that is, an ending that provokes a fresh start for the imagination. Fergus is a very different poet, estranged from himself by his discovery of all his selves. In powerful lines (unfortunately revised out of the poem) he feels in his heart the eternal battle of daemons and gods, suffers this pain, but has "no share in loss or victory." The poem is an urgent warning made to Yeats's imagination by itself, but not one that he could heed.

In the introductory poem of *The Rose,* Yeats demonstrates already the same struggle between his hunger for La Belle Dame's faery food, and a skeptical fear of the natural starvation the hunger brings, as it did to Keats's quester. The Rose is to come near, but to leave him still "a little space" for the natural odor of less occult roses to pervade. Come near, but not too near; this is the start of a characteristic pattern of vacillation. The source is more High Romantic than Pre-Raphaelite; Keats and Shelley, as few modern critics see, severely doubted poetry, and brooded on the natural cost of every imaginative victory. I take it that the deep source here is Wordsworth, and beyond him the Sublime tradition, for in Wordsworth the imagination is compensatory, and its recompense is for grievous natural loss. Yeats, throughout his poetry, unknowingly is profoundly indebted to Wordsworth's transformation of the Sublime mode, though of all Romantics Yeats was always most impatient of the dialectic of gain-through-loss. Yet he exhibited it constantly, as here in the early work, where already he finds the duality of imaginative fate he systematized thirty years later in Phase 17 of *A Vision.* Goll and Fergus and all the Rose-seekers are *daimonic* men, yearning to simplify through

intensity, but finding instead dispersal of being, and Yeats in creating them aspires to imagination through *antithetical* emotion
but attains only "enforced self-realization" or the self-victimization of self-portrayal. Goll and Fergus and Oisin are of the company of the poets of *Alastor, Endymion,* and *Pauline,* figures of
the youth not as virile poet but as baffled ephebe, frustrate pil-
grims who can dwell neither within nor without the Lower Paradise where poetry must begin, but where it cannot linger. Yeats
was an unusual late Romantic in learning these dangers quite
early, and sustaining their damages, as Johnson, Symons, Wilde,
Dowson, and other talented poets could not. In the long perspective, Yeats will be seen as the first Romantic poet after Browning
to succeed in the enormous, almost Titanic task of weathering his
own Romanticism without losing it, and thus losing his authenticity. Very few modern poets after Yeats make this difficult transition between the two major stages of the Romantic quest, from a
necessarily failed Prometheanism to a matured imagination that
has not cast off the enterprise of romance.

Evidence of the continued enterprise provides exuberance to
the vivid *Who Goes with Fergus?,* where Yeats for once fully in-
dulges the poet's Promethean dream. This is not the defeated Fergus of *Fergus and the Druid,* but a poet-king of wish-fulfillment,
who has pierced the wood's mystery and danced upon the shore,
in defiance of the sea's old cry of uncaring. To consider Fergus is
to know the power of imagination over nature, over even "dishev-
elled wandering stars," and knowing this we need brood no
longer upon any futurity, "hopes and fear," or "love's bitter mystery" (Yeats had been rejected once already, by Maud Gonne).
Yeats is not free, but rather movingly plays at the imagination's
freedom here.

The same dream of freedom animates the most renowned
(and now deprecated) of Yeats's early lyrics, *The Lake Isle of Innisfree.* But this poem, despite its obvious pleasures, is less intense
than *Who Goes with Fergus?,* and less moving, for lacking the dialectic of nature and imagination, the war between the sky and
the mind. We see again what Romantic tradition gave even the
young Yeats, to save him from inconsequence. Even Thoreau, the

reputed source for *The Lake Isle of Innisfree,* interests the attentive reader because the attained peace of solitude in *Walden* is a
mark of the power of mind over outward sense, a mark missing in
Yeats's plangent but drifting poem.

A related lyric, almost as famous, *The White Birds* is as much
adrift, yet lingers in the mind precisely because it is vitalized by a
violence from within, an impatience with all natural limitation.
But the poem's emblems are too much Shelley's, too little Yeats's,
and even the poem's central longings are derived from *Epipsychidion,* as though Yeats wished to flee to "a Danaan shore" with
Emilia Viviani rather than Maud Gonne. The evening star of infinite desire, identified by Yeats as Shelley's leading symbol, wakes
in the lovers' hearts "a sadness that never may die." Unfortunately, the poem forgets that its desire is not for this sadness, or for
anything natural, like "those dreamers," the lily and the rose.
The poem's aspirations are represented most inadequately by its
vision of white birds sustained by sea foam, and Yeats's recognition of his need to go beyond natural images of more-than-natural
desire is hardly conveyed here by his art.

This recognition had led him to his symbol of the Rose, about
which he made too many and too various prose comments. The
two that matter are written thirty years apart, and are equally
misleading. In 1895 the poems of *The Rose* were a solipsistic
pathway to "the Eternal Rose of Beauty and of Peace," but in
1925 the same Rose was a spirit that suffered with man, as opposed to the Intellectual Beauty of Shelley or the Heavenly
Beauty of Spenser.[9] As the Rose was also Maud Gonne, Ireland
(Dark Rosaleen), a central symbol of the Rosicrucian Order of
the Golden Dawn, a sexual emblem, the sun, and much else, it is
not a coherent image, and scarcely stimulates coherent discussion,
whether in Yeats or most of his scholars. The best suggestion is
Ellmann's, that the Rose in the Nineties had the function for
Yeats that the Mask fulfilled later, simply the image of desire, the
ultimate, *daimonic* form of what can be created and loved.[10] The
Rose, and then the Mask, are in Yeats what the emanation is in
Blake and the epipsyche in Shelley, and even the Interior Para-
mour in Stevens, perhaps even the Fancy in Whitman. Every

major poet in Romantic tradition has such a conceptual image, a varied displacement of the Muse herself. Yeats's true Mask or benevolent Muse was always what he was to name her in *A Vision,* "Simplification through intensity," his own version of the Wordsworthian-Coleridgean Secondary Imagination. His false Mask or destructive Muse, his Sphinx, was always what *A Vision* calls "Dispersal." In his early poetry the Rose is most directly derived from Shelley's Intellectual Beauty, in itself not a mystical entity but simply all of beauty that is apprehended beyond the range of the senses. Shelley's *Hymn to Intellectual Beauty* itself derives from Wordsworth's *Intimations* Ode, and so Yeats's light of the Rose-Sun is a grandchild of Wordsworth's "visionary gleam," a much more universal phenomenon than Yeats's fitful radiance or Shelley's unseen shadow.

Despite its title, *The Rose* group of poems emphasizes the negation rather than the affirmation of the quest for the objects of desire, the Human Abstract rather than the Divine Image, in Blake's terms. This is the deliberate contrast between *Crossways* and *The Rose* that Yeats designed when he grouped his earlier poems. Down to the culminating *The Two Trees,* the poems of *The Rose* are made to sustain the burden of the state Blake called Generation or Experience, a lower state than Innocence and yet a progression from it, a necessary step down. The most ambitious poem in *The Rose,* the narrative *Cuchulain's Fight with the Sea,* is a chant of Experience's triumph, particularly in its original form, as *The Death of Cuchulain.* This first *Death of Cuchulain* was improved greatly in revision, but the rhetorical gain is a thematic loss, obscuring Yeats's original design. The sea is the generative tide, the watery welter of mere Experience, but in it the Rose that is also the sun, that is also the man-god Cuchulain, must drown, even as Oisin is overcome in the strange third world of his poem. "Where the sun falls into the Western deep" Cuchulain must fall also. Powerfully as the revised poem ends, when Cuchulain hears "his own name cried;/And fought with the invulnerable tide," this is too inconclusive. In the original version, the end is inevitable, where the hero warred "with the bitter tide,/ And the waves flowed above him, and he died." This is a finer death than Cuchulain was to die in the vision of the aged Yeats, who no longer abode in the dialectic of Innocence and Experience.

Three more poems in *The Rose* have considerable value and importance. *The Man Who Dreamed of Faeryland* is replete with alchemical symbolism, which has excited scholars who delight in such *arcana,* but this is mere clutter, as it mostly is elsewhere in Yeats. The poem's strength is in its controlled bitterness, as befits a lament of Experience. For the poem's dreamer is Yeats himself as he would be, if he chose to burn to the socket, to meet the lingering death-in-life of those who will not take up the *antithetical* quest. This poem too was revised excessively, and needs to be read in its earlier version. The dreamer is in love, but a faery song "shook him out of his new ease." Subsequent visionary songs discontent him with the accumulation of this world's goods, and with revenge upon his mockers. His last naturalistic hope of solace is the oblivion of death, but a final song sung by grave-worms disturbs his last peace with a vision of apocalypse, until God "burns up Nature with a kiss." The poem's terror of its own irony is felt acutely in its last line: "The man has found no comfort in the grave." What Yeats achieved in this poem is a demythologized version of Blake's beautiful epyllion *The Book of Thel,* where the visionary voices rising out of nature attempt to comfort Thel, yet teach her instead a lesson she declines to learn, the necessity of descent into Experience. Yeats's dreamer has spent his life descending, but vision vexes his dull dream of life to nightmare, and he fails each test he must endure, learning only discontent and never the wisdom his descent might have taught him.

A greater bitterness, a magnificent one, pervades *The Dedication to a Book of Stories Selected from the Irish Novelists,* a cumbersome title for so grimly skilled a poem. But the *Dedication* I refer to is not the poem of 1890 but a re-written poem of 1924, a kind of prelude to *The Tower.* I do not find the 1890 *Dedication* as weak as Parkinson does; its metaphorical confusion works, and its sentimentality has an inverted bitterness that is satisfying because such complex and controlled self-glorification is rare, outside of Byron anyway.[11] Even this original *Dedication* shows us a tormented national consciousness, a nation "always growing Sorrow," charmed by itself to its own ruin. For these dreamers, wandering exiles, always weary spirits, though they love "the cause that never dies," are implicitly condemned for self-indulgence, for evoking from their poets "a honeyed ringing." And so Yeats sees himself as bearing his countrymen another "bell branch full of ease," like the one that came to Oisin in his third and final phase. Yeats had not studied Blake's ironies without some issue, and his apparent sentimentalism is subtle and a little dangerous.

But Parkinson is certainly correct in preferring the poem as we have it now, less subtle as I believe it to be. The crucial line, "I also bear a bell-branch full of ease," takes on immense force from the poem's context when Yeats goes on, in revision, to state its origin:

> I tore it from the barren boughs of Eire,
> That country where a man can be so crossed;
>
> Can be so battered, badgered and destroyed
> That he's a loveless man. . . .

This is so memorable a bitterness it would persuade any stone; the Yeats of 1890 could have taught the Yeats of thirty-five years after some cunning, perhaps, but no such power was available to the earlier self.

The Rose reaches nearest to symbolic precision in *The Two Trees,* a poem now generally admired despite the formidable nay-saying of Yvor Winters, to whom it was "obviously a bad poem . . . sentimental and stereotyped at every point." [12] Whether Blake's symbolism (which Parkinson, Kermode, and others rightly find here) accurately can be judged stereotyped, I doubt; that seems a poor word for it. [13] And the poem is hardly sentimental; it may suffer from a certain coldness, but not from excessive sentiment. The poem's sources are in Blake, or rather in Yeats's creative misinterpretations of Blake, and probably also in the scrambled cabalism of Mathers and allied adepts. I find disturbing the preference shown for the poem both by Maud Gonne and by Yeats, whose relationship the poem exists to commemorate. In that genetic context the poem takes on a fearful coldness, genuinely akin to some of Blake's greatest passages in *The Four Zoas* on the strife of Spectre and Emanation, and to the frightening manuscript lyric that begins: "My Spectre around me night & day."

The Two Trees has two twenty-line verse paragraphs, the first a Song of Innocence or Divine Image, the second a Song of Experience or Human Abstract. In the first, Maud Gonne is urged to gaze within, to find the holy Tree of Life growing in her own heart. There is nothing Blakean about this unless this were to be taken as an irony, since Blake saw only selfish "virtues" as growing in the natural heart. Even without the matching contrary in the poem's second half, there would be something equivocal in the poem's opening vision, particularly in its original form, despite Kermode's belief that this is one of the few early poems Yeats improved in revision. Songs of Innocence, in Yeats as in Blake, can fall into the category Blake called unorganized Innocence, or ignorance. Though the vitalism of Maud Gonne, her "joy," inspires her poet to "a wizard song," it also gives "the waves their melody," the incessant song that takes no account of his yearnings or the power of his creativity. There, in Maud's heart, "through bewildered branches, go/ Winged Loves borne on in gentle strife." The oxymoron does not alter the bewilderment or the strife, which is the lover's judgment upon what is most intrinsic to the beloved, and gives a subtly bitter flavor to his observation: "Thine eyes grow full of tender care," since what provokes her tenderness is not Yeats but a struggle within her own heart. Innocence here is a solipsism, and her centripetal gaze is consonant with an element in Romantic vision from Spenser through Shelley.

Still, this is preferred to her outward gaze, for "the bitter glass" of the poem's second half is Blake's Vegetable glass of Nature, and her self-absorbed Innocence suits her better than the barren fruit of knowledge, since like Thel she is unfit for Experience. The source here is certainly the Tree of Mystery from Blake's *The Human Abstract:*

> Soon spreads the dismal shade
> Of Mystery over his head;

> And the Catterpiller and Fly,
> Feed on the Mystery.

> And it bears the fruit of Deceit,
> Ruddy and sweet to eat;
> And the Raven his nest has made
> In its thickest shade.

> The Gods of the earth and sea,
> Sought thro' Nature to find this Tree
> But their search was all in vain:
> There grows one in the Human Brain

If Maud Gonne gazes too long upon the fallen world, the Tree may grow in her brain. Her joy is inward; nature for her is but "the glass of outer weariness," and Blake's "ravens of unresting thought" are only a threat to her, for thought would destroy her paradise, and her tender eyes would "grow all unkind." The poem is a warning to her, but surely the warning has a sardonic aspect, since either way her kindness is not for Yeats. On this reading, *The Two Trees* is the most bitter of Yeats's early lyrics, and a prophecy of many of his later attitudes toward his own frustrated love.

Near the end of his life, in *The Circus Animals' Desertion*, Yeats related the major themes of his early work directly to that frustrated love, particularly contrasting *The Wanderings of Oisin* as wish-fulfillment to the play, *The Countess Cathleen*, as "a counter-truth." *The Countess Cathleen*, written for Maud Gonne, is Yeats's first important play, but has little value in itself, no matter in which of its many versions one may read it. Nor is it at all clear, despite the labors of Ure and other scholars, just how *The Countess Cathleen* offers a counter-truth to the much more impressive *Oisin*, except that the poem chooses what Yeats will later call Self over Soul, Oisin over Patrick, while the play chooses the Countess over her poet-lover, responsibility over the dream, Soul or character over Self or personality. But, as Rajan sensibly complains, the play never makes this seem much of a choice, nor does it justify the description given of it in *The Circus Animals' Desertion*.[14] The Countess is moved in her sacrifice by pity, yet she is hardly "pity-crazed," and if Yeats was worried about the ef-

fects of hatred and fanaticism upon his beloved, he did not show
it in this play, as no one is less given to such excesses than the
shadowy Countess, who unfortunately resembles Christ rather
more than she does Maud Gonne. Nine or ten revisions did not
make *The Countess Cathleen* an interesting play or dramatic
poem. But there is a remarkable and revelatory moment in the
play's first version worth close regard, for it prophesies Yeats's
highly individual strength as a lyrical dramatist. In Scene II the
Countess (in this version spelled Kathleen) is introduced; she is
in her castle, with her foster-mother Oona, who seeks to rouse the
Countess from the sadness of brooding on famine by singing the
lyric, *Who Goes with Fergus?* As Yeats made the poem for Maud,
so in the play it was made for the Countess by the poet Kevin,
who vainly seeks to hold her back from sacrifice. Kathleen asks for
the song, is prevented for a time from hearing it, and does not linger long in her reverie after the song is sung. But as soon as she
can, she thinks back to it, only to reflect:

> My heart is longing for a deeper peace
> Than Fergus found amid his brazen cars.

The lyric, which to Yeats meant the triumph of dream, tempts
her deeply, but yields to the longing that will lead her to sacrifice.
By turning her nearer to devotional surrender through the play's
finest lyric intensity, Yeats does come close to making her a counter-truth to Oisin. That this comes through her brooding upon a
poem suggests, at the beginning, Yeats's central limitation and yet
most original resource as a dramatist.

This poignance is repeated in *The Land of Heart's Desire,* the
little play of 1894 which can be taken as Yeats's last unburdened
attempt to acknowledge the world of faery, in contrast to *The
Wind Among the Reeds,* where the burden is heavy, and the
heaviness becomes the theme. *The Land of Heart's Desire* has
nothing memorable except its final lyric, but this is the splendid
"The wind blows out of the gates of the day," where the wind resembles one of Blake's destructive but appealing winds of Beulah,
passively inviting and yet strong enough to uproot rocks and trees.
This wind's promise relates it also to Shelley's equivocal West

Wind, destroyer and preserver, for by it "The lonely of heart is withered away," a promise of fulfillment but also of death. This is the wind among the reeds that dominates the volume in which the early Yeats reaches conclusion, and bitterly finds the necessity for another beginning. After that, when he returns to drama, it is in a new century and in another spirit, momentarily set against continuity.

8: *The Wind Among the Reeds*

With *The Wind Among the Reeds,* published in 1899, as the century neared its turn and Yeats the middle of the journey, we have the culmination of all the earlier poetry. The later, extraordinarily elaborate poems in this volume show the very indirect influence of Mallarmé, through the mediumship of Arthur Symons. As the tragic decade of his generation's decline neared its close, Yeats felt "that there was something in myself compelling me to attempt creation of an art as separate from everything heterogeneous and casual, from all character and circumstance, as some Herodiade of our theatre, dancing seemingly alone in her narrow moving luminous circle." [1] The accent here remains that of Pater. The reference to Herodiade follows a quotation from Symons's version of Mallarmé:

> The horror of my virginity
> Delights me, and I would envelop me
> In the terror of my tresses, that, by night,
> Inviolate reptile, I might feel the white
> And glimmering radiance of thy frozen fire. . . .

This fascinated self-repulsion, centered in a hieratic context, is one of the shifting moods recurrent in *The Wind Among the Reeds,* a volume of love's defeat, and of the lover's subsequent offering of his passion to supernal and occult powers. Ellmann's view of *The Wind Among the Reeds* is that it is "a poetry where one sinks down and down without finding bottom," a judgment fairly based on Yeats's own description of his mental state in writing this poetry: "I had sometimes when awake, but more often in sleep, moments of vision, a state very unlike dreaming, when these images took upon themselves what seemed an independent life and became a part of a mystic language, which seemed always as if it would bring me some strange revelation." [2]

However unsatisfactory the verse of *The Wind Among the Reeds* proved to Yeats, or to many Yeats critics, it is a highly finished collection and its rich lacquer seems now to have protected it against time's decay. Yeats's dream of a stylized love, of an emotion not less urgent for its *antithetical* discipline, is realized here with formidable skill, while the Irish mythological baggage is remarkably light in the actual movement of the poems, particularly when contrasted to the ornate and redundant explanatory notes Yeats felt obliged to write for them.

The best of these poems is *The Secret Rose,* but several are almost as fine, including the justly popular *The Song of Wandering Aengus, He Remembers Forgotten Beauty,* the dream-poem *The Cap and Bells,* and the apocalyptic *The Valley of the Black Pig.* But more impressive than any single poem is the total design of the volume, which is again Paterian, and takes us back to Pater's vision of the Sphinx, his obsession with Leonardo's women, as well as to the critical outlook of Arthur Symons.

The Wind Among the Reeds is composed only of lyrics, thus setting a pattern for many subsequent volumes by Yeats. Not only does Yeats choose the lyric as his definitive vehicle here, but he seeks to perfect the kind of lyric he had sought for fifteen years, at times with real success. The perfection is one that wavers at the edge of an abyss, and may touch a limit of art. More than anything before it, with the single exception of Johnson's *The Dark Angel,* it represents the culmination of a particular sub-tradition within English Romanticism, which goes from a handful of poems by Coleridge and Keats through much early Tennyson on to the Pre-Raphaelites and the Tragic Generation. Pater, in his essay on *Aesthetic Poetry,* touches the definitive characteristic of this "afterthought" of Romanticism:

> One characteristic of the pagan spirit the aesthetic poetry has, which is on the surface—the continual suggestion, pensive or passionate, of the shortness of life. This is contrasted with the bloom of the world and gives new seduction to it—the sense of death and the desire of beauty: the desire of beauty quickened by the sense of death.

Unrequited love, the immediate theme of *The Wind Among the Reeds,* itself exemplifies a desire of beauty quickened by the sense of death. The beauty desired by Yeats at the turn of the century depends upon the death of desire, and on an end to time.[3] Yet unrequited love, and desire in any pragmatic sense, are very remarkably handled by Yeats in this volume. We need a fuller biography of Yeats, of a kind not yet authorized by his family, before we could hope to understand the exact relation of these love poems to Yeats's life during the years 1895 to 1899. The fullest account of Yeats's affair with Mrs. Shakespear is given by A. N. Jeffares, but it does not tell us enough.[4] All a reader needs to keep in mind is that Yeats, during these years, could not get free of his image of Maud Gonne, and this bondage destroyed an otherwise liberating love affair—with Mrs. Shakespear (Lionel Johnson's cousin, and at a later time Ezra Pound's mother-in-law).

Probably the most important external information one can have about *The Wind Among the Reeds* is the date of its publication, the last year of a century, and in particular of a century in which the anguished sense of the moment had become a peculiarly acute element in art and in life. A comment by Ian Fletcher, the great authority on the Nineties, is relevant:

> It is in the nineteenth century that the sense of belonging to a decade, to a generation, was developed. Not until the 1890s could Lord Henry Wotton have said to Dorian Gray "fin de siécle" and have received the antiphonal answer "fin du globe." Such tremors are common to ends of centuries, but the 1890s have more in com-

mon with the year 1000—a year of perfect numbers—or with the year 1600, than with the shrugging dismissal of, say, Dryden's *Secular Masque*. As the blank zeros of the calendar figure approached, the temporal uncertainties of the century merged in a diffuse, an irrational chiliasm.[5]

The temporal uncertainties of the century must have had an effect on the century's many visions of timelessness and its various counter-visions of endless recurrence. Here we are all of us still in surmise, with little that is certain in our studies. Pater's central idea of style is an idea of freedom from time, and perhaps all of aestheticism was a desperate protest against the menace of time that Romanticism had failed to dispel. Yeats's wind among the reeds has both Irish mythological and occult sources, as usual, but its main source is in Shelley's winds of destruction-creation, which blow all through his poetry, and in Blake's wind of Beulah that uproots stones and trees. Indeed, the main source of Yeats's volume is the not very esoteric *Ode to the West Wind*. The two dozen and more references to the hair of Yeats's beloved or of the faeries, which so much exercised the puritanical P. E. More and a number of critics after him, all go back to the locks of the approaching storm in Shelley's *Ode,* the locks being at once fiery clouds and the hair uplifted from the head of the fierce Maenad, the West Wind, which comes to visit upon the poet either the fate of Orpheus, or an apocalyptic restoration.

Yeats begins the volume by a vision of the faery host riding the wind, *The Hosting of the Sidhe*. His own comment explains that "Sidhe is also Gaelic for wind, and certainly the Sidhe have much to do with the wind. They journey in whirling winds, the winds that were called the dance of the daughters of Herodias in the Middle Ages, Herodias doubtless taking the place of some old goddess." [6] But Yeats's host is hardly the traditional Sidhe, including as it does Caoilte, a warrior of the Fenian cycle, and Niamh, the enticing beauty of *The Wanderings of Oisin*. This odd placement of warrior and ideal beauty is a clue to the meaning of the poem. The courage and splendor of the world have been taken up into the faery host, and so the poem can resolve itself in the rhetorical question:

> The host is rushing 'twixt night and day,
> And where is there hope or deed as fair?

Yeats has no answer, in this volume, but the odd strength of the volume is in his subtle, never quite spoken resistance to the "sweet everlasting Voices" that have appropriated all of human passion, and yet left a man suffering in and from time. *The Lover tells of the Rose in his Heart* and rejects "all things uncomely and broken"; the world is not shapely enough to provide fit context for his love, and he hungers to build a world more to the heart's desire. But this beautiful lyric tells against its singer, and our sympathies go out to everything he neglects; the cry of a child and the ploughman's steps, while we note how far this lover is from desiring a reality. He dreams of an image, and the image blossoms a rose in the heart's depths, and remains only an image. This is the condition of the "out-worn heart, in a time out-worn" of *Into the Twilight*, and it is expressed throughout the volume with a perfection that no lyrist in Romantic tradition had surpassed. Yeats aspired all his life to write a genuinely popular poetry, "popular" meaning "of the folk." His success came early, rather than late, in this regard anyway, for the only popular poetry is that which becomes popular, in the vulgar sense. The first essay in *Ideas of Good and Evil* is called *What Is "Popular Poetry"?*—written by Yeats in 1901, two years after the appearance of *The Wind Among the Reeds*. It is a splendid essay, and shows Yeats at his canniest:

> There is only one kind of good poetry, for the poetry of the coteries, which presupposes the written tradition, does not differ in kind from the true poetry of the people, which presupposes the unwritten tradition. Both are alike strange and obscure, and unreal to all who have not understanding, and both, instead of that manifest logic, that clear rhetoric of the "popular poetry," glimmer with thoughts and images whose "ancestors were stout and wise," "anigh to Paradise" "ere yet men knew the gift of corn." [7]

Yet there is a kind of "popular poetry" that Yeats does not recognize here, but to which he contributed not only *The Lake Isle of Innisfree,* but *The Song of Wandering Aengus,* and *The Wild*

Swans at Coole, and perhaps a few other lyrics. It is a kind that includes, in the nineteenth century, a handful of lyrics by Blake, Shelley, Keats, and Tennyson, and in the twentieth, probably only these lyrics by Yeats. The difficulty of characterizing the kind is itself a tribute to whatever it is that saves "all who have not understanding" from complete misunderstanding. There is a true poetry that is not "strange and obscure," that has a primal simplicity. It is, however, very rare, and it spoils the mass of readers "who have not understanding," since they always demand that all other poetry approximate it. Blake's and Shakespeare's songs are central instances of it; so is *The Song of Wandering Aengus.*

This was first published as *Mad Song,* in a tradition going back to the Elizabethans and Blake and issuing later in Yeats in the songs of Crazy Jane and Tom the Lunatic. Yeats used it as a song of Red Hanrahan also, but makes it the song of the god of youth, beauty, and poetry in *The Wind Among the Reeds.* Aengus is Yeats's god of lovers, in the sense that every man can say: "whenever I am in love it is not I that am in love but Aengus who is always looking for Edaine through somebody's eyes." [8] The strength of the lyric is that it finds inevitable expression for this universal compulsiveness. It echoes Keats and Morris, and overtly displays what is best in Pre-Raphaelite technique.

Its theme is the unappeasable quest for the *daimonic* beloved, a theme Yeats took from *Alastor* and was to alter, but never abandon. Here also the quest begins with the poet's imagination or madness, like the fire that grew in the spirit of King Goll, and again the quest begins in the natural world but cannot be completed there, for the beloved fades into the light of common day. The fire in the head of the first stanza is externalized in the glimmering girl of the second, kindled in place of the hearth flame. In the last stanza, the natural world is the frustrate repetition of lands, hollow and hilly, through which the vain quest has led. The fire of nature, sun and moon, has become purely visionary, the golden and silver apples to be plucked when the Hesperides have been reached, the quest fulfilled, the beloved attained. There is defeat in the poem, for the visionary hope of the last stanza is both stronger and more dangerous than despair would be. The hope is a madness, like Goll's and the god of love who sings this mad song is a dangerously compulsive god.

The obsessiveness of this god dominates the brief lyric, *The Lover Mourns for the Loss of Love,* where the "beautiful friend," Mrs. Shakespear, abandons the poet because his heart retains the image of his lost love, Maud Gonne. More impressive are the subsequent lyrics, where the compulsiveness of the poet expresses itself in the apocalyptic imagery of *The Wanderings of Oisin:*

> I would that the Boar without bristles had come from the West
> And had rooted the sun and moon and stars out of the sky
> And lay in the darkness, grunting, and turning to his rest.

Though the Boar here is simply the darkness following sunset, critics rightly see it as another prefigurement of Yeats's version of the Beast from the Sea, the animated Sphinx of *The Second Coming.* The longing for an End of the World here is the defeated lover's longing for an end to change through final change, and may suggest an unconscious sexual element in a poem like *The Second Coming,* where the frustrations of the poet appear to proceed from other anxieties. The most successful of these apocalyptic poems in the volume is *He Bids His Beloved Be at Peace,* where a Blakean directional symbolism is intermixed with more esoteric mythological material. Something of the astonishing strength of Yeats's earlier visionary endowment can be felt in his power here to vivify abstraction:

> The South is pouring down roses of crimson fire:
> O vanity of Sleep, Hope, Dream, endless Desire,
> The Horses of Disaster plunge in the heavy clay.

Though the rhetorical power of Yeats grows more incisive and self-chastened in his later and now more admired poems of apocalyptic longings, I think we may wonder finally where Yeats's genuine achievement is more clearly manifested, as between *The Wind Among the Reeds* and say, *Michael Robartes and the Dancer,* the most doctrinal of his volumes. Too often the doctrinal lyrics are vulnerable to the harsh accusations of Yvor Winters, who charges them with being too deeply moved by their own ideas, ideas Winters judges to be contemptible. Though the accusations are not wholly just, they border on a truth; Yeats's best critics generally defend such ideas only because they are Yeats's. The

ideas of *The Wind Among the Reeds* are universally human in
their concern, however esoteric the imagery of the volume becomes. Whether the word "ideas" is fully relevant to *The Wind
Among the Reeds* is perhaps a question, to which a reading of
The Cap and Bells may provide a useful answer. This is one of
Yeats's few poems based upon an actual dream, and always meant
a great deal to him. Ellmann accurately summarizes part of the
poem's meaning, in terms of its 'ideas":

> The jester, after first sending the queen the trappings of common
> romance, finally offers the cap and bells which are his alone, and
> she, obdurate before the familiar and grandiloquent gifts of heart
> and soul, yields when the jester sends what is most essential and
> individual in him.[9]

Ellmann, considering Yeats's revisions of the poem, is rightly
skeptical of the poet's claim that he wrote the poem exactly as he
dreamed it. But Ellmann's interpretation relies too much on
Yeats's own later interpretation, when the poet in lectures cited
The Cap and Bells as an instance of the right way to win a lady.
Whether the poem is essentially dream or not, it has a larger and
more sinister meaning, in its essential or intrinsic idea of the relation between jester and queen, or poet and Muse, Yeats and
Maud Gonne. The jester sends the soul out of his body; it rises
wise-tongued, even as the owls of wisdom call, and rises "in a
straight blue garment," the blue being the color of the spirit, as
in Mary's color. But the queen will not listen to wisdom, and the
jester sends his heart instead, the red garment of dream rather
than the blue of spiritualized thought, personality rather than
character, self rather than soul. When the voice of sweetness is rejected also (as Yeats had been rejected, personality as well as
character) the jester chooses death, or at least a kind of self-cas-
tration:

> "I have cap and bells," he pondered,
> "I will send them to her and die";
> And when the morning whitened
> He left them where she went by.

He sends his genius, which defines his manhood, and I assume
a terrible irony was involved when Yeats told his audiences this
was the right way to win a woman:

> She laid them upon her bosom,
> Under a cloud of her hair,
> And her red lips sang them a love-song
> Till stars grew out of the air.

What is this but a dream version of that central Yeatsian
image, out of the Decadence, of the dancer with the severed head?
True, she proceeds to gather up the heart and the soul, who set up
a cricket-song, "a chattering wise and sweet," but this is not to say
that she revives the presumably deceased jester. The dream-
poem's bitterness is one with the central emotion of the volume,
the defeated lover's rejection of nature and his longing for cataclysm.

The Valley of the Black Pig extends this longing to dream itself, the dream being of the Irish Armageddon. There is controlled hysteria in this poem, as in many of the brief lyrics that
follow, remarkably exquisite in their surface, but sexually tormented in their depths. The use of Golden Dawn imagery in
some of them is of no imaginative value, but gives us another
backwards clue of Yeats's motivations in seeking occult comfort,
having failed to attain the naturalistic completion of sexual love.
The most elaborate of the occult poems, though not the best
(which is probably the brief *He Hears the Cry of the Sedge*) is
The Poet Pleads with the Elemental Powers, which shows both
the formal and the mythological influence of Blake, resembling as
it does some of the interspersed songs of Enitharmon and Enion
in the early Nights of *The Four Zoas.* The poem is a densely
woven prayer, quarried from the ineffable Madame Blavatsky as
well as from Blake, and its precise sense is perhaps not to be ascer-
tained, but its general direction is clear. The cosmic serpent or
Polar Dragon, the coiled form of fallen nature, sleeps, and while
his vigilance is absent the elemental Powers (nameless, shapeless,
and Blavatskian) pull the immortal Rose from the Tree of Life,
Blake's Tree of Mystery. In the experiential state of darkness and

loss that results, the poet begs the Powers to protect his beloved from the temptations of the fallen, the Blakean "nets of day and night." The final stanza is curiously vaporous despite its elaboration:

> Dim Powers of drowsy thought, let her no longer be
> Like the pale cup of the sea,
> When winds have gathered and sun and moon burned dim
> Above its cloudy rim;
> But let a gentle silence wrought with music flow
> Whither her footsteps go.

It would be a loss not to see the poetic distinction of a stanza like this, even if we have to struggle to see its full relevance to the poem's despairing theme. The first four lines strain after a Shelleyan subtlety of vanishing imagery, in order to convey the desperate intensity of the lover's vision, in which the beloved moves always at the dim and fading margins of natural perception. The Keatsian paradox of the penultimate line is much less successful, but testifies again to the poet's obsessed desire, which is to remove his apprehension of the lost beloved entirely from the context of nature.

The principal virtues of *The Wind Among the Reeds* are concentrated in its finest poem, *The Secret Rose*. Yeats's own long note on this poem provides the reader with all the information necessary to identify the few arbitrary references; the real difficulties are also the poem's splendors. For the Rose prayed to in this poem is no longer the esoteric emblem of the poems in *The Rose* grouping in *The Countess Kathleen and Various Legends and Lyrics* (1892). The Rosicrucian particulars of the Golden Dawn symbolism have dropped away. It remains true that nothing in the poem works against an esoteric meaning, but the poem's concerns are no longer with the Rose but with the poet and his state of consciousness. Yeats begins as though he were still writing mystical addresses, as he had five years before:

> Far-off, most secret, and inviolate Rose,
> Enfold me in my hour of hours. . . .

This privileged hour is a state where questers "dwell beyond the stir/ And tumult of defeated dreams," like Oisin in his long repose. The questers and dreamers are named in a majestic catalogue; the Magi, Conchobar, Cuchullain and Fand, Caolte, Fergus, and then the nameless youth who quests after and finds a pastoral ideal:

> And him who sold tillage, and house, and goods,
> And sought through lands and islands numberless years,
> Until he found, with laughter and with tears,
> A woman of so shining loveliness
> That men threshed corn at midnight by a tress,
> A little stolen tress.

Yeats has no real source for this; it is his own beautiful fiction, a vignette attaining a visionary climax in a remarkable Romantic conceit, an idyll to be illustrated by Calvert or Palmer. The shining pathos here is that this is the poet's own defeated dream, and with a wholly satisfactory sudden transition the poet again addresses the Secret Rose:

> I, too, await,
> The hour of thy great wind of love and hate.
> When shall the stars be blown about the sky,
> Like the sparks blown out of a smithy, and die?
> Surely thine hour has come, thy great wind blows,
> Far-off, most secret, and inviolate Rose?

It is a great passage by any standards, and ends the poem greatly, and surprisingly, with the opening line now transformed into a genuinely open question. The passage suggests both the great wind of creation and destruction in Shelley's ode, and the violent imagery of the opening of *Night the Ninth, Being the Last Judgment* of Blake's *The Four Zoas,* while prophesying also the smithies of the Emperor in *Byzantium.* Like the other lost and defeated questers, the poet awaits now what he prayed for in the poem's opening, his hour of hours which will be also the universal apocalypse, when Los the poet-prophet will come again as Urthona the blacksmith of creation, and the star-world of Urizen shall be blown out and die:

> The Sun has left his blackness & has found a fresher morning
> And the mild moon rejoices in the clear & cloudless night
> And Man walks forth from midst of the fires the evil is all
>   consumd
> His eyes behold the Angelic spheres arising night & day
> The stars consumd like a lamp blown out & in their stead behold
> The Expanding Eyes of Man behold the depths of wondrous
>   worlds. . . .[10]

But, though he echoes Blake, Yeats ends the poem more in Shelley's skeptical if fierce spirit. "Destroyer and creator" Shelley names the wind, and he ends his ode with a subtle and open question. So, here at the end of *The Secret Rose,* Yeats ends also, and the "surely" that begins the penultimate line is already more of a question than an assertion, or is perhaps balanced unevenly between the two. Like Shelley, Yeats wants and does not want the great wind to rise. Something in the poet is more willing to understand an impulse always present in him, though usually an undersong at best. The Rose is best kept far-off, most secret, and inviolate, for if the hour of hours gives at last the sought love and creation, it must give also unsought hate and destruction, the end of nature and of human nature. Here also Yeats was more like Shelley than he was like the uncompromising and undoubting Blake. *The Wind Among the Reeds* stands consciously at the end of a century, and its dominant mood is "a diffuse, an irrational chiliasm," but playing against the mood is another strain in Yeats, one that he was never to abandon entirely, fortunately for him.

9: The Shadowy Waters

As in *The Wind Among the Reeds,* here Yeats reaches the full maturity of his earlier achievement. It is doubtful that any later poem by him contains as much of the whole man, or indicates the full scope of the poet's imaginative quest. Since *The Shadowy Waters* is frequently dismissed by Yeats's critics as over-decorative, mere Pre-Raphaelite verse, an example of what Yeats outgrew, they tend to consider it less fully than its difficulties and values warrant.

One basic problem in reading *The Shadowy Waters* is to decide just which text of the play or poem to read, as there are a number of principal alternatives now available to the reader. There is the dramatic poem of 1906, as Yeats finally approved it, in the *Collected Poems;* then the definitive "acting version," of 1907 and 1911, in the *Collected Plays;* then an earlier full text of the poem of 1900, to be found now most readily in an appendix to the "Variorum" edition of the poems; finally, the ur-version of 1894, evidently unfinished, recently edited from manuscript by David R. Clark.[1] Adding the variants in the earlier published versions to these, one finds the bewildering consequence to be that the different texts blend together in one's memory, which is perhaps as well, since such multiplicity is an accurate emblem for the difficulties that this very central and personal work gave to Yeats.

The first published *Shadowy Waters* was 1900, but Yeats seems to have had the work in mind when he was scarcely twenty, on the testimony of A. E., as cited by David Clark.[2] The incomplete version as edited by Clark, probably written in 1894, is in some ways a more rewarding and powerful poem or scenario for a poem than any of the complete versions that Yeats published, remarkable as all of them are, and so I begin with it here.

The hero of *The Shadowy Waters* is Forgael, a pirate and mage whose literary ancestry is clearly compounded out of Byron's Manfred, Shelley's Poet in *Alastor,* and Keats's Endymion. Like all these, Forgael is an uncompromising quester after an impossible beloved. Like Manfred, he has traffic with the dark powers, here the Fomorah or Seabars, eagle-headed creatures, and again like Manfred, he dominates the gods of darkness by his mysterious connection to the gods of light. Like the Poet of *Alastor,* Forgael rejects all earthly love in seeking his inhuman ideal, though in the published versions he is more like Endymion or Shelley's Laon in accepting an earthly love despite his quest.

The early Yeats, at his most characteristic and unsubdued, was fully as savage a poet as the old Yeats was to be. Indeed, the Yeats of *Purgatory* or *The Gyres* is almost mild compared to the poet of the unpublished *Shadowy Waters.* The Fomorah are cannibals, and the first *Shadowy Waters* is a barbaric work, bordering at times on the splendidly repulsive. Perhaps George Moore, who took credit for persuading Yeats to rid the poem of the Fomorah, was moved by considerations of humane tact as well as stagecraft. The Fomorah are bitter, dispossessed undersea creatures, now deformed into predatory bird-like beasts. Forgael feeds the victims of his piracy to them, not out of sadism or rancor, but out of a precisely apocalyptic indifference to the merely given world, natural and human. As the poem opens, Forgael has fallen into a swoon induced by his despair at being unable to disengage his dream of love from the realm of mirror-image, the natural world of *Alastor* and *Oisin*. The famished Fomorah prepare to feast upon him, but he awakens, and directs them with a new animus against the world, urging them to an apocalyptic destructiveness:

> Oh eagle-headed race, rush through the air
> Unhook the flaming shields and quench the world.

The shields are the creations of Forgael's own dream, earlier described by one of the Fomorah:

> And then I saw his dream float up and hide
> The heavens and burnished shields hang from the stars
> Mirror on mirror, and a flame that shook
> In the mid-air, and saw its loneliness
> Leaping from shield to shield. . . .

The world is to be destroyed, not because it is destructible and Forgael feels an Achilles-like rage against destructibility, but because nothing in it is adequate to the flame of Forgael's dream. In an extraordinary dialogue between Forgael and one of the Sea-bars, we hear a competition for supremacy in apocalyptic rage, easily won by Forgael who wishes for "that great hour/ That shall puff out demons and gods and men," the demons necessarily including the race of Seabars. Ironically frightened by this more comprehensive vision of destruction, they rush to what would be a vain battle against Forgael's magic, but are interrupted by the entrance of Forgael's sailors, who have heard music from a nearby ship. As the pirates' attack upon this ship proceeds, Forgael prays to a god of darkness for what Yeats will later come to call the Condition of Fire, a freedom not the self's in which nevertheless the self can share. He is granted a vision of "the shadows of unappeasable desire," a prelude to the appearance before him of two captives, Dectira a princess, and Aleel a poet (as in *The Countess Cathleen*). As Clark says, here are two Yeatses, Forgael and Aleel, the former an anti-self and the latter a sad reality, quickly slain by the brutal mage-pirate, who then uses his art to win the lady from her dead lover. Clark amasses evidence that demonstrates an uncompromising design Yeats surrendered in every finished version of the dramatic poem or play, which would have had Forgael, the lady won, abandon her finally to resume his solitary quest toward the true North of his unappeasable desires, the lonely death of the Poet in *Alastor* or of the demon in *Frankenstein*.[3] Studying all the finished versions of *The Shadowy Waters*, one comes to miss both the Seabars and Forgael's triumphant solipsism, respectively the active and passive forms of the same *antithetical* quest. We can surmise that Yeats himself was a little wary of his own savagery, quite aside from the censorious and witty criticism of George Moore.

If we turn next to the dramatic poem of 1900, the loss of pungency is felt immediately, but the gain in art is genuine, and the art is far from being mere lacquer. Yeats, writing a preface in 1933 for a collection of early articles, says that the first, unfinished *Shadowy Waters* had as theme the particular terror that filled him sometimes when he contemplated "the barrier between myself and other people." [4] This terror of his own solipsism is gone from all the finished versions of the poem, since Forgael loses his remorseless dedication to solitary quest. Yeats still considered the poem to be apocalyptic, saying in 1905 that the theme was to be found in "miracle, ecstasy, the impossible joy" that would suffice the mind at world's end.[5] The 1900 dramatic poem is better suited to sustain Yeats's statement than the 1905–6 poem, or the "acting version" of 1906–11, even though Yeats is citing lines he added in 1905. Despite the conclusions of two careful students of Yeats's revisions, Parkinson and Bushrui, I find a progressive imaginative loss with each fresh version of *The Shadowy Waters*.[6] A dramatic gain is continuous, and the "acting version" is certainly more actable than what came before. But *The Shadowy Waters* is more effective as poem than as play anyway, and more effective in 1900 than in its two principal later versions. After 1903 (Maud Gonne's marriage) Yeats was too bitter in his revisions not to violate the spirit of *The Shadowy Waters*. The middle Yeats was hardly the right custodian of the culmination of the vision of the early Yeats, and *The Shadowy Waters* suffered for it. The dramatic poem of 1900 has more nearly the right blend of savagery and control than the early, unfinished version, or the later, too-finished versions. In the remainder of this chapter, I discuss the poem of 1900, available to the reader on pp. 745–69 of the "Variorum" edition, edited by Allt and Alspach.

Ellmann's discussion of *The Shadowy Waters* gives a very full account of Yeats's overt, intentional symbolism in the poem, a symbolism that has little to do with the poem's imaginative strength, which is in deeper, more obsessive and inescapable patterns of meaning. The pattern of symbolism, as Ellmann says, "plays tag with boredom," but the poem is not boring, and offers more than "the nobility of its ideal and the virtuosity of its experimentation." [7] Where *The Shadowy Waters* is strongest is precisely in its mythopoeic aspect, directly derived from Shelley and Blake and the story of *antithetical* quest Yeats had made up for himself in his creative swerve from their influence. I have described the quest's general pattern in my first chapter, and Yeats's relation to Shelley and Blake in Chapters 4 and 5. *The Shadowy Waters* and *The Wanderings of Oisin* are the largest accounts of the quest Yeats gave his readers before *Per Amica Silentia Lunae* in 1917, and indeed the most ambitious single poems he ever attempted. When our "Modernist" fashions have ebbed, they may be valued more highly than Yeats himself or his students have valued them.

Not that Yeats ever escaped their obsessive appeal, whether in his recurrent return to their themes and problems, or in his relation to these early works themselves, for his later comments recognize their centrality. In 1933 Yeats said of Shelley and Tennyson, with considerable justice (as I must grant, reluctantly) that they had thought of the theater as being isolated from the authentic movement of literature, and so had written plays in which "they had tried to escape their characteristics." They ought, he said, to have created drama "in the mood of *The Lotus Eaters* or of *Epipsychidion*." [8] Clearly, this was the challenge Yeats attempted to meet in *The Shadowy Waters*, for the 1900 poem has the same relation to *Epipsychidion* that the unfinished 1894 poem has to *Alastor*. It is important to remember that Yeats met and fell in love with Maud Gonne in 1889. He first proposed marriage to her in 1891. Rejected, he tried again in 1894, and I believe the pain of the fresh rejection accounts in part for the savagery of the unfinished *Shadowy Waters* of that year, a savagery directed not only at Dectira (as she is spelled in that manuscript) but also, as Clark notes, at the courtly lover-poet, Aleel, the self Yeats rejects for the more masterful Forgael.[9] For five years, Yeats restrained his passion for proposals to Maud, and sought some solace elsewhere. But remorse for abandoning his impossible ideal overcame him in 1899, when he again proposed, with the usual results. The remorse, and the desperation of this proposal, are reflected in the publication of *The Wind Among the Reeds* in 1899. In 1900, Yeats again proposed, again suffered rejection, and returned to *The Shadowy Waters,* making his first complete version of the poem out of his apparent realization that the rejection was final. But the bitterness of the 1894 poem is far greater than any bitterness in the 1900 completed work, for Yeats assumed in 1900 that Maud would never marry any other man, even though he accepted finally that she would never marry him. This was a very different assumption than he had in 1894. Since Maud did marry, in 1903, Yeats's assumption was proved unreal, and there is subsequently a retreat from the erotic idealism of the 1900 poem in the 1906 revision.

This is, I admit, mere genetic surmise, but it helps explain why Yeats could not let himself abandon *The Shadowy Waters.* It does not explain the mythopoeic pattern of the poem, but the poem perhaps can help explain Yeats's love for Maud Gonne, and the erotic pattern of his life. The conception of *The Shadowy Waters* goes back at least to 1884, and precedes Yeats's earliest published poems in the *Dublin University Review.* Many childhood memories and impressions are mixed in *The Shadowy Waters,* as Clark and other scholars have noted.[10] William Pollexfen, the seafarer, found his way into the making of Forgael, as did not only poetic characters like Manfred, Laon, the Poet of *Alastor,* but the young Yeats's notion of Byron and Shelley themselves. Just as clearly, Dectora derives from Cythna, heroine of *The Revolt of Islam,* and from the Emilia who is apotheosized in *Epipsychidion.* But Yeats's dreamings of a decade, 1884–94, did not consolidate into the form of *The Shadowy Waters* until he had known and loved Maud Gonne for five years, and felt rejected by her for three. Dectora is a vision of Maud Gonne assimilated to several Shelleyan fictions, even as Forgael is a vision of Yeats himself assimilated to the major Shelleyan archetype of the poet-quester. The torment of *The Shadowy Waters,* genetically speaking, is not so much Yeats's baffled longing for Maud Gonne as it is his recognition, to use his later terms, that the *daimon* or *alastor* is his destiny, that he is cursed with the temperament of the *antithetical* quester, a victim of the Spirit of Solitude. There is no sexual love-making between Forgael and Dectora in any version of *The Shadowy Waters.* This is a crucial part of Yeats's swerve away from his Shelleyan sources, for Laon and the poet-protagonists of *Alastor* and *Epipsychidion* do possess the beloved, though this possession, by its very nature, cannot be long sustained. In Yeats, love and the means of love have drawn even farther apart, and the world of *The Shadowy Waters* cannot admit even a momentary sexual fulfillment.

As we have seen, the first, unfinished *Shadowy Waters* was a more uncompromising work than the poem of 1900, but it may be that just this savagery of spirit prevented any resolution for the original poem. In the 1900 poem, Forgael and Dectora conclude by sailing off together, but the princess is considerably more single-minded about making the final quest a joint venture than the mage is. As she insists: "I will follow you," he desperately protests: "Masters of our dreams,/ Why have you cloven me with a mortal love?/ Pity these weeping eyes!" It is remarkably parallel, despite the Yeatsian intensity and visionary context, to the resolution of Shaw's equally Shelleyan *Man and Superman,* where the overborne revolutionary goes on protesting even as he yields to his domesticated destiny. Indeed, there is perhaps an unintended humor in the closing lines of the 1900 *Shadowy Waters,* but it is not unacceptable to the poem's thematic concerns, if a little unfortunate for the unity of tone. Yeats wants the poem to be at once *Alastor* and *Epipsychidion,* which is impossible; the quester is both to reject every natural love, and yet is to embark on a visionary voyage to an Ultima Thule with an actual beloved. I assume that this reflects the curious compact made between Yeats and Maud Gonne, or that he somehow assumed had been made, to the effect that though the lady would not marry him she was not to love or marry anyone else. The last visionary voyage of

Forgael, made in the company of Dectora, presumably represented Yeats's own poetic and occult enterprise, as he persuaded himself it existed down to the awful shock of 1903, when the *epipsyche* suddenly became Madame MacBride. This surmise can be confirmed by comparing the close of the 1900 poem to the 1906 version, where Forgael is a much stronger character, and Dectora correspondingly weaker. There Dectora first attempts to persuade Forgael (once his magic has worked, and she loves him) to take her with him to some known land of peace, but fails to turn him from his quest and so yields herself to the quest and him together. In 1905 Maud separated from MacBride, and so was available as a spiritual possibility as Yeats worked at revising the poem, but something had gone out of his ardor.

The Shadowy Waters, in its 1900 version, should be read in this biographical context of Yeats's thwarted love, so as to illuminate that shadowy context. In the introductory lines, dated September 1900, Yeats salutes the shadowy ones he associates with Forgael's *daimonic* birds in the poem. They dwell in a Blakean Eden, "out of time and out of space," but perhaps gather round us in our moments of Shelleyan epiphany, visitations of the Intellectual Beauty, of "pale light/ Shining on water and fallen among leaves,/ And winds blowing from flowers." These echoes of Shelley's *Hymn to Intellectual Beauty* define the Shadow's nature in the very title, *The Shadowy Waters.* This is not so much the Blakean Shadow, identified falsely by Yeats with the Gnostic and theosophical Serpent of time, though as Yeats continued to revise the poem the Shadow became more and more the *daimonic* world. Primarily, it is the more innocent Shelleyan Shadow, that floats unseen among us in the *Hymn to Intellectual Beauty,* but does darken and widen in Shelley's poetry until it becomes the Shadow of our night, the earth's shadow cast up into the heavens, the sense of our own death-in-life that darkens even the stars, but ends at the sphere of Venus-Lucifer, evening and morning star, justly called by Yeats Shelley's most important symbol. *The Philosophy of Shelley's Poetry* and the first completed *Shadowy Waters* were both written in 1900, and frequently can be read as a commentary upon each other. Here for instance, is Yeats explaining Shelley's star-symbol, but commenting on *The Shadowy Waters* as well although he does not mention his own poem:

I was with a number of Hermetists, and one of them said to another, "Do you see something in the curtain?" The other gazed at the curtain for a while and saw presently a man led through a wood by a black hound, and then the hound lay dead at a place the seer knew was called, without knowing why, "the Meeting of the Suns," and the man followed a red hound, and then the red hound was pierced by a spear. A white fawn watched the man out of the wood, but he did not look at it, for a white hound came and he followed it trembling, but the seer knew that he would follow the fawn at last, and that it would lead him among the gods. The most learned of the Hermetists said, "I cannot tell the meaning of the hounds or where the Meeting of the Suns is, but I think the fawn is the Morning and Evening Star." [11]

These unlikely Hermetists are students of Shelley and Yeats, and have read *The Revolt of Islam, The Wanderings of Oisin,* and the just completed *Shadowy Waters,* at the least. In the stage directions of *The Shadowy Waters,* Forgael's sail is described as adorned by three rows of hounds, respectively dark, red, and white with red ears. The helmsman opens the poem by attributing Forgael's sorrow to the harp given the mage by "the fool of the wood," on an island where a red hound ran from a silver arrow. When Forgael later plays on the harp to win Dectora's love, she dreams of the arrows having slain the red hound. After she has fallen in love with Forgael, she has a vision of a red-eared hound following a hornless deer forever among the winds and waters, luring lovers "to the streams where the world ends." At the poem's close, when Dectora has secured Forgael for their now mutual quest, she possessively puts her arms about him addressing him as: "O morning star/ Trembling . . . like a white fawn." The hound symbolism may have a Vedantic touch in it (as Ellmann discovered),[12] but mostly Yeats takes it from his earlier imaginings in *Oisin,* where he attributes it vaguely to various Arthurian and Celtic sources, yet essentially invents it himself, perhaps with a backward glance at the Shelleyan symbolism of the hounds of Hades, the Furies who haunt Shelley's dreams of desire. The silver arrows are taken directly from Shelley's *To a Skylark,* where they represent the poet's synaesthetic hearing of the fading of the Morning Star into the dawn, in a magnificent passage Eliot pioneered in misunderstanding:

> Keen as are the arrows
>   Of that silver sphere,
> Whose intense lamp narrows
>   In the white dawn clear
> Until we hardly see—we feel that it is there.

The trembling fawn, also from *Oisin,* is Shelleyan again, being a prevalent image in his visions, but particularly in the description of Emilia's beauty in *Epipsychidion.* There remains, from the Hermetic vision in *The Philosophy of Shelley's Poetry,* only "the Meeting of the Suns," not employed in *The Shadowy Waters* but probably based upon Canto I of *The Revolt of Islam* where two glittering lights meet in the Temple of immortal spirits to become one clear, restored sun, the re-born and re-united martyred lovers, Laon and Cythna. The meaning of all this symbolism, in the Hermetic vision of the essay on Shelley, and in *The Shadowy Waters,* is simply that of Yeats's reading of the Shelleyan quest. Ecstasy, Yeats says while interpreting Shelley's *Rosalind and Helen,* is a kind of death, and he quotes from the intense passage where the harp's music unifies love, sleep, poetry, and death, ultimate source for the magic of Forgael's harp.[13] Ecstasy is the remorseless goal of the *antithetical* quester, yet ecstasy of a kind that dangerously transcends the world of object-relationships, and that threatens always to collapse into the Shadow or *alastor* of solitude, the vision-destroying bliss of solipsism. The black hound is that solipsistic intensity that destroyed Shelley's Poet in *Alastor,* and that Yeats knows the terror of in himself. When the hound dies, where the Suns meet, or Dectora enters, then the quester follows a red hound, the vision of sexual passion as an attempt to alter the voyage toward more-than-natural fulfillment. But the red hound too is slain, by a shaft of light from the Morning Star, spear or arrow of an *antithetical* desire that is generous, rather than solipsistic. Though the white fawn that is the Morning Star appears, the quester follows the white hound instead for a time, still loving the journey more than its destination. This is the redeemed or true quest, upon which Dectora and Forgael set out at the poem's close, with Forgael unable or a little unwilling to see that the white fawn by his side is his Morning Star, though the lady can see that he is hers.

The crisis of *The Shadowy Waters,* and its permanent fascination, is in the exchange between Dectora and Forgael when they have mastered the meaning of their symbolism, for here the central and lasting ambivalence of Yeats toward his own vision of Romantic love is definitively revealed. Forgael, speaking for Yeats, observes that all natural love "is but brief longing, and deceiving hope,/ And bodily tenderness." Dectora, speaking not for Maud but the Maud of Yeats's highly qualified wish-fulfillment of 1900, wonders why love is "so crazy that it longs/ To drown in its own image," for which Forgael has no answer but the streams at the world's end. His deepest desire remains that of the slain dark hound, to go to those streams alone, but the masters of his dreams, the *daimonic* Shadows, have cloven his heart with a mortal love. He accepts, though with tears, a compromised quest, as the heart-cloven Yeats had to accept it also. To see that Dectora is the quest's fulfillment is impossible for him; to go on without her is also impossible. She solves the dilemma by her sacrifice, going on the quest with him, at which the harp begins to murmur of itself, and Forgael revives to the altered quest, saying: "The harpstrings have begun to cry out to the eagles," which consecrates the transformed quest, ends the poem, and ends also Forgael's function as a poet. Maud Gonne, in her curious memorial essay, *Yeats and Ireland,* contrasts her road to her lover's, and admits that his "was more difficult, a road of outer peace and inner confusion, discernible in his later work." [14] It is to be seen also in the earlier work, nowhere more clearly than in *The Shadowy Waters,* yet there the inner confusion is more controlled and conscious than later. Though the *antithetical* quest, with its impossible demands, was to yield Yeats many more intricate inventions than *The Shadowy Waters,* none comes so near the division in his heart as the poem of 1900, written appropriately when he was in the middle of the journey.

10: The Middle Plays

Where There Is Nothing

The plays Yeats wrote during his painful middle decade (1900–1910) are on the whole superior to his poems of the same period. Even as the poems seem marred by over-reaction to the limit reached in *The Wind Among the Reeds,* so the plays suffer by the intense recoil from the extreme vision of *The Shadowy Waters. Where There Is Nothing* (1902–3) is an attempt to work out the implications of a Blakean-Nietzschean world-view in the context of an Ibsenite social drama. The result is very bad, but very important for an understanding of Yeats's creative mind, particularly in relation to Blake and Romantic tradition. Yeats rejected *Where There Is Nothing,* replacing it by *The Unicorn from the Stars,* where most of the writing is Lady Gregory's. In the original version of *Where There Is Nothing,* some of the writing is by Lady Gregory and Douglas Hyde, but the revised text seems altogether Yeats's. I agree with Ure that *The Unicorn from the Stars* has more coherent symbolism and better developed minor characters than *Where There Is Nothing,* but imaginatively it is a much less interesting play, and hardly Yeats's own.[1] And something crucial in Yeats's vision is lost, if we leave *Where There Is Nothing* out of the story, for the matter of the play, disengaged from its inappropriate form, retains its vitality, reminding us of a persistent impulse in Yeats largely blocked from 1900 to 1917, and severely modified thereafter.

This impulse is apocalyptic, and while it largely derives from Blake and Shelley, it was a genuine part of Yeats's consciousness, from his childhood on, and was responsible for the early and overwhelming effect that the poets of Romantic apocalypse had upon him. Yeats said of Paul Ruttledge, the hero of *Where There Is Nothing,* that his character was arid and dominating, and so unsympathetic.[2] Yeats was fairer to the character when he compared him to William Morris, "too absorbed and busy to give much of himself to persons," and said also that he possessed "a certain strength, a certain abundance," that emanates in "a kind of hard passion." [3] It is clear that Paul Ruttledge is in the line of Forgael, and beyond him of the Poet of *Alastor,* Prince Athanase, and Manfred, and ultimately of the major Romantics themselves, as Yeats conceived them. Like Forgael, Paul Ruttledge is Yeats as a man of action, attempting to transform reality into his vision.

Melchiori and other Yeats scholars have traced the development that leads from the stories of *The Secret Rose* on through *Where There Is Nothing* until it culminates in poems like *The Second Coming* and *Leda and the Swan.*[4] Ruttledge celebrates two hearaldic beasts as emblems of his apocalypse, a brazen, winged beast, with claws of iron and sapphire eyes, who will develop into the Egyptian Sphinx of *The Second Coming,* harbinger of "laughing ecstatic destruction," and a white unicorn, the Unicorn from the Stars, which was Yeats's title as a third grade adept during his sojourn among the Rosicrucians, in the Order of the Golden Dawn. Melchiori interprets Yeats's unicorn as "a scourge from above which will bring renewal, through ruin," which is consistent with Yeats's use of the emblem in *The Player Queen.*[5] The leading irony of *Where There Is Nothing,* and the play is hardly saved by it, is that the crazed country gentleman, turned first tinker, then monk, is neither Sphinx nor unicorn, but equally pathetic whether leading his gangs of folksy tinkers or credulous friars. Paul Ruttledge is the Don Quixote of Anglo-Ireland in the late nineteenth century, reading Blake and Nietzsche and William Morris as romancers of apocalypse, rather than the Don's romances of chivalry, and then rushing off with whole packs of Sanchos against the windmills of Church and State.[6] The play lacks only a Dulcinea, since Paul Ruttledge lacks the wit to so transform Sabina Silver, the tinker woman he marries. Arnold, whose Oxford scholar descended among the gypsies to escape the modern world and learn a secret lore, may have provided Yeats with a closer prototype, but the Scholar Gypsy, unlike Ruttledge, had the sense to remain a scholar in his descent.

Though the emphasis on the brazen beast as Laughter is roughly Nietzschean, the attack on "work" Ruskinian (or from Morris), and Ruttledge's sermon in Act IV clearly Tolstoyan (compare Tolstoy's pamphlet on the Sermon on the Mount, which Yeats cites in his notes), nevertheless *Where There Is Nothing* is Yeats's most Blakean work.[7] This is sometimes embarrassing, since Ruttledge has a way of quoting or paraphrasing Blake in irrelevant contexts, and a consistent literalism in misunderstanding Blake that is curiously at variance with Yeats's consistent occultizing in misunderstanding his precursor. But, as Yeats said in his notes to *The Unicorn from the Stars*, between his efforts and Lady Gregory's he hopes to have created a form that brings together Don Quixote and Sancho Panza, or Shelley and Dickens in the one body, as he says elsewhere. He calls this "yoking of antiquities, A Marriage of Heaven and Hell," but unfortunately the consequence is not a marriage but a grotesque coupling unsatisfactory to both modes, visionary romance and folk-farce.[8] The unhappy yoking-together of aesthetic contraries is not unique in Yeats, and issued finally in *The Herne's Egg* and some of the *Last Poems*, where the farce does not qualify but destroys the vision. In *Where There Is Nothing*, the vision is not much affected by Lady Gregory's folk realism, but everything realistic in the play is destroyed by the vision, so that we are left with certain kernels of Blake's abundance and hard passion, and of Nietzsche's astringent joy, and with nothing else whatsoever. A reader winces or ought to wince when Paul Ruttledge tells the magistrates that: "Some poet has written that exuberance is beauty, and that the roadway of excess leads to the palace of wisdom," and defends getting his tinkers drunk upon this basis.

Ruttledge is haunted by the music he hears, which he says "comes rejoicing from Paradise." It is the music of Blake's eternity, "made of the continual clashing of swords," but nothing Ruttledge says indicates that Blake meant intellectual warfare only. Ruttledge's (and Yeats's) wild beast is not Blake's or even Nietzsche's, but belongs to a consciousness that does not understand its own repressed longings for "iron teeth and brazen claws that can root up spires and towers." Though Ruttledge calls this beast Laughter, we more rightly name it hysteria, and have seen rather more of it than Yeats had by 1903. In his sermon to the friars, Ruttledge begins by preaching a simple antinomianism but passes to a severe local application of Blake's dictum that everything that lives is holy. State and Church must be destroyed because "the Christian's business is not reformation but revelation, and the only labours he can put his hand to can never be accomplished in time." Ruttledge does not see, as Blake did, that destruction is accomplished in time also, and so is no part of the labor of revelation. Ruttledge's final nihilism is a parody of Nietzsche rather than of Blake, as he exhorts his friars, like a current leader of student revolution, to "destroy everything that has Law and Number, for where there is nothing, there is God." Ruttledge repeats this formula as he dies, a martyr to Gnosticism but hardly to Romantic vision. As he himself says, every religious teacher before him has offered something to his followers, but he offers them nothing. But he does have one fine moment of insight, where he and Yeats understand Blake correctly. We remember Joyce's Stephen tapping his forehead, and saying it is there he must kill the king and the priest. So Ruttledge, also paraphrasing Blake on the apocalypse, tells his followers that it is inside our minds that the world must be destroyed: "it must be consumed in a moment inside our minds." Yeats is chastising himself for his own impatience, remembering it is in that moment, the pulsation of an artery, that the poet's work must be done. This is Ruttledge's only epiphany, and worth the rest of the play. *Where There Is Nothing* is one of those works that serve a poet by giving him opportunity to persist in his folly until he becomes, not wise, but a little warier of his own phantasmagorias, and so frees him, a little, of an obsession.

The King's Threshold

There are three versions of this moving play, published in 1904, 1906, and 1922. The play changed a great deal, not necessarily for the better, between 1904 and 1906; between 1906 and 1922, there were few changes in most of the play, but the ending was changed entirely, and a tragicomedy became a tragedy. In the earlier versions Seanchan the poet ends his hunger strike when the king yields, and restores to poetry its ancient rights at court. Seanchan starves himself to death in the 1922 version; Yeats says rather lamely in a note that he has given the play the tragic end he would have given it originally, had not a friend advised him to make it comedy.[9] I find very credible the suggestion of the textual critic Bushrui, that Yeats was influenced by the heroic Terence MacSwiney, Lord Mayor of Cork, who starved himself to death when imprisoned by the British in 1920.[10] With the hunger strike adopted as a patriotic political weapon in Ireland, Yeats could hardly maintain the earlier ending of his play. Synge had died in 1909, of a long illness, and the death of Synge lingered in Yeats's consciousness for many years. Yeats said of him that "he was one of those unmoved souls in whom there is a perpetual 'Last Day,' a perpetual trumpeting and coming up for judgment," which is very reminiscent of Seanchan.[11] In his notes to The King's Threshold, Yeats remembered that it was written when his Irish National Theatre Society was fighting hard to have pure art recognized by a community immersed in practical affairs, politics "and a propagandist patriotism." [12] It was natural, probably inevitable, that Yeats should have changed the end of the play as he did, for doing so after Synge was dead developed further a deep bitterness already central in the work.

Yet it is remarkable how little the change from comic to tragic ending matters, for there is no change in Seanchan himself. Ure greatly prefers the tragic ending, yet has difficulty demonstrating the necessity of it. The only change is in the king, who loses his nerve in the early versions, but not in the final one. Seanchan is in the line of Yeats's remorseless questers and founds his sense of the dignity and priority of poetry upon Shelley's *Defence,* and on *The Marriage of Heaven and Hell.* Where Paul Ruttledge is an unconvincing Romantic-Nietzschean apocalyptic, Seanchan is very persuasive, for he incarnates his own vision. Indeed *The King's Threshold,* particularly in its first version, seems to me the most undervalued of Yeats's plays, at least as a poem, for it does everything it attempts to do, and with economy and eloquence. Since what it attempts is to defend the rights of poetry against the world, it has no mean object, though probably it would have been better as a dramatic poem than a stage play, as Seanchan undergoes no dramatic development in it. Critics have compared him to the heroes of *Prometheus Bound* and *Samson Agonistes,* but the comparisons are hardly fair, both because *The King's Threshold* is modest in its scope and dignity, and because Seanchan is intrinsically less capable of dramatic evolution. Unlike Prometheus and Samson, Seanchan learns nothing in his ordeal, because his situation calls for simple though heroic obduracy, and nothing more. The divine world is outside the play; all that matters is a societal struggle between poetry and its enemies, which is too self-interested a theme for the greatest art, but more than adequate for *The King's Threshold.*

Shelley is the ultimate model for Seanchan, and *A Defence of Poetry* the deepest quarry for Sanchan's convictions. Poetry, connate with the origin of man, gives to mankind "the institutions of laws, and the founders of civil society, and the inventors of the arts of life." But the use of poetry, once past its initial gifts, is corrective: "Poetry is a mirror which makes beautiful that which is distorted." This is the doctrine taught by Seanchan to his pupils, that the poets display "images of the life that was in Eden," so that the world, gazing thereon, may bear "triumphant children." This is also the vision of Blake in *Jerusalem,* when he says that the world renews its powers by seeing all things "in the bright sculptures of/ Los's Halls." [13] Shelley's vision of the legislating poet as founder of civilization, and Blake's ironic account of how religions choose forms of worship from poetic tales, mingle in Seanchan's bitter contempt for the trinity of "bishops, soldiers, and makers of the law" that has driven him from the king's table.

The strength of the play is in the quality of Seanchan's bitterness. For the chief poet pleads "the poet's right, established when the world/ Was first established," and cannot yield without betraying all the poets who are yet to be. In the play's most famous speech, Seanchan compounds Shelley, Blake, Nietzsche, and Keats as he tells his scholars that poetry exults in the midst of apocalypse:

> Being the scattering hand, the bursting pod,
> The victim's joy among the holy flame,
> God's laughter at the shattering of the world,
> And now that joy laughs out and weeps and burns
> On these bare steps.

It does not lessen this eloquent passage to observe that its first line is Blakean, second Shelleyan, third Nietzschean, and last line and a half Keatsian, for these are controlled allusions and they mount up as a tremendous appeal to Romantic tradition. The first line, echoing Blake's lyric, "Thou hast a lap full of seed," emphasizes the poet as generous sower of life, yet reminds us also of Blake's bitterness, in finding the poet must pull up "some stinking weed." The second alludes to the martyrdom of Laon and Cyntha, and indicates Seanchan's resolution to follow them, if need be. The third is Zarathustra's terrible and prophetic laughter, appropriate for Seanchan as the singer of the great race that is to come. With the concluding Keatsian oxymoron, Seanchan stands upon the purgatorial steps as Keats did in *The Fall of Hyperion,* and we see suddenly that the king's threshold is akin to the porch of Moneta's temple. We will see Yeats employing an even more direct allusion to Keats's purgatorial confrontation with the Muse when he brings the Swineherd to the Queen in *A Full Moon in March.*

Seanchan's concern is with futurity, as befits a Shelleyan chief poet who is the hierophant "of an unapprehended inspiration." He has heard "murmurs that are the ending of all sound," and knows that the poets, provided they do not suffer their pride to be broken, cannot be driven out for good. "We come again/ Like a great wind that runs out of the waste," to destroy and to create. When he understands that, he is at bitter peace until the end, and so the end does not matter. For either way, whether the king yields or not, poetry must undergo an immediate, a temporal defeat. That is why Yeats, in revising to a tragic conclusion, could retain the closing lines of the earlier versions. The trumpets lifted up by Seanchan's pupils are "the trumpets which sing to battle" of the close of Shelley's *Defence,* trumpets that "feel not what they inspire; the influence which is moved not, but moves." Seanchan, in the first version's apparent triumph, knows that only the great race to come can triumph, only the long-throated swans who are far in the Unapparent. In the present, Blake's leprous God, Urizen, lord of the priest and the king, rules and thrusts his white hand out of the blue air, blessing the world with leprosy. In Urizen's sky, Yeats sets Shelley's sick moon: "Because it is the white of Leprosy/ And the contagion that afflicts mankind/ Falls from the moon." When, in the 1922 text, Seanchan dies, crying out "Dead faces laugh," it is no more nor less of either triumph or defeat than it was earlier. After Seanchan's youngest pupil chants the lines of the trumpet and great race, once Seanchan's closing speech, Yeats ends with the oldest pupil commanding a lowering of the trumpets. By 1922, Yeats had learned the esoteric wisdom that resolved, for him, the dilemma of poetry's temporal defeat and eternal victory: "Not what it leaves behind it in the light/ But what it carries with it to the dark/ Exalts the soul." But that, to me, defeats the play, and robs Seanchan of his glory. Seanchan's concern was not with what he could take into the death-between-lives, but precisely with what he could leave behind him in the light, for the poets after him. Yeats's modification of his own Shelleyan parable was characteristic, and profoundly saddening.

On Baile's Strand

Critics rightly praise *On Baile's Strand,* in both its very different versions (1903, 1906) as being Yeats's strongest tragicomedy, indeed his best play of the conventional sort. As 1900 to 1910 is Yeats's slough of despond as a creator, the *On Baile's Strand* of

1906 is his chief imaginative work of the decade, aside from *Adam's Curse* and one or two other short poems. Yet the play has few common readers, and what the critics mostly tend to praise in it are the barren splendors of its agile but contrived ironies, neatly spun but highly schematic sub-plot, and incontrovertible discipline of diction and ornament. I have nothing to add to the excellent formal analyses of the play that have been written, but of the deeper and more personal meanings I have read little to the purpose, except for some insightful remarks by Ellmann. As this book is a study of Yeats and Romanticism, I shall exclude much from the following brief discussion to concentrate on the two interlocking Romantic and intensely personal themes of the play, the war of father and son, and the bitterness of love between hero and Muse, when that love is as near to hatred as can be.

In the second part of *The Circus Animals' Desertion*, Yeats enumerated his "old themes" and "masterful images," choosing *The Wanderings of Oisin, The Countess Cathleen*, and *On Baile's Strand* for his illustrative texts. Remembering the end of *On Baile's Strand*, "when the Fool and Blind Man stole the bread/ Cuchulain fought the ungovernable sea," Yeats murmurs: "heart-mysteries there." He does not clarify these mysteries, in the poem or elsewhere, but Ellmann helpfully relates them to Yeats's self-indictment subsequent to Maud Gonne's marriage.[14] Yet the transmutation of experience here is profound, and the play's pattern shows no simplistic displacement of Yeats's frustration and bitterness. Similarly, his very complex, only partly conscious life-long struggle with his father's ideas is also rendered as a "heart-mystery" in the play, not easily available to psychoanalytic reduction. Most obviously, Yeats is not Cuchulain or Cuchulain's son; J. B. Yeats has no relation to Cuchulain's semi-divine, solar father; and Aoife has only a tenuous connection to Maud Gonne, despite Bushrui's shrewd observation that all of the revisions after 1903 tend to emphasize what is most negative in Aoife.[15] Less obviously, Cuchulain and Conchubar, Fool and Blind Man, do not make up a Yeatsian fourfold, on the analogue of Blake's division of the psyche, for while they all of them represent forces within Yeats himself, together they make up only a portion of him.[16] Yeats's fascinating letter of instruction to Frank Fay, who acted

Cuchulain, suggests a desire to identify himself with Cuchulain, but as the letter remarks, "when one creates a character one does it out of instinct and may be wrong when one analyses the instinct afterwards." The hero, Yeats tells his actor, is a little hard, "repellent yet alluring," and is allied to the fool. Conchubar is allied to the blind man, for he "is reason that is blind because it can only reason because it is cold." [17] This makes Conchubar the cold moon to Cuchulain's hot sun, an identification that seems to work for their shadows, Blind Man and Fool, particularly if we employ the schematic divisions of Yeats's later system. No consistent scheme emerges however for classifying the four principal characters of the play. Cuchulain is the hero in his glory, yet already in decline, longing for the renewal he obscurely senses in the young man he does not know to be his son. Conchubar is the ruler trapped in his own wiliness and fear of futurity, envious of Cuchulain's passion and vitality. The Fool and the Blind Man, despite the critics' praise, are not so well realized as Cuchulain and Conchubar. For the Fool must represent the solar forces that will replace Cuchulain after he dies, and the Blind Man the waning lunar malignancy that slays Cuchulain, but there is little in the speeches or actions of either figure to justify these representatives. They are a mystic geometry Yeats inserts into his play, in prophecy of a system not fully developed until decades later, and they trouble the play's deeper meanings as much as they help its theatrical actions. J. B. Yeats's dialectic of character and personality, always an immense influence upon his son's thought, is well illustrated by Conchubar and Cuchulain, but very obscurely shown, if at all, by the contrast between Blind Man and Fool. To examine this dialectic, in father and son, is to study also the "heart-mysteries" of *On Baile's Strand*.

Ellmann emphasizes the elder Yeats's uneasy skepticism, which found in poetry a refuge from itself, an absolute freedom from both convictions and the lack of belief. Poetry is the expression of personality, the whole man, brought into unity by the movement of moods, as opposed to the static unity of mere character.[18] Letters between father and son, in 1909–10, concentrate upon this distinction, which is developed in W. B. Yeats's 1909 diary, but J. B. Yeats had formulated the idea as far back as 1869, and taught it to the poet. Character, J. B. Yeats insists, is will power in action, but personality "is human nature when undergoing a passion for self-expression." [19] His son agrees, but is subtler in exposition. The will is comic, and personality tragic, an identification developed in the 1909 diary, where ecstasy is seen as "some fulfillment of the soul in itself," to be communicated only by tragedy, whose motives "are not related to action but to changes of state." [20] This more extreme, indeed arbitrary development of his father's thought must reflect the contrast between the two men that Ellmann's biography examines throughout, the natural harmony of the father as opposed to the son's inability to be at peace with himself, clearly the motive for a lifetime of questing after masks, or the Mask.

In 1899, J. B. Yeats wrote his son concerning "an amazing dream," in which he heard a sermon by his father (the Reverend William Butler Yeats, dead since 1862) and thought it "wonderful." The sermons of this first W. B. Yeats have not been published, and he seems in some sense to have been a splendid failure, like his painter son after him. J. B. Yeats had left his father's faith, and the dream's dominant motif appears to be the reconciliation of father and son:

> Last night I had an amazing dream—I thought I was listening to a wonderful sermon by my father—he and I afterwards walked up and down an old garden and to all my delighted compliments he only answered "it was very loosely constructed." I remember constantly trying to get hold of the M.S. that I might see his handwriting, which I have not seen for many years and which I have always wanted to see—my father was a man who excited strong affection. Afterwards came a lot of events causing to me great pleasure. A sort of dissolving view in which joy succeeded joy. At the end when all the rest had dispersed I found written on an unnoticed piece of paper the words, "The apple tree has been made free"—and all seemed to be a consequence of my father's sermon—[21]

After recounting his dream, J. B. Yeats broods on painting a picture, whose subject would be "the banquet of life," and later in the note to his son interprets the apple tree as the one that was in Eden. Even as this is his dream of reconciliation with his father, so the second W. B. Yeats's quest can be interpreted, in part, as his version of the universal dream of reunion between father and son. J. B. Yeats's own lifelong hope of more perfect execution as an artist is reflected in the dream's depiction and praise of the Reverend W. B. Yeats's artistry. One meaning of the dream may be that J. B. Yeats's uneasiness about his own art (he rarely could let a finished portrait stand, but through continual retouchings often reduced it to confusion) is revealed as allied to his sense of guilt concerning his own brilliant father's relative failure, guilt presumably augmented by his abandonment of his father's devout faith. In the dream the apple tree is made free, as though J. B. Yeats's own painting, free of anxiety, entered its own Eden. W. B. Yeats, the poet, in 1910 wrote to his father, saying he realized "with some surprise how fully my philosophy of life has been inherited from you in all but its details and applications." [22] He had inherited also his father's creative anxieties, since his lifelong revisions of his own work are clearly allied to his father's continual retouchings. But the poet was a stronger man, and a much more powerful imagination, than his father and grandfather, though probably no more brilliant than they were, as J. B. Yeats's letters and the reputation of the Reverend W. B. Yeats show.

The poet Yeats's relation to his father, as set forth by Ellmann, Jeffares, and Hone, was peculiarly difficult, but apparently never antagonistic. J. B. Yeats, an incurable optimist, incapable of remorse, was a very good man who imposed upon the poet, his oldest son, two burdens: the family's financial instability, and an endless flow of opinion, the more oppressive for its consistent brilliance, persuasiveness, originality, and lucidity. Since, as Ellmann says, J. B. Yeats had already assumed a revolutionary stance toward all late Victorian orthodoxies, the poet Yeats was in the unfortunate posture of the rebel's son, compelled to manifest his independence by a counter-revolutionary position. The poet's early timidity, and his permanent, indeed programmatic credulity, were both direct reactions to his father's vehemence and skepticism. Ellmann points also to the persistence of the Oedipal theme in the poet's work, enduring through the translations of Sophocles down to the play *Purgatory* at the end. Much remains to be understood about Yeats's handling of the theme, particularly in *A*

Vision's opposition of Oedipus and Christ, but while I hazard a few guesses in this book, such investigation is only partly within the bounds of my subject, Yeats's Romanticism.

Ahasuerus the Magus of *Hellas* was certainly a polar opposite to J. B. Yeats, when the young poet adopted him as prime image of sage or father-surrogate, even as the Poet of *Alastor,* the young man's other prime image, was an early opposite to himself. By the time *On Baile's Strand* was first written, W. B. Yeats was thirty-eight, and the apple-tree had been made free in his art, to some extent, but not at all in his life, with its titanic frustration of desire for Maud Gonne. The image of the apple-tree, though belonging to his father's actual dream, haunts Yeats's work, particularly with regard to Maud Gonne. *Autobiographies* beautifully introduces the lady by a wonderful memory: "Her complexion was luminous, like that of apple-blossom through which the light falls, and I remember her standing that first day by a great heap of such blossoms in the window." [23] That apple-blossom, associated with Aengus, god of love, pervades the early poetry, and lingers on in the later work, as in *Solomon and the Witch* where the moment of perfect sexual union, Chance and Choice coming together, is heralded by the cock's crow first heard "from a blossoming apple bough."

In the first version of *On Baile's Strand,* Conchubar reacts adversely to the presence of Cuchulain's entourage of swordsmen, harpists, and dancers by observing: "The odour from their garments when they stir/ Is like a wind out of an apple garden." [24] But the Cuchulain of either version, though an experienced amorist, has said farewell to love. His motive, unlike Yeats's, is not bitterness, but the self-realization of heroic solitude, the sense that he needs no one but his own expanded consciousness, his own life lived to the full. Yeats, by 1903, had come to condemn himself for the inability to yield to impulse, his lack of *sprezzatura,* a quality in which Cuchulain necessarily excels, but against which that hero sins when he yields to Conchubar and fails to credit his own affection for the young man he slays. The key genetic question to be asked about the interlocking themes of *On Baile's Strand,* father-son conflict and the love-hate of Aoife for Cuchulain, is whether Yeats had made an association, perhaps not consciously, between his evasive, qualifying temperament, which might have cost him Maud Gonne, and his defensive reaction to his father's overt vehemence.

On a more formal level, *On Baile's Strand* must be judged adroit in its dramaturgy, and poetically strong without, however, the highest distinction, for it is impeded not only by its too obviously schematic matching of characters, but by an imaginative incoherence as well. The heart-mysteries are impressive, and rightly connected, but hardly clearly defined. Cuchulain calls the past love between himself and Aoife "a brief forgiveness between opposites" and feels for the Young Man what he cannot recognize as paternal love, and yet cannot deny, an attraction of similarities tempered by the *daimonic* fascination of opposites, since the Young Man resembles his mother Aoife. There is thus a clear imaginative meaning to Aoife's hatred for Cuchulain and her sending of their son in revenge; the brief forgiveness between opposites has been long over, and the *daimonic* Mask or Muse can strike at the hero only by sending a younger version of himself against him. But what is the poetic meaning of Cuchulain's blind slaying of his son? It is not a simple reversal of a primal forbidden desire, as though Laius were to slay Oedipus, any more than *Sohrab and Rustum* is. Cuchulain neither realizes further his own heroic nature nor betrays himself by the act; horribly enough, the act is irrelevant to his personality, or vital aspect. Conchubar's wiliness, and mere circumstance, combine to impel the old hero to kill the new, and then himself, thus ending the heroic age in one meaningless catastrophe. The closing image of Cuchulain's career, in this play, is wholly appropriate, for he has been warring against the sea, against blind inadvertence, from his first entrance. In the larger symbolism, the sun-hero sinks into the murderous innocence of the sea, which drowns heroic innocence that a new *primary* age may come; to use Yeats's later term for it. The new age belongs to the descendants of Conchubar, who "have no pitch,/ No marrow in their bones," and necessarily are closer to the audience or readers than Cuchulain can be. Whether the critics are right to call the Cuchulain who fights the waves a madman, I am not sure, for is Oedipus mad when he blinds himself, or is he, like Cuchulain, perhaps passing a negative Last Judgment upon nature? The theme of the heroic does not sort well with the heart-mysteries of *On Baile's Strand,* and Yeats perhaps handled recalcitrant stuff in it, but still the play survives its own incongruities.

Deirdre

In *On the Boiler,* that very late and grotesque tract all good Yeatsians should re-read once a year, Yeats says he is haunted by certain moments of tragic ecstasy in his own plays and his friends', moments of performance, including "Mrs. Patrick Campbell in my *Deirdre,* passionate and solitary." [25] The play, its heroine, and its poet aspire to a condition they none of them attain, and I find difficult to understand the play's reputation with its critics. Yeats's remarks about his formal problem in the play may be applied to the whole effect made, that he is forced by this work away from his "capacities, experiences, and desires" and gives us "dry circumstance where there should be life." [26] Deirdre, he tells us, was the Irish Helen, and so has a touch of Maud Gonne, but she would be more persuasive if she had more. *On Baile's Strand* is much more interesting than *Deirdre* because Yeats allowed his personal bitterness to pervade Cuchulain's disaster. His bitterness is largely irrelevant to Deirdre's tragedy, as he chose to present it, but this choice was a mistake, for the heroine's personality and her play do not gain immediacy and universal interest by Yeats's uncharacteristic self-exclusion.

I discuss *Deirdre* here, quite briefly, because a note on it is a necessary part of a consideration of Yeats's Romanticism, and of the inevitable limitations as well as strengths his inescapable Romanticism brought him. Despite certain critics, Deirdre is scarcely a memorable personality, and her deliberate changes of mood as she fights for her own kind of honorable death could not deceive Naisi or Conchubar if either of her admirers were more than cardboard. A certain genuine naturalism, a oneness with her own body and its evidences, Yeats does manage to give her, a surprising achievement for him. But she fatally lacks individuality; we can believe that she is immensely attractive to all men, because myth and Yeats tell us so, but Yeats cannot show us her attractiveness. The reason for his failure is simple and of first importance; as a poet he can show us only one kind or aspect of women convincingly, and that is the Muse or her surrogate, the Mask as the object of the whole mind's desires. Deirdre, despite a few unconvincing hints, is not of the *daimonic* otherworld, as Cuchulain or Forgael is. The only memorable female personality in any of Yeats's plays is Decima in *The Player Queen,* and she is no Muse, but a naturalistic approach to the Mask. Despite the *daimonic* allusions of *The Player Queen,* Decima is the exception to my generalization, but though she is no Fand or Aoife from the other world, she has the natural qualities Yeats associated with women of Phase 14, verging on but distinct from the otherworld of Phase 15. And she is strong enough not only to dominate her odd play, but even to dwarf it.

Deirdre was beyond Yeats's powers, for he had no imaginative understanding of any woman who was not fatal for him, and he is not in love with Deirdre. The curse of Romantic drama is that it never understands except where it loves, and it loves only obsessively. Only four of *A Vision*'s phases are assigned female examples, and these are instructive. In the obsessive Phase 14 are "many beautiful women" in company with Keats and Giorgione, while the vehement Phase 16 contains "some beautiful women" in proximity to the exuberant grouping of Blake, Rabelais, Aretino, and Paracelsus. The assertive Phase 19 mentions "a certain actress," presumably Florence Farr, in conjunction with poetic men-of-action: D'Annunzio, Wilde, Byron. That leaves only the rather uninspiring Phase 24 where Galsworthy is assigned the august company of Lady Gregory, and Queen Victoria.[27] Deirdre is clearly of none of these phases, and Yeats's imagination finds her recalcitrant. She represents heroic love, totally fulfilled, menaced by fate and circumstance, but by no doubleness within, and requires a very different poet, whom she found, perhaps, in Synge.

When Deirdre seeks to deceive Conchubar, after Naisi's execution, that she may have the freedom to kill herself and thus escape Conchubar, she utters the only lines in the play in which Yeats's authentic bitterness comes to life. Women most worthy of desire choose men of power, she says, because the secret of mastery must involve what is most antithetical in such a woman's nature:

> Although we are so delicately made,
> There's something brutal in us, and we are won
> By those who can shed blood.

Certainly Yeats is thinking of MacBride's victory over him, and equally surely the lines are part of Deirdre's play-acting, and so wholly unrepresentative of her. But how much more vital a drama Yeats would have written if he had broken with the story's tradition, and allowed himself an Irish Helen closer to his deepest obsessions.

11: The Middle Poems

In the Seven Woods

Three volumes—*In the Seven Woods, The Green Helmet,* and *Responsibilities*—comprise Yeats's lyrical work from the turn of the century until the Great War of 1914. Fourteen years of what should have been a poet's prime, roughly the years from thirty-five to near fifty, represent only about one-eighth of Yeats's lyrical verse, though they include rather more than a quarter of his mature life. If one excludes the poems in *Responsibilities,* one finds Yeats showing fewer than three dozen lyrics for the first decade of the twentieth century, for the years between thirty-five and forty-five when so many major poets have done their best work. A few of these poems are superb—*Adam's Curse, The Folly of Being Comforted, No Second Troy, The Fascination of What's Difficult*—but most are indifferent work. Even *Responsibilities,* a stronger book than the two previous, has only a few outstanding poems—*September 1913, The Cold Heaven, The Magi.* Except for Wallace Stevens, who did not find himself, as a poet, until 1915, when he was thirty-six, no important poet of this century shows so startlingly late a pattern of development. It may be no accident that these are the major poets, in English, so far in the century; the burden that afflicts a major poet, always severe, has been augmented.

Since we are so slow to outlast our more tedious critical fashions, it will appear perverse when I suggest that Yeats's poetical achievement from 1885 through 1899 is more considerable than what followed in the fifteen years after. One of our slogans is that Middle Yeats is superior to Early Yeats, while Late Yeats (twenty-five years of it, from 1914 to 1939) improved with every year. This is nonsense, no matter how many academic critics repeat it. *The Wind Among the Reeds* is a better volume of poetry than Yeats was to write until *The Wild Swans at Coole,* and the poems collected in the *Crossways* and *The Rose* groupings are better than all but seven or eight of the poems of the whole middle period, which is the subject of this chapter. Again, as will be made clear, increasingly, the poetry of *The Tower* and *The Winding Stair* tends to be more in touch with justice and reality, Yeatsian tests for greatness, than are all but a few of the *Last Poems*.

Why is Middle Yeats so disappointing, even after one has rejected the New Critical fashion of reading it as at least a step toward the approved later style, but hardly as ambitious verse in its own right? The apparently simple answer is bitter and complex in its depths, and belongs to a larger phenomenon of modern poetry, a phenomenon of which the Yeats of 1900–1914 is the immediate ancestor, as Pound first recognized. Yeats, appalled by the personal wreck of his own Romanticism, attempted in his middle phase to become an anti-Romantic revisionist of English poetry, an attempt more familiar to us in Pound, Eliot, and Auden, than in Yeats, since they sustained their attempt and Yeats from 1917 on wisely did not. *The Tower* and *The Winding Stair,* despite the vagaries of New Criticism and the scholarship on Yeats done under its egregious influence, will be studied increasingly as what they are, as much monuments of Romanticism in English poetry as are *Jerusalem, The Prelude, Prometheus Unbound, The Fall of Hyperion,* or later, *Look! We Have Come Through!, The Bridge, Notes Toward a Supreme Fiction.* Middle Yeats is written against the grain, and despite his manifold theories Yeats could not prosper as poet in that way:

> Sweetheart, do not love too long:
> I loved long and long,
> And grew to be out of fashion
> Like an old song.

The sentiment is doubtless admirable, but who could prefer the expression to this:

> I would spread the cloths under your feet:
> But I, being poor, have only my dreams;
> I have spread my dreams under your feet;
> Tread softly because you tread on my dreams.

The sentiment is hardly possible, but the expression has the accent of mastery, and the mastery is that of a man in his own house. These examples are selected wholly at random, the first from *In the Seven Woods,* the second from *The Wind Among the Reeds.* Any reader can make dozens of such juxtapositions between the two volumes, and so uncover a truth that the critics of Yeats largely obscure: one is free to think that the movement between the two volumes is an improvement in attitude, but one is deficient in taste and judgment to think the movement an aesthetic advance.

In the Seven Woods contains one great poem, *Adam's Curse,* which dwarfs the rest of the volume. Most of its lyrics are expressions of mood; straining to avoid the overt symbolism of *The Wind Among the Reeds,* Yeats becomes oddly more indefinite and imprecise than he was in that generally misrepresented book. The loss of Shelleyan and Pre-Raphaelite color leaves a void, that the poet seems as yet resourceless to fill:

> I am contented, for I know that Quiet
> Wanders laughing and eating her wild heart
> Among pigeons and bees. . . .

The old rhythmic power and vividness of coloring is found only in the intensities of *Red Hanrahan's Song About Ireland,* but that is a poem composed in 1894. One poem besides *Adam's Curse* shows some success in an against-the-grain mode. The effectiveness of *The Folly of Being Comforted* is instructive, for it is of a kind that reveals the limitations of Yeats's new ambitions. The poem is a kind of Job's dialogue, between an "ever kind" Job's comforter of a friend, and the poet's heart or self, presaging the dialogues between soul, and self or heart in *The Winding Stair.* In *The Folly of Being Comforted* the "one that is ever kind" speaks the *primary* wisdom that Yeats's soul has now learned, or begun to learn:

> Time can but make it easier to be wise
> Though now it seem impossible, and so
> All that you need is patience.

But the objective work of time, grey hair and shadows about the beloved's eyes, cannot affect the heart's perceptions. To the heart, the autumnal beauty of Maud Gonne is more Promethean for its *antithetical* defiance of mere natural decay: "The fire that stirs about her, when she stirs,/ Burns but more clearly." Yet this is not triumph, for the first time in Yeats's work. Not only his spirit, but his imagination and sense of possible sublimity, are too limited by this mode. A more terrible passivity than ever before enters into him, and the poignant lyric ends with an outcry that belies itself, for the heart will know the folly of comfort whether the beloved turns her head or not.

Adam's Curse is one of Yeats's most persuasive and indisputable poems of the conversational style. Behind the poem is Shelley's remarkable version of the middle style, the conversational group that includes the *Letter to Maria Gisborne,* the closing quatrains of *The Sensitive Plant,* and aspects of *Julian and Maddalo, Rosalind and Helen,* and the late love lyrics to Jane Williams. Like the Shelley of these poems, Yeats in *Adam's Curse* assumes the existence of a community of love, with its ease of common rhetoric, implicit code of external gesture, and, most vitally, ethos of limitation, including the dignity of failure. There is high

design in the poem's closing evocation of a Shelleyan moon and
sea-shell, though these closing lines are deliberately set against the
Shelleyan vision of love, indeed are best read in counterpart to
the difficult raptures of *Epipsychidion:*

> We sat grown quiet at the name of love;
> We saw the last embers of daylight die,
> And in the trembling blue-green of the sky
> A moon, worn as if it had been a shell
> Washed by time's waters as they rose and fell
> About the stars and broke in days and years.
>
> I had a thought for no one's but your ears:
> That you were beautiful, and that I strove
> To love you in the old high way of love;
> That it had all seemed happy, and yet we'd grown
> As weary-hearted as that hollow moon.

Of all Yeats's love poems, *Adam's Curse* most shows the immense dignity that the poet's sense of love as an *antithetical* discipline could attain. Corinna Salvadori usefully invokes Castiglione as parallel to Yeats's unifying mood in the poem, for what
allies the poet's art to the woman's beauty is their mutual creative
recklessness, the *sprezzatura* or self-possession that accompanies
and hides mastery.[1] The unique greatness of *Adam's Curse* as a
poem (and surely Yeats never wrote better, though this was 1902)
is that it exemplifies this grace without bothering to celebrate it,
and then goes on to expose the severe limitations of this late version of courtly love. Poet and woman alike must labor to attain
beauty, but even achieved Unity of Being fails to sustain what
ought to have been a perfection of love.

Everything about *Adam's Curse* is precise and grave; setting,
manner, rhetoric, modulation of remarkably varied tone. This
precision and gravity define the early autumnal mood of *In the
Seven Woods*. Critics committed to the insistence that the later
Yeats is a modern poet and the earlier a twilight crooner generally find the start of a better Yeats here, as Eliot did when he
praised *Adam's Curse*. But this is a gratuitous reduction of a dialectical process, and has never cast much light on what finally

must be the crucial question; what is living, what is dead in the poetry of Yeats? *The Madness of King Goll* is a better poem than *The Gyres*, and *The Wanderings of Oisin* shows a power of sustained invention that Yeats never demonstrated again. *Adam's Curse* hardly could be improved; it is one of the undoubted poems of the language, and to see it as the start rather than the culmination of a poetic development is an arbitrary judgment, founded upon a momentary fashion in taste. Even scholarly myth may be exposed by time to be what Lec remarks all myth to be, gossip grown old.

To read *Adam's Curse* with full awareness of its values, is to see Yeats's poetic mind quite as fully as *Byzantium* allows it to be seen. *In the Seven Woods* begins to resolve the spiritual and poetic impasse of *The Wind Among the Reeds* and the first version of *The Shadowy Waters,* but only *Adam's Curse* prophesies the dimensions of the resolution. Yeats was thirty-seven when he wrote *Adam's Curse,* an age at which even the late-maturing begin to realize their powers. He had proposed marriage to Maud Gonne at least four times, in 1891, 1894, 1899, and 1900. *Adam's Curse* was written, according to Ellmann, before November 1902. Maud Gonne married MacBride in February 1903; infuriated and unhappy as Yeats was, he presumably had lost hope for himself in relation to the lady, and was shocked and hurt that she married at all, let alone a man of action. *Adam's Curse,* written a few months before this unsuspected marriage, appears to assume that "you and I" will never marry, whether one another or anyone else. The title refers to this assumption; Yeats's beloved is to bear Adam's curse, not Eve's; he and she are condemned to the respective labors of writing poems and being beautiful, and to the mutual labor of sustaining a courtly love relationship, "the old high way of love." Madame MacBride recorded the occasion when her sister Kathleen, "that beautiful mild woman, your close friend." remarked to Yeats that it was hard work being beautiful.[2] In the poem, it is more than hard work, and becomes an actual discipline.

Somewhere in the background of *Adam's Curse* can be heard the grimly eloquent passage of *Epipsychidion* in which Shelley declares he "never was attached to that great sect" whose doctrine is that of "the longest journey," marriage as an exclusive and confining relationship. In *Adam's Curse* the "great sect" has become "the noisy set/ Of bankers, schoolmasters, and clergymen/ The martyrs call the world." The world in *Epipsychidion* moralizes against the poet's sexual freedom; in *Adam's Curse* more fundamentally it attacks him as "an idler," misled not only by the nature of his labor but by his nonchalance in performing it. The world is too noisy to hear what only the laborers of beauty can express, but *sprezzatura* demands that the poet's voice, as well as the woman's, be sweet and low in this context. Adam's curse, for those striving after Unity of Being, is the fallen paradox that the finest things require the hardest labor. This would be only a poet's *apologia,* of necessarily mild interest, but for Yeats's subtle linkages between the poet's and the lover's disciplines. The poem begins in urbane discourse upon poetry itself, moves from the maker's art to the woman's labor to be beautiful, and then passes to the lover's highly oblique complaint of the failure of the old high mode of love. The noisy set of bankers and their clerkly friends win an indirect triumph; poets break their marrow-bones to a purpose, but courtly love indeed "seems an idle trade enough." With that admission, all grow quiet; the daylight and the summer die. Shelley's waning moon, assimilated to his sea-shell of Promethean prophecy, comes to an end together with that prophecy, washed in the breaking days and years of the unfathomable sea of Shelley's brief lyric, *Time*. Nothing in Shelleyan quest allowed for the possibility of unrequited love, never one of that poet's many sorrows.

The last stanza of *Adam's Curse* frequently is condemned by critics as a lapse into Yeats's bad, old manner, presumably of *The Rose* lyrics, or *The Wind Among the Reeds*. But this is a misreading of the poem, and an undervaluing of its consciousness of itself. The conversational opening modulates into the rhetorical violence of the poet's defence; after that the poem softens to the different *sprezzatura* of women's beauty, and the lover's defeat despite his *sprezzatura*. But the fine, apparently careless mastery of the *antithetical* lover no longer brings him, at the poem's close, the release, the sense of liberation that his discipline should assure. In the weary-heartedness of Yeats and Maud Gonne alike, the poem studies finally the limits of its own mastery, and hints at the troubles ahead for those who live so audaciously out of phase.

The Green Helmet

No poet ever wrote a poem in the consciousness that his labor was "transitional," a word for exegetes and not for poets. Aside from this, the poems of *The Green Helmet* (1910) are "transitional" only in that they lead to the more achieved volume *Responsibilities* (1914); they do not lead to the Yeats who was troubled out of his bitterness and apathy by the events of 1916, or was reborn as a High Romantic in 1917 and after. No single poem in *The Green Helmet* is an inevitable as *Adams's Curse,* but the flatness of *In the Seven Woods* is mostly gone, for Yeats grows more accustomed to his labors in a Jonsonian mode. Despite the suggestions of some distinguished critics, I find little Donne in Yeats. Even after his delight in the Grierson edition, his Donne remained the Donne of Romantic tradition from Coleridge to Symons, a poet who was a lesser Shelley (I am aware of the polemicism implicit in such a description, now-a-days). The "middle" Yeats, climaxing in *Responsibilities,* is a poet attempting work in the tradition of Jonson and of Landor, rather than of the somewhat allied line of Donne. There is a Byronic quality in Middle Yeats, and even a thwarted, or rather doomed attempt at cultivating an Augustan sensibility, a labor at a satiric mode closer to Byron's than to Byron's Augustan masters or to Pound (who praised Yeats for this quixotic enterprise).

The sequence of *The Green Helmet* is composed mostly of consciously retrospective poems on the lost relationship with Maud Gonne, but the volume opens with one of Yeats's rare dream poems. Though not the equal of *The Cap and Bells* in *The Wind Among the Reeds, His Dream* is still a fascinating lyric, in the manner of some of the nightmare visions of Coleridge. The dreamer sails a gaudy ship (his earlier intensity of love, or his earlier poetry, or likelier both), observed by a crowd upon the shore, who ask the identity of the shrouded figure they see on a gaudy bed (the ship itself?). They name the figure (due to its dignity of limb) "by the sweet name of Death," and the dreamer unwillingly takes up their song:

> Crying amid the glittering sea,
> Naming it with ecstatic breath,
> Because it had such dignity,
> By the sweet name of Death.

Maud Gonne here, by the terrible logic of nightmare, is the sweetly named Death (in descent from Coleridge's Death-in-Life) —"dignity of limb" is Yeatsian rhetoric invariably applied to her. The gaudy ship of Yeats's love-poetry, or poetic love, carries this death-principle, as the poet's audience or friends compel him to learn. Perhaps the motto for all the poetry of Yeats's middle period is in the desperate line: "What could I but take up the song?"

Of the half-dozen poems following, the principal fault is that they blend into one another, as do some later poems in *The Green Helmet*. The exception is the fierce *No Second Troy*, where the terror of the lover's sense of his beloved's *antithetical* beauty, "a kind/ That is not natural in an age like this," is conveyed by an audacious drum-roll of overstatement, swelling up into the grand climax of two rhetorical questions, always a strength in Yeats's work:

> Why, what could she have done, being what she is?
> Was there another Troy for her to burn?

Whether or not the reader accepts such an elevation, the poem is too strong to fail. Winters complained against Yeats's hyperbole in praising his friends, while granting that Maud Gonne "was a special case, for Yeats was in love with her; but his equation of Maud Gonne with Deirdre, Helen of Troy, and Cathleen ni Houlihan partakes of his dramatization of himself." [3] Winters meant this as negative criticism; it can be argued quite differently. If self-dramatization were always a poetic vice, all Byron and much Pope would have to be discarded also. What is inadequate about *The Green Helmet* and most of *Responsibilities*, compared to later Yeats, is insufficient self-dramatization, a lack of the self-possession and power that came to Yeats from 1917 on. Winters, as always, was a thoroughly consistent critic, with a clear knowledge of what he disliked, and a continuous faculty for perceiving the presence of a dreaded Romanticism, whether in Yeats or Stevens or Hart Crane. His unique excellence, among Yeats critics, was to see that Yeats's mature Romanticism did not need invention by any critic; the self-dramatization that Winters despised grew larger with every passing year of Yeats's poetry, from 1917 to 1939. *No Second Troy,* as Rajan notes, is a prophecy of poems like *The Second Coming* and *Leda and the Swan.*[4] Unfortunately it prophesies also the greater faults of those greater poems. Yeats leaps too quickly past his own argument in such poems; if impatience is necessary for apocalyptic poetry, the grounds for impatience still require externalization, as Blake never forgot. *No Second Troy* consists of four questions; none is genuinely open. This is as it must be, but the poem itself does too little to show why they must be closed.

More impressive in *The Green Helmet* is the different kind of bitterness shown in roughly the latter half of the volume, beginning with *The Fascination of What's Difficult,* ostensibly a complaint at "theatre business, management of men," but actually a concealed tribute to the discipline imposed upon the frustrated lyricist by the limitations of theater. For a man (and poet) of Yeats's extraordinary temperament, with its mingled caution and extravagance, the fascination of what is difficult is akin to the enchantment of romance. Though he blames this fascination for having "dried the sap out of my veins, and rent/ Spontaneous joy and natural content/ Out of my heart" he rightly praises what amounts to the same process in the wonderfully gnomic quatrain, *The Coming of Wisdom of Time,* worthy of Landor in its terrible simplicity of conclusion: "Now I may wither into the truth." Though one longs for a fuller voice than *The Green Helmet* as yet desires, prolonged reading grants the justice of Yeats's bitter pride in a poem like *All Things Can Tempt Me,* where at once he longs to be "colder and dumber and deafer than a fish" and yet begins to sense a new self-mastery in his craft: "Now nothing but comes readier to the hand/ Than this accustomed toil." Love, as the last poem in *The Green Helmet* recognizes, "is the crooked thing," and the disciple of Blake remembered that "the crooked roads without Improvement, are roads of Genius." [5]

Responsibilities

Ezra Pound praised *Responsibilities* for its "new robustness," welcoming Yeats to the work of literary satire: "There are a lot of fools to be killed." Fortunately, Yeats after *Responsibilities* invokes the satiric muse only upon overwhelming occasion, at least until the furies of *Last Poems*. Of the few strong poems in *Responsibilities*, only *September 1913* has satiric force, and even it is memorable for its wildness of lament that "Romantic Ireland's dead and gone." Though richer than the two preceding books of lyrics, *Responsibilities* scarcely deserves its reputation as a volume demonstrating any augmentation in Yeats's poetic power. One poem, *The Cold Heaven,* is comparable to his best work before and after; *The Magi* and *To a Friend Whose Work Has Come to Nothing* are also superb. But much of the volume is tendentious, and too much is special pleading. Is it of imaginative value to the possible reader that Yeats's ancestors "have left me blood/ That has not passed through any huckster's loin"? There are distressing portents in the book's introductory poem, compelling us to remember that the poet, more than twenty years later, indulged in dubious eugenic theories. Too many of the poems in *Responsibilities* exist "to prove your blood and mine," perhaps not the most appropriate of poetic functions in our age. Yeats had ample and splendid precedent, as he thought, in the Italian and English Renaissance, and before that one thinks of Pindar. But what was once appropriate now rings false, for lack of sustaining context. Sidney praises horsemanship, and we are moved by the praise; Yeats exalts it, and Winters is justly annoyed. The *sprezzatura* of one age too readily becomes the mindlessness of another, and those such as Yeats, who would hold back the tide, are battered by it.

So with Yeats's aristocratic disdain "of our old Paudeen in his shop" throughout *Responsibilities;* we read these poems, and wish that Yeats had been content to leave his counter-attack against

George Moore for *Autobiographies* to mount alone, since Yeats treated these matters better in prose. Against *Paudeen* and *To a Shade* Moore is unbeatable: ". . . and we looked round asking each other with our eyes where on earth our Willie Yeats had picked up the strange belief that none but titled and carriage-folk could appreciate pictures." [6]

September 1913 opens in that spirit, but is saved by Yeats's evocation of the supposed freedom and wildness of Ireland's "wild geese." Though these were mercenaries, and in no sense Romantic revolutionaries, the Yeatsian rhetoric successfully confounds them with genuine Irish revolutionaries of the Romantic period—Fitzgerald, Emmet, and Wolfe Tone, "all that delirium of the brave," anticipating the bewildering excess of love in the revolutionary martyrs of *Easter 1916,* who were to so profoundly shock the conservative Yeats by proving that Romantic Ireland was not dead and gone. What lifts *September 1913* above its rhetoric is the High Romanticism of its last stanza. The *sprezzatura* of the revolutionaries, in Yeats's vision, is that "they weighed so lightly what they gave." Time stales every cause whatsoever; only extravagance and recklessness, Yeats implicitly shows, remain memorable. What can go on living is what the Yeats of *Responsibilities* attempts to repudiate, but can no more surrender than Wordsworth could abandon his memory of the gleam. Maud Gonne was Yeats's experience of "the glory and the freshness of a dream." Hence the reader, returned to the time of the Romantic exiles, would discover the true cause of "all that delirium of the brave":

> You'd cry, "Some woman's yellow hair
> Has maddened every mother's son."

As before and later, in this matter Yeats rarely failed poetically. *A Memory of Youth,* a lesser re-working of *Adam's Curse,* still surpasses most of *Responsibilities* because the theme is so endlessly congenial to Yeats's imagination. But so much of *Responsibilities* is abortive work that the events of 1916–17 seem more and more fortunate, whenever the interrelation between Yeats's life and poetry is considered. The two set pieces in *Responsibilities, The Grey Rock* and *The Two Kings,* are Yeats's dullest

poems ever, before or after, on Celtic heroic matter; contrasted
with *The Wanderings of Oisin,* they demonstrate a shocking loss
of vigor and invention. The group of poems on beggars is only a
little better, except for *Running to Paradise,* where Yeats returns
to an earlier ballad strain with some success. *The Hour Before
Dawn,* the most ambitious of these poems, wastes extraordinary
descriptive skill upon a dreary debate between the claims of the
dream and the mundane world, an opposition Yeats fails for once
to vivify. A handful of lyrics partly redeem the remainder of the
volume. The epigrammatic strength and stoic knowingness of Landor, perhaps also of Jonson, are felt again in *To a Friend Whose
Work Has Come to Nothing,* probably Yeats's most enduring tribute to his indispensable patroness, Lady Gregory. Whether the
marmoreal muse of Landor is enhanced by the half-dozen other
lyrics in this kind is less certain, though *A Coat* compares favora-
bly with Tennyson's poem on the same theme, the major poet's
contempt for his superficial imitators. Yet in two lyrics, *The Cold
Heaven,* and *The Magi,* Yeats asserts his larger powers again.
Still, the greater of the two, *The Cold Heaven,* was first printed
in *The Green Helmet,* and no Yeats scholar, so far as I can see,
has attempted to date its composition, which I would guess is
well before 1912. *The Magi,* like its less successful companion-
poem, *The Dolls,* was written two weeks after the "delirium"
of *September 1913* and opposes to the lost Romantic Ireland
an apocalyptic presage of a mystery to come. As in *The Cold
Heaven,* the poem shows Yeats possessed by a wildness that declares an immediate authenticity.

   The Cold Heaven and *The Magi,* for all their brevity, are the
most memorable poems in *Responsibilities,* and stand with the
best in Yeats's lyric accomplishment. Both exhibit Yeats's uncanny power of incantation, with its associated persuasion that we
listen not to the voice of a single man, but a communal voice, or
primal sound of universal human process. Yet both poems are
lyric cries of the solitary ego, and *The Cold Heaven* is the freest
complaint of Yeats's defeated love for Maud Gonne, at least that
he ever suffered to be printed. What is most astonishing about
The Cold Heaven is not its admirable compression, packing so
much of a life's anguish into twelve lines, or even its precision in

conveying the suddenness of a vision's descent (a quality in which it surpasses more famous later poems like *The Second Coming* and *Leda and the Swan*), but the totality of its justice or fullness in presenting the self's unguarded encounter with its own remorse.

Both *The Cold Heaven* and *The Magi* begin with a glance at the sky, the cold heaven of winter, and the "dividing and indifferent blue" of an early autumn, respectively. The first is a vision of purgatorial burning ice, the second of "stiff figures in procession." The sky is a Romantic image of division and fall, of a covering that must be rolled away in the fullness of revelation. One thinks of Blake's obsession with the sky, "a void boundless as a nether sky" in the *Marriage,* and the many abominable skies of *The Four Zoas,* culminating in "the black incessant sky" of the apocalyptic Ninth Night, and contrasting with the redemptive "Sky is an immortal Tent built by the Sons of Los" in *Milton.* The "dark incessant sky" returns in *Jerusalem,* as reminder of the necessity for vision, even as the sky of *Prometheus Unbound* is the empire of Jupiter's world of remorse and self-contempt until his overthrow. Yeats stands beneath that Urizenic sky, a failed Promethean quester confronting the purgatorial mark of his own "fear and self-contempt and barren hope." Suddenly, unable to protect himself, he saw the cold heaven, delight to *antithetical* birds, but torment to the poet who could not sustain his self-annihilating quest for the impossible beloved. The sight itself suffices to drive wild not only the empty heart, but the imagination uneasily allied to the heart's defeat. In that wildness, all the immediate world vanishes, and only memory abides, memory of Maud Gonne. The crucial line, "And I took all the blame out of all sense and reason," governs one of the poem's two contending realizations, the Blakean and Shelleyan insistence that remorse cripples the imagination. The other realization is too strong to be overcome, the terror of the Sublime tradition, that loss has come through the encounter with an ultimate good that might have been gained: "Until I cried and trembled and rocked to and fro,/ Riddled with light." The last phrase is immensely suggestive, with its play on "riddled," as though the light of the cold heaven were the light of Maud Gonne's beautiful presence and spirit, at once an arrow (as in *The Arrow,* from the volume *In the Seven Woods*) and a Sphinx inducing profound sexual anxiety and human self-doubt. With the poem's final movement, in its last three and a half lines, the realization of loss dominates the struggle against remorse. In a conceit prophetic of *A Vision*'s dealings with the purgatorial after-life, the poem deliberately staggers to a terrible anti-apocalypse. Yeats's own spirit, coming alive again after the death-bed's "confusion," may go out naked beneath the skies, to continue the same terrible process of confrontation with its own blame. Though this is put as a question, the tone makes the question rhetorical, and ends the poem on the note of repetition, the cyclic dismay that will be suffered later by the fearful old man of the play *Purgatory.*

From this harrowing and effective vision of imaginative hopelessness, *The Magi* offers a grim token of release. In a note to *The Magi* Yeats called those "stiff figures in procession" forms complementary to "those enraged dolls" of the enigmatic and unsatisfactory *The Dolls,* certainly related to *The Magi* in genesis.[7] In *The Dolls* we hear a weak foreboding of the scorning aloud of common bird or petal by the poet's golden bird in *Byzantium.* The dolls reject a human babe as "a noisy and filthy thing," even as the Magi are unsatisfied either by the human babe they beheld "on the bestial floor" of the stable, or that babe's end in "Calvary's turbulence." Fortunately, there is more to *The Magi* than this.

Unlike *The Cold Heaven, The Magi* gives us both present and habitual vision; rather than "suddenly" we begin with: "Now as at all times." The Magi are frustrated, "the pale unsatisfied ones," the paleness suggesting repression, as though the Magi defer fulfillment of all their dreams and desires until the one massive consummation. They are also obsessive, "all their eyes fixed," and unnatural, in "their stiff, painted clothes," as though part of a roadside crèche. It does not make them more attractive that they are as immemorial as the sky's blue, and rain-beaten stones, for theirs is an eternity of being unsatisfied. They are weary, always, of the controlled and the known, and ironically weary of peace. In sum, they are Yeats's war-gods, like the Egyptian Sphinx of *The Second Coming* whom they prophesy. They offer release, to the Yeats of the peculiarly entitled *Responsibilities,* a man trapped in frustrate hopelessness, but even to Yeats they hint destruction also. Like him, they yearn for a new Dispensation, for an influx of a darkness welcome to those who are "riddled by light."

Responsibilities ends by coming full circle, in defence of self and companions against George Moore, taken as representative of the decadence of an *objective* age. Yeats mounts to invective, justified presumably by the larger, supposedly cultural issue. But justification becomes the problem in evaluating the "Closing Rhyme" to *Responsibilities,* and the volume itself, and perhaps even the whole of Yeats's middle phase.

The undeniably masterly invective against George Moore, whose autobiography skillfully portrays a delightfully ridiculous Yeats, has been handled very respectfully by the poet's scholars. Whitaker speaks of "the proud and precarious nature" of Yeats's "moral equilibrium" in this epilogue, and Ellmann finds "majesty and authority" in it.[8] Overtly quoting Ben Jonson, and adapting Erasmus to his own purposes, Yeats clearly tried for a rather serious effect here, and he would have been delighted to encounter in his exegetes such deference due to a poet of his degree. Still, other exegetes may wonder if this closing thrust does not connect to (and help explain) many of the faults of the *Responsibilities* volume. The wind among the reeds blows again here, but now inwardly, the poet claims, and it gives the poet what he needs, not inspiration, but a sense of community with the mighty dead, invoked throughout *Responsibilities*. Armed with that sense, the poet will hie him to Lady Gregory's, and under her roof will find that he can forgive even George Moore, who is merely an accident of historical decline. Moore is another sign that the present has fallen away from ancient ceremony, and so it is no wonder that notoriety (of the kind Moore enjoys and brings) replaces aristocratic "Fame," which has perished. Yeats "can forgive" because he has assumed the responsibilities of becoming the continuator of a living tradition, however dimmed it be in a world of Moores. That this fierce epilogue is self-congratulatory in tone is rather obvious; that Moore is injured in this name-calling is not. By the ordinary rules of criticism, it is hard to find the moral balance in Yeats's lines, and harder still to find them magisterial. Perhaps Moore may be allowed a word here, since it is not likely to be the last one anyway:

> As far as anybody could remember, he [Yeats] had always lived very comfortably, sitting down invariably to regular meals, and the old green cloak that was in keeping with his profession of romantic poet he had exchanged for the magnificent fur coat which distracted our attention from what he was saying, so opulently did it cover the back of the chair out of which he had risen. But, quite forgetful of the coat behind him, he continued to denounce the middle classes. . . .[9]

The dispassionate reader of *Responsibilities* could set this passage and the proud little poem, *A Coat,* against one another. "There's more enterprise/ In walking naked," or perhaps in the old green cloak of Romanticism, but probably not in that "magnificent fur coat" brought back from America.

12: Toward *A Vision:*
Per Amica Silentia Lunae

Anima Hominis

Yeats first intended to call this "little philosophical book" of 1917
An Alphabet, as though he meant it to be a key to the rudiments
of his imaginative work, or to the convictions upon which that
work was founded.[1] Starting with the poem *Ego Dominus Tuus*
(1915) as extended motto, the book divides itself into two reveries, *Anima Hominis* and *Anima Mundi,* the first dealing with the
Mask and the second with the relation of the Mask to the spiritual world, realm of *daimons* and the dead. In the total structure
of Yeats's work, *Per Amica Silentia Lunae* serves as introduction
to the visionary center, to the later poems in *The Wild Swans at
Coole,* and to *Michael Robartes and the Dancer, Four Plays for
Dancers,* and *A Vision* itself.

The cover design for *Per Amica Silentia Lunae,* done by
Sturge Moore at Yeats's suggestion, is the Rose, now a symbol of
the Mask, and thus a mark of deliberate continuity between the
earlier and later Yeats. In this surpassingly beautiful little book,
Pater and the Cambridge Platonist Henry More are made to join

hands, as though the creator of Marius had his true affinities not with the second Renaissance of Romanticism but with the *Theologica Germanica* and related works. *Per Amica Silentia Lunae* is a masterpiece in the tradition of the marmoreal reverie, worthy to stand beside Browne's *Urn Burial* and *Garden of Cyrus* or most of Pater. Except for the *Autobiographies,* it is Yeats's great achievement in prose, a book to be read and re-read, unlike *A Vision,* which we are compelled to study, but so frequently with regret.

The book begins with a brief, charming Prologue addressed to "Maurice," Iseult Gonne, with whom Yeats was, perhaps, half-in-love. Tone dominates here; the book, Iseult is told, completes a conversation her Persian cat interrupted the previous summer. There follows *Ego Dominus Tuus* (discussed in Chapter 13), a poem on the image of desire or Mask, the starting point for *Anima Hominis* even as the essay, *Swedenborg, Mediums, and the Desolate Places* is the starting point of *Anima Mundi.* The poem ends with a reference to a secret doctrine, which "the mysterious one," the double and anti-self, will read in the subtler language of the Shelleyan characters written on the wet sand by the water's edge, and which he fears to communicate to "blasphemous men." This suggestion of the hieratic is taken up in the opening sentence of *Anima Hominis,* where Yeats comes home "after meeting men who are strange to me." He fears to have caricatured himself, being unfit to move among what he calls, in Blakean language, "images of good and evil, crude allegories."

What follows is an eloquent prophecy of what Yeats was to call "The First Principle" of his aesthetic, written years later as part of a general introduction for a projected edition of his complete works. A poet always writes out of the tragedy of his personal life, but never directly to the reader, for "there is always a phantasmagoria." It may be mythology, history, or romance, but even poets as personal as Shelley or Byron never write as what they and we are, bundles of accident and incoherence. They have been "reborn as an idea, something intended, complete." But note, in this age of Eliot, Auden, and the New Criticism, that there is *no* escape from or evasion of personality in this phantasmagoria, which is indeed precisely what Blake and Pater called "vision" and the other major Romantics the Secondary or creative Imagination. The artist becomes "part of his own phantasmagoria and we adore him because nature has grown intelligible." Nature is a power separated from our creative power, until the poet makes nature intelligible to us, "and by so doing a part of our creative power." There follows the most powerful and self-confident proclamation of the High Romantic imagination made in our time, and surely one that the host of anti-Romantic Yeats critics ought to have pondered. Yeats's Romanticism, Tate asserted, would be invented by his critics. Yeats has forestalled us, grandly: "The world knows nothing because it has made nothing, we know everything because we have made everything." [2] So much for nature and God, and their merely Primary worlds.

Twenty years earlier, in *Anima Hominis*, Yeats was no less confident, but he was then a little warier at identifying himself with his anti-self, of being made one with his own phantasmagoria. Yet the wariness, even then, was poetic strategy, a crucial element in the vacillation necessary for Paterian style. The phantasmagoria is there as "an heroic condition," vision, justly compared to Dante's *Vita Nuova* where the "Lord of Terrible Aspect" says to Dante: *ego dominus tuus,* or to the landscape of the Lower Paradise in Boehme. Yeats makes a hieratic withdrawal from life, and finds himself as the poet-visionary proper, enjoying a heroic condition. He calls this a "compensating dream," but he means compensation in a Coleridgean rather than a psychoanalytic sense, judging by the major instances he gives, beyond himself. He admits cases of compensation, like that of Synge, who in ill-health delights in physical life, but his interest is in art as "an opposing virtue" rather than a therapy. Most profoundly, this idea of the "opposing virtue" creates a pattern of heroic desperation, which may be the most moving design in the mature Yeats. Though the pattern exhibits familiar elements—a withdrawal from experience into the *antithetical* quest, identified with Shelleyan poethood, the occult way, the war between men and women—a new clarity defines itself also. Against whatever he knew of Freud and what he knew of the Pre-Socratics, whose view that character is fate Freud shared, Yeats implicitly urges the contrary view that personality is fate, the *daimon* is our destiny. The purpose of this exaltation of self over soul is not to evade the tragic reality of the

Freudian and Pre-Socratic view, but to oppose it with another conception of freedom, one necessarily not available to more than a handful of artists, men whose work is a flight from their horoscopes, their "blind struggle in the network of the stars." On the simplest level of his deliberate illustrations of the "opposing virtue," Yeats is hardly convincing; he gives us the "irascible" William Morris as following "an indolent muse," the genuinely violent Landor pursuing calm nobility, and Keats, "ignorant, poor, and in poor health" thirsting for luxury. Not only are all of these quasi-mechanical compensations, but the Yeatsian notion of Keats is too absurd to be interesting. But in passing to Dante, who with Shelley is to dominate the description of Yeats's own Phase 17 in *A Vision,* Yeats returns to the true depths of his own *antithetical* conception. Thinking back to Simeon Solomon, painter and broken monument of the prelude to the Tragic Generation, Yeats remembers a Shelleyan phrase of Solomon's: "a hollow image of fulfilled desire." In Book iii, *Hodos Chameliontos,* of *The Trembling of the Veil,* Yeats distinguishes between the Mask or Image that is fated, because it comes from life, and the Mask that is chosen.[3] Though in *Anima Hominis* he says that all happy art is but Solomon's hollow image, he means by this that tragic art is happy, yet expresses also the "poverty" of its creator, this use of "poverty" being strikingly similar to Stevens's use of it to mean "imaginative need," or a need that compels the imagination to come into full activity. Dante, like Shelley, fights a double war, with the world and with himself. Yeats touches the heights of his true visionary argument, truer than any he makes in *A Vision,* when he praises an ideal poet for choosing the Mask as an opposing virtue, and so attaining the "last knowledge." When the poet has seen *and foreseen* the image of all he dreads, while still seeking the image of desire to redress his essential poverty, then he will have his reward:

> I shall find the dark grow luminous, the void fruitful when I understand I have nothing, that the ringers in the tower have appointed for the hymen of the soul a passing bell.[4]

The enormous plangency of this magnificent (and Paterian) sentence gains terrible poignance when set in the context of its genesis, February 1917, when Yeats was moving toward his fifty-second birthday, still unmarried, and not knowing he was to be married before the year was out.

Having attained to this "last knowledge," Yeats is free to explore the hollow image or *antithetical* self, and find there (with Plutarch's help) the figure of the *daemon,* who whispers in the dark with the poet's beloved, as Yeats's own *daemon* (hardly Leo Africanus, but the Spirit that Denies) whispered in the dark with Maud Gonne. Hence, "the desire that is satisfied is not a great desire," a harsh judgment that goes back to the values of *Alastor,* and to Blake's early engraved tracts. There rises from this the doctrine that Yeats insists the true poet shares with saint, hero, martyr: that only the *antithetical* man is not deceived, and so finds reality, "a contemplation in a single instant perpetually renewed," a privileged moment or pulsation of the artery, a time of inherent excellence, epiphany not of the Divine shining out of a natural babe, but of the mind's own power over everything that is merely given.

When Yeats has reached this point, at the close of the ninth section of *Anima Hominis,* his reverie would appear to be accomplished, his warfare done. But in four more sections, the subtlest in the book, the subtlest indeed that he wrote in prose, he passes inevitably to the problem of poetic originality, which is the problem of poetic influence.

Poet or sculptor, Yeats says, cannot seek originality; he will sing or mould after a new fashion anyway if he expresses *antithetical* emotion. This is unfortunately an evasion, and Yeats does not rescue himself from it by a bitter wit, when he finely insists that "no disaster is like another." So it seems to the lover, but hardly to the reader. Yeats is firmer when he implies that no originality can be sought deliberately, since the *daemon* is our enemy, and is interested only in our disaster, and not in what he can make of it. The *daemon* must be held off (he cannot be overcome) through the poet's true originality, which is the strong poet's creative misinterpretation of his strongest precursor. This is the burden of Section XI, which follows, and finds an image for Yeats's freedom by a *clinamen* that uses Blake as point-of-departure. Mentioning Balzac and "the Christian Caballa" as sources, but not Blake, the

section transforms a Blakean image of apocalypse from Plates
97–98 of *Jerusalem*. The dialectic of the transformation was
sketched in Section VI of *Anima Hominis*, which itself develops
convictions that dominated *Adam's Curse*, and emerged again in
Ego Dominus Tuus. The anti-self, which leads the poet to at least
the possibility of his fuller self, leads also to an uncovering that
promises release from time's burden, including the embarrass-
ments of poetic tradition. So Section VI associates St. Francis and
Caesar Borgia (a delightful conjunction) with the old nonchalance whose decay is lamented in *Adam's Curse*. Saint and man-
of-power alike make their creativity by turning from a lesser to a
greater mode of imitation, "from mirror to meditation upon a
mask," the *daimonic* Will they meet in *antithetical* reverie. In
Section XI the mirror is "the winding movement of nature" or
"path of the serpent," and the meditation upon the mask is the
straight line of an arrow shot into the heavens, aimed at the sun.
The winding path is associated with Blake's vision of Milton's
Shadow, the Covering Cherub, the burden of time including the
sinister beauty not only of the historical churches but of Milton's
own poetry, and of the beauty of all cultural tradition, Scripture
included, when Scripture is used to help cover our creativity, to
block the path to paradise. The arrow shot at the sun is the Cherub's uncovering, the originality of each strong, new poet, and in
Yeats's view is fired only by the poet who meditates upon a mask.

On Plate 97 of *Jerusalem* a revived Albion stretches his hand
into Infinitude and recovers his Bow. His fourfold flaming Arrow
finds its target in "A sun of blood red wrath surrounding heaven
on all sides around," a Sun composed of "the unnumerable Char-
iots of the Almighty," of the contraries reconciled, "Bacon & Newton & Locke, & Milton & Shakespeare & Chaucer," the empiricists
and the visionaries at last together.[5] In Section XI of *Anima
Hominis* Yeats speaks of "we who are poets and artists," unable to
reach into Infinitude, "not being permitted to shoot beyond the
tangible," and who are therefore subject to the endless cycle of desire and weariness, while living only for the sudden epiphany, the
vision that comes "like terrible lightning." Prophesying the mystical geometry of *A Vision* (before the revelation made through
Mrs. Yeats by ghostly Instructors), Yeats speaks of the winding

mathematical arcs that prick upon the calendar the life-span of even the greatest men. Beneath these Urizenic heavens we are condemned to "seek reality with the slow toil of our weakness and are smitten with the boundless and unforeseen." Our efforts, in feeling or in thought, are doomed unless we learn to meditate upon the Mask, which means we must renounce mere *primary* experience, even with its saving epiphanies, "leave the sudden lightning," give up nature or "'the path of the serpent" and thus take on the state of Blake's apocalyptic Man: we must "become the bowman who aims his arrow at the centre of the sun."

We confront here Yeats's *clinamen* in regard to his precursor, Blake; a creative misinterpretation overcomes poetic influence. In Blake's vision, to meditate upon a mask is only to be a Spectre vainly pursuing an elusive Emanation; this is natural religion, the worship of each day's unfulfilled desire. Here Blake is close to Freud, and Yeats opposed to both, even as Jung is opposed. Yeats begins Section XII of *Anima Mundi* by granting that the doctors are right in regard to certain dreams; unfulfilled desires and censoriousness can end in mere dream and nightmare, if they do not undergo the "purifying discouragement" that allows passion to become vision. But (whether we wake or sleep, in explicit echo of Keats) vision sustains itself by rhythm and pattern, and makes of our lives what it will. *Anima Hominis* ends, after this defiance of analytic reduction, with the poet's warning to himself. The imagination can wither, as in Wordsworth, most terrible of instances; rhythm and pattern, once found, are not enough. There must be fresh experience: "new bitterness, new disappointment," for the finding of a true mask, and prolonged meditation upon it, does not make suffering less necessary. It is Yeats's highly individual contribution to the Romantic Sublime, this insistence that continued loss is crucial. Without fresh loss, the Sublime becomes the Grotesque, and the poet only a pretender to the Mask.

Anima Mundi

Anima Hominis succeeds where Book I, *The Great Wheel*, of *A Vision* will fail, in giving a persuasive account of the necessity for finding a mask. Similarly *Anima Mundi* is more coherent and appealing than the later books of *A Vision* are, in showing us how the *antithetical* self can be related to the world of the dead. Partly, this superiority of *Per Amica Silentia Lunae* over *A Vision* is due to the extravagant over-elaborations of the later work, as contrasted with the simplistic reveries of a poet closer to his earlier thought. But I judge the larger difference to be that Yeats was a better literary theorist than he was an occultist. *A Vision* can be translated into aesthetic metaphors, as Mrs. Vendler shows, but a good deal of it obdurately resists such translation, or translates only by severe reduction. *Per Amica Silentia Lunae,* even in its more spectral second book, is closer to an aesthetic treatise, with poetic influence a more major concern in it than the vagaries of ghosts. Or rather, its ghosts are poetic ghosts, imprisoned imaginations and influences, like Shelley's, that linger and haunt and will not permit themselves to be lost.

Near the close of Section XII of *Anima Hominis,* Yeats says of his "vision" that "it compels us to cover all it cannot incorporate," and he means, to cover all of his life that seems merely accidental, and so irrelevant to meditation upon the Mask. Whether overtly or not, he is remembering the Shadow of Milton or Covering Cherub he had encountered in Blake. In my introductory chapter I sketched a theory of poetic influence (partly derived by me from Blake and Yeats) in which influence is seen both as blessing and as curse. The first comes about through the later poet's swerve away from his Great Original, by a revisionary act of misinterpretation, and such a process is illustrated by *Anima Hominis,* as I have tried to show. The second process, that of accepting the curse of the Original's (and tradition's) too-great achievement, is handled differently by Yeats than by any other poet I know, for perhaps no other major poet is so much of a Gnostic in his mature vision. In *Anima Mundi,* Yeats takes on the curse of poetic influence as a Gnostic adept would; he enters the Shadow of the Cherub not to redeem it (as Blake's Milton did) nor even to redeem himself, but to attain what he will come to call justice, a passionate fullness, not of experience or of being, but of an instantaneous knowing. There are triumphs of this momentary knowing throughout the later lyrics, and a prolonged defence of it in those books of *A Vision* that deal with history and the dead. The lyric triumphs and the defence (and the application of the attained Gnosis in some of the later plays) are more disputable than they would be if Yeats had been able to keep to the mood of *Anima Mundi,* but bitterness kept breaking in, and the eloquence of reverie was abandoned. In May 1917, Yeats had much cause for embitterment, yet a beautiful kind of slow wonder dominates *Anima Mundi,* and induces even the contrary reader to set aside his wariness. In temperament, Yeats has little in common with the Cambridge Platonist Henry More, who is so evident here, but he finds the art (as Pater did) to assume a mood he rarely sustained elsewhere. It is the mood of the beautiful sentence of Browne that Yeats quotes in his 1914 treatise, *Swedenborg, Mediums, and the Desolate Places,* a prelude to *Anima Mundi:*

> I do think that many mysteries ascribed to our own invention have been the courteous revelations of spirits; for those noble essences in heaven bear a friendly regard unto their fellow creatures on earth.[6]

In this spirit, *Anima Mundi* begins, with Yeats genially immersing his mind in "the general mind" of Eastern poets, Connaught old women, and mediums in Soho. From this, it is an easy step to the suspension of will and intellect, that images may pass before him. But these images, throughout the treatise, are not particularly random, and generally turn themselves into the central images of Romantic poetry. So, this first evocation attains its climax in the "immortal sea" of Wordsworth's *Intimations* Ode, and subsequent sections will end with references to Coleridge, Blake, Spenser, and Shelley. The *anima mundi,* though Yeats quotes from "More and the Platonists," not surprisingly turns out to be the general mind of Romantic poetic tradition, as Yeats has fused it together. The explorers who perhaps knew all the shores where Wordsworth's children sport appear to be the poets who found their first seminary in Spenser's Garden of Adonis, from which Yeats quotes two instructive passages. The women of Connaught and Soho are more than an amiable fiction, but something less than Yeats's Muses. And though we hear the vocabulary of the spiritual Alchemists in Section III, the table of elements given is Blake's, down to the bird born out of the simplifying, reductive fire, from which Mystery rises again at the close of "Night VIII" of *The Four Zoas*. Yeats goes on, in Section IV, to desire contact with "those minds that I could divine," but chooses to quote Coleridge's fine lyric, *Phantom,* so as to give coherence to those minds.

In so occultizing Romantic tradition Yeats merely gave birth to the bad line of pseudo-scholars who have been reducing Blake, Shelley, Keats, Spenser, and of course Yeats himself to esoteric doctrine in recent times. But his motive was more honorable than what animates these literary Rosicrucians. His *anima mundi* as a poet is not in itself at all original, and something in his creativity feared the Covering Cherub, the negative strength of Romantic tradition. Thus, in Section VI, he goes to Henry More and anonymous mediums for speculation upon the after-life, yet his pragmatic finding is the staple of Romantic poetry. Beauty, he tells us, is "but bodily life in some ideal condition," and he ends the section by quoting *The Marriage of Heaven and Hell:* "God only acts or is in existing beings or men." In between, he gives us the kernel of the after life as the soul's "plastic power" which can mould whatever "to any shape it will by an act of imagination." When, in his next section, he needs to image forth the *anima mundi* he resorts to the opinions of Shelley and to the central image of all English Romanticism, Spenser's Garden of Adonis:

> There is the first seminary
> Of all things that are born to live and die
> According to their kynds.

Though he holds that coherence is provided by the occult image, he can show us only a coherence made by the poets themselves. The dead, like the spiritists who study them, become metaphors for Romantic art, rather than principles who inform that art. So the freedom of the dead, or Condition of Fire, itself is able to illustrate nothing, but is clarified for us when Yeats quotes his own lyric, *The Moods,* from *The Wind Among the Reeds,* immensely more coherent than Section X, and enabling us to see what these "fire-born moods" are.

Yeats was rarely a self-deceiver, and I think plainly attempts to deceive us here, presenting us with rhetoric, by his own definition. He tells us that the dead are the source of everything we call instinct, and so of our passions, but what he means is that our passions imitate art, and that tradition has taken the place of instinct. Similarly, he wishes us to believe that we communicate with *anima mundi* through the famous and passionate dead, but what he means is precisely what the fiercely skeptical Shelley meant by the survival of Keats in *Adonais,* and he not only needs Shelley to explain his thought, but he must both distort the context and misquote when he cites *Adonais.* Shelley writes of the crisis of young poets:

> The splendours of the firmament of time
> May be eclipsed, but are extinguished not;
> Like stars to their appointed height they climb,
> And death is a low mist which cannot blot
> The brightness it may veil. When lofty thought
> Lifts a young heart above its mortal lair,
> And love and life contend in it, for what
> Shall be its earthly doom, the dead live there
> And move like winds of light on dark and stormy air.

This intricate stanza firmly holds to the Shelleyan attitude that is best described as a visionary skepticism, longing for imaginative survival yet remembering always: "All that we have a right to infer from our ignorance of the cause of any event is that we do not know it. . . ."[7] Yeats, despite his own temperamental skepticism, adopted always the contrary attitude, inferring from his ignorance a range of occult causes. In Section XIII of *Anima Mundi* he deals with "the most wise dead," who "certainly" return from the grave, and he remembers a doctrine of Henry More, on the music of the shades, that he had quoted in *Swedenborg, Mediums, and the Desolate Places.* He applies it here, saying that men have affirmed always "that when the soul is troubled, those that are a shade and a song: 'live there,/And live like winds of light on dark or stormy air.'" Shelley's context, the "there" of what Yeats quotes, is the uplifted heart of the young poet, and not the haunted state Yeats makes of it, while the misquotation of "live" for "move," whether deliberate or not, is immensely illuminating, as another instance of the happily perverse workings of poetic influence. One remembers Shelley's brief, pungent essay, *On a Future State,* where he remarks of the assertions made by those of "the secret persuasion" of an occult survival: "They persuade, indeed, only those who desire to be persuaded."

Shelley, as elsewhere in *Anima Mundi,* provides the key to Yeats's discourse: the "passionate dead" live only in our imagination, and their dream is only of our life. Alas that they do wear our colors there, though Yeats exultantly cries of them that they are rammed with life (itself a tag from another poet, Jonson). Though in *A Vision,* Yeats will depart from his uneasiness, and will postulate a world of the dead quite unlike the world of the living, here in *Per Amica Silentia Lunae* he is more of a poet and less of a necromancer, and he profits by his uneasiness, as do we. The Condition of Fire, with its purifying simplification through intensity, is precisely the Romantic Imagination, the burning fountain of *Adonais,* and the apparently mysterious Sections XV through XXI of *Anima Mundi* are an extended commentary upon *Adonais,* its stanza LIV in particular. The climax to this commentary, in Section XXI, is also the height of Yeats's visionary argument in *Per Amica Silentia Lunae.* Remembering that Shelley calls our minds "mirrors of the fire for which all thirst" Yeats asks the inevitable question, for Gnostic or naturalist alike, "What or who has cracked the mirror?" And, for answer, he turns to study his own self again, finding in the Paterian privileged moment his only true access to the *anima mundi,* and so presenting his genuine defence of poetry. What he describes is the basis of the poem *Demon and Beast,* but his description here is more in the Romantic tradition. If, in the pulsation of an artery or displaced epiphany, he finds himself "in the place where the daemon is," this is still no victory, until the *daemon* "is with me," a work the poet must perform for himself.

13: The Wild Swans at Coole

With the publication of the second version of *The Wild Swans at Coole,* in 1919, a deliberately "different" Yeats presented himself to his public.[1] He had married, and been found by the Instructors of *A Vision.* Marriage, to so occultizing a temperament as Yeats's, had to represent sea-change, but his poetry did not change as much as the man did, or felt he did. Five poems are important in the 1919 volume: two "texts for exposition," *The Phases of the Moon* and *Ego Dominus Tuus;* one personal, almost Wordsworthian lyric, the title poem; the grave and formal elegy *In Memory of Major Robert Gregory;* finally, the intensely visionary and difficult *The Double Vision of Michael Robartes.* None of these is a radical beginning for Yeats, though the Gregory elegy, rather than the doctrinal poems, comes closest to being a fresh invention. Certainly it, and the title poem, match the best work Yeats had done before 1916, except for a few superb poems, *Adam's Curse* and *The Cold Heaven* in particular.

The title poem, dated October 1916, rises from the complex mood in which Yeats began what was to be his last solitary year of bachelorhood. As Jeffares indicates, the poem's dominant emotion is not frustrated longing for Maud Gonne, but sorrow that the poet's passion for her is dead.[2] A man of fifty-one looks upon the same scene he saw at thirty-two. He comes to the scene again after having proposed marriage again to the same woman as nineteen years before, and after being refused, yet again. But his primary awareness is not of a dismal, almost ridiculous continuity, between an earlier and a later self. Discontinuity dominates, for the depression of nineteen years before was at the refusal, but the depression of 1916 is for *not* feeling depression at the continued refusal. His heart has grown old, and its soreness is that it should have aged.

This pattern is inherited indirectly from *Tintern Abbey*. Wordsworth both longs for and does not desire the raptures of an earlier phase, when he later returns to a crucially remembered landscape. Judiciously he balances loss and gain, the means of balance being the compensatory imagination, with its deeper autumnal music and sober coloring rising to take the place of a fled ecstasy. Between Wordsworth, who always evaded Yeats, and *The Wild Swans at Coole,* the essential link is the ambivalent Wordsworthianism of Shelley in *Alastor* and later poems, from the hymns of 1816 down to the death poem of 1822, *The Triumph of Life*. *Alastor,* as many critics have suggested, is a major source of *The Wild Swans at Coole,* which is perhaps the first poem in which Yeats swerves crucially away from the Shelleyan quest for the *daimonic* beloved. Of the two possibilities allowed by *Alastor*'s Preface, life burned away by the self-consuming quest or the heart burning coldly to the socket, Yeats fears now to have fulfilled the latter. When the doomed Poet, in *Alastor,* reaches the sea-shore, he begins to apprehend the desolation stalking him in the shape of his *alastor* or Spirit of Solitude. This apprehension follows the Poet's Spenserian vision of a solitary swan:

> A strong impulse urged
> His steps to the sea-shore. A swan was there,
> Beside a sluggish stream among the reeds.
> It rose as he approached, and with strong wings
> Scaling the upward sky, bent its bright course
> High over the immeasurable main.

His eyes pursued its flight.—"Thou hast a home,
Beautiful bird; thou voyagest to thine home,
Where thy sweet mate will twine her downy neck
With thine, and welcome thy return with eyes
Bright in the lustre of their own fond joy.
And what am I that I should linger here,
With voice far sweeter than thy dying notes,
Spirit more vast than thine, frame more attuned
To beauty, wasting these surpassing powers
In the deaf air, to the blind earth, and heaven
That echoes not my thoughts?"

This same passage from *Alastor* is a crucial influence upon *The Tower*, as will be shown later. In *The Wild Swans at Coole*, Yeats recalls it for deliberate contrast, for his depression and apparent loss is that he no longer shares this vision of the relation between poet and swan.[3] The Poet of *Alastor* sees in the swan an emblem of the subjective quest, but the quest realized as he, the Poet, never can realize it, precisely because his greater powers cannot be fulfilled by the inadequate context of nature, with its deaf air, blind earth, and unechoing heaven. Yeats too sees in the swans his *antithetical* quest fulfilled, but his regret is that for him the passionate or outward-bound aspect of the quest is forever over. It is of considerable critical importance that the stanza acknowledging this, now the fourth of five in the poem, was in the poem's first appearance the final stanza, so that the plangency of accepted defeat ended the poem:

Unwearied still, lover by lover,
They paddle in the cold
Companionable streams or climb the air;
Their hearts have not grown old;
Passion or conquest, wander where they will,
Attend upon them still.

Evidently, Yeats chose at first to put his emphasis here, upon his ancient love for Maud, the central passion of his life, being extinct. In revision, he took the poem's central stanza, and placed it last, altering absolutely the poem's significance:

> But now they drift on the still water,
> Mysterious, beautiful;
> Among what rushes will they build,
> By what lake's edge or pool
> Delight men's eyes when I awake some day
> To find they have flown away?

Ellmann speculates that, by putting this stanza at the end, "Yeats made it possible to read it symbolically so that his awakening would be his death." [4] This is possible, but unnecessarily stretched. Awakening here is not death but the end of *antithetical* consciousness, the complete breaking with the Shelleyan influence. The prophecy was not fulfilled, perhaps because such an awakening would have been a death-in-life for Yeats, even after love was dead.

In Memory of Major Robert Gregory

This ambitious elegy for Lady Gregory's son, killed fighting for the English, has inspired judgments ranging from Frank Kermode's to Yvor Winters'. Kermode's emphasizes the centrality of the elegy:

> It is a poem worthy of much painful reading, perhaps the first in which we hear the full range of the poet's voice; and with this heroic assurance of harmony goes an authentic mastery of design.[5]

Against this, set Winters': "I confess that I think it a very bad poem." [6] He found the writing slovenly, the structure loose, and the praise of Gregory excessive. The poem is not *Lycidas,* and hardly deserves a Johnsonian attack, though it has its pretensions and its faults. What is weakest in the poem is Gregory himself, more an Edward King than a Sidney. This would not have mattered if Gregory counted for as little in the poem as King does in *Lycidas,* but unfortunately he does count for more. What saves the poem is that Yeats's career matters more to it than Gregory's, a saving formula strenuously employed by Milton, and emulated by Shelley in *Adonais.* The elegy is most moving when it explic-

itly celebrates Lionel Johnson and Synge, and implicitly defends
Yeats's poetic development. The poet's apologia is the poem's culmination, in its best and last stanza, and its only difficult one. A
bitter wind shakes the shutter, and prompted by this *memento
mori* Yeats says he has tried to summon up the dead who are most
living for him. He implies that this would have been a work of
need and will, not of imagination, a kind of preparation for vision: "Until imagination brought/A fitter welcome." He has
failed, because the thought of the recent loss of Gregory "took all
my heart for speech." His heart it took perhaps, but not his soul,
which has made the poem out of the obsessive search for reality
that his heart or *daimonic* subjectivity necessarily continues to
thwart, that he may go on being a poet.

The definitive, wholly just commentary on the Gregory elegy
has been written by D. J. Gordon and Ian Fletcher, who avoid
the paths of Winters and of Kermode. They see what Winters
would not, that "uncertainties about the direction of Gregory's
talent and his future underlie the grave elaborations of Yeats's
beautiful 'appreciation'." [7] The use of Pater's word for his characteristic work, "appreciation," subtly indicates the profoundly
Paterian nature of the elegy though Gordon and Fletcher refer directly to Yeats's prose account of Gregory. I find this nature misrepresented by Kermode's commentary, which follows Gordon
and Fletcher in emphasizing the isolation of the artist as being
central to this poem also, as being Yeats's deliberate elegiac
theme, "his full exploration of the significance of Gregory's death
as the artist's escape." [8] But Gordon and Fletcher, like the elegy,
are closer to Pater, in trusting finally not to the sufficient image
but to the right sensation, a sharp flare felt rather than seen:
"consummation that is extinction; extinction that is a condition
of triumph." The difference between image and sensation may be
a difficult one, but the poetic strength of Yeats's elegy is founded
upon it.

Five men are involved in the elegy: Johnson, Synge, Gregory,
Yeats's maternal uncle, George Pollexfen, and Yeats himself.
Though the Great Wheel of *A Vision* was at most a spoke in
1918, the elegy is consistent with Yeats's later classification of personalities. Johnson presumably was an artist of Phase 13, Yeats of

the more fortunate Phase 17. George Pollexfen, horseman and occultist, can only be guessed at, but Synge was of Phase 23 and
Gregory, I surmise, of his mother's Phase 24, despite his many
characteristics drawn from the Romantic matrix of Phases 13, 14,
16, and 17. When Yeats, in his prose "appreciation" of Gregory,
sums up the thirty-seven-year-old man-of-action and artist, he
finds the war to have been a release for Gregory, release from the
burden of having to choose between perfection of the life or of
the work. In Yeats's technical terms, the choice would have been
between Phases, or since we cannot choose our Phase, between living in or out of phase. So, Gregory's time of warfare:

> . . . brought him peace of mind, an escape from that shrinking,
> which I sometimes saw upon his face, before the growing absorption
> of his dream, as from his constant struggle to resist those other gifts
> that brought him ease and friendship.[9]

If Gregory was caught between *antithetical* solitude and *primary* fellowship (though the dialectic actually is more austere
than this), he can be seen as standing between the poet Johnson
and the dramatist Synge, as Yeats in some sense (though closer to
Johnson) stood also. Differences of temperament, and of vocation,
have their function in the poem. Johnson's role in the poem is described with great precision by Gordon and Fletcher:

> Associated with and distinguished from Gregory by his remote
> scholarship and distant courtesy, Johnson is a type of the solitary
> artist unable to accept the burden of that solitude and unable also
> to accept absorption into the dream that creates solitude.[10]

Always, Yeats says in his elegy, we would have our new and
old friends meet, whether compatible or not. Johnson and Synge
are not compatible; Gordon and Fletcher again cannot be improved:

> From dreams, Lionel Johnson could escape only to still more
> impossible dreams. Synge escaped by celebrating the objective, a
> life antithetical to his own.[11]

Gregory was saved by death from a choice between the visions of Johnson and of Synge; the implicit and deepest theme of the elegy is that Yeats cannot escape the choice, but must found all his art upon an intense vacillation in choosing. If he chooses, definitively, he seems to fear the loss not only of part of his imaginative endowment but something also of his emotional nature. Writing in 1919, in *Reveries over Childhood and Youth,* he quoted his father as saying of the Yeatses:

> We have ideas and no passions, but by marriage to a Pollexfen we have given a tongue to the sea cliffs.[12]

George Pollexfen is in the poem as a voiceless sea cliff, "grown sluggish and contemplative," a fate the poet certainly escaped. There remains a puzzle in the elegy. The heart of the poem is in a passage closest to the Blake-Palmer-Calvert tradition that insisted we became what we beheld, and therefore beheld visionary landscape as opposed to corporeal outline. Yeats and Lady Gregory dreamed that the slain hero had been born to paint in that tradition.

> To that stern colour and that delicate line
> That are our secret discipline
> Wherein the gazing heart doubles her might.

These seem to me the most deeply moving lines in the poem, but they make the choice for Gregory that he did not live to make for himself, and that much else in the poem makes us doubt he would have made. Perhaps the lines need not be a puzzle, but another reminder that, in this elegiac vision of a Renaissance man, as in his visions of other ideals, Yeats knew already what he was to admit toward the end in *The Circus Animals' Desertion:* "It was the dream itself enchanted me."

Ego Dominus Tuus

The High Romanticism that prevailed in Yeats, despite his own misgivings, his Gnostic demonology of history, and his concessions to the spirit of the literary age, finds a perfect expression through the incantatory summoning of the *daimon* that concludes this poem:

> I call to the mysterious one who yet
> Shall walk the wet sands by the edge of the stream
> And look most like me, being indeed my double,
> And prove of all imaginable things
> The most unlike, being my anti-self. . . .

Splendid as this is, we wonder a little at it, as though the lines had been written by a committee of his exegetes, and not by Yeats himself. This is a touch too central, too much the expositional and doctrinal text Yeats had been working to achieve, and perhaps for too long a time. The passage expounds itself, as though the poet had become his own academy, his future critics. Yeats, a shrewd judge of his own work, worried about writing mere "texts for exposition." Yet *Ego Dominus Tuus* is better than that would imply for some of the same reasons that *Per Amica Silentia Lunae* is an achieved work of art, while *A Vision* is only one of the curiosities of literature. *Ego Dominus Tuus* (1915) is the starting point of *Per Amica Silentia Lunae* (1917), of which it forms the first section.

The poem's theme, like the treatise, is mastery; of what sort is the poet's, and how does he attain to it? Where *Per Amica* gives a dual answer—from his anti-self, attained through self-annihilation, and from the *anima mundi,* reached through vision—the poem gives a simpler but less imaginatively compelling reply. Mastery is the successful quest for the image, an image looking like oneself, but proving, of all imaginable things, to be the most unlike, or the anti-self. Removed from the poem's context, this must look more like helplessness than like mastery; its pattern indeed suggests Poe's *William Wilson* or Hoffmann's *The Devil's Elixirs,* as though Yeats too was a poet whose themes turned toward the destructive power of the imagination. But *Ego Dominus Tuus,* viewed standing close up, is understandably more in the pattern of *Alastor;* the poet seeks that mysterious one who will complete him, while being shadowed by the *daimon* of his Solitude. He finds, neither an emanative beloved, nor the mocking shadow of his quest, but rather a mastery that, in freeing him from natural limitation, renders him also unfit for continued natural existence. *Alastor* ends neither in bafflement nor in ordinary despair, yet its triumph is a splendid outrage of alienation, a dead end for the creative spirit. Yeats, as his lyric on the swans at Coole shows, was weary of such triumph, and *Per Amica* attempts another fresh start for the imagination. *Ego Dominus Tuus* is the kernel for *Per Amica*, in every sense, but lacks the treatise's reach after the universal, as shown in its necessary second part, *Anima Mundi*, where the self's quest for a more individual defeat is dissolved in the larger imaginative impulse that passes into the Condition of Fire. Between the winter of 1915 and the spring of 1917, the writing of *Ego Dominus Tuus* and of *Anima Mundi*, much had intervened—the Easter Rising of 1916, and the poet's brief, strange quasi-love for Iseult Gonne (to whom *Per Amica* is a kind of love letter, and preparatory leave-taking). Between the Rising, and the flare of the relationship with Iseult Gonne, came the last, almost ritualistic proposal to Maud Gonne. After *Per Amica* came marriage, and the vision of *A Vision*. Future and still better-informed criticism of Yeats than we have had should focus itself upon the two years from late 1915 to late 1917, for these were the most important in Yeats's imaginative life. Reading Hone, the authorized biographer, on these years is a little frustrating, for he finds Yeats both colder and more deliberate than anyone could have been in such circumstances. It is true that Yeats was no youth, but an immensely complex and distinguished man past fifty, yet the movement of thought and action is more of a tempest than the patient and impressively calm Hone would allow. Jeffares and Ellmann, the more critical biographers, both have too much to do in too few pages, between life and poetry, and do not speculate on these years.

The strength of *Ego Dominus Tuus* is that Yeats evades the constriction of his still rudimentary doctrine. *Hic*, the *primary*, objective soul or Owen Aherne-figure, is allowed something of the common sense of his stance. *Ille*, who has inherited the magic book of Michael Robartes, does not deny that he is "enthralled by

the unconquerable delusion,/ Magical shapes." This may echo
Arnold's Scholar Gypsy, urged by the poet to "keep thy solitude"
while "still nursing the unconquerable hope." Yet "delusion" is a
strong admission on Yeats's part. Elsewhere in his poetry Yeats
uses the word only once, when "delusions magical" are cast on
Cuchulain, the aim and result being his fight with the sea. Yeats
could have chosen "unconquerable illusion," as with the "manifold illusion" that hoops civilization together in the late poem,
Meru. But here, in *Ego Dominus Tuus*, he allows without argument, the *antithetical* quest to be termed delusion. Even *Ille*, just
before the final invocation of his anti-self, permits an objectivity
to destroy the possibility of his writing another book like that
of Robartes:

> Because I seek an image, not a book.
> Those men that in their writings are most wise
> Own nothing but their blind, stupefied hearts.

Still, Yeats went on to write *Per Amica*, and then *A Vision*,
and then a later, definitive version of *A Vision*. *Ille*'s admission is
ironic, for the wisdom he acknowledges is blind and stupefied, or
so he would believe, or have us believe. It is the wisdom presumably of nineteenth-century liberal humanism, of those who would
find themselves and not an image, and so have lost all conviction.
The subjective *Ille* again echoes *The Scholar-Gipsy* when he attacks the "modern hope" of self-discovery and self-expression:

> That is our modern hope, and by its light
> We have lit upon the gentle, sensitive mind
> And lost the old nonchalance of the hand;
> Whether we have chosen chisel, pen or brush,
> We are but critics, or but half create,
> Timid, entangled, empty and abashed,
> Lacking the countenance of our friends.

This is a profound complaint, and a reader of the earlier sections of the *Autobiographies* of Yeats will hear the personal reference in the last two lines. Essentially, Yeats is rejecting the
Wordsworthianism that was a powerful element in Victorian lit-

erary culture, with its champions in figures as great as John Stuart Mill and George Eliot. Hence the echo, deliberate or not, of the striking phrase "half create" from *Tintern Abbey:* Wordsworth declared himself a lover

> . . . of all the mighty world
> Of eye, and ear,—both what they half create,
> And what perceive; well pleased to recognise
> In nature and the language of the sense
> The anchor of my purest thoughts. . . .

Early in 1916, Yeats read or re-read most of Wordsworth's major poetry, reaching conclusions upon it strikingly like those of Hallam in his Tennyson essay that had so influenced the young Yeats. The conclusions are guarded, but severe:

> He strikes me as always destroying his poetic experience, which was of course of incomparable value, by his reflective power. His intellect was commonplace, and unfortunately he had been taught to respect nothing else. He thinks of his poetic experience not as incomparable in itself but as an engine that may be yoked to his intellect. He is full of a sort of utilitarianism, and that is perhaps the reason why in later life he is continually looking back upon a lost vision, a lost happiness.[13]

Hallam had opposed to Wordsworth's poetry of "reflection" the poetry of "sensation" as written by Keats and Shelley. To Wordsworth's "nature and the language of the sense" Yeats, in *Ego Dominus Tuus,* explicitly opposes a lost *sprezzatura,* "the old nonchalance of the hand," and implicitly chooses Shelley's "subtler language." *Ille* walks in the moonlight, to trace characters upon the sand, the image invented by Shelley to convey his "subtler language." In the 1925 *Vision* Robartes traced these characters on the sands of Arabia, and the 1923 poem, *The Gift of Harun Al-Rashid,* was printed in the first *A Vision* under the title of *Desert Geometry.* The source in Yeats is in his first Shelley essay, back in 1900, where the examination of Shelley's "ruling symbols" begins with the image of Cythna, archetype of Maud Gonne, tracing *antithetical* wisdom in the sands:

At a comparatively early time Shelley made his imprisoned Cythna become wise in all human wisdom through the contemplation of her own mind, and write out this wisdom upon the sands in "signs" that were "clear elemental shapes, whose smallest change" made "a subtler language within language." . . .[14]

Whether Yeats knew how he misinterpreted Shelley (or Wordsworth, or later in *Ego Dominus Tuus,* Keats) scarcely matters. These are the "misinterpretations" of Poetic Influence, instances of the *clinamen* or creative swerves. The source-passage in *The Revolt of Islam* presents a very different subjectivity than *Ille* pursues. Cythna comes out of the madness of ruined hopes, finds herself in solitude, and turns inward to find the power of the Romantic imagination:

> We live in our own world, and mine was made
>   From glorious fantasies of hope departed:
> Aye we are darkened with their floating shade,
>   Or cast a lustre on them—time imparted
>   Such power to me—I became fearless-hearted,
> My eye and voice grew firm, calm was my mind,
>   And piercing, like the morn, now it has darted
>   Its lustre on all hidden things, behind
> Yon dim and fading clouds which load the weary mind.
>
> My mind became the book through which I grew
>   Wise in all human wisdom, and its cave,
> Which like a mine I rifled through and through,
>   To me the keeping of its secrets gave—
>   One mind, the type of all, the moveless wave
> Whose calm reflects all moving things that are,
>   Necessity, and love, and life, the grave,
>   And sympathy, fountains of hope and fear;
> Justice, and truth, and time, and the world's natural sphere.
>
> And on the sand would I make signs to range
>   These woofs, as they were woven, of my thought;
> Clear, elemental shapes, whose smallest change
>   A subtler language within language wrought:
>   The key of truths which once were dimly taught
> In old Crotona;—and sweet melodies

> Of love, in that lorn solitude I caught
> From mine own voice in dream, when thy dear eyes
> Shone through my sleep, and did that utterance harmonize.

>   Canto VII, xxx–xxxii

Shelley's vision rising here from the wreck of hope is of the mind in its own place, unconquerable and unassailable, because its calm reflects all of reality, including sympathy, justice, truth, and other ideal goals. When Cythna calls the signs on the sand "the key of truths," Shelley does not mean a solipsistic truth but the entire world *Ille* rejects, the world "that is our modern hope." Yeats takes from Shelley, as always, only what he needs, to employ against the nineteenth-century poetic humanism Yeats seeks to overturn. Mill, who can be taken as the best representative of the attitudes *Hic* inadequately embodies, justly linked Wordsworth and Shelley in his regard. But what Hallam and Yeats found in Shelley is there, a poetry of sensation that offers, not objective ideas, but subjective conceptual images. Yeats divides, as always, the means of Shelley's poetry, from its revolutionary and humanistic ends.

This excursus, into Wordsworth and Shelley, ought to illuminate *Ille*'s attack upon the modern artists who "are but critics, or but half create." The kernel of the poem is *Ille*'s "by the help of an image," and the question formed by the poem is: "How much help is an image"? Wordsworth, in his difficult variation upon the Sublime mode, was willing to yield up the early image of desire, hoping for the abundant recompense of a maturer vision. Yeats is caustic in calling this "a sort of utilitarianism"; perhaps it was, but a utilitarianism of the spirit. *Hic* does not argue, at this point, the case for nineteenth-century poetry. He will do that later in the poem, presenting the natural humanism of Keats. More cunningly, he puts forward "the chief imagination of Christendom," Dante, who in *A Vision* will occupy the most fortunate of phases for a poet, Phase 17, where Unity of Being is most possible, and where the other major poets in residence are Shelley and Yeats himself. Dante is supremely relevant partly because his *Convivio* is one of the apt models for both *Per Amica* and *A Vision*, but mostly because the *Comedy* can be thought of as an utter self-finding. *Ille's* answer is as unsatisfying as Yeats's account of Dante in *Per Amica* is. The Dante of the poem, we are asked to believe, is a "spectral image" opposite in being to the natural man Dante. Though the example is unconvincing, the principle *Ille* extracts is expressed with Yeats's most majestic and unanswerable rhetorical authority:

> The rhetorician would deceive his neighbours,
> The sentimentalist himself; while art
> Is but a vision of reality.
> What portion in the world can the artist have
> Who has awakened from the common dream
> But dissipation and despair?

How different the last three lines of this passage are from the first three. The last three evoke the Tragic Generation, while we would hardly associate the first three, as Yeats clearly does, with the poetry of Dowson and Johnson, moving and permanent as the best of it is. Whatever the "art" described in *Per Amica* is, we cannot call it "a vision of reality," unless we agree with Yeats's late proposition:

> Reality is a timeless and spaceless community of Spirits which perceive each other. Each Spirit is determined by and determines those it perceives, and each Spirit is unique.[15]

Yet *Ille's* rhetoric is too strong for our skepticism; our struggle against it is "the struggle of the fly in marmalade." What has begun in Yeats is that marvelous style one fights in vain, for it can make any conviction, every opinion even, formidable out of all proportion to its actual imaginative validity. Thus, when *Hic* offers Keats, with his love of the world, his deliberate happiness, as being neither rhetorician nor sentimentalist, *Ille*-Yeats replies with a wholly inadequate late Victorian misrepresentation of Keats, in no sense even a creative misinterpretation, but the verbal gesture remains convincing. We know, as Yeats hardly cared to know, that Keats was not an "ignorant" man who made "luxuriant song," but Yeats makes it difficult for anyone to see his nonsense as being just that here, nonsense.

What savés *Ego Dominus Tuus* from its own unfairness of judgment is more than powerful rhetoric however, for the final exchange between *Hic* and *Ille* concerns what matters most in the poem: the value of the *antithetical* image. *Hic* speaks the conventional wisdom of Poetic Influence, but not the truer wisdom one must grant Yeats as having learned:

> A style is found by sedentary toil
> And by the imitation of great masters.

Ille knows the esoteric truth of Poetic Influence, that a style (in the largest sense of style) finds a strong new poet not by imitation but by the *antithetical* swerve, which for *Ille* leads to "the mysterious one," the anti-self. The poem has come full circle, returning to the "magical shapes" of a doctrine of visionary images, to the emblems of tower, lamp, open book, moonlight, and the grey sand by a shallow stream. *Ego Dominus Tuus* is not one of Yeats's great poems, but it is surely one of his most central and troubling.

The Phases of the Moon

This poem, despite its eloquence, is something closer to a "text for exposition" than *Ego Dominus Tuus* is. Commentary upon much of it would be superfluous, as my book attempts a very full commentary upon *A Vision,* which expands upon this poem of 1918. There are incidental insights in the poem, however, valuable not only for understanding *A Vision,* but much of Yeats thereafter, and a brief overview may help to bring these out.

Ego Dominus Tuus implied that a poet's mastery came in seeking and finding the inevitable or *daimonic* image, a double of the self in appearance, but opposite to the self in nature. Such an image is peculiarly divided against itself, for it must mean the reverse of what it seems. One sees why poets who read realities in appearances, Wordsworth and Keats, are inimical to the poem's doctrine. Blake, for whom nature was an imposture, and Shelley, for whom nature was at best equivocal, at worst an involuntary deceiver (the "Shape all light" in *The Triumph of Life*), are clearly more congenial to *Ille*'s vision. In *Ego Dominus Tuus* the *daimonic* image is the mysterious one who will interpret to Yeats (or his surrogate) the characters in the sand, which will lead the poet past the compensatory psychology of *Per Amica* and into the more just, because more complete, psychology-cosmology of *A Vision*. But Yeats never developed, in the poem or the treatise or later, his indistinct image of his own anti-self. Why? Surely we ought to expect, whether in verse or prose, an account of "the mysterious one"? Yeats shied from it, almost superstitiously, perhaps believing that to encounter his double-but-opposite, as Shelley's Zoroaster did when walking in a garden (in *Prometheus Unbound*) or Shelley himself by tradition did, just before drowning, would be to meet his own death. Aesthetically, the potential difficulties were daunting enough. *A Vision* disappoints for many reasons, as I shall demonstrate in the next two chapters, but one frustration it provides is particularly acute. Yeats so elaborately disguises its self-referential aspects, that we are left to find the book's meaning for the poet's life and art by various sleights of translation. Where *Per Amica* is, as I have attempted to show, among much else a study of Poetic Influence, *A Vision* chooses to shelter itself under the interlocking shadows of the Sphinx (or Yeats's concealed love-torments) and of the being Yeats called the Shadow, and identified with Blake's Covering Cherub (or Yeats's concealed torment of blocked-imagination, or case of Poetic Influence). This double process of concealment is already at work in *The Phases of the Moon,* and makes the poem less of a poem than it might have been.

Aherne and Robartes, in the poem, are tiresome properties, easy ironies by which the poet may mock himself. Robartes expresses contempt for poets in general, as well as Yeats; they have found "mere images." Yet the irony is as much bent against the occult Robartes; they sought only images, and the "true song, though speech" the occultist chants is the huge, mere image of the Great Wheel. As my next chapter expounds the Wheel, with frequent reference to this poem, most of it may be neglected here. The double irony again needs to be noted now. Critics rightly focus upon the cryptic account Robartes gives of Phase 27, the

Saint, because there is a hint of escape from the Wheel's turnings here:

> Hunchback and Saint and Fool are the last crescents.
> The burning bow that once could shoot an arrow
> Out of the up and down, the wagon-wheel
> Of beauty's cruelty and wisdom's chatter—
> Out of that raving tide—is drawn betwixt
> Deformity of body and of mind.

In Blake's *Milton,* one finds the fullest and likeliest source for Yeats's twenty-eight Phases, in the twenty-eight Churches that mark off the divisions of fallen human history. In less schematic form, this Blakean Wheel or Circle of Destiny is presented in *The Mental Traveller,* cited by Yeats as a prime source for *A Vision.* When Blake's Milton, the archetypal poet, resolves to descend again into history and nature (having become disillusioned with the orthodox Eternity he desired, and attained) he is compelled to put on the Shadow or Covering Cherub, a twenty-seven-fold darkness under which we dwell. The Twenty-Seventh Church is called "Luther," the Protestant phase of Blake's own time, and equivalent to Yeats's Phase 27, or the Saint. For both Blake and Yeats the twenty-seventh fold of the Shadow offers the possibility of release, but Blake passionately means it, while for Yeats it is only another irony. For Blake, the twenty-eighth Church is Apocalypse; else the Circle must turn round again. For Yeats, the Wheel must turn around again always, so Phase 28 is the Fool, deformity of mind, a last waning before the darkness of a terrible god, Phase 1. This is the complex irony of the close of *The Phases of the Moon.* The laughter of Aherne, at the expense of Yeats, is a hollowness, for the finder of mere images, the poet, never expects to find anything but endless cycle, the spinning of the Great Wheel by the Gnostic composite god of history, deity of a meaningless death (for who, in Yeats's systematics, can die?) and an absurd life (for who, in Yeats's kind of heroic vision, can live meaningfully?). Perhaps *The Phases of the Moon,* despite its frequent brilliance and invariable eloquence, is more than a little hollow too, fit vehicle for the humor of Yeats's Aherne, and of Yeats.

The Double Vision of Michael Robartes

Though Yeats was willing to regard this poem also as a text for exposition, it succeeds doubly, within the context of system, and entirely by itself. It occupies the place in Yeats's work that a poem like *The Mental Traveller* has in Blake's, though the comparison is hardly fair to Yeats. Blake's ballad, like at least two other poems in the Pickering Manuscript, *The Crystal Cabinet* and *The Golden Net,* seems to have been written partly as an experiment, to see how well Blake could present the outlines of his central story without resorting to the technical formulations he had invented. *The Double Vision* has the fascination of the hieratic, as Yeats intended it should, but it lacks the other aesthetic strength of Blake's manuscript ballads, the apparent simplicity that makes the difficulties of those poems so attractive.

Yeats opens in the dark of the moon, and with a power appropriate to the inhuman Phase 1. The blank eyes of some demiurge watch its own restless fingers pounding "the particular," until the cold spirits of Phase 1 become the men of Phase 2. Though the first section of *The Double Vision* compels only a cold admiration, Yeats is astonishing in his control of his own emotion here. Whitaker rightly says that this first vision "is that of *primary* monism," [16] hardly a sympathetic vision for Yeats, but rarely does Yeats write with such descriptive accuracy of one of his own abstract states-of-being as he does here. Lines seven through sixteen of this section appear to be spoken by "the cold spirits" of Phase 1, who feel relatively little, but who can observe their own creators with great particularity, and who win over the demiurges the pre-human victory, pathetic in its limitations, of feeling that "they do not even feel . . . triumph that we obey."

With the opening of the second section, Yeats accomplishes one of his most agile tonal modulations. Robartes enters the poem, with a vision by the light of the full moon. Between Sphinx and Buddha, knowledge without love and love without knowledge, a girl dances, celebrating the mystery of incarnate beauty, the triumph of art in Phase 15. In Shelleyan terms, the dialectic is that of the separated Prometheus and Asia, with the dancer in between as the equivalent of the mythic infants of Act IV, the Apocalypse of *Prometheus Unbound*. In Blake the parallel is in the merely natural cycle of oppositions between Urizen and Luvah-Orc, but Blake would have scorned Yeats's female dancer as a substitute for his hammer-bearing Los. Yet the analogue holds; Shelley's infants, Blake's Los, and Yeats's girl all outdance thought, and all bring the human body to a perfection beyond any available in natural incarnation:

> For what but eye and ear silence the mind
> With the minute particulars of mankind?

The second line is essentially Blake's; the first, which Blake would have rejected, is Yeats's legacy from Coleridge and Wordsworth through Shelley, reversing as Shelley grimly does the Lake Poets' theme of the power of the mind over outward sense. Perfection of the dancing girl's body silences the mind; Phase 15 will suffice. Blake's pulsation of an artery, his moment in each day that Satan's Watch Fiends cannot find, has not been revealed to Yeats, let alone to Robartes, but is re-created magically by the presence of Sphinx, Buddha, and dancing-girl together:

> In contemplation had those three so wrought
> Upon a moment, and so stretched it out
> That they, time overthrown,
> Were dead yet flesh and bone.

So far there is much arbitrariness, and little indisputable greatness in the poem. With the third section, the meditation of Robartes upon his double vision of Phases 1 and 15, a lyrical greatness is manifested. Robartes suddenly speaks for Yeats the visionary, trapped between the inescapable determinism of the objective world, and the unattainable freedom of art, an amalgam of beauty and love as cold as the objective reality, colder perhaps as the hopeless ideal must be cold. Robartes has seen his dream-beloved, his own Helen, "who never gave the burning town a thought." He has seen an epitome of our condition, the "commonness" in Hamlet's double sense of "common," that dominates our frenzy, that is, our thought and images. His reaction is that of the lover of Romantic tradition; the complaint, the self-abnegation of kissing the stone, but the triumph also of having "after that arranged it in a song." Though no freer, he is less ignorant; he has his reward. We see in him the man of *A Vision*, who can attain knowledge of process, but no freedom from the labyrinth process makes.

14: *A Vision:*

The Great Wheel

It is possible to read *A Vision* many times over, becoming always more fascinated with it, and still to feel that Yeats went very wrong in it, that the book, with all its inventiveness and eloquence, nevertheless is not adequate to Yeats's own imagination. This feeling need not be a reaction against the mere complications of the work. Even when *A Vision*'s categories prove barren, they have a way of illuminating some odd corner of another's poetry. More germane to a reader's uneasiness may be a sense that the book is nothing if it is not wisdom literature, yet it is sometimes very unwise.

Yeats was always writing mythologies, and it may therefore be said that he was always writing some *ur*-version of *A Vision*, many years before he conceived of his mythology proper. That would make *A Vision* something of a culminating work for him, and I am afraid that it is. We must be wary of Yeats when he shows his own uneasiness by grotesque self-referential ironies in the introductory parts of the book, and even more when he has the Instructors say that they have come primarily to give him metaphors for poetry. Critics are too happy with this last evasion, as it sanctions their own escape from handling the awkward matters in Yeats, by which I refer not to the theosophy but to the inhumanity, or the calculated anti-humanism of much in the poet from at least *A Vision* on to the *Last Poems.*

One illuminating study of *A Vision,* by Helen H. Vendler, attempts to save the book by arguing that it is essentially an account of aesthetic experience, a poetics, rather than an esoteric philosophy in its own right.[1] I wish that this were true, and perhaps at moments Yeats wished it also, but it is not. *A Vision* would be a richer book if it confined itself to the life of the poetic mind, and it would have given our age another poetics to vie with the one sketched by Stevens in his essays and aphorisms, or with the more formidable poetics of Valéry. The book's most thoroughgoing defender, on its own terms, is Whitaker, who expounds it as serious and brilliant philosophy of history, albeit history as seen by a self-conscious subjective brooder, whose dialogue with history is a discipline largely for the self.[2] I think that this is to read the book as it must be read, but I dissent from the judgment. *A Vision* as a work of literary intellect compares poorly with *Zarathustra,* or even with much of Carlyle or Emerson, though it gains stature when juxtaposed with allied subjective confessions of its own age, say with Jung's *Memories, Dreams, Reflections* or with Lawrence's *Fantasia of the Unconscious.* Like those testaments, it is a polemic against the time of what Philip Rieff has called "Psychological Man," the time of Freud and the Reality Principle. *A Vision* is most heavily indebted to Blake, but it is not at all a Blakean book, *A Marriage of Heaven and Hell* for our century. Its vitalism, like all modern vitalisms since Rousseau's, is a protest against reductiveness, against the homogenizing of experience, but its dialectics are themselves reductive, and tend to diminish man.

It is of some importance to clarify a stand against *A Vision,* since it is, at the least, a beautiful book, a considerable if flawed major poem. Yeats lavished upon it, particularly in its second version, the full wealth of his Paterian rhetoric, and the book is as eloquent as *Marius the Epicurean* or *The Renaissance,* and will survive as they have survived, if not quite with the more abundant life of similar works by Browne and by Burton, to which it has been compared. The case against *A Vision* cannot be made in the name of any discursive discipline whatsoever, but only in that of Yeats's own poetic tradition, only by comparing him to his masters in vision. Critics have called *A Vision* a cosmology or an "anatomy" in genre; what matters is that it expresses itself as another language of faith, a protest against the analytic attitude. We have scores of contemporary irrationalisms, and some are more brightly colored than others, which does not make them useful or admirable. Yeats's mythology has affinities, a few deliberate, many accidental, with dank crankeries too readily available elsewhere, most massively in the arcane speculations of Jung and his cohorts. Jung is a bad Romantic poet, Yeats a great one who suffered, in *A Vision*, a failure in vision. Failures in vision can be judged, and measured, only against vision, and in what follows I measure Yeats's book against Blake's epics, its most direct ancestors, and Shelley's *Prometheus Unbound*, another forerunner. The comparison may be a touch unfair; why not against Poe's *Eureka* or Pound's *Cantos* or Graves's *The White Goddess* or Spengler, all of whom have been invoked by scholars of *A Vision*? Because Yeats never stopped writing commentaries on Blake and Shelley, is the answer, *A Vision* being one more such commentary. A better reason still is that of mere source scholarship; for all Yeats's quasi-erudition, in which his critics of the occult persuasion have followed him, the substance of *A Vision* is quarried largely out of Blake (or one should say Yeats's Blake) with a number of structural hints added from Shelley. Just as Yeats grossly exaggerated the relation of Blake and Shelley to esoteric traditions, so his followers, or rather a group thereof, have magnified Yeats's dependence on the *arcana* that constituted only another stimulus for his work. Yeats was writing a Sacred Book in *A Vision*, and if we think back to the sacred writers he names in his career we will find them primarily literary and central in their traditions— Blake, Shelley, Morris, Pater, Balzac and Nietzsche count for more in *A Vision*, and in Yeats's poetry, than do Blavatsky, Mathers, Swedenborg, Thomas Taylor, Agrippa, and the secrets of the Golden Dawn. There is, it must be acknowledged, one serious defence of Yeats's occultism, stressing not the doctrines in themselves but the experience of their psychological meanings, set forth largely in Jungian terms. This is again by Whitaker, and a critique of this defence will be a strand in the study of *A Vision* that follows.

Even analytical maps of the mind become mythologies; perhaps the Freudian mythology of ego, superego, id, libido, imago, is the only one now held in common by Psychological Man. The following table is peculiar, but may eventually simplify discussion. The Freud is there only as common mythology; all the equivalences are rough, but they will be found to work:

A Vision	*The Four Zoas*	*Prometheus Unbound*	*Freud*
Will	Urizen-Satan	Jupiter	Superego
Mask	Luvah-Orc	Bound Prometheus	Libido
Creative Mind	Urthona-Los	Unbound Prometheus	Ego
Body of Fate	Tharmas-Covering Cherub	Demogorgon	Id
Daimon	Emanation	Asia	Imago

To understand this table, we need to start with Yeats's deepest requirement of every idea, including ideas of human psychology. Yeats is a quester, and he seeks simplification through intensity. The goal is almost universally Romantic; it is Wordsworth's and Coleridge's; it is not alien to Shelley, Byron, Tennyson, even Arnold; but it does not suit Blake and Keats and Browning and Whitman, who delighted in an endless diversity of natures and phenomena, who embraced multiplicity with gusto. Though Yeats had a more ebullient temperament with every year of his long life, his ideal of the imagination always remained a Wordsworthian or Coleridgean one, and not Blakean at all. In *A Vision* the ideal is Phase 15, the full moon, where "all thought becomes an image and the soul/ Becomes a body," which is not greatly different from "that serene and blessed mood,/ in which . . . we are laid asleep/ In body, and become a living soul" and thus "see into the life of things." The point of epiphany in *A Vision* is at one with the same point in *Tintern Abbey* or *The Ancient Mariner*. Yeats too wishes to see the edge of things waver and then fade out; hopes to see the field of objects narrow into one radiant image; seeks a gleam that he recalls from the rev-

ery that sustained him at Sligo, in the pain of his awkward childhood. Ellmann records an early Shelleyan fragment, in which the
adolescent Yeats has found already the fundamental Wordsworthian epiphany, "a lake of glittering light":

> Yet thou[gh] I am cursed with immortality
> I was molden with a human nature
> With the centuries old age came on me
> And weary of flying from the wrath of nations
> I long since crossed the mountain
> Seeking some peace from the worlds throbbing
> And sought out a little fountain
> Plaining because no nymph had decked his valley
> And then I spoke to it a word of might
> And it heard the oreads language
> It spread a lake of glittering light
> Then once more I spoke that tongue
> And there rose a stately island
> Bright with the radiance of its flowers. . . .[3]

This is Yeats's first known (or anyway written) encounter
with Phase 15, where "the reverie has been sufficient of itself."
Yeats's description of Phase 15 is inspired commentary upon his
own early fragment, which he probably had forgotten: "The
being has selected, moulded and remoulded, narrowed its circle of
living, been more and more the artist, grown more and more 'distinguished' in all preference." [4] Both the poetic instance and the
abstract comment are Wordsworthian; one remembers the poet's
dream in Book V of *The Prelude,* where the fleeing Arab sees
"the waters of the deep/ Gathering upon us," but Wordsworth,
"looking backwards when he looked," saw instead "a bed of glittering light." By the light of the Yeatsian full moon, one sees
again "the visionary gleam." Probably the most Yeatsian vision in
a poem not by Yeats himself is this, in a late fragment of Coleridge:

> But that is lovely—looks like Human Time,—
> An Old Man with a steady look sublime,
> That stops his earthly task to watch the skies;

But he is blind—a Statue hath such eyes;—
Yet having moonward turn'd his face by chance,
Gazes the orb with moon-like countenance,
With scant white hairs, with foretop balk and high,
He gazes still,—his eyeless face all eye;—
As 'twere an organ full of silent sight,
His whole face seemeth to rejoice in light!
Lip touching lip, all moveless, bust and limb—
He seems to gaze at that which seems to
    gaze on him! [5]

Here a human figure leaves the realm of the human, is absorbed into Phase 15, and acquires citizenship in the world of Yeats's *Byzantium*. In Coleridge's fragment, this vision is juxtaposed to one of Limbo, which is remarkably like Yeats's Phase 1, a plastic state of what Blake called non-entity. Most simply, the opposition in Yeats between Phase 15 and 1 is the Coleridgean or Wordsworthian contrast between the Secondary, creative Imagination, and the death-in-life of the world without imagination. But this takes us to the fundamental desires of Romanticism, and to the large matter of the use of Romantic poetry.

The most admirable restraint of imagination, in our time, is to be found in the writings of Freud, who does not quest after a cure that cannot be found. He offers neither Unity of Being, nor the simplicity of the Condition of Fire. Yet he understood that poetry might be a discipline roughly parallel to psychoanalysis, one in which the poet and his reader, like the analyst and his patient, would find not cure but a balance of opposites, not ultimates beyond knowledge but self-knowledge, not a control over fate but self-control. There are a few modern poets, of the highest achievement, who have the Freudian wisdom that accepts limitation without prematurely setting limits; Stevens, I think, is the major example of this diminished but authentic Romanticism, which might be called still a possible humanism. But Yeats and Lawrence, among others, could accept no limits, any more than Blake and Shelley could. Blake, and the younger Yeats, both faced priesthoods of reason inimical to a visionary art, but the later Yeats and Lawrence did not. Philip Rieff illuminatingly says "that the notion of a man's being natively artistic is central to

Freud," [6] and insofar as the later Yeats followed Lawrence in turning against the intellectual spirit of the age, it is legitimate to wonder if the turn was necessary. It is one of Blake's advantages that we side with him against the intellectuals whom he caricatures; when Yeats rages, say in *On the Boiler* or some of the letters to Dorothy Wellesley, we turn away, or should.

Wordsworth saw himself as at least a teacher, perhaps a prophet. Blake appears to have found his prophetic vocation in his thirty-third year, when he formulated his dialectics in *The Marriage of Heaven and Hell,* and he kept to that self-recognition until he died. Shelley was an intellectual skeptic, and struggled against his own prophetic calling, but we remember the dithyrambist of the *Ode to the West Wind* and *Prometheus Unbound,* and the orator of *A Defence of Poetry* as a prophet, perhaps despite himself. *A Vision* is technically an apocalypse; that seems to me its actual genre, rather than cosmology or anatomy or aesthetic treatise. Whether Yeats generates the moral authority to match his undoubted rhetorical authority is problematic, but *A Vision* does try to pass a Last Judgment on its own age, and its own poet.

The aesthetic ideal of *A Vision* has its clearest affinities in Wordsworth and his school; Arnold would have understood the book, if he could have allowed himself to suffer through it, as he had suffered Carlyle and Ruskin. But the view of man in *A Vision* has no affinities in Wordsworthianism. Cosmology and psychology go together, and Blake was Yeats's starting point in them. Yeats's earliest prose draft of *A Vision,* in peculiar but valid sense, is Volume One, "The System," of *The Works of William Blake,* by Edwin J. Ellis and Yeats. Here, rather than in Blake's actual dialectic of the contraries, is the seed of *A Vision:*

> The mind or imagination or consciousness of man may be said to have two poles, the personal and impersonal, or, as Blake preferred to call them, the limit of contraction and the unlimited expansion. When we act from the personal we tend to bind our consciousness down as to a fiery centre. When, on the other hand, we allow our imagination to expand away from this egoistic mood, we become vehicles for the universal thought and merge in the universal mood. [7]

Here are the Yeatsian conceptions of *antithetical* and *primary,* the thrust toward individuality, and the counter-movement toward unity. This is Yeats's double gyre, the troublesome hourglass shape that tends to madden or anyway bore readers of *A Vision* who are looking for passion and insight, and sometimes find themselves staring at an empty geometry. Yeats visualizes the process of life as a double cone, moving in just one direction at a time, yet always containing the opposite direction within itself. As the directional thrust gains momentum, the counter-movement begins within it, starting from the base of the first cone and going back through it. The rotation of this double-cone produces a total circular movement, or cycle, divided by Yeats into twenty-eight phases, governed by the moon, partly because of the moon's association with sexuality and with the Romantic imagination.

Expositions of *A Vision* tend to move on rather too quickly from this starting point, frequently with the aid of diagrams that do not aid me, and I will not reproduce any of them here. Nor ought discussion ever to get too far from Yeats's starting point, if only because Yeats never got far himself. The time to question *A Vision* is at its start, with its curious assumptions, curious I mean *within* its own poetic tradition, and in its fundamental image. What precisely is Yeats trying to say about human life, and has he found an adequate image for his insight, if it is one? Though much esoteric apparatus has been imported into earlier discussions of *A Vision,* I am not aware that these questions have been met.

Yeats presents his Great Wheel or cycle of lunar phases as at least a double allegory; every individual life, and all of Western history, since for Yeats as for Emerson all knowledge reduced to biography. This allegorical image assumes a Fall, but as this Fall is neither Christian nor Romantic in Yeats, but theosophical or Gnostic, it provides certain problems in value and coherence that must be met now. Blake and Shelley both posited a Fall of Man where the more naturalistic Wordsworth and Keats did not, but their versions of the Fall are neither orthodox Christian nor Gnostic, though Yeats confounded Blake with Blavatsky and would not see the difference. For Blake and the Gnostics, as opposed to orthodoxy, the Creation and the Fall are one event. It is in meeting a fallen world, in learning how to live in history, that Blake and the Gnostics, and so Blake and Yeats part (as do Shelley and Yeats also). To Yeats, the fallen world or shadow of history contains the *daimon* of the *antithetical* or subjective man, of the poet who seeks to redeem time. So the other self, that can lead one toward Unity of Being, is both natural and temporal, and must be met by an embrace of the shadow. Yeats does not seek to exorcise the shadow by clarifying it, or by compelling it to a full manifestation of itself. This is deliberately Yeats's choice; it is the crucial moral choice that the Gnostic makes for himself. Not to see that Blake makes quite another choice from the start is not to see Blake, and makes a mockery of the life and work of a prophet who was as great a moral figure as Ezekiel or Jeremiah. To Blake the shadow or serpent was a selfhood, but not the "other" or creative self; it was the stifler or Covering Cherub, the separating or inhibiting force of nature and history, sanctified by an inadequate version of reason, and by an unjust organization of society.

The present book is a study of Yeats in relation to Romantic tradition, or as a kind of case history testing a theory of poetic influence. The emblem of that theory is the Covering Cherub, a figure in Ezekiel crucial to Blake's symbolism, and central also to Yeats's, under the more generalized metaphor of the shadow. Yeats, as was shown earlier, interpreted Blake's Covering Cherub as the "mask of created form in which the uncreated spirit makes itself visible," and thought that Blake "praises or denounces this Covering Cherub according to whether he considers it as a means whereby things, too far above us to be seen as they are, can be made visible in symbol and representative form, or as a satanic hindrance keeping our eager wills away from the freedom and truth of the Divine world. It has both aspects for every man." [8] That is good theosophical doctrine, but not Blake, for Blake never praises the Cherub any more than an orthodox Christian praises Satan. To employ a Blakean distinction made by Northrop Frye, between cyclic and dialectical symbolism, Yeats is interpreting a dialectical figure as though it were cyclic, and naturalizes an apocalyptic image, or more simply, finds the *daimonic* where Blake saw the demonic, the genuine death of the imagination. [9] This point requires laboring, for just such labor is the main concern of Blake's poetry. The Covering Cherub is not a means of redemption for Blake, any more than he was for Ezekiel, or than "the shadow of night" was for Shelley.

The argument between Yeats and Blake, or Yeats and Shelley, is of course not an argument that a critic can or should join, but the function of a critic is to demonstrate that it *is* indeed an argument. Yeats is demonstrating the way poetic influence tends to work when strong poets are involved; he is inventing his precursors. Yeats's Golden Dawn name, *Demon Est Deus Inversus,* was taken in the hope that by it "with the Divine Aid I may at length attain to be more than human, and thus gradually raise and unite myself to my Magus and Divine Genius." [10] Aside from the mumbo-jumbo aspect of this, it reminds one of Blake's stern warning, that seeking to become more than human we become less. *A Vision* is not as far away from a calculated anti-humanism as its admirers should want it to be. It is this element, a Gnostic reaching after some place on a scale-of-being that is other than human, that distinguishes Yeats's subjectivity not only from Blake's or Shelley's, but from any of the major Romantic quests for truth, from Goethe and Wordsworth through to Emerson and his American descendants. Setting aside his characteristic "vacillation" (who but Yeats could have made such a habit into a continual poetic strength?) is it perhaps time to ask whether Yeats ever sought truth at all?

A Vision is an apocalypse, and the purpose of an apocalypse is to reveal the truth, and so help stimulate a restoration of men to an unfallen state. The Gnostic poet enters the shadow in order to gain knowledge that will hasten the Judgment. In Yeats's interpretation of Blake's brief epic, *Milton,* Milton is seen as that Gnostic poet, at work redeeming his own shadow, saving a nature he had prematurely condemned. Again the interpretation is closer to Jung than to Blake, for in the poem what matters is the confrontation between Milton and the shadow, his own Satan, in which the temptation of Satan is rejected, and history is dismissed. Blake's vision of history, like Shelley's, ends in the realization that all historical conception of truth are like all doctrinal conceptions: false. Milton—Blake's Milton—learns the pragmatic spiritual wisdom that Blake knew so well; the language of faith is not that of the imagination, and the poem must not become a sacred book, the vision only of another "Church," to be drawn into the cycles of history. Blake at least was not formulating a religious psychology, as Yeats I think always was, and as Jung more explicitly did. If Yeats's symbolism is a therapeutic one, and it comes uncomfortably close to Jung by being so, then Yeats, unlike Blake, by attempting to be something more than a poet perhaps became less than one, despite the extraordinary persistence and coloring of his work.

Yeats, like Jung, and like Lawrence, found himself prophesying a hidden divinity, not the hidden God of the Christians, but what Martin Buber grimly calls the "composite god" of the historicists and Gnostics, the god of process, a dehumanizing divinity. The God of Wordsworth's Nature, the Human Form Divine of Blake, the Restored Man of Shelley—

> Man, one harmonious soul of many a soul,
> Whose nature is its own divine control,
> Where all things flow to all, as rivers to the sea. . . .

—whatever these are, they are no part of the "composite god." It is a darker Romanticism that Yeats comes to represent, and perhaps there is something Celtic, even Druidic about it. Yeats, Jung, and Lawrence were not Fascists, not at least in any merely crude way, but they help us understand why Blake's conception of "Druidism," of a universal natural religion, is a kind of prophecy of Fascism. In Blake's sense of the term, Yeats and Jung and Lawrence are all natural religionists, all founders of new mysteries, hoping to save man by teaching him the true symbolism of the irrational, the supposedly curative powers of phantasmagoria. Any deep reader of Blake now knows—thanks to the work of Damon, Frye, Erdman, and Fisher in particular—what Yeats and Lawrence never wanted to know, that Blake had no quarrel with a genuinely critical and thorough rationality (as opposed to all rationalisms). There are deep differences between Blake and Freud, but an impassable gulf divides them both from the sustained irrationalism of Yeats and Jung.

This excursus is meant to recall my earlier discussion of *Per*

Amica Silentia Lunae, and its Jungian affinities. But the Jungian analogues to Yeats's myth now must serve a very different function, the illumination of Yeats's purposes in *A Vision,* and in all of his subsequent celebrations of the *antithetical* self. The *anima mundi,* for Yeats, cannot be reached without an embrace of the shadow, without putting on Satan. But the *anima mundi,* like the collective unconscious, reveals itself only to the Gnostic adept, the alchemical poet, because its universality is a saving construct of the therapeutic idealist, of the subjectivist driven in on his own desperation. I am trying to suggest that the Romantic Imagination was a final form of Protestant inwardness, but that Yeats and Jung were not apostles of that tradition, but of a natural religiosity that is its opposite. The clearest understanding of the hypothesis of the collective unconscious that I know is to be found neither in the Jungian exegetes nor in its Freudian attackers, but in the sociologist Rieff:

> In Jung's sense, Christianity is unique only insofar as every religion is unique, each being "individuated" in its particular combination of religious images. From this special sense of uniqueness, Jung launches his argument for the essentially private character of all true religion as it erupts, paradoxically, from the collective unconscious. Although these religious images differentiate themselves from the collective unconsciousness, they are merely particular varieties of it. The collective unconscious, therefore, is the predicate of individuation. Jung's psychology of the unconscious is not, as it might appear, a version of the pietist doctrine of the inwardness of all religious feeling, irreducibly personal—and almost uncommunicable. On the contrary, the unconscious is Jung's psychologically functional equivalent of communities and, in fact, derives its content from the culture. It is in the sense of a derivation *from,* and *individuation* of the cultural community, that the unconscious is "collective." [11]

In the light of this explanation, it is possible to understand better both Yeats's flirtations with Irish Fascism, and his more lasting hope for the folk, with its attendant hatred of the half-educated.[12] Yeats's apocalypse is not a Protestant one, in the broad sense that the apocalypses of Blake and Shelley were; Yeats was neither an overt Christian, nor as deeply indebted to Christian traditions as many of his critics have thought. Yeats's "individuation" is the quest for Unity of Being, and at the end of the quest one finds neither a more human man nor God the Father, but rather an individual fantasy that precedes or hopes to precede a fantasy of the uncultured, a new natural religion. It is only in this sense that Yeats was a prophet, and we ought, all of us, to be a little less ready than we have seemed to be to take Yeats as a spiritual authority. The starting point of *A Vision* is Yeats's consciousness of man's fall into division, and his determination to restore man to unity, but even in that starting point the vision of man has diminished, and we need to ask at what price the restoration to unity is to be bought. I have tried to come full circle so far in this discussion, to return now to Yeats's opening image, his vortex, and the conception of psychological types upon which it is founded.

As a conceptual image, Yeats's double gyre has a clear Blakean source in Blake's vortex, particularly as it is employed in *Milton,* though at first the gyres and the vortex appear to deal with very different matters, Yeats's ostensibly relating to processes, and Blake's to problems in perception. But for Blake, and for Yeats, mental things were alone real, and the purely corporeal was an imposture of the rationalizers. The Great Wheel and its component gyres are movement, judgment, thought, but this is all as it is perceived, a mental reality reaching us through our relation to it. Blake's image of the vortex is perhaps his most comprehensive, as it is an identity with the apparently disparate images of the serpent or labyrinth of the natural world, or Covering Cherub, and with the cosmic egg or mundane shell that is the whole of creation. The vortex or spiral, seen from eternity, opens into mental reality; the same vortex, seen from our fallen, buried position, is the labyrinthine serpent. Similarly, Yeats's double gyre, seen from eternity, is the symbolic or cabalistic rose he had invoked throughout the 1890's. Here also, Blake uses the imaginative and the natural as contraries, and Yeats oddly, does not, though his Great Wheel of a rose is only minimally a rose.

Yeats's gyres, though he begins *A Vision*'s Book I by a reference to Empedocles's Discord and Concord, do not arise out of the

contraries, as Blake's vortex does. Blake's vortex probably began
as a Swiftian satire upon the vortices of Descartes, since nothing
could have seemed more pernicious to Blake than the Cartesian
theory of vortices, with its insistence that all motion was circular,
there being no vacuum for matter to move through. Cartesian
matter is capable of indefinite division and extensiveness, like Urizenic matter, and unlike the Minute Particulars of Blake's vision
of reality. When Blake's Milton enters his own Shadow, Blake intends us to understand that this is a purgative *descent* of the imagination, for Milton knowingly thus enters into illusion. In the
world of vision, which Milton self-sacrificingly abandons, for a
time, a perceiver is able simultaneously to be at the apex of perception and also at a distance from the object he perceives.
Blake's vortex image pictures eternal or visionary consciousness as
a whirlpool, at the center of which is every object of perception.
When the perceiver wills to move to the apex himself, as Milton
does, he objectifies himself, and the circumference he has abandoned rolls up behind him, the whirlpool of consciousness thus
being transformed into a Newtonian or Cartesian globed solidity.
Blake's vortex therefore rises out of the dialectical contraries of
the imaginative man and his Shadow or Spectre. Yeats's gyres rise
rather out of an entirely cyclic movement that he held to be present in every human consciousness, a movement of pure process,
in which subjectivity and objectivity constantly interpenetrate,
and then spin around, each within the other. Though Yeats of
course preferred always the subjective movement, whether in history or in his own consciousness, he did not overtly conceive "subjectivity" and "objectivity" as dialectical entities, in the Blakean
or any other moral sense. This was necessarily to the good, as *A
Vision* would hardly be improved by any intensification of its implicit moral judgments, but it creates a difficulty for the reader
from the start, as Yeats's "subjectivity" and "objectivity" are not
exactly what we might expect of those words. Dictionaries tell us
that "subjective" means "having its source in the mind" or "personal and individual," while "objective" means "treating of outward things or events." Though Yeats would have accepted such
definitions, who could guess that he would proceed then to employ "objective" as a synonym for "sentimental"? Or that the

"objective," re-named the *primary,* should be judged "that which serves," while the "subjective," re-named the *antithetical,* "is that which creates"? Yeats decided, as far back as we can trace him, in favor of the lunar movement toward heightened subjectivity and individuality as opposed to the solar movement toward intensified objectivity and unity with others. "Decided" is possibly misleading, as we do not choose our temperaments or even, if we are authentic, our traditions, and Yeats's temperament and tradition alike were High Romantic.

It seems clear that Yeats always tended to define life as moving either toward the lonely ecstasy of the artist or toward the communal wisdom of society. In a letter written a few months before his death, he associated the possibility of a union between ecstasy and wisdom and the idea of "true death":

> This idea of death suggests to me Blake's design (among those he did for Blair's *Grave* I think) of the soul and body embracing. All men with subjective natures move towards a possible ecstasy, all with objective natures towards a possible wisdom.[13]

The perilous and idealistic intensity of that statement is justified by the imminence of death. The same intensity is to be found in another of Yeats's starting points toward his division of souls into subjective and objective, the Preface to *Alastor,* written when Shelley, on bad medical advice, mistakenly expected death at twenty-three:

> But that Power which strikes the luminaries of the world with sudden darkness and extinction, by awakening them to too exquisite a perception of its influences, dooms to a slow and poisonous decay those meaner spirits that dare to abjure its dominion.[14]

The "luminaries," Shelley's version of the subjective, move toward the ecstasy of a self-destructive "intensity and passion," a more glorious end than "those unforeseeing multitudes who constitute . . . the lasting misery and loneliness of the world," which the objective might claim as wisdom. This is a rather fearful Either-Or, yet Shelley never mitigated it to any considerable degree in his later works. To Yeats, whose adolescence was essentially Shel-

leyan, it seemed a dialectical division that needed very little modification, particularly when he encountered it again in Browning's
essay on Shelley. His technical synonyms for Browning's subjective and objective, *antithetical* and *primary,* show a certain ruthlessness in the intensification of this division. *Antithetical* would
seem to mean "secondary" only in the sense of Coleridge's Secondary Imagination; the *primary* has a metaphysical priority, but the
antithetical is the creative principle, marked by its name as being
in direct opposition to any "objective" view of the world. One
might wish that Yeats had been clearer on this opposition, or at
least more detailed. Yeatsian "subjectivity" sometimes just means
self-consciousness, but sometimes takes on the particular flavor-
ings of esoteric tradition, as Jungian "subjectivity" does. Many
critics have noted that Jung, like Yeats, associates "objectivity"
with Christianity, and "subjectivity" with Western heterodoxy
and with Indian exaltations of the Self. Yeats and Jung have their
broad Gnosticism in common, which in itself would account for
their similarity here, but they also possess in common the rather
dubious habit of wanting to have their "subjectivity" taken both
ways, so that it is not always possible to see exactly where their
use of the term ceases to be descriptive and becomes eulogistic.
For recent readers, "subjectivity" has taken on a special status as
a value-word because of Kierkegaard, a peculiar irony since Kierkegaard, from a Yeatsian viewpoint, is a major monument of
Christian "objectivity."

What terms ought Yeats to have used? Not "aesthetic" and
"natural," as some critics of *A Vision* have suggested, since that
would confine the area into which the book ventures, and not the
Blakean "visionary" and "corporeal," since Yeats was given to deliberate (and poetically fruitful) "vacillation" in all questions of
epistemology. "Imaginative" and "reductive" might have done as
well as any terms, but are less metaphorical and certainly less interesting than *antithetical* and *primary.* Wallace Stevens, in his
version of this Romantic dialectic, uses the re-imagining of the
First Idea or spring vision, as against the intolerable First Idea itself, or winter vision, but Stevens had both the poetic advantage
and personal burden of his humane gloom, the Freudian naturalism of *The Auroras of Autumn* and *The Rock.* Yeats's superna-

turalism was thoroughgoing enough to demand and perhaps even sustain the proud force inherent in the loaded term *antithetical*.

A Vision might be a more moving and intrinsically valuable book if Yeats had allowed its dialectic to be a truly open one, if it really were a dialogue between his *antithetical* Self and his *primary* Soul, if the questing Oisin were still to be disputed by the aggressively Christian Patrick. But *A Vision* has the temper of Gnostic apocalypse, and something long thwarted or partly thwarted in Yeats insists upon getting its whole way at last in this treatise. *Per Amica Silentia Lunae* has a balance that *A Vision* willingly forsakes, except in a few remarkably insightful passages, particularly in the glimpses of Heracles that we are allowed. These glimpses, as several critics have remarked, reveal to us a purely imaginative hope that most of *A Vision* lacks, or is too impatient to propound.[15] Yeats, in the "Dedication" to the book's first printed version, connects his purpose to the "practical object" that first led him to arcane systems: "I wished for a system of thought that would leave my imagination free to create as it chose and yet make all that it created, or could create, part of the one history, and that the soul's." [16] This is a difficult statement, if we are to take *A Vision* (as Yeats asks us to) as indeed being such a system. Yeats credited the Greeks, and Dante, as having enjoyed a system in this sense. Evidently, Yeats meant a coherent body of ideas that gave an adequate account of all psychic and historical complexities. Blake was the first and perhaps still is the only poet who did this for himself, despite the many attempts since. Blake had conceptual powers unique among the poets, and Yeats did not.

Yeats in *Vision* A, explained the Four Faculties or psychic components in every man, rather more clearly than he does in *Vision* B. The systematic mythology of *A Vision* depends upon the two Tinctures (as Yeats called his contraries of *antithetical* and *primary*) and the Four Faculties of Will, Creative Mind, Body of Fate, and Mask:

> By *Will* is understood feeling that has not become desire because there is no object to desire; a bias by which the soul is classified and its phase fixed but which as yet is without result in action; an

energy as yet uninfluenced by thought, action, or emotion; the first matter of a certain personality—choice. If a man's *Will* is at say Phase 17 we say that he is a man of Phase 17, and so on. By *Mask* is understood the image of what we wish to become, or of that to which we give our reverence. Under certain circumstances it is called the Image. By *Creative Mind* is meant intellect, as intellect was understood before the close of the seventeenth century—all the mind that is consciously constructive. By *Body of Fate* is understood the physical and mental environment, the changing human body, the stream of Phenomena as this affects a particular individual, all that is forced upon us from without, Time as it affects sensation.[17]

We do well to examine this paragraph with a polite skepticism as to the charged terms Yeats has employed. Will and Mask are *antithetical* terms; Creative Mind and Body of Fate are *primary*. Will is described by Yeats as though it were the purest potential of energy, to become desire when an object is encountered. Yet Yeats does mean "will," and even roughly what Freud called "superego." Yeats's Instructors called the Will the Ego, but Yeats helpfully explains the confusion in terms:

> I have changed the "creative genius" of the Documents into *Creative Mind* to avoid confusion between "genius" and *Daimon;* and "Ego" into *Will* for "Ego" suggests the total man who is all *Four Faculties. Will* or self-will was the only word I could find not for man but Man's root. If Blake had not given "selfhood" a special meaning it might have served my turn.[18]

Yeats means that his Will is Blake's Urizen, but not necessarily in Urizen's fallen form of the Selfhood or Satan. In *Vision* B, the Will is reduced almost to Blake's Spectre of Urthona, the mundane anxiety of the Selfhood as worker:

> The *Will* is very much the Will described by Croce, when not affected by the other *Faculties* it has neither emotion, morality nor intellectual interest, but knows how things are done, how windows open and shut, how roads are crossed, everything that we call utility. It seeks its own continuance. Only by the pursuit or acceptance of its direct opposite, that object of desire or moral ideal

which is of all possible things the most difficult, and by forcing that form upon the *Body of Fate,* can it attain self-knowledge and expression.[19]

This last sentence is excellent paraphrase of Blake's *The Four Zoas.* What emerges from the complexity of Yeats's hesitations on the Will is his characteristic "vacillation" between Blakean and Gnostic versions of the Selfhood (or Spectre, or Shadow of Desire). Yeats wants his Will (and his other Faculties) to be both cyclical and dialectical as an entity, wants to compound the "normal ego" and the superego, so that a more human potential in every man, and a mere temporal anxiety that mocks the potential, can scarcely be separated. That *A Vision* (and Yeats's subsequent poetry) should show this compounding is probably a dramatic gain, but again at the expense of clarity.

The man of every phase of *A Vision* is an *antithetical* quester, despite the provision made for objective men by Yeats's system. We are governed, in every way that mattered passionately to Yeats, by the *antithetical* faculties of Will and Mask, the superego and the libido. It is as though *Prometheus Unbound* were to be only the barren and bitter struggle of Jupiter and the bound Prometheus, as though *The Four Zoas* were to be the record only of Fall, the cyclic struggle of Urizen-Satan and Luvah-Orc. The primary faculties do not move Yeats's imagination; *Vision* A makes Creative Mind "all the mind that is consciously constructive," excluding the shaping spirit of imagination, and the Body of Fate only "all that is forced upon us from without, Time as it affects sensation." In the more guarded definitions of *Vision* B, the same preferences are revealed:

It will be enough until I have explained the geometrical diagrams in detail to describe *Will* and *Mask* as the will and its object, or the Is and the Ought (or that which should be), *Creative Mind* and *Body of Fate* as thought and its object, or the Knower and the Known, and to say that the first two are lunar or *antithetical* or natural, the second two solar or *primary* or reasonable. A particular man is classified according to the place of *Will,* or choice, in the diagram. At first sight there are only two *Faculties,* because only two of the four, *Will* and *Creative Mind,* are active, but it will be presently seen that the Faculties can be represented by two opposing cones so drawn that the Will of the one is the Mask of the other, the *Creative Mind* of the one the *Body of Fate* of the other. Everything that wills can be desired, resisted or accepted, every creative act can be seen as fact, every *Faculty* is alternately shield and sword.[20]

One way of understanding this is to observe how the equivalents are fleshed out by Blake and Shelley in *The Four Zoas* and *Prometheus Unbound,* since Yeats uses his system only in lyrics or short plays. In Blake, the conceptualizing Urizen is the Will and the rebellious Orc (fallen form of Luvah, the Zoa of passion) the anti-will, or Mask, while Los takes up the work of Creative Mind and the chaotic, torn former integral being, Tharmas, constitutes the Body of Fate. The story of the epic, *The Four Zoas,* is a dialectical one in which the two contrary movements—further Fall and the struggle toward apocalypse are constantly in process. The *antithetical* figures, Urizen and Luvah-Orc, bring about the Fall into division; the *primary* figures, Los and Tharmas, at length compel a Last Judgment to begin. In Shelley, again it is the Will and the Mask, Jupiter and Prometheus Bound, who cause the Fall; it is a transformed, unbound Prometheus who becomes Creative Mind, and with the instrumentality of the shapeless Demogorgon, Body of Fate, moves to apocalypse.

Both *The Four Zoas* and *Prometheus Unbound* reach their resolutions by way of a renunciation, for each poem undergoes a transformation from one kind of quest to another, from Promethean or Orcean quest to a more mature and inward struggle. The questing libido and the censorious superego cease to be at the center of struggle; the ego, at strife with itself, and allied with a new version of the id, becomes crucial. Yeats's myth, in *A Vision,* stays at the *antithetical* or Promethean level, and avoids this later struggle between *primary* forces. One thinks back to *Per Amica Silentia Lunae* (from which Yeats said his Instructors took the term *antithetical*); there the *antithetical* is "the anti-self," and the Mask or Promethean image comes out of baffled quest only:

The poet finds and makes his mask in disappointment, the hero in defeat. The desire that is satisfied is not a great desire, nor has the shoulder used all its might that an unbreakable gate has never strained. The saint alone is not deceived, neither thrusting with his shoulder nor holding out unsatisfied hands . . . For a hero loves the world till it breaks him, and the poet till it has broken faith. . . .[21]

Yeats, and his whole individuality is in this preference, makes his system for the poet and hero, and begins by predicating their defeat. Beyond Promethean quest, for him, there is only the cyclic renewal of quest, and the renewed necessity for heroic defeat. *A Vision* exists to pattern the drama of defeat, for its apocalypse is the hopeless judgment of gnosis. In *Vision* A, Yeats described the "Drama of the Faculties" in a passage blurred in *Vision* B:

One can describe *antithetical* man by comparing him to the *Commedia del Arte* or improvised drama of Italy. The stage manager having chosen his actor, the *Will,* chooses for this actor, that he may display him the better, a scenario, *Body of Fate,* which offers to his *Creative Mind* the greatest possible difficulty that it can face without despair, and in which he must play a role and wear a *Mask* as unlike as possible to his natural character (or *Will*) and leaves him to improvise, through *Creative Mind,* the dialogue and the details of the plot. He must discover a being which only exists with extreme effort, when his muscles are as it were all taut and all his energies active, and for that reason the Mask is described as "a form created by passion to unite us to ourselves." [22]

The problem is precisely to define that being which the *antithetical* man must discover. But, badly as either version of *A Vision* does at such definition, Yeats has emphasized that only *antithetical* man can quest after completeness. His quest will take disturbing forms, as Yeats acknowledges in a revealing section called "Discords, Oppositions and Contrasts," where "deception" is made a synonym for "desire," and it is made clear that the best we can hope for is "to come to a double contemplation, that of the chosen Image, that of the fated Image." Not the achievement of quest matters, but the questing; one remembers Yeats's beautiful sentence about Spenser, the ancestor of internalized or High

Romantic quest: "Deafened and blinded by their [Ariosto's and Tasso's] influence, as so many of us were in boyhood by that art of Hugo that made the old simple writers seem but as brown bread and water, he was always to love the journey more than its end, the landscape more than the man, and reason more than life, and the tale less than its telling." [23] The *antithetical* man, like Spenser, loves the journey more than its end, for its end is the equivocal double contemplation of the Image. Here we encounter the darkest yet most vital of *A Vision*'s complexities, the relation, within the Image of desire, between Mask and *daimon*, and we need to pause before we proceed to the lesser complexity of the Great Wheel, or complete cycle of phases of the moon that the interlocking gyres combine to form. More than exegesis of *A Vision* is involved, for the mythology of this relation is Yeats's version of the Oedipus Complex, of the encounter between libido and imago, or in Shelley's terms, Prometheus and Asia, or Blake's, Orc and Enitharmon. *A Vision* never gets far from the peculiar burden that Romantic love created for Romantic poetry, the burden of the right relation between poet and Muse. In *Vision* B, the *Faculties* are defined in terms of each man's *daimon*, and are thus further internalized:

> The *Four Faculties* are not the abstract categories of philosophy, being the result of the four memories of the *Daimon* or ultimate self of that man. His *Body of Fate*, the series of events forced on him from without, is shaped out of the *Daimon's* memory of the events of his past incarnations; his *Mask* or object of desire or idea of the good, out of its memory of the moments of exaltation in his past lives; his *Will* or normal ego out of its memory of all the events of his present life, whether consciously remembered or not; his *Creative Mind* from its memory of ideas—or universals—displayed by actual men in past lives, or their spirits between lives.[24]

It is difficult, even with the aid of *Per Amica Silentia Lunae* and *Vision* A, to give an accurate description of Yeats's myth of the *daimon*, for Yeats had the subtle conviction that relations with one's Muse are most fruitful when deliberately equivocal. Pragmatically, as a working poet, he seems to have been right, and in modern warfare between poet and Muse Yeats is the largest single victor (a comparison with Graves or Auden is instructive). Here at least Yeats was the fortunate inheritor of High Romantic tradition, particularly of the heroic struggles with the Muse throughout Blake's work, and in the testaments of Keats and Shelley, *The Fall of Hyperion* and *The Triumph of Life*. The closest ancestors of Yeats's *daimon* are the Emanations of Blake, the Epipsyche of Shelley, and the progression of Muse-figures in Keats, from the moon-goddess of *Endymion* through to Lamia and Moneta. There are no suggestions in Shelley that the Muse herself is destructive until the poet's last work, though in *Adonais* the inability of the Muse to aid her son and lover is stressed. But in the equivocal "Shape all light" of *The Triumph of Life* Shelley at last attained a vision of the Muse (in a bitter sense, Wordsworthian Nature) as destroyer:

> And still her feet, no less than the sweet tune
> To which they moved, seemed as they moved, to blot
> The thoughts of him who gazed on them, & soon
>
> All that was seemed as if it had been not,
> As if the gazer's mind was strewn beneath
> Her feet like embers, & she, thought by thought,
>
> Trampled its fires into the dust of death. . . .

Keats's encounters with the *daimon* had always their equivocal element, which is intensified in *Lamia* and attains a climax in the menacing harshness of Moneta in *The Fall of Hyperion*. Blake's distrust of the Muse is without rival among the poets; he does not invoke her without chastising her, and his various accounts of the relation between poet and Muse, Los and Enitharmon, culminate in the fearful internal warfare of *Jerusalem*. Something of a Blakean pattern I have traced already, in earlier chapters, in Yeats's love poems, from his beginnings through *The Wild Swans at Coole*. But Yeats's doctrine of the Muse attained its first full statement in the *daimon* of *Per Amica Silentia Lunae*. The *daimon* at first in *Per Amica* is spoken of as though it can be of the same sex as the poet, but a note written (or dated) February 1924 distinguishes between the impermanent *daimon*, who may be an illustrious dead man, and the permanent, presumably always of the opposite sex, and promises more on the matter in *A Vision*.[25] Yeats wrongly believed that Blake had founded sexual love on spiritual hate, evidently basing this doctrine on some remarks by Blake that Crabb Robinson characteristically garbled.[26] Yeats's obsession with *The Mental Traveller*, reflected throughout *A Vision*, was based on the reading-in of this doctrine into the poem's opening stanzas. In *Per Amica* the doctrine is stated boldly, saving itself from palpable nonsense by great eloquence:

> When I think of life as a struggle with the Daimon who would ever set us to the hardest work among those not impossible, I understand why there is a deep enmity between a man and his destiny, and why a man loves nothing but his destiny. In an Anglo-Saxon poem a certain man is called, as though to call him something that summed up all heroism, "Doom eager." I am persuaded that the Daimon delivers and deceives us, and that he wove that netting from the stars and threw the net from his shoulder. Then my imagination runs from Daimon to sweetheart, and I divine an analogy that evades the intellect. I remember that Greek antiquity has bid us look for the principal stars, that govern enemy and sweetheart alike, among those that are about to set, in the Seventh House as the astrologers say; and that it may be "sexual love," which is "founded upon spiritual hate," is an image of the warfare of man and Daimon; and I even wonder if there may not be some secret communion, some whispering in the dark between Daimon and sweetheart. I remember how often women when in love grow superstitious, and believe that they can bring their lovers good luck; and I remember an old Irish story of three young men who went seeking for help in battle into the house of the gods at Slieve-na-mon. "You must first be married," some god told them, "because a man's good or evil luck comes to him through a woman." [27]

There is too little emphasis on this fascinating relationship in *Vision* B. In *Vision* A, there is a remarkable section, called "The Daimon, the Sexes, Unity of Being, Natural and Supernatural Unity," which fully develops *Per Amica*'s doctrine of the *daimon* as Muse. In *Per Amica* the *daimon* is a taskmaster, who sets the poet and hero the goals of their quests, delivering them from inconsequence, but deceiving them as to their doom. The deliverance and the destiny can come only through sexual love, through an alliance of *daimon* and beloved. But in *Vision* A, the alliance is much more pungently stated as an actual identity:

> Man's *Daimon* has therefore her energy and bias, in man's *Mask*, and her constructive power in man's fate, and man and *Daimon* face each other in a perpetual conflict or embrace. This relation (the *Daimon* being of the opposite sex to that of man) may create a passion like that of sexual love. The relation of man and woman, in so far as it is passionate, reproduces the relation of man and *Daimon*, and becomes an element where man and *Daimon* sport, pursue one another, and do one another good or evil. This does not mean, however, that the men and women of opposite phases love one another, for a man generally chooses a woman whose *Mask* falls between his *Mask* and his *Body of Fate*, or just outside one or other; but that every man is, in the right of his sex, a wheel, or group of *Four Faculties*, and that every woman is, in the right of her sex, a wheel which reverses the masculine wheel. In so far as man and woman are swayed by their sex they interact as man and *Daimon* interact, though at other moments their phases may be side by side. The *Daimon* carries on her conflict, or friendship with a man, not only through the events of life, but in the mind itself, for she is in possession of the entire dark of the mind.[28]

It follows, from this remarkable passage, that a man's dreams and inspirations are the expressions of his *daimon*'s energy, and that he must not struggle against this dark energy if he hopes to attain Yeats's lifelong goal, Unity of Being. The *antithetical* quester must be content to exhaust himself in a struggle with his destiny, in the knowledge that he can never win, that his fate must be his only freedom. At Phase 17 on the Great Wheel of incarnations, Yeats's phase as we will see, Unity of Being is most possible, as there the *daimon* is most *primary*. But to be a man and poet of Phase 17 is to have Yeats's version of the tragic sense of life, for one must lose the women one loves, confronted always as one is by a recalcitrant Muse.

With this notion of the tragedy of an individual fate, we reach the most famous and readable part of *A Vision*, the commentary

on the Great Wheel and its twenty-eight Incarnations, or Embodi-
ments as Yeats first called them. There are of course only twenty-
six Incarnations, since Phases 1 and 15 are not human. Though
Yeats left Phase 1 for last, after Phase 28, I propose to discuss it
first here and then go on to a discussion of the opposing Phase 15.
From there the discussion passes to the phases clustered around
15, concentrating on 17, the phase of Yeats, Shelley, and Dante,
and only then will we come to the scheme of the whole sequence
of phases. My procedure is not so arbitrary as it may seem; Yeats
was repelled by Phase 1, fascinated by 15, 17, and 23 (the phase
of Synge), but interested in the other phases largely because of
their relationship to the crucial ones.

The irony of Phase 1 being the state of pure objectivity is that
no description of it is possible "except complete plasticity," as
Yeats remarks. There is no Will: "Thought and inclination, fact
and object of desire, are indistinguishable (Mask is submerged in
Body of Fate, Will in Creative Mind), that is to say, there is complete passivity, complete plasticity." What is Yeats talking about?
His critics tend to let Phase 1 alone, and certainly it is not a particularly attractive sort of a Limbo. But it has its aesthetic power:

> Under blank eyes and fingers never still
> The particular is pounded till it is man.
> When had I my own will?
> O not since life began.

Of this mysterious condition, the dark of the moon, we can
surmise the following. It is raw material for any supernatural
agency to work upon, and so will respond to any energy that cares
to choose it for object. This is Yeats's womb of nature, strikingly
unlike the dialectical equivalents in Dante, Milton, Blake, because it is morally unallied. It is not wholly unlike Spenser's vision of substance in the Gardens of Adonis, and it has an affinity
also with the material world in Shelley's *Adonais,* particularly
with Shelley's vision of a recalcitrant dross that vainly tries to resist the One Spirit's plastic stress, as the Spirit sweeps through the
dull dense world.

Of Phase 1, Yeats remarks that "there may be great joy; but it is the joy of a conscious plasticity." It ought to be said, for the benefit of readers who can discover Yeats to have been, in some sense, a Christian poet, that Phase 1 clearly is the realm of those who have succeeded utterly in surrendering their wills to the Will of God, and have become what Yeats, in the last word of Book I of *A Vision,* calls "automatic." Of these automatic beings, Robartes cruelly sang in *The Phases of the Moon:*

> Because all dark, like those that are all light,
> They are cast beyond the verge, and in a cloud,
> Crying to one another like the bats;
> But having no desire they cannot tell
> What's good or bad, or what it is to triumph
> At the perfection of one's own obedience;
> And yet they speak what's blown into the mind;
> Deformed beyond deformity, unformed,
> Insipid as the dough before it is baked,
> They change their bodies at a word.

The language here is that of Blakean intellectual satire, as directed against the denizens of an orthodox Heaven that to Blake was only a Selfhood-communion in Ulro, home of Ultimate Error, of a paradoxically will-less solipsism. Yeats too is not grotesque without satirical purpose; the ultimate goal of objective, sentimental, Christian, democratic, nineteenth-century-humanist man is to be so much communal dough for the kneading "that it can take what form cook Nature fancies." Phase 1 is a supernatural state but, if we are to credit Yeats, it is the goal to which the ideals of our debased culture are leading us, a Limbo or abyss of mass servitude and insipidity. To quarrel with Yeats as visionary satirist here is not a critic's privilege, but we should be clear that what he thus condemns must include the larger part of our supposed values. His vision of the sentimental Hell to which a liberal and Christian humanism leads is a barbaric one, but it has the force and persuasiveness of genuine passion.

At the risk of battering the gates of the commonplace, I will expatiate upon this vision, particularly in contrast to the saving vision of supernatural subjectivity, Phase 15. For Yeats's apparent esotericism tends to shield his critics from making finely obvious just what he is doing. The contrast between Phases 1 and 15 is Yeats's only genuine dialectical distinction in the whole of *A Vision;* the other distinctions are merely cyclic. The preference for Phase 15 over Phase 1, so depicted by Yeats that it is an outrageously necessary preference, is a more extreme polemic against everything that is not art than can be found anywhere else in British Romantic tradition. To find anything like its equivalent, we would have to go to the most extreme gestures of French Symbolist tradition, seeking out those few figures who do not save their polemics against all reality principles by some degree of irony or 'Pataphysical wit. Yeats's genuine occultism and Gnosticism is involved in his polemic here, and clearly distinguishes his dialectic from Blake's, which superficially it resembles. For Yeats's Phase 15 is not Blake's Eden, any more than his Byzantium is Blake's Golgonooza or City of Art. The phase of the Full Moon belongs to Blake's Beulah with its dream of indefinitely prolonged forms of love and beauty, a dream that Yeats of course, like Blake, knows to be illusive. But Yeats, as a poet of Phase 17, accepts the tragedy of loss as his Last Judgment, where Blake does not. Yeats is thus armored against all that is not poetry, including everything in existence that claims a value without possessing an intrinsic beauty. There is a terrible if obscure eloquence in the concluding passage of Yeats's description of Phase 15, an eloquence many of Yeats's admirers might give themselves to pondering:

> Where the being has lived out of phase, seeking to live through *antithetical* phases as though they had been *primary,* there is now terror of solitude, its forced, painful and slow acceptance, and a life haunted by terrible dreams. Even for the most perfect, there is a time of pain, a passage through a vision, where evil reveals itself in its final meaning. In this passage Christ, it is said, mourned over the length of time and the unworthiness of man's lot to man, whereas his forerunner mourned and his successor will mourn over the shortness of time and the unworthiness of man to his lot; but this cannot yet be understood.[29]

The *antithetical* forerunner here I take to be Oedipus, while the successor is whatever hero will attempt to overcome the Sphinx, to assert the primacy of Personality over Nature, in the dark New Age of our time to come. Perhaps, as Yeats says, this cannot yet be understood, but he gives us enough clues for a provisional understanding, when we examine closely his account of Phase 15. There is, to cite *Byzantium,* a state of death-in-life or life-in-death in Phase 15, the vacillation in deciding between the two being again customary in Yeats. Since, in Phase 15, we find "Body and soul cast out and cast away/ Beyond the visible world," a kind of dying must take place, either art or the phenomenal world yielding to the other, and it is the world that yields. This is, of course, a very extreme view, and needs to be distinguished from both earlier and contemporary Romantic accounts of the relation between imagination and nature.

The radical instance of this opposition between *antithetical* image and *primary* phenomenon is given by Yeats in the letter to Ezra Pound that helps to introduce *A Vision:*

> I send you the introduction of a book which will, when finished, proclaim a new divinity. Oedipus lay upon the earth at the middle point between four sacred objects, was there washed as the dead are washed, and thereupon passed with Theseus to the wood's heart until amidst the sound of thunder earth opened, "riven by love," and he sank down soul and body into the earth. I would have him balance Christ who, crucified standing up, went into the abstract sky soul and body. . . .[30]

The image of Christ going up into the abstract sky, there to become Jehovah-Urizen, is Blakean; the preference for the savior who descends into the earth is also Romantic, and has its analogues in Shelley and Keats as well as Blake. The "new divinity" proclaimed by *A Vision* is that unnamed "successor" to Christ who is prophesied at the close of the account of Phase 15. Oedipus is the poetic Image dreamed by the *daimonic* Will, but Christ is natural, and suffers the purgation that the natural, even in its best aspect, must undergo when it meets the Image of complete beauty. Phase 15 is a supernatural one, and yet is incarnated in the fictive hero Oedipus, more than in any other single figure, Oedipus being at once a God, a poetic hero, the supreme instance of tragedy, the greatest single *antithetical* quester through gnosis and finally, quite neatly, a splendid embodiment of Yeats's own obsessive relation to his natural father, the painter John Butler Yeats. There is a difficult sense in which Yeats identified his own quest with that of Oedipus, whom he praises because he chose to know "nothing but his mind, and yet because he spoke that mind fate possessed it and kingdoms changed according to his blessing and his cursing. Delphi, that rock at earth's navel, spoke through him, and though men shuddered and drove him away they spoke of ancient poetry. . . ." [31] There are no references to Freud in Yeats (though he is reported to have talked about Freud and the relation of the unconscious to art in 1916), and one can only wonder how aware the poet was of the reductive pattern involved in his choice of Oedipus as hero.[32] Ellmann has demonstrated the complexity of the relation between Yeats and his father, and the depth of the intellectual influence John Butler Yeats had on the poet's quest for Unity of Being, which indeed was a concept first formed by the father.[33] To the poet, Oedipus was Greek or Western Man, emancipated from Asiatic formlessness and servility, but also emancipated from his immediate forebears by virtue of his godhood. But, though like Christ a Son of God, Yeats's Oedipus need not suffer the purgation oddly attendant upon Phase 15, as Christ must. What Christ needs to purge is his compassion, a *primary* flaw from which Oedipus, like Yeats, is free. Yeats wants a Byzantine Christ, free of humanity, capable of perfect absorption into Phase 15, a God of art. The aesthetic reverie, for Yeats, transcends contemplation, and purges away the whole of the natural man. That, so far as I can understand it, is why there is a purgatory just beyond Yeats's earthly paradise, rather than just before it, as in Dante. The pattern here is like that in Keats and Shelley again, as in the structure of *The Fall of Hyperion* and *The Triumph of Life*. The pattern matters most in each poet's vision of sexual love, and returns us, in Yeats, to the problematic relations between poet and *daimon*.

Yeats does not intend Phase 15 to be a description of the state-of-being of a work of art, or of a more perfect sexual intercourse than we know in nature, or of death-in-life or life in or after death. All of these are analogues to Phase 15, and are invoked or implied in *Byzantium,* which is Yeats's great poem of Phase 15, but the phase itself alas is occult, and its account of a transformed or magical body undoubtedly owes something to Swedenborg and something even to the Rosicrucian obfuscations of the Order of the Golden Dawn. It is really fit stuff for Yeats's spooks to have instructed him in, and difficult to accept as being after all what it is, the center and repository of value in Yeats's system. What, in imaginative or human terms, does it come to, what can it show us? And is it indeed, as Yeats insisted, the goal of his quest, his own version of the use and end of Romantic art, of the redemptive and compensatory imagination? The devoted reader of Yeats must come to some answer to these questions, when he ponders this crucial passage, for it is the heart of Yeats's "official philosophy":

> Now contemplation and desire, united into one, inhabit a world where every beloved image has bodily form, and every bodily form is loved. This love knows nothing of desire, for desire implies effort, and though there is still separation from the loved object, love accepts the separation as necessary to it own existence. *Fate* is known for the boundary that gives our *Destiny* its form, and—as we can desire nothing outside that form—as an expression of our freedom. Chance and Choice have become interchangeable without losing their identity. As all effort has ceased, all thought has become image, because no thought could exist if it were not carried towards its own extinction, amid fear or in contemplation; and every image is separate from every other, for if image were linked to image, the soul would awake from its immovable trance. All that the being has experienced as thought is visible to its eyes as a whole, and in this way it perceives, not as they are to others, but according to its own perception, all orders of existence. Its own body possesses the greatest possible beauty, being indeed that body which the soul will permanently inhabit, when all its phases have been repeated according to the number allotted: that which we call the clarified or Celestial Body.[34]

The first sentence here appears to be an exemplification of Freud's essay on the relation of poetry to day-dreaming, but the difficult second sentence removes the first from the realm of wish-fulfillment or what Blake would have called the Beulah-couch of repose. Yeats was grounded in Blake well enough to insist on disjunctiveness even in his paradise. The Blakean dialectic of Prolific and Devourer, with its insistence on a bounding outline (the Devourer) lest the exuberant Prolific expire in an excess of its own delights, is behind the next sentence, which leads on to the subsequent points emphasizing the coalescence of the object-world into "all orders of existence." There remains the transformed subject or perceiver, and one expects to learn something important about the relation of the poet and lover and hero to their own visions, to poem and beloved and goal of quest. Admittedly the relation, which amounts to the stance of the poet before his own beloved and achieved fiction, is a difficult one to convey, and Romantic poets from Wordsworth to Stevens verge dangerously near to an apparent exaltation of solipsism when they attempt to show the freedom they have found. But that is the burden of the dialectic of love in any Romantic poet; his final obligation to us is somehow to demonstrate that he can make all things new, and then marry what he has made. He goes to this marriage not as he was or is but as what he will be, or always is about to be; as bridegroom he offers what Wordsworth calls "possible sublimity." There are poems by Yeats in which he mounts to these heights; *A Vision,* at its cynosure, falls short of them. Whatever "the clarified or Celestial Body" is (not being a Rosicrucian adept, I do not know what it is), we want and need something quite different at the center of *A Vision.* When Blake speaks of a Risen Body, brought about through an improvement of sensual enjoyment, we can discover what he means, both imaginatively and reductively. But Yeats's Celestial Body (as likely derived from the *Seraphita* of Balzac as anywhere else) is opaque both as image and as concept.

Yeats is closer to *A Vision*'s real center in his extraordinary description of Phase 17, his own phase and Shelley's, and perhaps equally illuminating in his account of Phase 16, Blake's. In certain respects, we can take these phases as being representative of all twenty-six of the human Incarnations in *A Vision,* and by studying them can hope to discover what matters most about the other phases as well. What matters least is all the technical material, such as the rules for discovering True and False Masks, Creative Mind, and so on, as these are both arbitrary and inconsistent. About the only rules worth remembering in *A Vision* are that one is placed by the phase of one's Will, and that one's Mask, being in direct opposition, is always fourteen phases removed from the phase of the Will. Creative Mind and Body of Fate are necessarily fourteen phases apart also, as oppositions. Since Will and Creative Mind are on different quests in Yeats, they *move* in opposite directions always, but can never be in direct opposition. Yeats distinguishes two directional thrusts in his spinning wheel or hour-glass, toward Nature from Phases 1 to 15, and toward God from Phases 15 back to one. But "toward God" is a rather misleading phrase, unless one accepts a Gnostic Godhead, as the phases after Phase 23 make clear, since in them "when the individual intellect lingers on, it is arrogance, self-assertion, a sterile abstraction, for the being is forced by the growing *primary tincture* to accept first the service of, and later an absorption in, the *primary* Whole, a sensual or supersensual objectivity." [35] The goal of this absorption we have seen already, in the supernatural but also sub-human degradation of the dough-like plasticity of Phase 1. One of the really profound insights of *A Vision* follows on Yeats's realization that this "service" is an abnegation:

> When the old *antithetical* becomes the new *primary,* moral feeling is changed into an organisation of experience which must in its turn seek a unity, the whole of experience. When the old *primary* becomes the new *antithetical,* the old realisation of an objective moral law is changed into a subconscious turbulent instinct. The world of rigid custom and law is broken up by "the uncontrollable mystery upon the bestial floor." [36]

The use of the last line of *The Magi* relates this passage to Yeats's obsessive theme of Annunciation, which is the underlying myth of *A Vision.* What the passage makes clear is that *both* movements, toward God or toward Nature, lead away from moral feeling and moral law. Both movements are Gnostic (with Jung again providing the most accurate analogue) in that they are founded upon a more radical moral dualism than Christianity could ever sanction. Both of the winding paths in his gyres lead, for Yeats, to a supernatural salvation that devalues all human existence. Here also his system was inadequate to the dialectical resources of Yeats's own poetic mind, and critics have been accurate in generally agreeing that the late poems are more imaginative and more humanly relevant than *A Vision*.

The personal as opposed to the structural center of *A Vision* is Phase 17 rather than 15, and Yeats's imagination asserts itself always when he is most personal. The man of Phase 17 is called "the *Daimonic* man" because his Will only is in position to express *daimonic* thought directly; he only can hope to attain Unity of Being. The Mask he seeks, in its authentic form, Yeats calls "Simplification through intensity," leading on to the Simplicity or Condition of Fire. But this True Mask must rise out of the Body of Fate of "Loss," even as libido rises out of id. In Wordsworthian and Coleridgean terms, which are immensely relevant here, the poet's Imagination is Compensatory, a saving and simplifying gain rising out of experiential loss. But out of loss rises also the parody of simplification through intensity, which Yeats calls "Dispersal," the ultimate fate of the Romantic Imagination. The Mask of the *daimonic* Will is from Phase 3, where we find not so much a man as the pastoral image of Romanticism, natural man open to seasonal delight and without the nostalgia for permanence, living in Blake's pulsation of an artery or "eternity's sunrise":

> Seen by lyrical poets, of whom so many have belonged to the fantastic Phase 17, the man of this phase becomes an Image where simplicity and intensity are united, he seems to move among yellowing corn or under overhanging grapes. He gave to Landor his shepherds and hamadryads, to Morris his *Water of the Wondrous Isles,* to Shelley his wandering lovers and sages, and to Theocritus all his flocks and pastures; and of what else did Bembo think when he cried, "Would that I were a shepherd that I might look daily down upon Urbino"? Imagined in some *antithetical* mind, seasonal change and bodily sanity seem images of lasting passion and the body's beauty.[37]

This is the Yeats who is legitimately the last High Romantic, the poet in his humane greatness, who sets all our reservations aside and helps us to live our lives. The passage, in its thought and coloring, joins itself to everything finest in Yeats, and to the tradition Yeats pioneered in understanding, the Romantic pastoralism of Landor, Shelley, Blake, Palmer, Calvert, Keats, and Morris, the poets and painters of the lower Paradise, in its internal-ized Romance phase. Yeats's true Mask, like Shelley's, is the Image of solitary wisdom in a natural context, either the wandering lover who is the Poet of *Alastor,* or the sage Ahasuerus of *Hellas.* This Image is the simplification through intensity of a manifold of images, of everything in pastoral romance that is a vision of Innocence, of change without decay and the body's wisdom.

The false or dispersed Image dominates poems like *Adonais* or *The Triumph of Life,* on this view, where seasonal change is emblematic of the death of human love and bodily beauty is only a mask that process strips off, to reveal the transience of passion and the insanity of the body. The Creative Mind of the *daimonic* Man of Phase 17 is from Phase 13, the phase of the Sensuous Man, of the Tragic Generation of the Nineties, of Beardsley and Dowson and of their master Baudelaire. Yeats thus explains the bond as well as the difference between himself and the artistic companions of his youth, though he had too much tact, or genuine love for Lionel Johnson, overtly to assign him here. The true form of this intellectual aestheticism is "Creative imagination through *antithetical* emotion," the uneasy ideal of Yeats's personal life; the false form is "enforced self-realization," the actual burden of Shelley's life, and of Yeats's. The *Body of Fate,* exchanged with that of Phase 27, is "Loss," but the loss is immensely dignified by its association with the intellectual martyrs, Socrates and Pascal, oddly joined as examples of the Saint or man of Phase 27.

At the close of his account of Phase 16, Blake's phase, Yeats gave a hint that his own love was for the Image, and not for the fury and the mire of human veins:

> From this phase on we meet with those who do violence, instead of those who suffer it; and prepare for those who love some living person, and not an image of the mind, but as yet this love is hardly more than the "fixed idea" of faithfulness. As the new love grows the sense of beauty will fade.[38]

For the *daimonic* Man, love of the actual is not yet possible; indeed such love makes Unity of Being impossible. In the phases just before the supernatural Phase 15, mental images are distinct from one another, still subject to further knowledge of an external world. In Phase 16, mental images flow toegther, but with frenzy, "breaking and bruising one another," whereas in Yeats's phase "all now flow, change flutter, cry out, or mix into something else," yet remain undamaged. "The *Will* is falling asunder, but without explosion and noise. The separated fragments seek images rather than ideas. . . ." [39] This is Yeats's rationale for finding, not the impassioned myth that Blake found for his Mask, "but a *Mask* of simplicity that is also intensity," the way of Shelley and of *The Wanderings of Oisin.* And, with more immediacy, it is Yeats's definitive interpretation of his own passion for Maud Gonne, his own fated and necessarily defeated quest for the Shelleyan epipsyche. The *Body of Fate* is "Loss," derived from the Saints of renunciation. It is the labor of the Body of Fate to defeat the imagination, to make "simplification through intensity" impossible. "The being, through the intellect, selects some object of desire for a representation of the Mask as Image, some woman perhaps, and the Body of Fate snatches away the object." [40] Yeats is thinking of Maud Gonne, and also of Shelley's lengthy procession: Harriet, Mary, Claire, Emilia, Jane. Since, as Yeats now acknowledges, the Creative Mind is the ego or Los of the *antithetical* man, and so his Imagination proper, it is Creative Mind that must replace each shattered image by some new image of desire. The test for Unity of Being is the Imagination's power to relate apparently disparate entities, first the lost image to the new image; next, the circumstances of earlier loss to the new image; finally, the circumstances threatening the new image to the being's own unity. This is the heroic task of the *daimonic* Man, and is what Yeats believes himself to have accomplished in his mature poetry.

This accomplishment Yeats attempts to see plain by contrast with the "failure" of Shelley to be in phase with himself, to accept "Loss" as the *daimonic* Man should, by seeing the Body of Fate that opposes him as it really is. Shelley's greatness as a poet, for Yeats, is that despite this failure he "yet returns again and again to these two images of solitude, a young man whose hair has grown white from the burden of his thoughts, an old man in some shell-strewn cave whom it is possible to call, when speaking to the Sultan, 'as inaccessible as God or thou.' " [41] These are Athanase and Ahasuerus again, the two Images that sufficed for Yeats's definition of himself as poet, the youthful quester with age's wisdom, the ancient sage who has conquered time. But, out of phase, Shelley yields to nightmare, Yeats insists, thus falling short of his own genius, and failing to be a new Dante, as Yeats implies he himself has or will become. To be in phase, for the poet of Phase 17, is to have the Vision of Evil, which Yeats seems to define as being able to conceive of the world as a continual conflict. I have considered elsewhere the necessity that compelled Yeats to deny Shelley a Vision of Evil, even in *Prometheus Unbound* which clearly is suffused by it, if we are to accept Yeats's definition of what it is. Another sense of the conflict between Yeats and Shelley is more relevant to my discussion here, and again it enforces the distinction between the Gnostic apocalypse of *A Vision* and the humanistic hope of *Prometheus Unbound* and *The Four Zoas*. The Vision of Evil that Yeats possesses goes beyond conceiving the world as a continual conflict, for it leaves little or no value to abide upon the field of conflict; the good is in Phase 15, where there can be disjunction, but no continual conflict. The *daimonic* Man can have what Yeats praises Landor for having, as much Unity of Being as his age permits, and he may have in full measure the Vision of Evil, but he still must struggle in a material world whose very existence is an affront to the Imagination, and in which the Imagination itself knows only loss. His struggle, according to Yeats, cannot affect or modify that world. Dante, as Yeats says, found divine justice and the heavenly Beatrice, having lost the world's justice and the Beatrice he loved. Yeats's divine justice is of the Gnostic sort Kafka shows us in his novels, and Yeats's heavenly Beatrice is the *daimon,* who stage-manages the Great Wheel as an individual life, which expresses the *daimon*'s Will, and not our own. Yeats's faith is that the *daimon* is a man's ultimate self, but the faith is a little desperate or at least reckless. Recklessness, of the Renaissance *sprezzatura* sort, is the essence of Yeats, and very attractive rhetorically, but in the structure of *A Vision* it tends to help make the Vision of Evil a Kafkan rather than a Dantesque one. *A Vision* is a work of its age, and the religion of art in our time has become Gnostic, so Yeats is hardly to be censured. But, again, there are both aesthetic and human difficulties in a Gnostic vision that Yeats does not meet.

Phase 17 belongs to Yeats and Shelley, for Yeats recognized that he was more like Shelley than like Blake, though he had strained to make himself a Blakean poet. Blake stands between the phase of complete beauty and the phase of the *daimonic* Man. The *daimonic* Man is necessarily something of a skeptic, as Shelley emphasized he was, and Yeats uneasily admits to being. But Blake, the greatest exemplification of Phase 16, is the Positive Man. His Mask is from Phase 2, where energy just begins, emerging from the terrible preternatural absorption of Phase 1. It is a Mask of the child, with a child's fierce and aimless energy, "of physical life for its own sake." Yeats evidently confuses Blake's idea of Innocence with more primitive notions here, and the curious result is that Blake's true Mask turns out to be "Illusion," his false one "Delusion," which does not seem at all adequate to the actual Blake, but shows us a great deal about what Yeats wanted Blake to have been. Excited, incoherent, confused; this is the Blake of nineteenth-century caricature, but not the poet of *Milton* and *Jerusalem*. Everything about the intentional structure of Phase 16 suggests that Yeats wishes to reduce Blake to this caricature. The Creative Mind of Blake is the Los of his major poems; here (from Phase 14) it is "Vehemence" at its best, "Opinionated will" at its worst. And, by the oddity of Yeats's system, Blake's Body of Fate is from Phase 28, the phase of the Fool of God, of an all but total absorption. Though Yeats shows a valuable and original insight by associating Blake in Phase 16 with Rabelais and Aretino (the association with Paracelsus can be excused, though Paracelsus is largely dismissed in *The Marriage of Heaven and Hell*), the insight is only partial, or perhaps partially expressed. The major aspect of Blake as great satirist and great caricaturist is rightly expressed, but the cosmic and redemptive humanism that Blake shares with Rabelais is ignored. Yet Yeats is closer to the center of Blake in the description of Phase 16 than he ever was before or after. It is a dazzling insight to see the parallels between the comedy of Aretino and of Rabelais and the mythology of Blake, and there is no finer description of Blake's mythology than to say that in it we "discover symbolism to express the over-flowing and bursting of the mind. There is always an element of frenzy, and almost always a delight in certain glowing or shining images of concentrated force: in the smith's forge; in the heart; in the human form in its most vigorous development; in the solar disc; in some symbolical representation of the sexual organs. . . ." [42] Yeats significantly weakens the strength of this by ending: "for the being must brag of its triumph over its own incoherence," but that hardly alters the accurate eloquence of the passage, with its brilliant rhetorical progression of "force," "forge," and "form." As in this passage, there is something of the same deep split in the description of Blake's phase as in that of Shelley's. Shelley fell short of Unity of Being through lacking the Vision of Evil, and Blake must fall short of it through the inescapable limitations of his phase. Extraordinary to say of the phase of Blake and Rabelais that "capable of nothing but an incapable idealism (for it has no thought but in myth, or in defence of myth), it must, because it sees one side as all white, see the other side all black," as though Rabelais and Blake were deluded idealists in a drama by Ibsen.[43] Yeats's discomfort with Blake, as with Shelley, proceeds from a struggle within himself, or rather with his own *daimon* or Muse. The description of Phase 16 attains its illuminating climax in an account of "some beautiful women," of whom Maud Gonne presumably was one:

> Here too are beautiful women, whose bodies have taken upon themselves the image of the True *Mask,* and in these there is a radiant intensity, something of "The Burning Babe" of the Elizabethan lyric. They walk like queens, and seem to carry upon their backs a quiver of arrows, but they are gentle only to those whom they have chosen or subdued, or to the dogs that follow at their heels. Boundless in generosity, and in illusion, they will give themselves to a beggar because he resembles a religious picture. . . .[44]

Out of phase they are Venus and choose Vulcan, as Maud Gonne chose MacBride. Yeats assigns beautiful women, as such, to only the two phases we might expect, 16 and 14, on either side of the phase that is complete beauty. To Phase 16 are assigned "some beautiful women," while in Phase 14 are "many beautiful women," welcome company for Keats and Giorgione, the artists exemplary of the phase. Giorgione, about whom nothing subsequently is said, is there I surmise because of Pater's essay upon "The School of Giorgione," in which the School is assimilated to the vision of the *Ode on Melancholy,* and Yeats's revisionary idea of Keats defines the phase, as his brilliant caricatures of Blake and Shelley define Phases 16 and 17. The beautiful women of Phases 14 and 16 are there because in a clear, fortunate, and almost saving sense they are what *A Vision* is about, when it does not pursue its Gnostic personal quest for the Celestial Body or its Gnostic historicist quest for the "composite God" of process and cyclic decline.

Yeats's own women, I would guess, he assigned usually to Phase 14, particularly "Diana Vernon," the principal sexual affair of his life before his marriage. We can understand better now the dialectic implicit in *The Wind Among the Reeds,* discussed earlier, for the conflict there in Yeats's soul between the images of Maud Gonne and "Diana Vernon" is also the contrast between Phases 16 and 14 in *A Vision.* I surmise that the description of Phase 14 is largely drawn from "Diana Vernon":

> At Phase 16 will be discovered a desire to accept every possible responsibility; but now responsibility is renounced and this renunciation becomes an instrument of power, dropped burdens being taken up by others. Here are born those women who are most touching in their beauty. Helen was of the phase; and she comes before the mind's eye elaborating a delicate personal discipline, as though she would make her whole life an image of a unified *antithetical* energy. While seeming an image of softness and of quiet, she draws perpetually upon glass with a diamond. Yet she will not number among her sins anything that does not break that personal discipline, no matter what it may seem according to others' discipline; but if she fail in her own discipline she will not deceive herself, and for all the languor of her movements, and her indifference to the acts of others, her mind is never at peace.[45]

Beautiful and difficult as it is, the passage and what follows it are only an entrance to a much more complex matter in Yeats, and one of his greatest strengths, the quest for the meaning of a woman's beauty, the quest of Shelley's Poet in *Alastor* and of Shelley himself in *Epipsychidion*. The women of Phase 14 or 16 are those whom Yeats saw as most crucially suffering the dualism that Romanticism came to heal: "Their beauty dropped out of the loneliness/ Of body and soul." In his Note on *The Only Jealousy of Emer* Yeats relates "the greatest beauty visible to human eyes" of Phases 14 and 16 to "Castiglione's saying that the physical beauty of woman is the spoil or monument of the victory of the soul, for physical beauty, only possible to subjective natures, is described as the result of emotional toil in past lives." [46] Phase 14 is the phase of obsession, its Will being wholly obsessed, its Mask taken from the last phase, 28, which Yeats calls "a folding up," where the Image somehow fades into itself as befits the Fool or Child of God. Truly found, this is a Mask of "Serenity," but otherwise of "Self-distrust." The Creative Mind, from the Blakean Phase 16, a phase of violent scattering, is violently willful at best, and full of terror at worst. Most striking is the Body of Fate, which offers what Yeats elsewhere calls the "honey of generation" or Stevens the "honey of common summer." [47] "The *Body of Fate,* derived from the phase of the utmost possible physical energy, but of an energy without aim, like that of a child, works against this folding up, yet offers little more of objects than their excitement, their essential honey." [48] Yeats is caricaturing a heroic naturalism in Keats and Wordsworth that he chooses not to understand, even as he describes an extraordinary kind of woman, or perhaps a poet's vision of a kind of woman. The obsessed poet or beauty of Phase 14 has "Enforced love of the world" as Body of Fate, a transfigured version of the state of being of Phase 2, a phase Yeats characterizes by citing *The Mental Traveller:*

> But when they find the frowning Babe,
> Terror strikes through the region wide:
> They cry "The babe! the babe is born!"
> And flee away on every side.

This is precisely what Yeats calls it, the Beginning of Energy, with the terrified reaction of the world to a fresh birth of libido.

"Enforced love of the world" in this context is defeat, the perpetual cycle of defeat that man undergoes in Blake's poem, as he struggles vainly to overcome the world by renewing it. So Yeats, in his subtle commentary on Phase 2, deprecates both the Aesthetic visionaries of Phase 13 and the naturalistic Romantics of Phase 14 as being too weak to deal either with the energy of renewed life or the recalcitrant context of nature:

> Seen by those lyrical poets who draw their *Masks* from early phases, the man of Phase 2 is transfigured. Weary of an energy that defines and judges, weary of intellectual self-expression, they desire some "concealment," some transcendent intoxication. The bodily instincts, subjectively perceived, become the cup wreathed with ivy. Perhaps even a *Body of Fate* from any early phase may suffice to create this Image, but when it affects Phase 13 and Phase 14 the Image will be more sensuous, more like immediate experience. The Image is a myth, a woman, a landscape, or anything whatsoever that is an external expression of the *Mask*.[49]

This is an excellent description of the pervasive lyrical mood of Dowson and Johnson, and an extraordinarily inept account of Keats, let alone Wordsworth. Yeats's Keats is the Keats of Victorian convention, the caricatured Keats of Arnold and Swinburne, hardly the poet of *The Fall of Hyperion* or the great odes. Yeats generally learned to read the major Romantic poets for himself; his reading of Shelley in "The Philosophy of Shelley's Poetry" owes something to Browning's essay and perhaps something else to Todhunter's fine book (Todhunter and Yeats read *The Triumph of Life* correctly, whereas Bradley and most subsequent criticism read it so as to ignore its despair), but it is in the main astonishingly original and profound. But of Wordsworth all Yeats sees is a man "shuddering at his solitude" and filling his pages "with common opinion, common sentiment," while reducing mankind "to a few slight figures outlined for a moment amid mountain and lake."[50] This is not even interesting caricature, nor can anyone now recognize Keats from Yeats's remark that in him "intellectual curiosity is at its weakest." Sensuous reverie is all that Yeats grants Keats, whom he dismisses in an abstract summary that baffles analysis: "The being has almost reached the end of that elaboration of itself which has for its climax an absorption in time, where space can be but symbols or images in the mind." [51] If applied to the *Ode on a Grecian Urn,* for one example, this summary may seem to be exactly contrary to the truth, and it seems fair to conclude that Yeats assimilates Keats and Wordsworth to "many beautiful women" in his pages on Phase 14, rather than assimilating the beautiful women to the poets, as he does in drawing Maud Gonne into the vortex of Blake and Rabelais in Phase 16.

If we return now to the women of Phase 16, and contrast them to those of Phase 14, we ought to be in a position to understand Yeats's theory of female beauty and a great deal about his highly individual dialectics of love. The regal ladies of Phase 16 have the menace of being so Positive in all things that they approach madness in their intellectual hatred (for which see *A Prayer for My Daughter*) and potentially in their sexual frenzy, almost like Maenads to the poet's Orpheus. They are therefore the most dangerous of Muses, and Yeats quotes from himself to illuminate the paradox of their faithful unfaithfulness, when he observes they "die convinced that none but the first or last has ever touched their lips, for they are of those whose 'virginity renews itself like the moon.'" [52] Yeats goes on to imply that their bodies have greater perfection than the beauties of Phase 14, thus accounting for "something imperfect in the mind, some rejection of or inadequacy of *Mask,*" for there must be a radical disjunction when the body is so close to the clarified perfection of Phase 15.[53] The clue to the contrast between this impossible but truly *daimonic* Muse, and the gentler, less ideal Muse of Phase 14 is their relative positions with regard to supernatural perfection. Maud Gonne, the *daimonic* Muse, comes *after* Phase 15 and is thus in the first phase of those who do rather than suffer violence. "Diana Vernon" and the other Muses of Phase 14 suffer violence; they are victims of the indeterminate energy of the Body of Fate. At the least, Yeats as a man of Phase 17 is telling us that he was Maud Gonne's victim, as "Diana Vernon" and others were his. But he is rather deliberately, though obliquely, exposing something more interesting than that. How much briefer the description of the beauties of Phase 16 is than that of Phase 14, for the women of

Phase 14 are Yeats's actual Muses, with whom he has been to bed, and not the destructive *daimonic* Muse he has confronted only in aspiration and in the nostalgia of frustrate lust. (Mrs. Yeats is not among the Muses, but is in Phase 18, "the Emotional Man," which might be called Yeats's domesticated phase, since his wife and father join Goethe and Arnold there.) The women of Phase 16 "seem to carry upon their backs a quiver of arrows," and their attractiveness depends upon unattainability, and their arbitrariness (". . . they turn termagant, if their lover take a wrong step in a quadrille where all the figures are of their own composition and changed without notice when the fancy takes them").[54] The woman of the *daimonic* ideal is described with a certain flavor of bitterness on Yeats's part, and we would hardly know that the system enshrines her as the ultimately inevitable Muse if we had only the presentation of the Great Wheel of incarnations to guide us. For the actual fascination of Romantic love, we need to go to the subtle interpretation of Phase 14, to find "those women most touching in their beauty," from Helen of Troy to the women Yeats has known in love. Here the kernel is in the formula from Castiglione already cited, with Yeats's mythopoeic transformation of it into his doctrine of reincarnation. To extract the innermost meaning of *A Vision,* we need to be able to relate the poet's *antithetical* quest to his beliefs in the after-life, and to his quasi-historical obsessions. These latter have occupied the attention of Yeats's more scholarly and intelligent exegetes, which is rather a pity, for the true synthesis of *A Vision* is centered elsewhere, on the individual soul's history in relation to its own past lives. The Great Wheel is perhaps best regarded, we can now see, as a system of personal and poetic influence, or table of possible reincarnations. The *antithetical* quest is for beauty, and then through beauty not to truth but to the soul's own sublimity, its heightened sense of itself. The last stage of this quest, for Yeats, leads in parallel courses through sexual love and the writing of poetry, until the poet learns the tragedy of sexual love, which is the perpetual and solipsistic virginity of the soul and the tragedy of a poetic career, which is that a poet is in the condition of other men—he can incarnate the truth, but he cannot know it. Yeats courageously insisted that we begin to live when we conceive of life as tragedy, but his own life and poetic career indicate that we cease to live when we can no longer conceive a possible sublimity for ourselves, and for Yeats tragedy was not sublime enough. There was enough of the genuine apocalyptic in Yeats, as in Lawrence, to make him something other than a tragic artist. Blake insisted that the tragic and the apocalyptic modes were in opposition, and *A Vision* is Blakean enough to be uncomfortable with any tragic definitions of the highest art.

It is difficult now to conceive of a doctrine less imaginatively stimulating to most of us than that which holds our qualities to be determined by our supposed past incarnations. We can play with such notions, but they have become grotesque. I do not know of a good poet in English who held the view besides Yeats, except for Beddoes, to whom metempsychosis was something of an obsession. Yet Beddoes treats it at least as grotesquely as he does everything else. Yeats was to handle reincarnation in the manner of Beddoes in his play *The Herne's Egg*, but not in *A Vision*. What does it mean, imaginatively, to say that a woman's beauty derives from the emotional toil that she underwent in past existences? If the body's beauty is the soul's triumph over the body, then is the body's ugliness the body's triumph over the soul? *Sailing to Byzantium* and its attendant poems in *The Tower* seem at first to exemplify this pernicious dualism, but Yeats is too skilled an ironist to allow any poem the burden of so simple and drastic a dualism. The beauty of Phase 14 is the beauty of female reverie, intent only upon itself; it needs nothing and somehow suggests it will give nothing. Why does it fascinate?

> . . . and after,
> Under the frenzy of the fourteenth moon,
> The soul begins to tremble into stillness,
> To die into the labyrinth of itself!

The labyrinth is the Blakean clue we need and returns us to *A Vision*'s single image, the whirling gyres which from the fallen perspective are the labyrinth of each individual, merely natural existence. Yeats's own self-insight anticipates commentary:

> Old lecher with a love on every wind,
> Bring up out of that deep considering mind

All that you have discovered in the grave,
For it is certain that you have
Reckoned up every unforeknown, unseeing
Plunge, lured by a softening eye,
Or by a touch or a sigh,
Into the labyrinth of another's being;

Does the imagination dwell the most
Upon a woman won or woman lost?
If on the lost, admit you turned aside
From a great labyrinth out of pride. . . .

There are better reasons, even in Yeats, for avoiding the plunge into the labyrinth of another's being. The temptation, for Yeats, was particularly intense if the labyrinth was a beautiful woman of Phase 14. Perhaps the lines from *The Tower* just quoted, in which the "woman won" is probably "Diana Vernon" and the "woman lost" Maud Gonne, ought to be read as meaning that the imagination shies away from dwelling upon the woman won because subsequently Yeats turned aside from her. Certainly the reasons given for turning aside do not apply to Yeats's relations with Maud Gonne, nor could it be said accurately that Yeats turned aside from her anyway. Yeats's biographers may have made too little of "Diana Vernon"; *A Vision* owes more to Yeats's experience of her than it does to Maud Gonne.

To sum up the meaning and importance of Phase 14 is to see how precarious, inadequate, and immensely moving an image Yeats's version of Romantic love must bring us to contemplate. The images of desire that Phase 14 gives us are akin to the images of Blake's Beulah or the earthly paradises of Keats and Shelley and of *The Wanderings of Oisin*. They are apart from all other images:

When we compare these images with those of any subsequent phase, each seems studied for its own sake; they float as in serene air, or lie hidden in some valley, and if they move it is to music that returns always to the same note, or in a dance that so returns into itself that they seem immortal.[55]

These are images belonging to a realm where all contraries are equally true, and no progression is possible. Though this is a state of sexual love, it is also a state of what Yeats, following

Blake, could have termed Unorganized Innocence. The idealized love of his own natural existence Yeats had located elsewhere, in Phase 16, and he married in yet another phase, but he placed his memories of an achieved sexuality in the phase of naturalistic Romanticism, as if to make of his own past life the best kind of an allegory. If the beauty of Phase 14 is dependent upon the emotional toil of past existences, then Yeats could hope to found a poetic beauty upon his own emotional past.

We have examined the five phases most crucial to the Great Wheel—13 through 17—and must look at only a few more before moving on to the other books of *A Vision*. As one goes around the Wheel from Phase 18 through Phase 22, there is a necessary falling-away from the possibility of Unity of Being. In Phase 18, the Emotional Man, exemplified by Goethe and Arnold, Yeats is sardonic, for he disapproves the flight from Romanticism of these poets:

> The nightingale will refuse the thorn and so remain among images instead of passing to ideas. He is still disillusioned, but he can no longer through philosophy substitute for the desire that life has taken away, love for what life has brought. The *Will* is near the place marked Head upon the great chart, which enables it to choose its *Mask* even when true to phase almost coldly and always deliberately. . . .[56]

"Philosophy" here means a system like *A Vision,* or Blake's myth, or the near-myth studied in Yeats's "The Philosophy of Shelley's Poetry." The poets of Phase 16 or Phase 17, like Blake, Shelley, and Yeats "forget their broken toys" and so are not reduced, like Goethe and Arnold, to loving "what disillusionment gave." Many of Yeats's critics have tried to make him into Goethe or Arnold, and present us with a Yeats who loves the wisdom given by disillusionment, which would have infuriated him. He sought always "emotional wisdom," and desired to be a sage, like Ahasuerus of *Hellas,* and not "a wise king," the ideal of Goethe and Arnold.

With Phase 19, the Assertive Man, we come to Byron and Oscar Wilde, who are farther away from Yeats but more attractive to him, because he sees them as frustrated men of action, and the soldier or activist, like Kevin O'Higgins, was a secret ideal for

Yeats. But he shrewdly finds a masochism in them also, and observes that they can never complete themselves in Unity of Being, "for they have found that which they have sought, but that which they have sought and found is a fragment." [57] The acuteness of this is more than balanced by the oddness of Phase 20, the Concrete Man, of Shakespeare, Balzac, and the poet of action, Napoleon. This is a phase of ambition, in which the imagination is not content with making a heterocosm, but enters the world it makes and becomes a part of it, and has the strength to "compel it to seem the real world where our lives are lived." [58] But Yeats has no insight he can communicate here as to how this is done, and nothing to match the sweep and originality of the scattered remarks on Balzac and Shakespeare elsewhere in his writings.

Only in Phase 23 is Yeats's own imagination stirred again by his Great Wheel, at least until he comes to the last darkened phases, 26 to 28, of Hunchback, Saint, and Fool. The description of Phase 23, the Receptive Man, Synge and Rembrandt, has tremendous vitality, and a kind of imaginative puzzlement, as Yeats struggles to understand the attraction for him of an art so different from his own, and yet not in any way a creative opposite to him. The Creative Mind of the Receptive Man, when truly operative, is what Yeats was to deny to the lyric poet when he excluded Wilfred Owen from *The Oxford Book of Modern Verse,* "Creation through pity." [59] Owen, despite his limitations, was a great poet, and a purer Romantic visionary than Yeats. A contrast between Owen's *The Show* or his *Strange Meeting* and *The Second Coming* or *Leda and the Swan* exposes a subtle fault in Yeats's poems of vision, the inability to create as much through compassion as through other emotions. Whether Synge possessed this power as fully as Owen is questionable, even in *Riders to the Sea,* but it is refreshing to see Yeats moved and even disconcerted by the presence of this gift in Synge. It may be that Phase 23 is the only creative phase of the Wheel that is free from the tinge of solipsism, for the artist now "must free the intellect from all motives founded upon personal desire, by the help of the external world, now for the first time studied and mastered for its own sake." [60] Hence Synge is the Receptive Man, the man who "wipes his breath from the window-pane, and laughs in his delight at all the varied scene." This is the artist that John Butler Yeats had wanted his son to be, but the poet had followed another path, taking Blake and Shelley as *antithetical* fathers, and refusing a creativity in which pity is inseparable from wisdom. Synge fascinated Yeats because both men had undergone an aesthetic Second Birth into life, but Yeats had done it in the manner of Shelley's Poet in *Alastor,* while Synge had sought his true self and not that other, the *antithetical* self of Yeats's quest:

> In Synge's early unpublished work, written before he found the dialects of Aran and of Wicklow, there is brooding melancholy and morbid self-pity. He had to undergo an aesthetic transformation, analogous to religious conversion, before he became the audacious, joyous, ironical man we know. The emotional life in so far as it was deliberate had to be transferred from Phase 9 to Phase 23, from a condition of self-regarding melancholy to its direct opposite. This transformation must have seemed to him a discovery of his true self, of his true moral being; whereas Shelley's came at the moment when he first created a passionate image which made him forgetful of himself. It came perhaps when he had passed from the litigious rhetoric of *Queen Mab* to the lonely reveries of *Alastor*. *Primary* art values above all things sincerity to the self or *Will* but to the self active, transforming, perceiving.[61]

No other passage in *A Vision* shows so just a balancing between two rival modes of art. The description of Phase 23 needs to be read together with the section on "The Death of Synge" in Yeats's *Autobiographies,* and the stanza on Synge in *The Municipal Gallery Revisited*. The combined effect is both a tribute to an artist who was capable of finding his Mask among actual men, consciously choosing "the living world for text," and an oblique, haunted confession of longing on Yeats's part for a stance not possible to him. What Yeats knows through the counterforce of Synge is something more of the spiritual cost of Romantic art.

Everything most hostile to Romantic art is concentrated by Yeats into his description of the three last phases, as the moon wanes into its darkness:

> Hunchback and Saint and Fool are the last crescents.
> The burning bow that once could shoot an arrow
> Out of the up and down, the wagon-wheel

Of beauty's cruelty and wisdom's chatter—
Out of that raving tide—is drawn betwixt
Deformity of body and of mind.

The image here is from the climax of Blake's *Jerusalem,*
where the burning bow of Los shoots arrows of intellect and desire, to hasten the apocalypse.[62] Here the bow is drawn between
deformities so as to act as a barrier against revelation, or any saving movement in the self or nature. *Antithetical* and *primary* are
becoming wholly separated from one another, and soon self and
soul will hold no dialogues. In this condition the imagination
dies, and every fresh deformity is a further barrier against vision.
Unity is sought by the creatures of the waning moon, but this is
not Unity of Being (which itself is an Image of images) but
rather a unity rejecting every image of desire. The Hunchback of
Phase 26 "would, were that possible, be born as worm or
mole." [63] Incredibly, Yeats places Blake's Ezekiel here, misunderstanding a parable in *The Marriage of Heaven and Hell,* or more
likely, again deprecating a kind of moral prophecy he uneasily
evaded. Phase 27, the Saint, is almost as peculiarly exemplified,
for do Socrates and Pascal find their joy in being, doing, and
thinking nothing? Yeats's conception of sainthood is as poverty-
stricken as his views of God or the soul; the divine not only moves
beyond our antinomies, but comes as a baneful solarity that devastates the imagination. Unredeemed Gnosticism exacts its terrible price in *A Vision* as we come round the Great Wheel to its
last phase, where the natural man reappears as the Fool, who is
malignant, "out of jealousy of all that can act with intelligence
and effect." [64] To risk banality is an exegete's obligation here;
the Fool is not just the crazed "Child of God" whose many shapes
can be found "from the village fool to the Fool of Shakespeare";
he is precisely what Yeats calls him, the Natural Man as *A Vision*
sees natural man, "a straw blown by the wind, with no mind but
the wind and no act but a nameless drifting and turning." [65]
We have not come round the whole of the Great Wheel, since
next to nothing has been said of Phases 2 through 12, but enough
has been investigated so as to allow some conclusions about Book
I of *A Vision,* before analysing the four remaining books of

Yeats's apocalypse in the next chapter. The gyres and the wheel make up Yeats's principal symbol, and the aim of this discussion has been to reach a point where that symbol could be understood and evaluated in relation to what it seeks to represent. If the Great Wheel "is every completed movement of thought or life, twenty-eight incarnations, a single incarnation, a single judgment or act of thought," then the symbol potentially must be totally coherent, for it is of no value if we cannot gain insight into what it pictures, by understanding it. In design, at least, the symbol has the potential it requires, for it seems the inevitable symbol for existence conceived as a doubled quest, either toward the *primary* absorption of objective unity or the *antithetical* solitude of subjective individuality. The double vortex contains its own counterpoises, as it spins perpetually in the circular movement of thought. It does seem to me that Yeats added little of his own to Blake's symbolism here, but his acute recognition that Blake provided apt images show an exemplary aesthetic tact and a fruitful kind of poetic influencing. The limitations of Yeats's symbol, as he employed it in *A Vision*, emerge starkly, however, from a close comparison with Blake's ancestral use of it. Here is one instance, from the brilliant and difficult poem *Europe:*

> . . . when the five senses whelm'd
> In deluge o'er the earth-born man; then turn'd the fluxile eyes
> Into two stationary orbs, concentrating all things.
> The ever-varying spiral ascents to the heavens of heavens
> Were bended downward; and the nostrils golden gates shut
> Turn'd outward, barr'd and petrify'd against the infinite.
> Thought chang'd the infinite to a serpent; that which piteth:
> To a devouring flame; and man fled from its face and hid
> In forests of night; then all the eternal forests were divided
> Into earths rolling in circles of space, that like an ocean
>   rush'd
> And overwhelmed all except this finite wall of flesh.
> Then was the serpent temple form'd, image of infinite
> Shut up in finite revolutions, and man became an Angel;
> Heaven a mighty circle turning; God a tyrant crown'd.[66]

The "mighty circle turning," called Heaven by the Angels or orthodox, is Blake's Circle of Destiny or Yeats's Great Wheel.

Blake divides the historical phases of the Circle into Churches, Yeats into Incarnations, twenty-eight in each case. The "ever-varying spiral ascents" become the Winding Stair upon which Yeats mounts as he follows the motions of his whirling hour-glass; for Blake they are the apocalyptic sense of hearing, the poetic sense, fallen into time's bondage. The infinite of eternal vision falls into the labyrinthine serpent whom Yeats sought as his Shadow or *daimonic* otherness, while creative compassion, "that which pitieth," becomes Yeats's Condition of Fire, of simplification through intensity. Man flees to the wilful mental darkness in which he is terrified by Tygers of his own negative creation, but to Yeats these forests are the symbol he seeks, for they become his "image of infinite/ Shut up in finite revolutions," the system of *A Vision.* What Blake presents as disaster Yeats accepts as revelation. The "serpent temple" of Blake's vision is Yeats's symbol for a possible poetic faith. Blake implies the dialectical necessity of choice; this is the Fall, but the Imagination can reverse the Fall. Yeats makes explicit a cyclic necessity, which he implies the imagination must accept.

The image of the double-gyre, and the Great Wheel, is comprehensive enough to be coherent, but any great poet's apocalypse of imagination asks coherence to be complete, and *A Vision*'s symbolism lacks completeness, nor will its remaining four books add what Book I lacks. Yeats's symbolism cannot be detached from human life and its possibilities, because Yeats has embraced too much in that symbolism. But life and its possibilities demand immensely more than Yeats's negations masquerading as contraries will allow; our sense of possibility insists upon the prospect of the Sublime, of a state beyond the false extremes of the phases clustering about Phase 1, and those clustering about Phase 15. If Yeats had confined his sense of human possibility to what Book I of *A Vision* permitted, he might still have been a poet, but hardly the Last Romantic he proclaimed himself to be.

15: *A Vision:*

The Dead and History

Emerson identified the Sphinx with nature, and his curious poem *The Sphinx* is another precursor to aspects of *A Vision*. Emerson thought the poet could unriddle the Sphinx by a perception of identities among the diverse particulars nature presented. If Yeats read Emerson on history, and he is likely to have done so, he would have encountered a very Yeatsian defiance of natural mystery: "This human mind wrote history, and this must read it. The Sphinx must solve her own riddle. If the whole of history is in one man, it is all to be explained from individual experience." Emerson and Yeats both believed "there is one mind common to all individual men," a mind sovereign and solitary, whose laws were immutable and could be discovered by men. Yet to read Emerson's essay on history and *A Vision* together is to see how rapidly the affinity between these poetic theorists of history is dissolved. Where Emerson kept away from system, and turned to poetry for his history, Yeats enters the labyrinth of system, and turns for knowledge to the dead. A fit epigraph for the aspects of *A Vision* this chapter discusses, perhaps for all of the book, can be found in Emerson's *Journals:*

Miss Bridge, a mantua maker in Concord, became a "Medium," and gave up her old trade for this new one; and is to charge a pistareen a spasm, and nine dollars for a fit. This is the Rat-revelation, the gospel that comes by taps in the wall, and thumps in the table-drawer. The spirits make themselves of no reputation. They are rats and mice of society. And one of the demure disciples of the rat-tat-too, the other day, remarked that "this, like every other communication from the spiritual world, began very low." It was not ill said; for Christianity began in a manger, and the knuckle dispensation in a rat-hole.[1]

"The spirits make themselves of no reputation"; Book II of *A Vision*, "The Completed Symbol," begins by apologizing for having delayed unwittingly in giving us the Four Principles, the innate ground of the Four Faculties that we have studied already. Either the spirits were frustrated, or the poet was careless. The Principles are Husk, Passionate Body, Spirit, and Celestial Body, corresponding in *daimonic* existence to Will, Mask, Creative Mind, and Body of Fate in human existence, as Yeats conceives it. Having learned one barbaric terminology, the reader is reluctant to learn another, but Yeats has his justification, even as Blake did when he created both an eternal and a temporal mythology. Blake's Faculties are Orc, Satan-Jehovah (in a brilliant compounding of the opposites of the orthodox), Los, and the Covering Cherub, the fallen forms of the Zoas or primal beings; Blake's Principles are the eternal forms of the same beings; Luvah, Urizen, Urthona, and Tharmas. The double mythology in each poet is necessary because vision, in their sense, is always at least double, of the experiential world and the world of Giant Forms (to use Blake's phrase) from which experience has fallen away. The Faculties or fallen Zoas are "man's voluntary and acquired powers and their objects;" the Principles or unfallen Zoas are "the innate ground" of our powers, centered in our consciousness even as the powers are centered in our wills.[2] Yeats's most direct passage of explanation is dense, and demands explication:

The *Principles* are the *Faculties* transferred, as it were, from a concave to a convex mirror, or vice versa. They are *Husk, Passionate Body, Spirit* and *Celestial Body. Spirit* and *Celestial Body* are mind and its object (the Divine Ideas in their unity), while *Husk* and *Passionate Body,* which correspond to *Will* and *Mask,* are sense (impulse, images; hearing, seeing, etc., images that we associate with ourselves—the ear, the eye, etc.) and the objects of sense. *Husk* is symbolically the human body. The *Principles* through their conflict reveal reality but create nothing. They find their unity in the *Celestial Body.* The *Faculties* find theirs in the *Mask.*[3]

We must recall that the Faculties are voluntary, in the sense that we accumulate them in the course of our experience. Not that we are free to will them, but they reside in what Yeats calls Will, which is more of an accumulated superego. The Husk, being an intrinsic Principle, always existent, is a kind of transcendental superego; if we can think of what a god's own censor might be, we have something close to Yeats's Husk. When Yeats says, darkly, that *"Husk* is symbolically the human body," he is recalling what I judge to be the Blakean origin of the term, in the great line from the apocalyptic *Night the Ninth* of *The Four Zoas:* "and all Nations were threshed out and the stars threshed from their husks." [4] Yeats re-wrote the line as the epigraph to his *Crossways* group of early lyrics ("The stars are threshed, and the souls are threshed from their husks," a strong line but written by Yeats and not, as he says, by Blake), and since the revision of Blake presumably was an unconscious misremembering, the implied interpretation of Blake's "husk" would make the Husk the human body, as it is in *A Vision.* "My body is that part of the world which my thoughts can change," Lichtenberg remarks, in making much the same point that Yeats makes about the Husk. Husk is sense in sense's aspects of impulses and images, which shape the body and make it the manifestation of the unconscious, as a phenomenological psychiatrist might say, or of a transcendental superego, as the occultist Yeats in effect would say. The objects of sense come together in Passionate Body, the transcendental form of the Mask or questing libido. But, whereas the Faculties find their union in the Mask, the Principles cannot find theirs in the Passionate Body, for the conflict of the Principles is revelatory but not creative, and the Passionate Body remains always a manifold of sensations, subject to natural entropy.

Though a touch strained as symbolism, these first two Principles are not difficult to apprehend. But Spirit and Celestial Body,
eternal mind and its object, are much more opaque to the understanding than eternal sense and its object. Partly this is because
they dominate the world of the dead or, as Yeats terms it, "the
period between lives." Spirit or unfallen mind is what Blake calls
Urthona, or Coleridge (following the Kantians) "reason." This is
not so much the consciousness of any particular visionary—be he
poet or philosopher—but visionary consciousness itself, and perhaps Yeats should have called it The Spirit, if he had to use the
misleading word "spirit" at all. Celestial Body, the object of the
Spirit, is not as badly named since it means "the Divine Ideas in
their Unity," and these Ideas for Yeats are Neoplatonic. Blake
called his equivalent symbol Tharmas, the original unity of all
the Zoas or warring beings in his pantheon. Like the unfallen
Tharmas, the Celestial Body is a collective entity in the form of
energy, rather than anything corporeal, and can best be thought
of as a kind of transcendental id, even as the Spirit is a transcendental ego. "Transcendental," because we are now in the world of
daimons and of the dead, and not of natural men, and also because we are now in the world that Yeats wants to call reality.
When we die, consciousness passes from Husk to Spirit, and so
only the imagination survives the ruin of sense. The Spirit turns
from the objects of sense, or Passionate Body, "and clings to Celestial Body until they are one and there is only Spirit; pure mind,
containing within itself pure truth." Or, very simply, Yeats is saying that after death we become all Imagination.

But for Yeats, the Imagination is daimonic, and this makes it
impossible to understand Books II and III of A Vision without
struggling with the meaning of Yeats's daimons. Husk is not
human sense, but "the Daimon's hunger to make apparent to itself certain Daimons, and the organs of sense are that hunger
made visible. The Passionate Body is the sum of those Daimons."
This kills the deepest interest we can feel in Yeats's mythology at
this point, for there are no psychological correlatives to this part
of the mythology, as there abundantly are when we read of the
Faculties in Book I. The distance from human analogues is still
greater when Yeats speaks of Spirit as "the Daimon's knowledge,

for in the *Spirit* it knows all other *Daimons* as the Divine Ideas in their unity. They are one in the *Celestial Body*." This then is not human knowledge, except insofar as our knowledge is revelation or *daimonic* thought, the thought of the poet of Phase 17 when he approaches most closely to Unity of Being. One mark of Yeats's vivifying power is that suddenly he is able to raise his own abstractions into an intensity of imaginative concern, mostly by invoking the central tropes of Blake's great ballad, *The Mental Traveller:*

> The *Spirit* cannot know the *Daimons* in their unity until it has first perceived them as the objects of sense, the *Passionate Body* exists that it may "save the *Celestial Body* from solitude." In the symbolism the *Celestial Body* is said to age as the *Passionate Body* grows young, sometimes the *Celestial Body* is a prisoner in a tower rescued by the *Spirit*. Sometimes, grown old, it becomes the personification of evil. It pursues, persecutes, and imprisons the *Daimons*.[5]

As a note to this passage, Yeats refers us to *The Mental Traveller,* but the reference is redundant. Though Blake presents a more inclusive dialectic in the poem, covering the relations of man to every confining context, Yeats is not mistaken in following out one strand only, the wars of love and jealousy fought between poetic consciousness and the Muse. The Female of *The Mental Traveller,* Yeats takes as the composite form of his *daimons,* and the passage just quoted relies for its coherence on this identification. Because poet and Muse are fated to meet only in opposition, the human and the *daimonic* alternately persecute one another. Yeats characteristically sides with the female figure in Blake's poem, a point obscured by some earlier critics of *A Vision.* Thus, in the passage above, the male of the poem momentarily is the Celestial Body, and the female the Passionate Body. Translated, Yeats's passage reads: the poetic mind cannot know the ultimate forms of poetic thought until it perceives these first as sensuous forms, which exist so as to provide a bridge or ladder between poet and archetypes. But there is an opposition between the forms of thought and of sense, and if either expands, it must be at the other's expense. As a poet's mind comes closer to the ultimate forms, the sensuous ones recede, as at the opening of *Byzantium.*

"The unpurged images of day" belong to the Passionate Body; the image, "more shade than man, more image than a shade," belongs to the Celestial Body, which dominates in the night, or the death that for Yeats is only an interval between lives. In *A Dialogue of Self and Soul,* when the Soul summons the Self to climb the ancient winding stair of Yeats's Tower, the purpose of the steep ascent is to rescue the Celestial Body, held prisoner through the long day of the poet's life that is drawing to its end. Yet those same archetypes, grown old in their unity, can so reduce the Passionate Body as to tyrannize over the *daimons,* for even the Muse cannot bear altogether to be cut off from the sensuous realm or, as Yeats phrases it, "the *Daimon* seeks through the *Husk* that in *Passionate Body* which it needs." [6]

Yeats cares about only the two Principles that govern the dead, because Husk and Passionate Body not only disappear when life is over, but are past and present respectively during life, while Spirit and Celestial Body are always to be realized, are the future. Yeats knows two futures, the dead and history, and most of *A Vision* after Book I is a sustained meditation on one of these or the other. Though the Yeatsian vision of history begins to be expounded in Book II, after the definition of the Principles, this exposition belongs mostly to Books IV and V, while the world of the dead is examined in Book III. For convenience of discussion, I turn now to Book III and the dead, after which I will return to Book II before describing the major aspects of Yeats's theory of history.

Book III, "The Soul in Judgment," is uniquely the book of the *daimon* and so belongs to the Muse, and it would be a comfort if this meant the book concerned aesthetic process, as Helen Vendler tried to demonstrate. Unfortunately, Yeats is perfectly categorical in making this his Book of the Dead, and a dismal book it is. I am haunted, each time I read it, by memories of Wallace Stevens's fine insistence that poetry is a satisfying of the desire for resemblance:

> What a ghastly situation it would be if the world of the dead was actually different from the world of the living and, if as life ends, instead of passing to a former Victorian sphere, we passed

into a land in which none of our problems had been solved, after all, and nothing resembled anything we have ever known and nothing resembled anything else in shape, in color, in sound, in look or otherwise. To say farewell to our generation and to look forward to a continuation in a Jerusalem of pure surrealism would account for the taste for oblivion.[7]

These are the remarks of a poet who believed that "the brilliance of earth is the brilliance of every paradise." "The Soul in Judgment" portrays not a paradise, but a purgatory, though it is surely the oddest purgatory ever imagined by a poet. The spirit of Book III was best conveyed by Yeats himself, in conversation with Dorothy Wellesley:

> He had been talking rather wildly about the after life. Finally I asked him: "What do you believe happens to us immediately after death?" He replied: "after a person dies he does not realize that he is dead." I: "In what state is he?" W.B.Y.: "In some half-conscious state." I said: "Like the period between waking and sleeping?" W.B.Y.: "Yes." I: "How long does this state last?" W.B.Y.: "Perhaps some twenty years." "And after that" I asked, "what happens next?" He replied: "again a period which is Purgatory. The length of that phase depends upon the sins of the man when upon this earth." And then again I asked: "And after that?" I do not remember his actual words, but he spoke of the return of the soul to God.[8]

This is simpler than Book III's account of the dead, and considerably more conventional in its moral implications. Yeats, in Book III, divides "the period between death and birth" into six states:

1) The Vision of the Blood Kindred
2) Meditation
3) Shiftings
4) Beatitude
5) Purification
6) Foreknowledge

The Vision of the Blood Kindred is a farewell to the world of sense, of unpurged images, to the Passionate Body and those bound to us through it. The Meditation is a state in which Husk and Passionate Body vanish, their place taken by Spirit and Celestial Body. There are three phases in the state of Meditation: the Dreaming Back, the Return, and the Phantasmagoria. The dead, in The Vision of the Blood Kindred, say farewell to things as they are, to the whole universe of impulses and images. What follows, in the Meditation, is a vision of the completed life under the aspect of coherence, the bundle of impulses and images, appetites and moods, now gathered together as an achieved form. Certainly Yeats's hidden analogue for the Meditation is the act of making a poem, as *Byzantium* shows, but the Meditation itself is not a creative state. Rather, it is a troubled and imperfect process, in which creativity rids itself of organic sense only through long and painful dreams of the past, the Dreaming Back. For the unpurged images of day remain stubborn; they may recede, but they do not vanish, and so long as they are present the Spirit clings to them and cannot find the Celestial Body, as it must. When the Dreaming Back is over, the Spirit enters the Return phase of the Meditation, which:

> . . . has for its object the *Spirit's* separation from the *Passionate Body,* considered as nature, and from the *Husk* considered as pleasure and pain. In the *Dreaming Back,* the *Spirit* is compelled to live over and over again the events that had most moved it; there can be nothing new, but the old events stand forth in a light which is dim or bright according to the intensity of the passion that accompanied them. They occur in the order of their intensity or luminosity, the more intense first, and the painful are commonly the more intense, and repeat themselves again and again. In the *Return,* upon the other hand, the *Spirit* must live through past events in the order of their occurrence, because it is compelled by the *Celestial Body* to trace every passionate event to its cause until all are related and understood, turned into knowledge, made a part of itself.[9]

The resemblance at the close of this passage to the Self's culminating stanza in *A Dialogue of Self and Soul* is palpable. What should be noted is that the Dreaming Back is closer to the poetic process than the more spiritually advanced Return is. We are compelled to recognize again, in pondering a passage like this, that *A Vision* is not primarily a study of poetic consciousness, but a Gnostic scripture or apocalypse. Why should the Celestial Body, or Divine Ideas in their Unity, compel the Spirit to such a measuring and tracing of causes? Yeats's answer would be that this is a condition if freedom is to be attained. But is it a poetic condition? The purgatorial notion of intense memory as a painful necessity is to be followed by a pernicious casuistry, and the result is to be freedom. Yeats falls down imaginatively in finding the process of liberation, yet his aim is imaginative in the highest degree, for he sees that the Spirit's freedom is entirely in its own gift. Movingly, he cites William Morris, to him "the happiest of the poets," as he thinks of "the Homeric contrast between Heracles passing through the night, bow in hand, and Heracles, the freed spirit, a happy god among the gods." The passage he quotes, in Morris's translation, is much more Morris than Homer:

> And Heracles the mighty I saw when these went by;
> His image indeed: for himself mid the gods that never die
> Sits glad at the feast, and Hebe fair-ankled there doth hold,
> The daughter of Zeus the mighty and Hera shod with gold.[10]

Heracles as image walks in Hades, but his true imaginative form is among the blessed. It is a sharp descent from this to Yeats's subsequent observation that "after its imprisonment by some event in the *Dreaming Back,* the *Spirit* relives that event in the *Return* and turns it into knowledge, and then falls into the *Dreaming Back* once more." The cycles of *The Mental Traveller,* which Yeats does not want to escape, are hardly presented by Blake as being the true form of imagination, but precisely as the image of fallen man rotating in the hell of nature. For Yeats, the freedom of the complete Meditation is a "more happy or fortunate . . . next incarnation," hence the necessity of the third phase, of "what is called the *Phantasmagoria,* which exists to exhaust, not nature, not pain and pleasure, but emotion, and is the work of *Teaching Spirits.*" The Phantasmagoria is a parody of poetry, even as the Return is an antithesis of poetic imagination. For the Phantasmagoria is simply our capacity for nightmare, the Spirit's hideous ability to see itself tortured by flames and persecuted by demons, the very real Boschian hell of failed vision. Yeats speaks of the Phantasmagoria as completing "not only life but imagination," a use of "completing" which does not reveal the poet in the fullness of his freedom.

The Gnostic coloring of Yeats's Book of the Dead darkens further after this, for the Spirit is still unsatisfied after the Phantasmagoria, and requires the third state, the Shiftings, before it casts off moral good and moral evil as being irrelevant to its own freedom. What is "shifted" here is simply the whole morality of a man—"In so far as the man did good without knowing evil, or evil without knowing good, his nature is reversed until that knowledge is obtained." This, for Yeats, is the start of "true life" or freedom, lived in the presence of the Celestial Body. The model here is certainly the Blake of *The Marriage of Heaven and Hell*, but the result is parody of Blake, whose rhetoric may look like this simplistic Yeatsian antinomianism, but whose dialectic in the *Marriage* exposes the inadequacy of all mere moral inversions. But Yeats sees himself as having married good and evil together, and his alternate name for the next stage, the Beatitude, is the Marriage. The Beatitude is described both as a state of unconsciousness, and as a privileged moment of consciousness, a time of complete equilibrium or wholeness, clearly akin again to the aesthetic analogue which Yeats has been picking up and dropping almost at will.

The Spirit is now prepared for its perfection, before the movement toward rebirth begins. Yeats calls this fifth and perfect stage the Purification, but his term must be understood very narrowly, for the perfection is rather narrow itself. One thinks of the line revised out of the manuscript of *Byzantium:* "all my intricacies grown sweet and clear," for what the Spirit has been freed of, in this Purification, is all complexity, and not just the sensuous complexities of blood and mire. "All memory has vanished, the *Spirit* no longer knows what its name has been, it is at last free and in relation to *Spirits* free like itself." [11] I think it important to recognize here that the aesthetic analogue has dropped out again, for while the Celestial Body now dominates, a new Husk and Passionate Body have been born. Translated, that means we are both in a supersensuous and a sensuous realm, which means that the state is now occult, opaque to the resources of Yeats's language anyway. We are being told about somehow existent beings, and not about fictive ones. As might be predicted, Yeats is forced into obscurantism, and his description of the Purification is less coherent than it seems. But it is also the only description in *A Vision* that matters nearly as much as the earlier description of Phase 15, and a commentator on *A Vision* is obliged to enter into its difficulties.

What is the Spirit's purpose, for Yeats, which is only another form of the question, what can be achieved in the world of the dead, or the space between lives? Yeats insists upon purpose here; "the *Spirit* must substitute for the *Celestial Body,* seen as a Whole, its own particular aim." [12] The Protestant element in Yeats, which is mostly the residual Protestantism preserved in the poetic tradition of English Romanticism, is dominant here, and not his esoteric Neoplatonism, for which the seeing as a Whole of the Celestial Body would more than suffice. When the purified Spirit has substituted its own particular aim for the Celestial Body, "it becomes self-shaping, self-moving, plastic to itself, as that self has been shaped by past lives." Yeats necessarily is interested only in unique natures (like those of lyrical poets of the seventeenth phase) and a Spirit possessing such a nature cannot be reborn until the appropriately unique circumstances exist to make rebirth possible. An extraordinary notion begins to be shaped; the unique Spirit may linger in the Purification for centuries, while it attempts to complete various syntheses abandoned, perforce incomplete, in its past life. Yeats is sensible enough to insist that "only the living create," which means that the Spirit must seek out a living man to assist it in completing such syntheses, as for instance Yeats's Instructors sought him out to teach him the system "not for my sake, but their own." This casts a fine illumination upon *All Souls' Night,* the celebratory verse epilogue of *A Vision,* for presumably it implicitly salutes Yeats's own Instructors, who are made free by the poet's completion of his book to leave the Purification and reach the Foreknowledge, the stage of being directly before rebirth.

Yeats has been approaching his own center of vision again, and suddenly he takes us to it. "The *Spirit's* aim, however, appears before it as a form of perfection, for during the *Purification* those forms copied in the Arts and Sciences are present as the *Celestial Body*." In one sense, this is again Yeats's recognition that only the living create, though here the recognition is disguised by its backward presentation, as we are told that the Celestial Body provides the archetype that human creativity copies. But we, and even Yeats, know these forms only through the arts and sciences, which is closer to the point of Yeats's source here, Blake's "the bright sculptures of Los's Hall." [13] Yeats's deep concern here is with his own lifetime desires as a poet, for which he now seeks (but scarcely achieves) a definitive rationalization. The Spirits' aim is perfection, but they can find such perfection only by acting in unison with one another, an ironic reversal of Yeats's distinction between living men, where the *primary* are condemned to communal desire, and the *antithetical* to a proud solitude (the distinction defined for Yeats by the "Preface" to Shelley's *Alastor*). The form of perfection for the dead "is a shared purpose or idea." Musing on this community of Spirits, Yeats suddenly clarifies more than he might have known, or been comfortable in knowing:

> I connect them in my imagination with an early conviction of mine, that the creative power of the lyric poet depends upon his accepting some one of a few traditional attitudes, lover, sage, hero, scorner of life. They bring us back to the spiritual norm.[14]

Shelley haunts this passage, which indeed recalls not only *The Philosophy of Shelley's Poetry,* but also the account of Shelley's self-discovery as a poet in the description of Phase 17. Yeats's vision of perfection in his death-between-lives is a transcendental version of his lifelong vision of a possible poet, of the Shelley-free-of-limitations that he himself aspired to become. The condition of freedom (as much freedom as Yeats's system could allow) is the gift of the Romantic imagination, of simplification through intensity, here and in Eternity. Necessarily Yeats invokes the Thirteenth Cone, which he expounded in Book II, but which we have refrained from examining until now, at this climax of *A Vi-*

sion. Speaking of the Spirits, in their Purification, Yeats binds together his immanent and transcendental realms, the worlds of the Faculties and of the Principles:

> They may, however, if permitted by the *Thirteenth Cone.* so act upon the events of our lives as to compel us to attend to that perfection which, though it seems theirs, is the work of our own *Daimon.*

A Vision sees its God or "the ultimate reality . . . symbolised as a phaseless sphere." [15] This sphere is called the Thirteenth Cone, a happily Urizenic name for God. Behind this name is Yeats's complicated myth of history, a fuller account of which is best postponed to a discussion of Books IV and V. Only a few rudiments are necessary for understanding the Thirteenth Cone. Each Great Wheel of twenty-eight incarnations is also conceived as a historical cycle or gyre of some twenty-two hundred years. Twelve such gyres form a single Great Year of twenty-six thousand years, on the model of the Platonic Year (which was, however, thirty-six thousand years, as Yeats knew).[16] But the historical geometry of *A Vision* still awaits us in later books; the immediate meaning of the Thirteenth Cone, for Books II and III, is man's freedom, or all of freedom that Yeats desires, anyway. Insofar as a gyre is an individual human life, it always intersects its own double, and the point of intersection determines a corresponding and opposite point on the other gyre. This corresponding point on the other cone "is always called by my instructors the Thirteenth Cycle or *Thirteenth Cone.*" [17] Yeats is always difficult when he speaks of deliverance, and we need to attend him closely:

> It is that cycle which may deliver us from the twelve cycles of time and space. The cone which intersects ours is a cone in so far as we think of it as the antithesis to our thesis, but if the time has come for our deliverance it is the phaseless sphere, sometimes called the Thirteenth Sphere, for every lesser cycle contains within itself a sphere that is, as it were, the reflection or messenger of the final deliverance. Within it live all souls that have been set free and every *Daimon* and *Ghostly Self;* our expanding cone seems to cut through its gyre; spiritual influx is from its circumference, animate life from its centre.[18]

The Ghostly Self Yeats had defined earlier as the *daimon* "when it inhabits the sphere," that is, the *daimon* withdrawn by the Thirteenth Sphere to itself.[19] Critics have described the Thirteenth Cone as the re-entry of God into Yeats's system, but that hardly helps in defining it. Yeats ends the passage above with an illuminating reference to Shelley, while the use he makes of circumference and center is very close to Blake's in *Jerusalem*.[20] For Blake and Shelley freedom lay not in the will, but in the imagination which struggled with the will. In Blake, the Yeatsian will is the Spectre of Urthona, who struggles with Los the creative mind; in Shelley, the will is Prometheus still trapped by hatred for Jupiter, who is will incarnate, and in Shelley we are doomed to become whatever we are unwise enough to hate. For Yeats, freedom is neither in the will nor in the imagination, but only in the inexplicable intervention of miracle, the Thirteenth Cone. Though there is genuine incoherence in this intervention, Yeats saves himself from the full consequences of that incoherence by his customarily subtle vacillation, which is his form of the Byronic "mobility," or his own version of a kind of *sprezzatura*. Only the Thirteenth Cone delivers us from the cycles of time and space, but Yeats is a half-hearted Gnostic, and rather wary of such deliverance. He triumphs over his own system by not always wanting to be one of those "souls that have been set free." Like his own Spenser, he loves the journey, and not the destination.

We left the death-between-lives at the close of the fifth stage, or Purification, where Yeats tells us that the Thirteenth Cone, our freedom, may permit the purified Spirits to so act upon us that we are compelled to become poets, "to attend to that perfection which, though it seems theirs, is the work of our own Daimon." Here the Spirits become, not quite a composite Muse, but a complete Mnemosyne, or mother of the Muses. But we are not to assume their benevolence, which is part of the point of the sixth stage or poise before rebirth, called the Foreknowledge. The Spirit (presumably most, or almost all Spirits) must be reborn, but not until the state of Foreknowledge substitutes for the perfection of the community of Spirits the next incarnation, which must be completely known as a vision, and be accepted by the individual Spirit. The next incarnation, for Yeats, is very arbitrary, and has nothing to do with our previous performances, being merely decreed by fate. And the Spirits, here also, are liable to make themselves of no reputation, but are "frustrators," like the beings who keep scrambling the airwaves between Yeats and his Instructors. Indeed, they operate as a kind of group superego; they play a part, Yeats says, "resembling that of the 'censor' in modern psychology." [21] In the Foreknowledge, the only power the Spirit has is to delay indefinitely its own rebirth. Yet, if the Thirteenth Cone chooses to help (we are not told why it should), the Spirit "can so shape circumstances as to make possible the rebirth of a unique nature," like presumably another lyrical poet of the seventeenth phase. That completes the technical account of the death-between-lives in Yeats, and if he had left it there, it would be rather too much less than would suffice. Fortunately, he makes something of an imaginative recovery in the remaining sections (X through XII) of Book III.

The last sentence describing the Foreknowledge reminds us that the Book is called "The Soul in Judgment": "During its sleep in the womb the Spirit accepts its future life, declares it just." "Just" in what sense? And how does Yeats mean us to interpret his use of "expiation"?

> The more complete the expiation, or the less the need for it, the more fortunate the succeeding life. The more fully a life is lived, the less the need for—or the more complete is—the expiation.[22]

This is very Emersonian, and very effective, and clearly Yeats is persuasively re-defining "expiation," which appears to mean something like "using up the entire human potential, including all the capacity for significant emotion." If this is so, then the Spirit, declaring its future life to be "just," declares it to be more aesthetically complete, fuller, than the lives it lived before. Similarly Yeats himself, introducing *A Vision,* when he says of his gyres that "they have helped me to hold in a single thought reality and justice," means an aesthetically gratifying wholeness by "justice." Yeats found something of this "justice" in Lawrence's *The Rainbow* and *Women in Love,* novels he pioneered in admiring greatly. "Justice" is a grim quality in *The Mental Travel-*

ler also, and I suspect Yeats admired that poem so intensely because, like Lawrence in his best novels, it seems to bring its persons together again and again until all possible passionate relations are exhausted. In Yeats the supernaturalist (the Lawrence of the tales is a supernaturalist also) the possibility of passionate relations is expanded to include the *daimon,* and Romantic love is even explained as "expiation for the *Daimon,* for passionate love is from the *Daimon* which seeks by union with some other *Daimon* to reconstruct above the antinomies its own true nature." [23] On this account, all love must fail, and Yeats's own frustration in loving Maud Gonne is ascribed to a supernatural necessity. Little wonder that Yeats adds, with a finely savage urbanity: "We get happiness, my instructors say, from those we have served, ecstasy from those we have wronged." [24]

In this dubious ecstacy, founded upon victimage, the obscure final section of "The Soul in Judgment" finds its subject. Section XII expounds two relationships, called Victimage for the Dead and Victimage for the Ghostly Self or for the *daimon* absorbed into the purified Spirits. *"Victimage for the Dead* arises through such act as prevents the union of two incarnate *daimons* and is therefore the prevention or refusal of a particular experience, but *Victimage* for a *Spirit of the Thirteenth Cone* results from the prevention or refusal of experience itself." [25] "Victimage" here means the opposite of the "justice" that is completion; to be victimized is to be denied the fullness of possible experience. Most simply, Victimage for the Dead is what Blake attacked in the "Proverbs of Hell" in his *The Marriage of Heaven and Hell.* To nurse an unacted desire is to murder an infant joy in its cradle, and victimizes the dead, in the ironic sense of the self-victimization of the dead-in-life. But the deeper Victimage, for the Spirit of the Thirteenth Cone, or the Divine Freedom, is a greater perversity of the spirit, and comes from Yeats's vision of death-in-life as the ultimate enemy of the imagination. Yeats comes closest to Blake and Shelley here, but is prevented from identifying with them by his perfectly sincere Gnosticism.

When the Spirit of the Thirteenth Cone is starved, it revenges itself upon refused experience, and tortures the unwilling dross of nature by inflicting upon nature a frustrate spirituality, which in turn produces only a greater asceticism or refusal of experience. This hideous cycle Yeats calls Victimage for the Ghostly Self, and says of it that it is "the sole means for acquiring a supernatural guide," which illuminates a dark aspect of *Byzantium,* and perhaps several other major lyrics as well.[26] Yeats's particular interest is reserved for a harsher state: "Sometimes, however, *Victimage for the Ghostly Self* and *Victimage for the Dead* coincide and produce lives tortured throughout by spirituality and passion." A life so tortured, never to break into fulfillment, is a life of cruelty and ignorance (cruelty to the self, ignorance toward others), and though Yeats says that such a life is evil, it is for him a kind of necessary evil, for it alone "makes possible the conscious union of the *Daimons* of Man and Woman or that of the *Daimon* of the Living and a *Spirit of the Thirteenth Cone,* which is the deliverance from birth and death." [27]

It is not without considerable revulsion, or at least skepticism, that most readers (I trust, perhaps naïvely) could entertain such doctrine, for Yeats is not persuasively redefining cruelty and ignorance. He means cruelty and ignorance, in the contexts of spirituality and passion. As to passion, it is difficult to argue with any strong poet's dialectic of Romantic love, however savagely presented, and Yeats meets any protest in the matter of spirituality by coldly remarking: "All imaginable relations may arise between a man and his God." With that warning, Yeats is ready to pass from the dead to history, for his vision of history is his central relation to his God, a Gnostic "composite God" of process and entropy, whose cruelty answers our ignorance.

"The Great Year of the Ancients," Book IV of *A Vision,* has no admirers, while Book V, "Dove or Swan" rightly does. "Dove or Swan" is the only part of *A Vision* that can be judged an aesthetic achievement in its own right, though it is not as beautiful as *Per Amica Silentia Lunae.* "The Great Year of the Ancients" is a ramble but a ramble around two ideas Yeats could neither clarify nor discard, though their value to him in organizing poems and plays was always partly vitiated by their essential incoherence. The Great Year is, for Yeats, the promise of Eternal Recurrence, and the dialectic between *antithetical* and *primary* (Caesar and Christ, in Book IV, as derived from Mommsen) the promise of return to a world-order closer to his heart's desires. Blake made his myth of the Seven Eyes of God (characteristically drawing upon Scripture, and not an occult source) for reasons Yeats insisted upon misunderstanding. *The Mental Traveller,* and other cyclic poems down to (but not including) *The Four Zoas* were intended by Blake not as promise or comfort but as moral prophecy in the Hebraic tradition, as terrible depictions of what was and what would be unless men awoke to their own humanity. For Blake the Great Year of the Ancients, like every other vision of mere recurrence, was a dehumanizing idea, and a reading of Book IV of *A Vision* necessarily shows Blake to have been correct. Nietzsche is a formidable antagonist for Blake when he insists upon the heroism necessary to endure the idea of Eternal Recurrence, but Yeats is manifestly less formidable when he adopts the Nietzschean principle that there is no redemption from recurrence. Section XVII of Book IV is the paradigm of the whole, and will stand for it here. Yeats awaits the *antithetical* intellectual influx:

· At the birth of Christ religious life becomes *primary,* secular life *antithetical*—man gives to Caesar the things that are Caesar's. A *primary* dispensation looking beyond itself towards a transcendent power is dogmatic, levelling, unifying, feminine, humane, peace its means and end; an *antithetical* dispensation obeys imminent power, is expressive, hierarchical, multiple, masculine, harsh, surgical.[28]

This is a contrast, despite its masking terms, between death-in-life and vitality, a Romantic dialectic irrelevantly transferred to an alien context. The contrast, as Yvor Winters insisted, is of no value in itself; one can go further, and ask if the contrast, so applied, is not a barrier even to aesthetic values? To Yeats, it was a value because it became a condition for his creative freedom; thus, the passage just quoted precedes a citation of the Sphinx, the "gaze blank and pitiless as the sun," of *The Second Coming,* here called by Yeats the actual intervention of the *"Thirteenth Cone,* the sphere, the unique." Whenever Yeats anticipated the approaching influx, he anticipated also his own creative maturation. The only importance Book IV of *A Vision* has for the stu-

dent of Yeats is just this; we must see that our horror is his ecstasy, his as poet even if not as man.

When the student of Yeats passes on to Book V of *A Vision,*
"Dove or Swan," he can be grateful that the poet has taken over
completely from his astral Instructors. The defences of *A Vision*
by such Yeats scholars as Whitaker and Mrs. Vendler are convincing when "Dove or Swan" is in question. Like *Per Amica Silentia
Lunae,* "Dove or Swan" is a superb and controlled marmoreal
reverie, worthy of Sir Thomas Browne or of Pater (who suggested
to Yeats more than its mood). The central belief of "Dove or
Swan" is well summarized by Whitaker: "the acceptance of history is at one with freedom and creativity." [29] Though Whitaker
denies that "Dove or Swan" is deterministic, since it leaves to
the contemplative poet the inner freedom of his reverie, a more
objective reading of the book makes clear that Yeats is involved
in self-contradiction.[30] This is certainly no more damaging than
self-contradiction is to many prose-poems. We have to judge
"Dove or Swan" not by its coherence and insight as serious philosophy of history (as such, it is merely maddening) but as a reverie
upon such a philosophy, a reverie beautifully proportioned and
eloquently adjusted to many of our deepest imaginative needs.
Where the first four books of *A Vision* fail such judgment, "Dove
or Swan" triumphs, and provides the entire work with as much of
a purely aesthetic justification as it can be said to have.

"Dove or Swan" is flanked by two lyrics, *Leda and the Swan*
and *All Souls' Night,* which define between them the extraordinary range of the book, from the rape of Leda to the poet Yeats
drinking wine at midnight, at Oxford in the autumn of 1920. The
Christian Era is approaching its end, sinking into rigid age and
the final loss of control over its own thought:

> A civilisation is a struggle to keep self-control, and in this it is
> like some great tragic person, some Niobe who must display an al-
> most superhuman will or the cry will not touch our sympathy. The
> loss of control over thought comes towards the end; first a sinking
> in upon the moral being, then the last surrender, the irrational cry,
> revelation—the scream of Juno's peacock.[31]

Yeats grants Christian civilization the opportunity to expire in tragic dignity, but has no doubt that it must soon expire. He proceeds to trace three great wheels of time—2000 B.C. to A.D. 1, A.D. 1 to A.D. 1050, and A.D. 1050 to the present day, or 1925. The first, or cycle of classical, *antithetical* civilization, reaches Phase 12 of the Great Wheel in the sixth century B.C., attaining personality but as yet no intellectual solitude, which for Yeats is the prime condition if lyric poetry is to be possible. Still a good Pre-Raphaelite, Yeats locates a Pre-Phidian stage (Phidias = Raphael) of art, a first discovery of solitude (Phases 13 and 14) "with a natural unsystematised beauty like that before Raphael." [32] This art Yeats compares with Greek philosophy before Anaxagoras, and with the lost dramatists who wrote before Aeschylus and Sophocles, "both Phidian men." The age after Phidias is the art of Phases 16, 17, and 18, the art clustered round Unity of Being. Yeats recognizes three historical manifestations of Phase 15—Phidias, the artists of the reign of Justinian, Raphael. The phases just after, in each case, are those of the poets who meant most to Yeats, himself included. Partly, Yeats is exalting the Romantic art to which he adheres, but partly he is engaged in a much more valid and interesting activity, which is explaining Romanticism's conception of itself as renaissance not only of the Renaissance, but also of the two great periods earlier of which the Italian Renaissance was itself a renaissance, Periclean Athens, and Byzantium under Justinian.

It is in this explanation that "Dove or Swan" joins a vital tradition, and perhaps serves as its culmination. Yeats follows Pater in his Romantic versions of the Renaissance and of Athens, and derives his Byzantium from the French and English revival of interest, in the 1880's and later. Yeats's Byzantium, as Gordon and Fletcher have shown, is very close to Oscar Wilde's remarks on Byzantine art in "The Decay of Lying." [33] Wilde read the essay aloud to Yeats on Christmas Day 1888, with lasting effect upon Yeats, subtly analyzed by Ellmann in his *Eminent Domain*.[34] Wilde, rather than Pater (from whom, however, in this as in every other respect, Wilde derived) is the immediate source for the distinction between Caesar and Christ, upon which much of *A*

Vision is founded. Condemning "our own imitative spirit," Wilde praised "Orientalism, with its frank rejection of imitation, its love of artistic convention, its dislike to the actual representation of any object in nature." This is of course Romantic Orientalism, and the Byzantium of Wilde and Yeats is in some ways closer to the moonlit world of the *Arabian Nights* than to mere history.

There are, for Yeats, as for Pater and Wilde, three full moons in the history of the arts. Yeats has the confidence to fix their dates, and the dialectical cunning to remind us that these eras of Phase 15 are also times of Phase 8 or 22 in larger cycles, and so times of trouble as well as of achievement. Or rather, to come closer to Yeats, the achievement is a resolution of the struggle of opposites that makes for the trouble:

> Each age unwinds the thread another age had wound, and it amuses one to remember that before Phidias, and his westward-moving art, Persia fell, and that when full moon came round again, amid eastward-moving thought, and brought Byzantine glory, Rome fell; and that at the outset of our westward-moving Renaissance Byzantium fell; all things dying each other's life, living each other's death.[35]

The age of Phidias is for Yeats a relatively cold splendor. With the Incarnation, an extraordinary intensity enters into "Dove or Swan," particularly in one Paterian passage ambiguous and eloquent enough to have achieved an independent fame, justly due its high purple:

> We say of Him because His sacrifice was voluntary that He was love itself, and yet that part of Him which made Christendom was not love but pity, and not pity for intellectual despair, though the man in Him, being *antithetical* like His age, knew it in the *Garden*, but *primary* pity, that for the common lot, man's death, seeing that He raised Lazarus, sickness, seeing that He healed many, sin, seeing that He died.[36]

The tone of this passage is perhaps too complex for mere analysis, the complexity being due to Yeats's vacillation, which here approaches oscillation, between belief and unbelief. There is a similar puzzle in Pater's attitude toward Christianity as a supreme example of "the religious sentiment," in the concluding pages of *Marius the Epicurean,* a book Yeats had absorbed with rare completeness. Read closely, the passage is in the tradition of Blake's rejection of "pity" and Shelley's of "remorse," and appears to question the spiritual value of the Incarnation for the imaginative or *antithetical* man. Like Blake and Shelley, Yeats finds more in Christ than "that part of Him which made Christendom." As a polytheist, Yeats does find in Christ "love itself," but also a human *antithetical* imagination, the poetic mind of Phase 22, the phase evidently of the man Jesus, and of Flaubert, of Herbert Spencer and of Marx, of Swedenborg and of Dostoevsky (and of Darwin!), an astonishing company, selected with fine willfulness, and erratic but genuine insight. The man of Phase 22, whose Will is balanced between ambition and contemplation, may

> . . . become a destroyer and persecutor, a figure of tumult and of violence; or as is more probable—for the violence of such a man must be checked by moments of resignation or despair, premonitions of balance—his system will become an instrument of destruction and of persecution in the hands of others.[37]

Like Blake and Shelley, Yeats sets himself against the "system" of Christendom, while positing a Jesus more imaginative than Christendom worships. And he sets himself also against Christian love, too near allied to pity and too dangerously akin to remorse, for pity and remorse deaden the visionary imagination. This is perhaps the deepest lesson Yeats had learned from Blake and from Shelley, that creativity and love for a poet of the phases just past the full moon, poets who quested for apocalyptic Unity of Being, could come only through a difficult process of self-remaking, in which some of the prime apparent virtues of Christian tradition had to be redefined or even repudiated. The dance of opposites, which Yeats took too literally, is a metaphor of that remaking, and not the process itself. In one of his most remarkable self-revelations, Yeats converts his literalism of the imagination into another valuable insight, defining the difference between Christian love and his own:

Love is created and preserved by intellectual analysis, for we love
only that which is unique, and it belongs to contemplation, not to
action, for we would not change that which we love. A lover will
admit a greater beauty than that of his mistress but not its like, and
surrenders his days to a delighted laborious study of all her ways
and looks, and he pities only if something threatens that which has
never been before and can never be again. Fragment delights in
fragment and seeks possession, not service; whereas the Good Sa-
maritan discovers himself in the likeness of another, covered with
sores and abandoned by thieves upon the roadside, and in that
other serves himself. The opposites are gone; he does not need his
Lazarus; they do not each die the other's life, live the other's
death.[38]

Though this is marred by its formulaic ending (which must
weary in time, surely, even the most devoted Yeatsians) it has in
abundance the beauty of surprise. For Yeats's love is a cold passion, fostered by analysis. We love, he speculates, because our intellect tells us we have come upon uniqueness. This is hardly Romantic love, which knows that all things need to be made new before the imagination can marry what it has made. In Yeats's
terms, Romantic love belongs to action, for Yeatsian love desires a
stasis of the object of desire. Yeats is being true to his pervasive vision, for his love is Gnostic, fragment possessing fragment in desperate pursuit of the whole. The true center of Yeats's view is
that this love is involuntary, though made by analysis, for analysis
converts the lover's sense of the uniqueness of the mistress into
love, but cannot make that sense. By the dialectics of *A Vision* the
sacrifice of the seventeenth phase is involuntary, but that of the
twenty-second voluntary. Yeats is fated not to be a Christian.

Once past his account of the beginnings of Christendom, Yeats
is not stirred again, all through the decline of Rome, until the
rise of Byzantium. By postulating a historically idealized version
of his City of Art, Yeats follows the lead of Shelley in *Hellas*
rather than Blake in *Jerusalem*. Blake's Golgonooza, like Spenser's Cleopolis, is a vision of what might be, not of what was. Shelley, in singing of an idealized Greece, was still skeptical enough
not to commit himself to historical detail:

> Temples and towers,
> Citadels and marts, and they
> Who live and die there, have been ours,
> And may be thine, and must decay;
> But Greece and her foundations are
> Built below the tide of war,
> Based on the crystalline sea
> Of thought and its eternity;
> Her citizens, imperial spirits,
> Rule the present from the past,
> On all this world of men inherits
> Their seal is set.[39]

Yeats's Byzantium is both built below, and yet swept by, the tide of war. The city begins to interest Yeats "the moment when Byzantium became Byzantine and substituted for formal Roman magnificence, with its glorification of physical power, an architecture that suggests the Sacred City in the Apocalypse of St. John." [40] In the vision Yeats now allows himself, a historical city existed where belief flowered supernaturally into art, the art of "some philosophical worker in mosaic" showing forth divinity "as a lovely flexible presence like that of a perfect human body." Whitaker finds a qualification here and throughout Yeats's description of Byzantium, but such qualification is not evident to me.[41] Certainly Yeats is not simple in his historical mythicizings, but if ever he wrote without ironical intent, it was certainly here:

> I think that in early Byzantium, maybe never before or since in recorded history, religious, aesthetic and practical life were one, that architect and artificers—though not, it may be, poets, for language had been the instrument of controversy and must have grown abstract—spoke to the multitude and the few alike. The painter, the mosaic worker, the worker in gold and silver, the illuminator of sacred books, were almost impersonal, almost perhaps without the consciousness of individual design, absorbed in their subject-matter and that the vision of a whole people.[42]

The admission as to poets is not so much an ironic qualification as it is an anxiety-reaction, since the historical evidence baf-

fles Yeats. The Renaissance was hardly free of theological contro-
versy, yet its languages did not grow abstract to inhibit its poets.
Unable to find the great poetic period at this full moon, Yeats
contents himself with the fulfillment of his communal ideal
through the visual arts. If the entire passage be transposed into a
description of an idealized poetry, we can see what Yeats hoped
for in his own work. The poet speaks to multitude and esoteric
group alike, and with an almost impersonal voice. It is difficult to
see this fulfilled in any actual poet, Dante for instance is hardly
without consciousness of individual design, but Yeats's dream is a
moving one nevertheless.

As waking dream or Paterian reverie Yeats's description of Byzantium is most effective, but that it is conscious reverie need not
render it ironical. Not Byzantium itself is being described, but the
vision of a City of Art that runs through English Romantic tradition, from Blake and Shelley through the late phase of which
Yeats is the culmination, the movement of Ruskin, Morris, and
the Pre-Raphaelites. Because of the fame of the two *Byzantium*
poems, Yeats critics have made more of Byzantium than Yeats
himself did. The later Yeats tended to find only two full moons in
the history of civilization, Greece and the Renaissance, and
placed more stress upon Greece.

From Byzantium to the Renaissance is, for Yeats, a story of
cultural decline, one that is a little surprising for the heir of the
Pre-Raphaelites and their medieval Romanticism. But Yeats's Romanticism is not of the Gothicizing variety; he is the involuntary
heir of Wordsworth in his longing for creative solitude, and he associates poetic solitude with the breaking-up of religious syntheses.
The longing "for a solitary human body" as an erotic ideal becomes fused, for Yeats, with "something we may call intellectual
beauty or compare perhaps to that kind of bodily beauty which
Castiglione called 'the spoil or monument of the victory of the
soul.' " [43] This is hardly Shelley's "intellectual beauty," which
was to be apprehended just beyond the range of the senses, but
is a direct sensuous ideal: "Intellect and emotion, primary curiosity and the *antithetical* dream, are for the moment one."
This might be Pater on the Renaissance, the difference being not
in any Yeatsian irony of apprehension, since an *antithetical*

dream is a self-conscious one, but in the more direct assertion of Unity of Being that Yeats allows himself.

When the perfection of Phase 15 is past, Renaissance art loses its disinterestedness in "a sudden rush and storm." Power is purchased at the cost of knowledge, and "the Soul's unity has been found and lost." With this dispersal, Yeats begins an account of English poetic history that constitutes the last movement of "Dove or Swan." The history, from Shakespeare to the Generation of 1914, is one of decline, but of a dialectical kind, as befits Yeats's system. Where no negative criticism entered Yeats's remarks on Dante, the description of Shakespeare is refreshingly equivocal:

> I see in Shakespeare a man in whom human personality, hitherto restrained by its dependence upon Christendom or by its own need for self-control, burst like a shell. Perhaps secular intellect, setting itself free after five hundred years of struggle, has made him the greatest of dramatists, and yet because an *antithetical* age alone could confer upon an art like his the unity of a painting or of a temple pediment, we might, had the total works of Sophocles survived—they too born of a like struggle though with a different enemy—not think him greatest. Do we not feel an unrest like that of travel itself when we watch those personages, more living than ourselves, amid so much that is irrelevant and heterogeneous, amid so much *primary* curiosity, when we are carried from Rome to Venice, from Egypt to Saxon England, or in the one play from Roman to Christian mythology? [44]

Shakespeare's age is Phase 16, but he lives out of phase, being a man of Phase 20. Because he was out of phase, according to Yeats, Shakespeare became a dramatist rather than a lyric poet or man of action "drunk with his own wine." The great tragedies show Yeats not Unity of Being, but rather "a crowd of men and women who are still shaken by thought that passes from man to man in psychological contagion." Yet these personages, Yeats quietly concedes, are "more living than ourselves." Shakespeare's art caused always a feeling of unrest in Yeats, as indeed it had to, the feeling helping to save Yeats from writing a kind of drama in which he must have failed. For Yeats was too genuinely apocalyptic to live easily with any conceptions of tragedy that the Renaissance had developed; a difficulty that needs to be met when discussing Yeats's later plays.

After Shakespeare, the major English poets do not baffle Yeats's categories so badly, the sad result being that his remarks on them in "Dove or Swan" are less interesting. Milton, for the Romantics the poetic father who had to be overcome, is for Yeats only an attempted return, made too late, to the outworn synthesis of the Sistine Chapel. Milton's fault, we are told, is in his negative attitude toward classical mythology, and he is dismissed for "his unreality and his cold rhetoric." The mystery of Poetic Influence remains, for Yeats is to Blake and Shelley what they are to Milton, a son who makes himself strong by creatively misinterpreting the father. In Milton, Yeats acknowledges "the music and magnificence of the still violent gyre," which is more than J. B. Yeats would recognize. Like his corporeal father, the poet Yeats felt that Milton had entertained too many opinions, a curious prejudice on the part of two of the most opinionated of men.

The world of Cowley and Dryden is, for Yeats, one in which "belief dies out." A weary world "begins to long for the arbitrary and accidental, for the grotesque, the repulsive and the terrible, that it may be cured of desire." [45] The accent is that of Pater describing Rome in its Decadence; for Yeats this later decadence goes from 1650 to 1875, Phases 19, 20, and 21 of an ebbing gyre. In this Yeats sees three epicycles—Augustan and the Age of Sensibility, Romantic, post-Romantic. For the first, at this point in his life, Yeats has little regard: "It is external, sentimental and logical—the poetry of Pope and Gray, the philosophy of Johnson and of Rousseau—equally simple in emotion or in thought, the old oscillation in a new form." [46] The oscillation between *The Dunciad* and *The Bard,* and between the wisdom of Johnson and of Rousseau, has rarely been so undervalued or so misunderstood. A wonderful critical recovery is made when Yeats describes the onset of Romanticism (without using that term). In Yeats's theory, Romanticism is only a foreshadowing of the revelation that is soon to come, but only through reading this shadow can knowledge be found:

In frail women's faces the soul awakes—all its prepossessions, the accumulated learning of centuries swept away—and looks out upon us wise and foolish like the dawn. Then it is everywhere. . . . In poetry alone it finds its full expression, for it is a quality of the emotional nature (*Celestial Body* acting through *Mask*); and creates all that is most beautiful in modern English poetry from Blake to Arnold, all that is not a fading echo.[47]

Yeats sees his own role as carrying expression of "the new emotion" over into an overt *antithetical* wisdom, of which Blake, "Coventry Patmore at moments," and above all the Nietzsche of Eternal Recurrence were the forerunners. This role is uniquely reserved for him in the period from 1875 to 1927, for reasons that the later version of *A Vision* cannot explain, because it excludes the last few pages of "Dove or Swan." In the first published *Vision* of 1925, Yeats examines his literary contemporaries in those pages. In 1925 we are at Phase 23, "the first where there is hatred of the abstract, where the intellect turns upon itself." Brooding on the art of Pound, Eliot, Joyce, Pirandello, Yeats does not find any mastery of *antithetical* wisdom but only a "technical inspiration" that wholly separates "myth—the *Mask*"—from fact. That was never his way, he implicitly insists, and he shows more sympathy for the mystical communalism of Peguy and Claudel, little as he resembles them in aspiration. Looking ahead to the waning phases of our gyre, Yeats utters the only one of his prophecies that chills me, for its insights are convincing and ominous:

I forsee a time when the majority of men will so accept an historical tradition that they will quarrel, not as to who can impose his personality upon others but as to who can best embody the common aim, when all personality will seem an impurity—"sentimentality," "sullenness," "egotism,"—something that revolts not morals alone but good taste. There will be no longer great intellect for a ceaseless activity will be required of all; and where rights are swallowed up in duties, and solitude is difficult, creation except among avowedly archaistic and unpopular groups will grow impossible.[48]

This is a Romantic vision of the death of desire, an extension of the implicit darker prophecies of Shelley's *The Defence of Po-*

etry. Mankind moves toward a democratic and *primary* Decadence, unfavorably contrasted to the Decadence of the ancient world and his own day traced by Pater. The new influx of irrational force will awake into life not the apocalyptic forms dreamed by the prophets—Milton's and Blake's Human Form Divine, Nietzsche's superman, Patmore's New Catholic—"but organic groups, *covens* of physical or intellectual kin melted out of the frozen mass." In this coming horror Yeats looks for salvation to a small band of imaginative men, like himself, who will develop "a form of philosophy" like that roughed out in *A Vision*. This philosophy "will call that good which a man can contemplate himself as doing always and no other doing at all." This is too curious an ethic to bear commentary, and as always there are two rival strands in Yeats's apocalyptic anyway, one which would best suit a kind of amalgam of Carlyle and a Rosicrucian, or the later Lawrence, and a rather different one that is pure Blake and Shelley. The latter one is allowed a luminous but momentary expression when Yeats says: "Men will no longer separate the idea of God from that of human genius, human productivity in all its forms," but the Fascist-Gnostic amalgam dominates the conclusion of the original "Dove or Swan." [49] Thus we are told that men of learning, wealth, and rank "will be given power, less because of that they promise than of that they seem and are." But even these Elect "once formed must obey irrational force," yield themselves to "fanaticism and a terror" and, best of all, "oppress the ignorant—even the innocent—as Christianity oppressed the wise."

It is a relief then to return to the revised *Vision* to read the mellower conclusion that Yeats composed during 1934–36, where we find the aged poet sitting in his chair turning a symbol and not a civilization over in his mind. "Dove or Swan" is a majestic reverie, but more than a disconcerting one, for the *daimons* sometimes show greater exuberance in it than Yeats does. But in "The End of the Cycle" we hear a personality meditating, as we did in *Per Amica Silentia Lunae,* and this personality is rich and somber enough to doubt all speculation, its own included. The Thirteenth Cone or God is in every man and is his freedom, and it keeps the secret of futurity, as its ancestor Demogorgon did: "The deep truth is imageless." So self-admonished, the Blakean and

Shelleyan imagination asserts itself in Yeats and ends *A Vision* with the greatest and most humanistic of his insights, more definitively expressed for being an open question addressed to the poet's own vacillation:

> Shall we follow the image of Heracles that walks through the darkness bow in hand, or mount to that other Heracles, man, not image, he that has for his bride Hebe, "the daughter of Zeus, the mighty, and Hera, shod with gold"? [50]

"Man, not image" is a Blakean and Shelleyan motto, but hardly an inscription on the gate into Byzantium.

16: Four Plays for Dancers

At the Hawk's Well

To understand Yeats's relation to the Noh drama (the fundamental form of *Four Plays for Dancers* and later *The Death of Cuchulain*) we should turn to the important essay of 1914, *Swedenborg, Mediums, and the Desolate Places*. The very late *An Introduction for My Plays* (1937) emphasizes the poet's "delight in active men" but scants his deeper concern for the appropriate dramatic form. *Certain Noble Plays of Japan* (1916), the beautiful introduction to the Fenollosa-Pound translations, is extraordinarily self-conscious even for Yeats, a Paterian reverie in its own right. It emphasizes "an aristocratic form," as though the central difficulty for Yeats's dramatic imagination was social. Remarkably, this form is associated with "the arts of childhood," and Yeats is again centrally in the Romantic tradition when he says that "only our lyric poetry has kept its Asiatic habit and renewed itself at its own youth." [1] He is thinking, as he says, of the "most typical modern verse," such as *Kubla Khan* and the *Ode to the West Wind,* and we see that he is searching for a dramatic form that is equivalent to those poems.[2] Cultivated "accomplishment" or Noh is both childlike and noble, in Yeats's view, and primarily expresses intensity of movement, of body and of spirit. Clearly Yeats (unlike Pound) assimilates Noh to the Romantic tradition. Of its soldier-audiences, he imagines a consciousness combining Walter Pater and Achilles (delightful blend), and to find an equivalent of what he takes to be Noh's "rhythm of metaphor" he turns inevitably to "Shelley's continually repeated fountain and cave, his broad stream and solitary star."[3] I suggest that Yeats, however astonishingly, found in Noh what the Romantics had sought for themselves but failed to find, a form for drama that suited their intricate sensibilities. Shelley, highly conscious of the need, began to find it in Calderon, scenes from whose *Magico Prodigioso* he translated, and whose influence is to be felt in the late fragments of an unfinished drama that Dr. Garnett entitled *The Magic Plant*. Yeats sought, by his own admission, a dramatic form in which the moods of *The Book of Thel* or *The Sensitive Plant* might be depicted. This means a drama revealing states-of-being rather than states-of-mind, which is probably impossible, but Yeats must be allowed the honor of working in *Four Plays for Dancers* at one of the limits of literature.

The formal problem is illuminated by the context in which it is presented, in *Swedenborg, Mediums, and the Desolate Places.* Primarily that essay is an embryo of *Per Amica Silentia Lunae,* itself the *daimonic* alphabet that led to *A Vision.* Yeats writes in the Swedenborg essay of the *daimons* and the dead, and looks for artistic illustrations of what has "more dimensions than our penury can comprehend."[4] He finds it in Noh, to which Pound had introduced him, just the winter before. Clearly, Yeats had listened to Pound's readings as to so many winters' tales, such as he might hear from his Soho mediums or Lady Gregory's Western Irish peasantry. Noh seemed to him to solve the formal difficulties of bringing the occult, folk superstitions, and Romantic imaginings onto the one stage with representations of living men and women. An art that can permit apparitions their vividness rarely has been an art of the stage, and Yeats could not fail to respond to the opportunity Pound had offered him.

The paradox of a formal invention is that it sometimes works best in a poet's initial mastery of it, even as he engages in the process of learning it. This is the paradox of *Four Plays for Dancers,* Yeats's finest achievement in the drama. The first two ventures by Yeats in the Noh, *At the Hawk's Well* and *The Only Jealousy of Emer,* are the best plays he ever wrote, and stand as artistic accomplishment with the best of his lyric poetry. *The Dreaming of the Bones* and *Calvary* are slighter work, but still superior to most of the plays that came after them. As Yeats grew more assured, he allowed himself the dangerous extremes of direct presentation of his convictions, and equally direct self-parody. But in *Four Plays for Dancers,* his formal tentativeness served him well, impelling him to re-imagine some of the consequences of his convictions, and helping him to work with a radiant suggestiveness. Here the lofty emotion of the *antithetical* quester in his high solitude attains the embodiment of simple but intense action, and every contrast upon stage is a successful variation upon a central metaphor. In reading *At the Hawk's Well* in particular, we sense that the poet's imagination is again wholly at one with his themes (in defiance of his own theories) precisely as Shelley's was in *Alastor,* or his own was earlier in *The Wanderings of Oisin* and *The Shadowy Waters.*

The immediate sources of *At the Hawk's Well,* with one exception, do not matter, as the essential invention is Yeats's own. Here the exception is William Morris, the principal literary influence upon Yeats after Shelley, Blake, Pater, and perhaps Balzac. Behind Yeats's adaptation of the Noh is not only his Paterian aesthetic and the desire to find a form for a drama of the Shelleyan quest, but the world of Morris's late prose romances, particularly *The Well at the World's End* and *The Water of the Wondrous Isles.* This influence, first studied by Birgit Bjersby, is clarified by Yeats's moving essay on Morris, *The Happiest of the Poets* (1902):

> In *The Well At The World's End* green trees and enchanted waters are shown to us as they were understood by old writers, who thought that the generation of all things was through water; for when the water that gives a long and fortunate life, and that can be found by none but such a one as all women love, is found at last, the Dry Tree, the image of the ruined land, becomes green. To him

indeed as to older writers Well and Tree are all but images of the
one thing, of an "energy" that is not the less "eternal delight" because it is half of the body.[5]

The softening of Blake in that last sentence is an instance of
Yeats's caution, as also of his swerve away from Blake. *The Marriage of Heaven and Hell* had not spoken of an energy that was
merely half of the body:

> Energy is the only life and is from the Body and Reason is the
> bound or outward circumference of Energy.
> Energy is Eternal Delight.[6]

Here, in any case, are the central images of *At the Hawk's
Well,* Dry Tree and Well of long and fortunate life. In 1896,
Yeats had reviewed *The Well at the World's End,* and had made
the review his memorial to Morris, dead in that year. The review
contrasts Shelley, "the type of the poet," who pursued the dream
into the bitter waters, questing always for 'the sense of the perfect," to Morris who "accepted life and called it good." [7] Because
Yeats knew himself, despite all struggle, to be of Shelley's phase,
he longed the more intensely for the abundant world of Morris's
romances. This abundance is of desire satisfied, quest fulfilled.
When Yeats spoke of these prose romances as having "the same
curious astringent joy" as Nietzsche and Blake, he referred not to
any actual quality of Morris's work, but to his own affective,
highly *antithetical* reaction to them. "Curious astringent joy" is
an excellent characterization of the tone pervasive in *At the
Hawk's Well,* a tone strikingly at variance with the overt action
of the play. The joy is Cuchulain's, Yeats's, the attentive reader's,
in each case a joy rising out of the acceptance of a temporal frustration, but joy all the same. In this play, Yeats is again a master,
and all imaginative readers his debtors.

I do not think that the play takes moral heroism as its precise
subject. Cuchulain is of course the hero proper for Yeats, as Shelley is the poet proper, and so a play on Cuchulain is necessarily a
play about heroism even as Yeats's essays on Shelley are essays
about the nature of poetry itself. But this play is closer to Yeats
than any he had written since *The Shadowy Waters;* it rises from

his permanent sorrows as Morris's romances rise from the long frustrations of his marriage to Jane Burden. Neither Yeats nor Morris, though each lived long and fortunate lives, in terms of accomplishment, considered himself "such a one as all women love." In the abundance of the prose romances, Yeats recognized what he and Morris lacked, the luck of the true quester who can afford to reject many false loves in the accurate confidence that he will not only find the true beloved, but be accepted by her.

At the Hawk's Well displaces this recognition into another realm, not Morris's florabundant world but the *daimonic* wastes of the Sidhe, the dancers who cheat every quester. Cuchulain enters these wastes with a flamboyance no experience, *daimonic* or natural, can reduce. His true encounter is not with the Guardian of the Well, but is in the future, with Aoife, leader of "the fierce women of the hills." The Guardian performs the role she has in Morris, and yet for Cuchulain she is only a prelude. Morris describes

> . . . how she liveth yet, and is become the servant of the Well to entangle the seekers in her love and keep them from drinking thereof; because there was no man that beheld her but anon he was the thrall of her love, and might not pluck his heart away from her to do any of the deeds whereby men thrive and win the praise of the people.[8]

Even so, Cuchulain watches the hawk-like dance of the Guardian of the Well, until he is in thrall, and then follows the dancer away from the well just as the water for which he quests comes in. But he shows no regret when he emerges from the trance of fascination, for the dancer has gone to rouse up Aoife and the Amazonian women who follow her, and the quest is nothing to Cuchulain when he hears the clash of arms again. As the stage direction emphasizes, directly he has said: "I will face them," he goes out "no longer as if in a dream." It is not a heroism for the hero to achieve self-recognition, but something that lies beyond heroism. I am surprised always, in reading the play, at the extraordinary force of Cuchulain's call as he shoulders his spear: "He comes! Cuchulain, son of Sualtim, comes!" The splendor of this would be lost if Cuchulain did not so sublimely put it in the third person.

In context, the effect is overpowering, and demonstrates the play's deepest concern, which is with the incarnation of the heroic character. Here Yeats is highly original; Romantic tradition afforded him myriad instances of the incarnation of the poetical character, but none for the self-recognition of the hero. The hero, like the poet, is not born, but is re-born, incarnated, in a consciousness prepared to receive him. What Yeats gives us is a remarkable displacement of Romantic tradition, a hymn to intellectual courage rather than to Intellectual Beauty, while maintaining Shelley's notion of "intellectual" as meaning "beyond the senses." Cuchulain is the lucky quester, "such a one as all women love," but he too is intended as one of the deceived, by the Sidhe. His triumph is that he is not cheated, because he has no consciousness of deception. He moves toward fulfillment by self-recognition, and goes out to battle and to shoulder the eventual curse of the Sidhe—to defeat Aoife, beget a son upon her, unknowingly slay that son, and die at last an exhausted and indifferent death. But, as this play leaves him, he moves toward the heights, in the exultation of receiving his life's role, of incarnating the hero.

This is the climax of the play, but for all its strength it is not the play's dominant element or value. More memorable still is the play's context, the waste lands against which Cuchulain flares. The hero goes to the triumph of his equivocal victory and necessary *daimonic* defeat, but the reader's consciousness lingers with "a well long choked up and dry" and the Old Man who has watched the well vainly for fifty years. It is not possible to forget that Yeats had lived fifty years when he started to write the play, however wary we are of biographical interpretations. The water, if drunk, gives a long and fortunate life, at the least; perhaps even the immortality promised by the rumor that has brought Cuchulain to the bare place. We do not know; it may be only rumor, for the Sidhe deceive. But Yeats himself dwells, until 1917 anyway, in the ruined land. The water is, as everywhere in Yeats, "the generative soul," image of life's miracle even to a Gnostic. The Old Man is not Yeats, nor any part of him, but he is an image of what Yeats fears to become. The mask of age Yeats desires some day to wear is the ageless mask of Ahasuerus of *Hellas*, old Rocky Face, oracle of secret wisdom, not the cowardly, degrading mask of the Old Man waiting endlessly by a dry well. Three times already the Old Man has fallen into the sleep induced by the hawk-dance of the Guardian; the play shows us a fourth. Our intimation of the Old Man's failure comes to us as it should through the play's chief action. We watch the hawk-dance; it moves the Old Man to sleep, and Cuchulain to sexual desire. The Old Man awakens to a more awful bitterness; Cuchulain comes out of the dream of desire to the joy of self-proclamation, and the lust of battle. Strong and clear as this fable is, it intimates also the old wisdom Yeats had learned in his High Romantic youth: there are two destructions, one dusty, one bright, and no salvation. One can burn to the socket, or pursue the poet's fate, questing after the dream while shadowed by the *alastor,* avenger and dark brother. *At the Hawk's Well* is the hero's parable, but its meaning for Yeats is in another kind of persistence, one that can say in pride: I made my song out of "a mouthful of sweet air."

The Only Jealousy of Emer

At the Hawk's Well has the beauty of austerity; its pattern is simple and its diction stripped. This simplicity exposes it to exactly contrary interpretations; to Wilson and Rajan for instance it is a work of spiritual defeat, while to Mrs. Vendler its theme is moral heroism.[9] My own view, as presented above, is closest to Ure's, for whom it is a play about the hero's courage betraying the hero.[10] Since Cuchulain does not know loss, I read him as having suffered no loss, but only the gain of self-recognition, which necessarily precludes a long and fortunate life anyway. Yet, there is no "correct" interpretation of *At the Hawk's Well.* The play's rounded perfection finds one flat shadow or another depending upon the rival planes of our criticism, to borrow a figure from Wilson Knight. Part of Yeats's meaning in the play is the ambiguity of our responses to Cuchulain, hero of Phase 12 (as Wilson rightly says), responses that expose our own probable phases on the Wheel.

   The Only Jealousy of Emer is a very different work, as intri-

cate as *At the Hawk's Well* is simple. Here the problem of interpretation becomes conversely a rivalry of necessarily simplistic
judgments, and this too is legitimately part of Yeats's meaning.
For *The Only Jealousy of Emer* is at the heart of Yeats's system,
the mystery of Phase 15, and the power of that phase is the power
of the Romantic Imagination. The manifold of sensation is con-
densed to the heightened image of unity, yet this belongs, as Shelley says of the flames on the Witch of Atlas's hearth, to each and
all who gaze upon, and one critic's simplification through intensity is not another's. Here Yeats's intricacies have not grown sweet
and clear, not all of them anyway, yet he triumphs again in the
dramatizing of them. It is very difficult to choose between *At the
Hawk's Well* and *The Only Jealousy of Emer,* whether as play or
poem. Nothing else in Yeats's drama matches them. I prefer *At
the Hawk's Well,* but that shows only that I am more at home
with a drama or poem of self-recognition, than one of self-sacrifice. The self-sacrifice of Emer does not save Cuchulain; no one is
saved in Yeats, except through the fullness of the *dreaming-back*
and the acceptance of necessary reincarnation. But then self-recognition could not save Cuchulain either, unless becoming oneself is
as much salvation as heroism requires.

The Will of Phase 12, we must remember, is called "The
Forerunner" because the phase is fragmentary and violent. Repre-
sentative of Cuchulain's phase is Yeats's intellectual hero, Nietzsche, and the True Mask or salvation of Nietzsche and
Cuchulain (or Yeats, when he can adopt their extravagance) is
"Self-exaggeration." The False Mask, to which Nietzsche suc-
succumbed in life and Yeats's hero in his last play, *The Death of
Cuchulain,* is "Self-abandonment." [11] Yeats, like Shelley, suffered
the Body of Fate of Phase 17, "Loss," but the Body of Fate for
Nietzsche and Cuchulain is the less tragic one of "Enforced intellectual action." The relevance of these categories should be apparent in the following account of the play.

True to phase, Cuchulain "is a cup that remembers but its
own fullness," for the hero, because "wrought to a frenzy of desire
for truth of self" is able to believe supremely in those values that
personality creates in character's despite. Yeats's hero, because he
is uniquely the man who has overcome himself, need not prove

his victories. What then remains for his *antithetical* quest? "Noble extravagance," is Yeats's stirring answer; the hero must pay for his fullness. Yeats does not bother to say why, but allows us to abstract the cost from the accomplishment; the hero has achieved an *antithetical* fullness that nature does not permit, and for this expulsion of nature he is punished tyrannically by nature, to adapt an apothegm of Goethe. Nature strikes back at the hero at the only point possible, through the Image:

> The man follows an Image, created or chosen by the *Creative Mind* from what Fate offers; would persecute and dominate it; and this Image wavers between the concrete and sensuous Image.[12]

There is the pattern of *The Only Jealousy of Emer:* Cuchulain must waver between two Images, the concrete one of Emer or Eithne Inguba, and the purely sensuous one of the Woman of the Sidhe, representative of Phase 15, even as the earthly women are of Phase 14, or the nearest the hero could encounter in his quest for a woman of complete beauty. We need to remember that the hero is not the poet, and so his relations with the Sidhe are not the poet's relations with the Muse. This is the central problem of *The Only Jealousy of Emer,* for any reader's interpretation of the play must turn upon the reader's judgment as to which of Cuchulain's possible fates is necessarily preferable, in the play's own context. Is it imaginative gain or loss that the hero is reclaimed from Fand, Woman of the Sidhe? Even more simply, how are we to take the play's title? Emer's only jealousy is of Fand, and results from her realization that Bricriu's taunting question to her is self-answering: "but do those tire/ That love the Sidhe?" Are we, as readers, expected by the play to condemn this jealousy, or to value it as the basis of Emer's self-sacrifice? *Per Amica Silentia Lunae,* written the year before the play was conceived, associates the quests for the Mask by poet and hero, yet keeps them distinct:

> The poet finds and makes his mask in disappointment, the hero in defeat. The desire that is satisfied is not a great desire, nor has the shoulder used all its might that an unbreakable gate has never strained. . . . For a hero loves the world till it breaks him, and the poet till it has broken faith. . . . The poet or the hero, no matter

upon what bark they found their mask, so teeming their fancy, somewhat change its lineaments. . . .[13]

Yeats has broken up his earlier dream-self of *The Shadowy Waters* into two separate but allied components; what was Forgael is now partly Cuchulain, partly Yeats. The reality-principle is at work, operating in *The Only Jealousy of Emer* after Yeats's marriage. Immensely difficult as it must be to relate the play to Yeats's life, we at least can see that the play was not possible until after his marriage. The sensuous image of Fand is the still-hovering vision of Maud Gonne; the division of the concrete image between Emer and Eithne Inguba may be the fantasy of the still recently married man, wavering between his wife and Iseult Gonne, to whom *Per Amica Silentia Lunae* was a kind of love letter, and a plangent farewell. *The Only Jealousy of Emer* is a farewell also, to Yeats's dream of a life lived with a Muse, whether by poet or potential hero. But the farewell is ambiguous, for the *antithetical* quester in this poet will not die. When he wrote an introduction for the later prose version of the play, *Fighting the Waves*, Yeats concluded that his quest could not conclude:

> "Everything he loves must fly," everything he desires; Emer too must renounce desire, but there is another love, that which is like the man-at-arms in the Anglo-Saxon poem, "doom eager." Young, we discover an opposite through our love; old, we discover our love through some opposite neither hate nor despair can destroy, because it is another self, a self that we have fled in vain.[14]

Certainly this is more self-comment than commentary on Cuchulain in the play. I think the play less than coherent dramatically because we cannot know whether to wish Cuchulain to end with Fand, or with his wife and mistress, whether he ought to belong to the Condition of Fire, or to the Terrestrial Condition. But what confuses dramatically may enrich lyrically, and the play seems stronger as symbolic poem because we cannot establish our sympathies with any assurance. Cuchulain is one of the "Doom eager," as befits so violent and amorous a man; Yeats is, and is not. Can we speak of defeat or victory, whether for the *daimonic* or the human world, in this play? Or is it that Yeats, having chosen a wife, must now grant less to the *daimonic* world than ideally he would have wished to grant?

The world of Fand possesses "the murderous innocence of the sea," against which Cuchulain fought in *On Baile's Strand* and in Yeats's early poem on the hero's death. In fighting the sea, Cuchulain confirms his role as heroic ideal, since the battle is hopeless; the sun must set in the waves. But Cuchulain cannot be slain by the sea, and *The Only Jealousy of Emer* is an *antithetical* Resurrection, not from scattering to a unity, in Blake's manner, but from Dionysiac frenzy to an illusive natural calm, in which the hero cannot possibly abide. On the level of action, the play is a natural victory, but Yeats was certain that every natural victory belonged either to the beast of desire or the demon of hatred, and so depended upon *antithetical* energies in any case. Yet a natural victory is an occult defeat, even if brought about through the bestial desires of Cuchulain and his women, and the *daimonic* hatred of Bricriu for Fand, and occult defeats are so rare in Yeats as to be very precious. Hence, our troubled response as readers is to admire Emer for her self-sacrifice, though it is motivated by her greater jealousy of Fand than of any natural rival, and so is based upon what Blake had taught Yeats to despise as the selfish virtues of the natural, possessive heart.

Blake is one of the few poets who would have celebrated a defeat for the Muse as an imaginative victory, for Blake invoked the Daughters of Beulah only to admonish and chastise them. Yeats however is more typical in being a celebration of the Muse, whatever the human cost, and *The Only Jealousy of Emer* therefore records Fand's defeat as an imaginative catastrophe. As none of the play's human characters, the hero and his two women, contribute to that consciousness of imaginative defeat, it seems clear that the work divides into play and poem at its close, with the dramatic force conflicting with the poetic meaning, by which I do not mean the esoteric meaning as imagined by Wilson and those critics who accept his account of the play.[15] The only dramatic sense of loss at the play's close is Emer's, and the common reader's, for he is impelled to sympathize with her as a victim of dramatic irony. Her moral heroism (granting, for a moment, such a description) saves Cuchulain from the Otherworld, but only for the pragmatic sake of Eithne Inguba. But, in terms of the play's imaginative design, Cuchulain has been saved from everything that is most to be desired, the *daimonic* beauty and perfect love of Fand's full moon, that perfect consummation of the sun-hero and the moon-beauty that would free the hero from the cycles of retribution and rebirth he must continue to suffer. I do not see how one can avoid the conclusion that *The Only Jealousy of Emer* fails as drama, unlike *At the Hawk's Well*, or *On Baile's Strand*, though as extended lyric it is at least equal to the former and clearly superior to the latter. Perhaps occult and dramatic defeat are related in the play, as are natural and lyrical victory, odd as such combinations must be in Yeats.

The immense imaginative strength of *The Only Jealousy of Emer* results from its coherence and insight in handling Yeats's most difficult theme, the genesis of love and beauty in Phases 14 and 15. In his Notes on the play, Yeats emphasizes this thematic concern, his "convictions about the nature and history of a woman's beauty," centering on Castiglione's formula, "that the physical beauty of woman is the spoil or monument of the victory of the soul." This victory, Yeats insists, is itself occult, for it is "the result of emotional toil in past lives." Difficult as this is conceptually, it is clarified by the beautiful opening lyric of *The Only Jealousy of Emer*. Blake's opening quatrain in *The Book of Thel* is used by Yeats to suggest the necessity for a descent into experience deeper than any one incarnation can accomplish. The mole knows what is in the pit, but the toils of measurement necessary to make a woman's beauty go "beyond eagle or mole/ Beyond hearing and seeing," into "the labyrinth of the mind," the cycle of incarnations in history. Yeats uses two characteristic images for woman's beauty, white sea-bird and sea-shell, both going back to his early love poetry, both Shelleyan (though the shell image here, as Whitaker discovered, comes most directly from a poem of Edwin Arnold) [16] and both coming out of the vortex of murderous innocence. Both stanzas of the song, frail bird and fragile shell, emphasize the moment of daybreak, when Shelley's star of infinite desire fades into the experiential dawn of the sun. In each stanza, woman's beauty is associated with calm daybreak after a stormy night. The night is our world, daybreak Fand's beauty, when the natural sun of Cuchulain may be absorbed by her greater light. This deliberately is set against natural sense, and is the "toils of measurement," the "discipline" or "bonds no man could unbind" that alone raise or drag into being woman's loveliness. The echo of the *Ode on a Grecian Urn* (noted by Mrs. Vendler) is undoubtedly deliberate, for Yeats's notion of woman's beauty is being paralleled to Keats's unravish'd bride's legend of pursuit and escape.[17] "What pursuing or fleeing,/ What wounds, what bloody press,/ Dragged into being/ This loveliness?" answers Keats's "What wild ecstasy?" with a Dionysiac rhetorical question. The emotional toil of past existences then must mean the ecstasy of fullness in experience that beautiful women have known more completely than all others in earlier incarnations. The justice of beauty is thus a movement from fullness to fragility, for "a strange, unserviceable thing" has known much service in its earlier lives. This may mean that the beauty of Cuchulain's women, the touching beauty of Phase 14, is necessarily never at peace and can bring Cuchulain no peace. The sea raises beauty but also throws it upon the shore, drags it by force into a being too frail to withstand the sea's fury. But the beauty of Fand is the sea's own beauty, "inhuman, of the veritable ocean," allied to the beauty of Phase 15 as the tides are to the moon. I take this as the difficult meaning of the opening song, and of the entire play in its aspect of extended lyric; Yeats, and Cuchulain, must abide in the troubled beauty of the Terrestrial Condition. A greater, less fragile beauty, beckons in the stormy sea, but we are to turn from it.

The plot, such as it is, of the play has been fully discussed by earlier critics, and I will not rehearse it again here. It emphasizes Cuchulain's passivity, as though his trance suggests the hero's essential helplessness, when contested for by beings of Phases 14 and 15. Of Fand, the plot gives us one essential vision, the need of the Muse to escape her own solitude, about which Mrs. Vendler has written with insight.[18] As I understand the play, Fand's tragic mistake is to have chosen hero rather than poet (as Maud Gonne erred also). By falling in love with Cuchulain, she has not chosen a true opposite, and so does not obtain the erotic object she requires if her *daimonic* intensity is to be completed. For Cuchulain is not a poet-like hero; his actions do not express Fand's image even if Yeats's poem does. She needs a Forgael, and Yeats can no longer create one for her. When she dances for Cuchulain, she thinks she dances for the young and passionate man who desired her at the Hawk's Well, but she is tragically mistaken. As Cuchulain brokenly says: "my memories/ Weigh down my hands, abash my eyes"; the hero grows old, but the Muse, like the dead, moves "ever towards a dreamless youth." The poor Muse, in Yeats's grim fable, is self-deceived, for while Cuchulain may still be heroic (though there is not the slightest evidence in the play to show this), he is singularly lacking in exuberance, in that Blakean energy that is Eternal Delight. Exuberance, Blake said, is beauty; Fand is exuberant, but Cuchulain is no longer beautiful. I disagree then with Mrs. Vendler; Fand is no longer "Cuchulain's natural kin," and the hero, alas, has been domesticated in Emer's world.[19] We may, at this point, choose to remember again that the poet had been domesticated also. Domestication here follows the pattern that Shelley knew and feared, and against which Blake protested with an immense passion; to have a wife, for hero or poet, is to become lost in a labyrinth of "intricacies of blind remorse," to be made impure by many guilty memories. The mistaken Muse, Fand, thinks that Cuchulain can join her in the occult or imaginative world that has purged its remorse, but he cannot. In the play's final version, the choice is made for Cuchulain, but an earlier text makes clear that Cuchulain would make the same choice for himself. Mrs. Vendler ascribes his choice to resentment and scorn of Fand, and Yeats's nervousness at thus offending the Muse is seen by her as the grounds for revision.[20] It may be so, but there is another possibility. Does he scorn her fear of memory, or does he not rather fear to be without memories? When he says that "there's a folly in the deathless Sidhe/ Beyond man's reach," does he mean "courage" when he says "folly"? Fand says she is ashamed to have chosen a man "so knotted to impurity" and by "impurity" she appears to mean mere "nature." Fand is defeated because the *antithetical* hero is exposed as a natural man, a reduction the more affecting for the "intricacies of pain" it reveals in Yeats himself.

The Only Jealousy of Emer ends with a difficult song that expresses Fand's bitter grief and Yeats's acute sense of his vision's

limitation. Fand, the Woman of the Sidhe, is the "statue of solitude,/ Moving there and walking," a phantom with a beating
heart, like the Christ of *The Resurrection*. That heart cannot be
stilled at last, despite the bitter reward it has received, which is
the loss of Cuchulain. For the Muse's lovers are faithless: "He
that has loved the best/ May turn from a statue/ His too human
breast." Cuchulain too was human, all too human; the Forerunner is not always a Zarathustra. We are asked to attend to the suffering of the bereft Muse, and while it is difficult to feel sympathy
for an occult grief, Yeats is unique enough among the poets almost to compel it in us. Even the Sidhe may be betrayed; the
Belle Dame wither, in spite of her beauty, on the cold hill's side.

The Dreaming of the Bones

Though the least famous of the *Four Plays for Dancers,* whether
as play or poem, *The Dreaming of the Bones* is particularly interesting in the context of Romantic tradition. The play has been
read as versified Cornelius Agrippa by Wilson, who oddly compares it to Blake's *Tiriel,* presumably because he regards the latter as versified Cornelius Agrippa also.[21] But the play has nothing in common with *Tiriel,* though it has its affinities with Blake,
and even more with Shelley. Critics rightly regard *The Dreaming
of the Bones* as the closest approach Yeats made to the Noh form,
in this case to "the Noh of spirits." The best of these studies is by
David R. Clark, and I will avoid further reference to the problem
of form here.[22]

The Dreaming of the Bones, by being closer to the Noh, is
necessarily more of an extended lyric than the other plays for dancers. Its theme is not purgation, but rather the blocking of purgation by remorse, a major Romantic theme Yeats had inherited
primarily from Shelley's polemic, and secondarily from Blake's attack upon "pity" and the other selfish virtues of the natural heart.
The lovers in Yeats's play, as he himself commented, "have lost
themselves in a . . . self-created winding of the labyrinth of conscience."[23] In *The Municipal Gallery Revisited,* Yeats was to
praise Kevin O'Higgins as "a soul incapable of remorse or

rest." [24] Before that, in what seem to me his two finest poems, *Vacillation* and *A Dialogue of Self and Soul,* he had struggled with remorse as an ultimate antagonist to his imagination. In the rejected stanza of *Coole Park and Ballylee, 1931,* which became *The Choice,* Yeats wrote of "the day's vanity, the night's remorse," as though remorse were the conscience's vanity. When Blake, in "Night VIII" of *The Four Zoas,* says that "Desperate remorse swallows the present in a quenchless rage," he sums up his case against the false virtue of natural contrition.[25] With Shelley, the polemic against remorse is a veritable obsession, but humanistic in its liberating purpose. Remorse, in Shelley's poetry, is equated with self-contempt, which destroys the imagination. The single passage in Shelley, attacking remorse, which is likeliest to have affected Yeats most deeply is Cythna's address to the Mariners in Canto VIII of *The Revolt of Islam.* Cythna, we know, was Yeats's prototype for Maud Gonne, the dream woman he loved before Maud appeared to merge with the Shelleyan vision. For Maud Gonne as for Cythna, the pure purposes of the revolutionary excluded all possibility of remorse, and Yeats was deeply influenced by his beloved's temperament. Cythna denounces "the dark idolatry of self," the "vacant expiation" of remorse. Blake's "Desperate remorse swallows the present in a quenchless rage" is paralleled by Cythna's: "The past is Death's, the future is thine own." [26]

In the mythology of *A Vision,* the dead can be redeemed from remorse through a fullness of the past recaptured, a purging justice of completeness in the *dreaming-back.* But the ghosts of *The Dreaming of the Bones* are not redeemed from their remorse, for the young revolutionary soldier is as remorseless as the dreadful old man of *Purgatory,* and will not forgive the dead, who cannot learn to forgive themselves. Blake and Shelley did not deal in ghosts, but Yeats's ghosts are usually lively enough, and the Romantic polemic against remorse is relevant to them. All mumbo-jumbo aside, Yeats's purgatorial process is structurally in the Romantic topology, for the traditional purgatory (as in Dante) is placed just before the Earthly Paradise, which must be gained by a mounting of the purgatorial steps. In the Romantic topological displacement, the Earthly Paradise is placed just before purgatory, rather than just after it. So, in Keats's *The Fall of Hyperion*, Keats first sojourns in the regained Garden of Eden, and then suffers his purgatorial confrontation on the steps of Moneta's shrine. Similarly, Blake's equivocal state-of-being, Beulah or lower paradise, is first a place of fulfilled desire, and then becomes a purgatorial trial for the imagination. Dante's Paolo and Francesca are agonizingly together but separate, as are Yeats's Diarmuid and Dervorgilla, but Yeats's lovers had known more of the earthly paradise of lovers' union, and are tortured more terribly by the endless purgatory of their mutual remorse.

On its surface, *The Dreaming of the Bones* seems remote from Yeats's deepest concerns, and is a cold work, merely formulaic in its occasional intensities. Its 1916 revolutionary setting is gratuitous, and Yeats's thoughts on Ireland's freedom from air pollution are imaginatively deadly ("we have neither coal, nor iron ore,/ To make us wealthy and corrupt the air"). The play is saved by its persuasive conviction that shades are more passionate than the living. Though the young revolutionary has fought in the Post Office, it is the ghostly lovers who wear heroic masks, for the soldier lacks imagination, dismissing the dead as those who "fill waste mountains with the invisible tumult/ Of the fantastic conscience," a presage of his later failure to forgive, which is a failure of vision. When the lovers dance before him, they offer the soldier his supreme chance to cast out fanaticism and hatred, but though he almost yields, he ends in an ugly obduracy, cursing the temptation. To forgive would be to cast out remorse, for hatred is a kind of inverted remorse, and is the soldier's own "dark idolatry of self." Yeats had seen that hatred disfigure Maud Gonne, and other women of surpassing excellence, and in his more visionary and redemptive moods he understood such hatred as a blight upon Ireland.

The final song of the play makes clear that the blight withers imagination. Music is heard on the night air, and the bitter dreams of dead lovers "darken our sun." Remembering the lyric that concluded *The Land of Heart's Desire*, Yeats hears again the wind that blew out of the gates of the day, but now it is not the lonely of heart who is withered away. "Our luck is withered away," for the luck of a people cannot survive the related furies of hatred and remorse. *The Dreaming of the Bones* suffers from its lack of personal intensity, but it is Yeats's most imaginatively telling parable for his own nation.

Calvary

Yeats's Christ is his own uneasy creation, despite some abortive attempts by critics to relate this figure to Blake's Jesus. The uneasiness is felt throughout *Calvary,* a difficult play to characterize or enjoy, though not difficult to understand, if understanding merely means reducing into Yeats's formulas. If it means something more imaginatively active, then *Calvary* has its mystery, but the mystery belongs more to Yeats's idea of Christ as the *primary* gyre, than it does to the simplistic confrontations that form the play. I have discussed the *antithetical* quest rather fully in this book, as any student of Yeats must. *Calvary* compels a fuller consideration of the *primary* than any other work by Yeats, for Christ (though an abstract one) is the god of the *primary* cycle, even as death appears to be the god of the *antithetical.* Yeats was imaginatively free (though with indifferent results) in writing about death, but though not quite in fetters when writing about Christ, he betrays a curious nervousness for so credulous a mystagogue.

I have expounded the *primary* in my first chapter on *A Vision,* but wish to make a fresh start here. Yeats's terms have not lost all their rhetorical shock value, which is greatly to Yeats's credit, but standing back from his terms is therefore a valuable safeguard, if we would ruminate upon them dispassionately. Though Yeats, as I indicated in my opening chapters, founded his distinction between dispensations upon his creative misinterpretation of Blake, the swerve from Blake is so great that sustained parallel studies of Blake and Yeats are never likely to prove fruitful. Yeats's ideas of contrary dispensations or world-epochs are more in the Gnostic pattern, and so result in the very un-Blakean dialectic of Christ having power over our epoch, but not over the one that will succeed us. Our epoch, soon to end, has exalted the rational, but paradoxically has tried to make self-surrender, or the soul's triumph over self, a rational ideal. Yeats's Christ is the god of this paradoxical, perhaps impossible *primary* quest, founded upon the conjunction of Mars and Venus. Character, formed through self-surrender in war and love, triumphs that it may yield itself to the universal, and so lose its separateness. Viewed as impulse rather than rational imitation of a Savior, this quest leads to a Dionysian ecstasy, which is not the ecstasy that Yeats seeks, as he wishes to create rather than transcend forms. The blend of elements in Yeats's syncretic system defies the common reader's expectations, for who could have prophesied that Yeats would range himself with the Apollonian against the Dionysian?

If Yeats's Christ is the divine goal of our impulse toward unity, it would follow that he would not be much concerned with the accidents of personality, among whom heroes and poets are to be numbered. The conjunction of Jupiter and Saturn, power and un-self-consciousness, produces heroes like Oedipus, who by knowing nothing but their own minds come to know everything. This is the antithesis of Yeats's Christ, who begins by knowing everything and would abolish every individual mind, and whose apparent ecstasy resolves itself as wisdom. The *primary,* in Yeats's formulation, cannot desire what it lacks, for by lacking nothing, it can only pity everything that is not itself. Yeats's Christ belongs to Phase 15, necessarily (though this is Phase 15 of the *primary* cycle) because so radically unified a being must be of that only phase where such unity is possible, yet Christ cannot abide in Phase 15, even a *primary* Phase 15, for his impulse is Dionysian, and he must withdraw all other being to his own, by imparting his being to all others. This is the odd Yeatsian rationalization for the Incarnation, and accounts for much of the resentment expressed by Lazarus and Judas in *Calvary.*

We ought now to be able to understand Yeats's curious association of Christ with science and the rationalization of society, which allowed Yeats to league the Christians and the Marxists in the same camp of the objective, or "those who serve." So the Russian Revolution was for Yeats the last of the Christian revolutions, while the Fascist counter-revolutions were *antithetical* indications of influx, of the approaching post-Christian cycle. Against the science of the *primary* rationalist, Christ, Yeats sought to establish his own New Science, with *A Vision* as central text. Cuchulain, Celtic contemporary of Christ, was to be exalted as his antithesis, a program Yeats happily abandoned quite early on. But the increasing decadence of Cuchulain as hero, highly evident in the plays for dancers and culminating in *The Death of Cuchulain,* seems to have compelled Yeats to bring Christ upon stage also, that his limitations might be revealed. So *Calvary* is the complement to the plays of the Hawk's Well and Emer's jealousy, and we are invited to juxtapose the ironies of *antithetical* defeat with the greater ironies of *primary* apparent victory.

In his notes to *Calvary,* Yeats tells us that objective men "are never alone in their thought, which . . . always seeks the welfare of some cause or institution," while subjective men are free to quest for the unique and personal.[27] This makes Christ sound rather like an executive of a benevolent Foundation, and we need not be surprised that Yeats goes on to emphasize "the objective loneliness of Christ" which can never be self-sufficient. As Yeats goes on to say, the play surrounds Christ with all those he cannot save, precisely because they are or long to be self-sufficient, lonely perhaps but subjectively lonely, needing only their own shadows, at most. Yeats's source, as several critics have shown, is a parable of Oscar Wilde, to which Yeats can add little.[28] But Wilde knew something about intellectual despair, and something about the reality of evil; Yeats knew nothing of either, and *Calvary* would be offensive if it were not so cunningly ironic as to qualify all its own intensities.

As a play, *Calvary* does not exist, for nothing happens in it; even in *The Dreaming of the Bones* there is the one event, when the soldier refuses to forgive the lovers, but there is nothing comparable in *Calvary.* We have a parable of Wilde's elaborated into a symbolist poem, but do we have a making of Yeats's own? *Calvary* consists of an opening lyric, three confrontations—between Christ and Lazarus, Judas, the Roman soldiers respectively—and a closing lyric. The two lyrics are greatly superior to the three intervening episodes, which show Yeats as a novice in the art at which Browning was a master, for Lazarus and Judas will remind an attentive reader of such monologists as Karshish and Cleon, a reminder not flattering to Yeats.

Rather than risk a dramatization of the Passion, Yeats has the tact to distance us from Calvary's turbulence by making the play Christ's own *dreaming-back.* Christ encounters his own victims, for as the god of the *primary* cycle he is responsible for everything in it; this is Wilde's witty insight, not Yeats's. The complaint of Lazarus and Judas is not that Christ has failed to save them, but that his love has damned them by taking from them all that was unique and personal. Mrs. Vendler says that Christ has made them what they are; I would modify this only by saying that the making was a creation-fall, marring more than it gave, or as Mrs. Vendler says later, ruining them.[29] The subjective birds of the opening and closing lyrics have not been marred, but they do not belong to Christ's *primary* dispensation, and are holding on tenuously in solipsistic self-absorption until the new influx takes place. In the meantime, "God has not died for the white heron," but presumably for all those whom he made and marred. These include Lazarus and Judas, who reject his sacrifice, and Martha and the three Marys, who wail, as Blake would have said, on the verge of non-existence. But how is Yeats justified in excluding his natural men, the Roman soldiers who are shown as gamblers on the Great Wheel of the cycles? Though his notes explain that these worship Chance, that hardly makes them free of the *primary* gyre.[30] To be indifferent is not to be self-sufficient; it is only not to know that one is dependent. This makes Christ's despair at the soldiers' unconcern quite unconvincing, and much the weakest moment in the play.

Calvary fails as a poem despite its ironies of apprehension, for its coherence is purchased by its hollowness. All Yeats's rhetorical skill and long-nurtured symbolism do not suffice to make its poverty of invention compelling, or its reductive and tendentious ideas profound. Yeats is defeated by his own temerity, for even an abstract dreamer-back of a Christ is too strong a figure to tolerate this play's indignities. To show a passive and defeated Cuchulain is within the bounds of Yeats's abilities; to exhibit an ironically self-defeated Christ would demand too much from a greater poet and dramatist than Yeats. A wealth of accumulated association is not to be overthrown by one myth-maker, as Blake wisely saw when he chose to assimilate Christ to his own vision by making him the central image of the saving imagination, the Los-Blake-Jesus of the last chapter of *Jerusalem*. *Calvary* can be admired for its ambition, but its accomplishment does not match its audacity.

17: Michael Robartes
and the Dancer

Placed as it is in Yeats's career between two much richer volumes, *The Wild Swans at Coole* and *The Tower,* this would be a justly neglected book if it were not for the fame of *Easter 1916* and *The Second Coming.* Beyond these, the volume's strongest poems, *Demon and Beast* and *A Prayer for My Daughter,* serve as ironic prologue and tendentious epilogue for *The Second Coming,* while the other lyrics largely fail, whether as political poetry or as explorations of the poet's vision of *daimonic* love. The volume's unifying theme is hatred, political and sexual, hatred being a passion that Yeats, like his *persona* Ribh in the later *Supernatural Songs,* studied with great diligence, but also with a certain saving wariness.

The title poem, despite its genuine wit, fails through archness and triviality, adding nothing to the wisdom of *Adam's Curse.* But *Solomon and the Witch* and *An Image from a Past Life* fail for a more genuinely disturbing cause, related to the failure of some of the later poems in *The Wild Swans at Coole. Solomon and the Witch,* for all its deftness, is too slight to sustain the difficult dialectic of chance and choice that even the play *Calvary* bears much better, while the exquisite poem on the vision of "a sweetheart from another life" relies too much for its coherence on Yeats's complex note explaining the "Over Shadower or Ideal Form." Texts for exposition, as Yeats wryly called such poems, rarely cease to be texts for exposition after they are expounded.

Easter 1916 is a puzzling poem, despite the clarity of its rhetoric and the remarkably high quality of the commentaries devoted to it; puzzling because even its excellences are uncharacteristic of Yeats. Like his masters Blake and Shelley, Yeats is both a political and a visionary poet, and like them he is usually best when the visionary greatly outweighs the political in the amalgam of the poetry. But *Easter 1916* is as much an exception in Yeats's canon as *The Mask of Anarchy* is in Shelley's or *The French Revolution* in Blake's. There is vision in *Easter 1916,* in the "terrible beauty" born out of motley, the utter change and transformation brought about by the sacrificial intensity of Connolly and the other martyrs of revolution. But vision is not the strength of the poem, which excels in a sober coloring of accurate moral description, a quality normally lacking in Yeats. *Easter 1916* is a model of sanity and proportion, and is genuinely Yeats's eighteenth-century poem, in telling contrast to the extravagance and arbitrariness of later poems like *Blood and the Moon* and *The Seven Sages,* where the Augustan aspiration is at odds with much ill-sustained moral posturing and personal fabling.

The transition between *Easter 1916* and its lesser pendants, and the visionary poems clustered around *The Second Coming,* is provided with real skill by the placing of the slight but very sensitive lyric, *Towards Break of Day.* Here the theme is shared phantasmagoria, as in *Solomon and the Witch,* yet the dream material is more universal than the esoteric matter of the earlier poem, and Yeats thereby maintains proportion. As in the political poems, Yeats displays the careful bitterness of a maturely balanced man as he studies the nostalgias and concludes reasonably: "Nothing that we love over-much/ Is ponderable to our touch." In contrast is the "bitterer sleep" of his wife's vision, with its hint that her husband fails her dreams.[1] We are moved closer by this to the tremendous visionary bitterness of *The Second Coming,* and the uneasiness at such intensity shown by *A Prayer for My Daughter* and the more amiable *Demon and Beast.*

Demon and Beast

Yeats refreshes most, necessarily, when he allows the natural man a voice. *Demon and Beast* is a moving poem, but is especially appealing because only a literal handful of Yeats's poems speak against the *antithetical,* as this does. The greatest in this kind, by Yeats, are *Vacillation* and *The Man and the Echo,* but they are near attempting the Sublime, at least in theme. *Demon and Beast* has a deliberate homeliness, and a cunning clumsiness about it. Though centered upon Pater's privileged moments or secularized epiphanies, the poem manages to avoid intensities. After so many heraldic birds—swans, herons, hawks, peacocks—a non-symbolic gull and a mere duck charm us:

> To watch a white gull take
> A bit of bread thrown up into the air;
> Now gyring down and perning there
> He splashed where an absurd
> Portly green-pated bird
> Shook off the water from his back;

It is even a pleasure to find "gyre" and "perne" in so amiable and apparently relaxed a context. Intellectually, the context is not relaxed, for Yeats remains certain that all natural victories belong not to nature, but to either of the poem's *antithetical* forces, the beast of subjective passion or the demon of intellectual hatred.[2] Yeats goes far beyond his *antithetical* precursors, Blake and Shelley, when he insists again, in this otherwise uncharacteristic poem, "that never yet had freeman/ Right mastery of natural things." This insistence prophesies the next poem in this volume, *The Second Coming,* with its opening image of the falconer or freeman losing his mastery of the falcon or natural thing. Yet, here in *Demon and Beast,* Yeats strives to retain, if only for half a day, a natural sweetness wholly at variance with his mythology of self.

The poem's demon is "crafty," and governs his "hatred," which generally is directed against the *primary* or objective

world; the beast is "loud," governing "desire," but this is not desire capable of "natural victory," but the Shelleyan desire to find
more in this world than any can understand, the self-consuming
desire of the Poet-Wanderer of *Alastor*. Both demon and beast ha-
bitually plague the poet; he spends his life whirling about the
labyrinth of fruitless hatred for what is, and unappeasable desire
for what can never be. The poem exists to celebrate a highly mu-
table moment of release, a brief freedom from the *antithetical*
quest, as celebrated in the first stanza. Release from hatred is
studied in the second stanza, and from "being no more demoniac"
in the third. Free of the "loud beast," Yeats finds that "all men's
thoughts grew clear/ Being dear as mine are dear," while momentary liberation from the demon (Yeats might as well have written
daimon) permits "a stupid happy creature" to "rouse my whole
nature." A remarkable transfer of cross-categories takes place
here. Insight and tolerance become possible in regard to the
thoughts of others, when *antithetical* desire is stilled, while affective response in sympathy with nature is liberated by freedom
from *antithetical* thought and its attendant hatred. Though Yeats
is being true to his dialectic of opposites living each other's death,
dying each other's life, he moves us not by his fidelity to his own
categories, but because he writes out of a psychological truth, or
at least the truth of his own psychology.

When he turns, in the fourth stanza, to a stress on the limitations of his naturalizing epiphany, Yeats necessarily moves us less.
It is difficult to believe that *every* natural victory belongs to *daimonic* thought or desire, and a little chilling to have the poet attribute the privileged moment to "mere growing old." There is
mitigation when the stanza ends with the poet's heartfelt wish
somehow to prolong the moment.

Demon and Beast is poetically most impressive where it is
most difficult, in its fifth and last stanza:

> O what a sweetness strayed
> Through barren Thebaid,
> Or by the Mareotic sea
> When that exultant Anthony
> And twice a thousand more

> Starved upon the shore
> And withered to a bag of bones!
> What had the Caesars but their thrones?

"Nothing" is the answer to that final, rhetorical question, for the Caesars represent here all those who live only by the Prolific, and without the Devouring, to apply a relevant dialectic from *The Marriage of Heaven and Hell*. The stanza's point is oblique, but very strong. Sweetness of the *primary*, natural kind, such as has come to Yeats in this poem, comes *as sweetness* only to *antithetical* men, whether to poets and thinkers like Yeats and Pater, ascetics of the spirit, or to more extreme spiritual athletes like St. Anthony and similar desert monks of the barren Thebaid. Exultation comes only to the starved, not to the Caesars on their thrones. *Demon and Beast* ends as *apologia* for a life dominated by demon and beast, but the defence of the myth of poetic subjectivity has gained unusual dignity by all that the poem concedes to the natural man.

The Second Coming

Increasingly this is seen as Yeats's central poem, and not only by exegetes, but by whatever general literary public we still have. The Johnsonian respect for the common reader must enter into any fresh consideration of *The Second Coming*. Though I will indicate limitations of the poem, my concern here is not with its limitations, but with the nature of its power. My prime subject, as throughout this book, is Yeats's Romanticism, particularly with regard to the austere and terrible melancholy of Poetic Influence within that tradition. As much as any other poem by Yeats, *The Second Coming* bears its direct relation to Blake and Shelley as an overtly defining element in its meaning. The poem quotes Blake and both echoes and parodies the most thematically vital passage in Shelley's most ambitious poem, *Prometheus Unbound*, as a number of critics have remarked.[3]

The manuscripts of *The Second Coming*, as given by Stallworthy, are something of a surprise in relation to the poem's final text.[4] Yeats is writing (according to Ellmann) in January 1919, in the aftermath of war and revolution.[5] His mind is on the Russian Revolution and its menace, particularly to aristocrats, to *antithetical* men. In a way instantly familiar to a student of Blake and Shelley, as Yeats was, the Revolution suggests an apocalypse, and the time of troubles preceding it. But unlike his Romantic precursors, Yeats is on the side of the counter-revolutionaries, and his apocalyptic poem begins by seeing the intervention against revolution as being too late to save the ceremoniously innocent: "The germans are . . . now to Russia come/ Though every day some innocent has died." In his grief for these innocents, Yeats laments the absence of those Blake had satirized as Albion's Angels, the champions of reaction: "And there's no Burke to cry aloud no Pitt." With no one to lead them against revolutionary violence: "The good are wavering," while the worst prevail.[6]

Donald Davie has remarked that the title of Yeats's poem is a misnomer, since Christ's advent was not for Yeats the First Coming.[7] I wish to go further, and suggest that the title is not only a misnomer, but a misleading and illegitimate device for conferring upon the poem a range of reference and imaginative power that it does not possess, and cannot sustain. The poem should have been called *The Second Birth,* which is the wording Yeats first employs in its drafts: "Surely the great falcon must come/ Surely the hour of the second birth is here." Two lines later Yeats first cried out "The second Birth!" and later in revision altered "Birth" to "Coming." [8] As he revised, Yeats evidently thought of associating his vision in the poem both with Christ's prophecy of his Second Coming and with Revelation's account of the Antichrist. I propose the argument that the poem, even as he revised it, does not justify this portentous association. It remains a poem about the second birth of the *antithetical* Divinity or spirit, and a few verbal changes did not alter the poem's conception enough to give a full coherence to its intended irony of reference. Kierkegaard, in the thirteenth thesis of the defense of his *The Concept of Irony* says that irony is like vexation over the fact that others also enjoy what the soul desires for itself. This is worth remembering in judging the irony of *The Second Coming,* and in brooding upon Poetic Influence.

Yeats's poem is a vision not of the Second Coming, but of the Second Birth of the Sphinx, not of Thebes but of Memphis, not the Riddler and Strangler but the one-eyed Divinity of the Sun: "An eye blank and pitiless as the sun," as the draft has it.[9] This is the male Sphinx who had haunted Yeats ever since he had read Shelley's *Ozymandias* in his youth, as distinct from the female Sphinx who had served as a Muse of Destruction for the poets and painters of his Tragic Generation. The Egyptian Sphinx is a kind of demonic parody of one of the Cherubim of Ezekiel's vision, the Cherub taken by Blake as the archetype of his Urizen, whose "stony sleep" in *The Book of Urizen* is used by Yeats in the poem as a description of the dormant state-between-births of his "shape with lion body and the head of a man." [10]

In *The Book of Urizen* that Giant Form falls, unable to bear the battle in heaven he has provoked. To ward off the fiery wrath of his vengeful brother Eternals, he frames a rocky womb for himself:

> But Urizen laid in a stony sleep
> Unorganiz'd, rent from Eternity
>
> The Eternals said: What is this? Death
> Urizen is a clod of clay.[11]

During this stony sleep, Urizen writhes in his rocky womb, going through seven ages of creation until he emerges in a second birth as fallen man, man as he is, as we are. This is man become the Sphinx of Egypt, a demonic parody of what man was, the Living Creatures or Cherubim of Ezekiel's vision.

Yeats's poem then is about the second birth of Urizen or the Egyptian Sphinx, but in a context of revolutionary and counter-revolutionary violence, the literary context of Shelley's *Prometheus Unbound,* among other Romantic apocalypses. We need not believe that Yeats's use of Shelley here is any more unintentional than his use of Blake. The moral climax of Act I of *Prometheus Unbound* is the speech of the last Fury to the crucified Titan. The Furies have shown Prometheus visions of the failure of the French Revolution, and the failure of Christ's sacrifice. But the last Fury unfolds a worse torment:

> In each human heart terror survives
> The ravin it has gorged: the loftiest fear
> All that they would disdain to think were true:
> Hypocrisy and custom make their minds
> The fanes of many a worship, now outworn.
> They dare not devise good for man's estate,
> And yet they know not that they do not dare.

What follows is Shelley's central insight; an insight of the Left that Yeats proceeds to appropriate for the Right:

> The good want power, but to weep barren tears.
> The powerful goodness want: worse need for them.
> The wise want love; and those who love want wisdom;
> And all best things are thus confused to ill.[12]

> The best lack all conviction, while the worst
> Are full of passionate intensity.

Other echoes of Shelley are at work also, before *Ozymandias* and *The Book of Urizen* are recalled. "Things fall apart; the centre cannot hold" takes us to the tremendous lament for Mutability from *The Witch of Atlas,* when the Witch rejects all natural love:

> The solid oaks forget their strength, and strew
> Their latest leaf upon the mountains wide;
> The boundless ocean like a drop of dew
> Will be consumed—the stubborn center must
> Be scattered, like a cloud of summer dust.[13]

Because the center cannot hold, natural love cannot endure, and the Witch will not accept the unenduring. Prometheus, the figure of endurance, can scarcely bear the condition that Yeats grimly accepts, the rending apart of power and knowledge, of good and the means of good. Both Shelley and Yeats are noting the weakness of their own camps; Shelley sees the spiritual schizophrenia of his own revolutionary intelligentsia, and Yeats, writing still *before* the rise of Fascism, sees the lack of fervor of the ruling classes. In a dubious afterthought, Yeats later claimed *The Sec-*

ond Coming as a prophecy of Fascism, but if this was so, then the moral urgency we have assigned to prophecy would have to be reviewed. Conor Cruise O'Brien is the inevitable authority on the politics of Yeats, and he reminds us that "The *Freikorps* on the Polish-German border were at this time trying to do exactly what the Black and Tans were doing in Ireland and the *Freikorps* were the direct and proudly acknowledged predecessors of Hitler's Nazis." [14] The *Freikorps,* I would assume, are the Germans who are "now to Russia come" of Yeats's draft, and clearly this is for Yeats his *antithetical* defence against the *primary* "blood-dimmed tide." The greater terror to come, the apocalyptic shape or Egyptian Sphinx to be reborn, may frighten the poet as he does us, but what I hear in the poem is exultation on the speaker's part as he beholds his vision, and this exultation is not only an intellectual one.[15] But this is where critics must disagree in reading, and discussion needs to be conducted more closely.

Christianity, largely irrelevant to the poem, is dragged into its vortex by Yeats's title, and his change of the Second Birth into the Second Coming. This has resulted in some critical arbitrariness, such as Jeffares's comment on the poem's opening:

> The falcon represents man, present civilisation, becoming out of touch with Christ, whose birth was the revelation which marked the beginning of the two thousand years of Christianity.[16]

A juxtaposition of this interpretative remark with the two opening lines is not encouraging. All those lines tell us is that the falconer has lost control of his falcon, not because the bird wills disobedience, but because it has spun too far out to hear its master. Powerful as the ensuing lines may be, they are not wholly coherent, in terms of following upon this initial image. It seems likelier that the falconer, rather than the falcon, represents man, and the falcon his mastery of nature, now in the act of falling apart. The center is man; he cannot hold the falcon to an imposed discipline, and the widening gyre is therefore one with the loosing of anarchy upon the world. Anarchy is "mere" because the value-systems that could judge it portentous are being overwhelmed. What seems to me the poem's first real difficulty enters

with "the ceremony of innocence." What is it? By the most legitimate rules of interpretation, one looks nearest to hand. If the
best lack all conviction, it is because conviction must be ceremoni-
ous (in Yeats's view), and the rituals by which conviction is
taught to "the best" are not being observed. Yeats is a ritualist in
Pater's manner, where the ritual may be the best part of the belief, the only operative technique for fostering conviction. Radical
innocence, according to the matched poem, *A Prayer for My
Daughter,* is the soul's solipsistic knowledge of its own autonomy,
and is born only out of ritual, "where all's accustomed, ceremoni-
ous." The question then becomes, why does the falconer's loss of
control over the falcon betoken a lapse in the maintaining of ritual, and we thus face a dilemma. Either the opening image reduces to an emblem of ceremony, which trivializes the entire
poem, or else it does refer to man's mastery over nature, in which
case Yeats has not provided any demonstration that a loss of such
mastery necessarily leads to the abandonment of elitist ritual. Either way, an aesthetic difficulty exists, which critics continue to
evade.[17]

With the second stanza, heretofore evaded difficulties crowd
upon the detached reader, if he can resist not only Yeats's heroic
rhetoric but also the awed piety of the exegetes. The poet (or
poem's speaker) says "surely" revelation, the uncovering of apocalypse, is at hand, but what *in the poem* justifies that "surely"?
Mere anarchy does not always bring on revelation, and we would
all of us be scarred with multiple apocalypses by now if every
loosing of a blood-dimmed tide had compelled a final reality to
appear. Presumably the poet's repetition of "surely" merely indicates his own uncertainty, but nothing in the poem justifies the
subsequent and merely misleading outcry that the Second Coming, with all of its traditional reverberations, is upon us. In fact
the Second Birth of the Sphinx of Egypt, *even in the poet's personal vision* or private apocalypse, is what comes upon him, and
us. This is not unimpressive in itself, and the most indisputable
lines in the poem proclaim the origin and nature of the vision.
Difficulty enters again when the vision ends, and Yeats claims an
access of knowledge, if not of power, on the basis of his vision. He
claims to know one thing, and pretty clearly a related fact, by pre-

senting the second part of his knowledge as a climactic rhetorical question. For twenty centuries the Sphinx or Urizen, demonic parody of angelic or imaginative man, has been vexed to nightmare by the Incarnation, by the perpetual image of a myth of *primary* salvation (how to keep *A Vision's* terms out at this point, I do not know). This nightmare of Christian history is over, even as Enitharmon's dream of the Christian centuries ends in Blake's *Europe,* when Orc is re-born as the French Revolution. The Egyptian Sphinx is the rough beast who slouches toward Bethlehem to be re-born, not born, in place of the re-birth of Christ. Once the initial shock is set aside, Yeats's closing image is surely replete with difficulties. Christian apocalypses do not visualize the Child born again at Bethlehem; that is not the Christ of Revelation. There is imagistic desperation in Yeats's closing rhetorical lunge. Has he earned his ironic reversal of his own arbitrary use of the Christian reference? And is his closing image coherent in itself? In what sense will the rough beast be "born" at Bethlehem? Clearly, not literally, but is it legitimate then to use "born" for what would actually be a demonic epiphany?

The power of *The Second Coming* is not called in question by these smaller questions, but perhaps its artistry is. Winters was justified in observing that

. . . we must face the fact that Yeats's attitude toward the beast is different from ours: we may find the beast terrifying, but Yeats finds him satisfying—he is Yeats's judgment upon all that we regard as civilized. Yeats approves of this kind of brutality.[18]

But Winters was too idealistic when he concluded from this that a great poem could not be based, even in part, on "a homemade mythology and a loose assortment of untenable social attitudes." Much major poetry has been founded, in part, upon such odd materials. And one needs to dissent from Winters's judgment that the ideas of *The Second Coming* are "perfectly clear." There is a puzzle about the entire poem, which is why Yeats risked as much arbitrariness and incoherence as the poem possesses. The reason is somewhere in the dark area that the still undeveloped critical study of poetic influence must clarify. Yeats's swerve away from his precursors, in *The Second Coming* as elsewhere, is in the direction of a Gnostic quasi-determinism. The meaning of *The Second Coming* turns upon Yeats's deliberate misinterpretations of apocalyptic poems like Blake's *The Book of Urizen, Europe,* and *The Mental Traveller,* and of Shelley's *Prometheus Unbound* and *The Witch of Atlas. A Vision* deliberately associates *The Second Coming* and *The Mental Traveller,* and Yeats's late essay on *Prometheus Unbound* explicitly chides Shelley for not sharing the attitude of the speaker of *The Second Coming:*

> Why, then, does Demogorgon . . . bear so terrible a shape? . . .
> Why is Shelley terrified of the Last Day like a Victorian child? [19]

What *The Mental Traveller* reveals is the hopelessness of cycles, unless the Imagination dares to break through them. As for Demogorgon, his shape is not terrible, and does not trouble the sight, because he is a formless darkness, the agnostic's vision of historical reversal. Yet he does speak, unlike Yeats's Sphinx, and what he says is a considerable contrast to *The Second Coming:*

> To defy Power, which seems omnipotent;
> To love, and bear; to hope, till Hope creates
> From its own wreck the thing it contemplates; [20]

To do this, Demogorgon simply concludes, is to be free. What the contrast between Shelley and Yeats, or Blake and Yeats, suggests is the problem not of humaneness in apocalyptic poetry, but of freedom even in the context of apocalypse. To Yeats, like any other Gnostic, apocalypse is the fiction of disaster, and *The Second Coming* is an oracle of an unavoidable future. What is a Last Judgment for, in the vision of Yeats's precursors? "A Last Judgment is not for the purpose of making Bad Men better but for the Purpose of hindering them from oppressing the Good with Poverty & Pain." [21]

There is something in the power of *The Second Coming* that persuades us of our powerlessness. Other poems of Advent by Yeats, including *Leda and the Swan,* share in this characteristic. The common reader suffers many mysteries, whose very menace makes for an augmented influence upon him. It is hardly the function of criticism to deny these mysteries, but it need not be the role of criticism to celebrate them. If the good time yet comes, as the faith of Blake and Shelley held it must, *The Second Coming* may impress the common reader rather less than it does now.

A Prayer for My Daughter

As a formal celebration, rather than a prayer, this is a highly satisfactory poem. It elaborately displays the Yeatsian *sprezzatura,* disguising rigorous pronouncement of doctrine as so much rumination. Though it makes much of casting out hatred, social hatred is an undersong through much of the poem, which has the virtues and faults of its implicit polemic. In terms of *Demon and Beast,* one could say that *The Second Coming* is written by Yeats's loud beast, and *A Prayer for My Daughter* by his crafty demon. Where *The Second Coming* gives us a nightmare image as his vision of desire, this celebratory prayer presents a version of family romance as fulfillment of his *daimonic* hatred of the contemporary world.

We all of us have or ought to have a group of poems we admire greatly but dislike. There is so much high art in *A Prayer for My Daughter,* admirably set forth by the Yeatsians, that the poem compels great respect. *Under Ben Bulben,* and some other famous poems by Yeats, will be seen someday as structures of cant and rant, but *A Prayer for My Daughter* has the ritualistic strength of Spenser at his strongest, no matter what it is that here informs the ritualism. As a wholly coherent work, it disarms formalist criticism, and further possesses an excellence rarely attained by any poem of celebration, by providing an epitome of the values it praises and desires. In its eighty lines we are given a complete map of Yeats's social mind, at least of that mind in the act of idealization.

I find generally that a search for latent psychic content in Yeats's poetry is an unrewarding quest, inappropriate to so thoroughly finished a body of work. He knows too well what he is about, and his *daimonic* mythology makes manifest very fully and knowingly what might be the unconscious in a lesser poet. But *A*

Prayer for My Daughter may be one of those rare poems by Yeats that reveal more then even his *daimon* could know. Its actual subject is not the new-born Anne Butler Yeats but Maud Gonne, and the bridegroom who ends the poem in so movingly archaic a fashion is Yeats himself, making in a phantasmagoria the marriage he was denied in life, yet ironically marrying only his own soul.

The poet who has walked in the wind, praying for his daughter, is afflicted by "the great gloom that is in my mind." For the sea-wind's scream grants a vision as disturbing as the sight of *The Second Coming,* but one that the poet does not care to describe:

> Imagining in excited reverie
> That the future years had come,
> Dancing to a frenzied drum,
> Out of the murderous innocence of the sea.

The oxymoron suggests that "innocence" in this poem has nothing to do with harmlessness or blamelessness. As Yeats moves, with no transition, to the thought of Maud Gonne's beauty, and her archetype, Helen's, it is a reasonable surmise that one "innocence" in the poem is being redefined persuasively, to mean a quality closely associated with a woman's murderous beauty. But this innocence, of sea or of Maud Gonne, Helen and the sea-born Aphrodite, is what Blake called "unorganized," and therefore an "impossibility," because it dwells with ignorance and not with wisdom.[22] The higher, organized innocence of Blake Yeats calls "radical," and presumably it cannot be murderous. Yet Yeats's description of it is not only remote from Blake, but from any reality that is not solipsistic:

> The soul recovers radical innocence
> And learns at last that it is self-delighting,
> Self-appeasing, self-affrighting,
> And that its own sweet will is Heaven's will;

Such a soul does not hate, we can grant Yeats, but is it autonomous or merely autistic? There is a deep withdrawal in the poem, born of a lifetime's frustration, sexual and cultural, but finally a frustration of vision, a failure to uncover the Covering Cherub or anxiety-principle that blocks free creation and the fulfillment of the soul's most authentic desires. The description of radical innocence returns Yeats to his deepest and most sustained but also most despairing insight, the perpetual virginity of the soul.[23] Though the poem ends by finding refuge for the poet's daughter, or emanative soul, his imagination, in a house built above the tides of war, like the visionary Athens of *Hellas,* this refuge at best will house two radically innocent souls, each self-delighting, self-appeasing, self-affrighting. One wonders how or why these souls will need one another, and how each will manage after learning the exuberant lesson that its own sweet will is Heaven's will? What each must learn, finally, are the wares peddled in the great houses of the spirit as much as in the thoroughfares of communal realities. The soul's radical innocence, for Yeats, is also condemned to know at last that

I shall find the dark grow luminous, the void fruitful when I understand I have nothing, that the ringers in the tower have appointed for the hymen of the soul a passing bell.

18: Later Plays

The Player Queen

Yeats began *The Player Queen* as early as 1907–8, at the time when his earlier thoughts about the *antithetical* quest were evolving into his doctrine of the Mask, to be developed a decade later in *Per Amica Silentia Lunae.* The play baffled him, until the idea of writing it as farce came to him (perhaps through Ezra Pound) in 1914.[1] Even then, he could not complete it until 1919, and there may have been further revisions before he published it in 1922. Many commentators have puzzled over it after him, for the play's wildness makes it attractive, and its theme of the *antithetical* self is so clearly central to the understanding of Yeats. The play, as only a few of the commentators have acknowledged, is unfortunately not coherent, but that helps make it another of Yeats's involuntary and powerful self-revelations, an ironic turn for this of all plays. Apocalyptic farce is a peculiar mode; Yeats tried it again in *The Herne's Egg,* with even less success and as little coherence. One question worth asking about *The Player Queen* is why Yeats was ready to change it to farce; another, what then is

Yeatsian high seriousness, if the doctrine of the Mask cannot be pondered for long without a saving irony? Farce is always just around the corner in late Yeats and this is not necessarily an aesthetic virtue.

Yeats said, in 1922, that *The Player Queen* was his only work, "not mere personal expression," written for twenty years that was not Irish in subject-matter.[2] We can recall that *The Shadowy Waters,* despite its traditional names and Shelleyan symbolism, was Yeats's only major work up to 1900 that was purely his own invention. The symbolism of the quest-voyage is Shelley's, but the story is, in every sense, Yeats's own, his personal revelation of self. *The Player Queen* is also Yeats's invention, and is as revealing. Though the indefatigable Wilson has given us the esoteric meaning of *The Player Queen,* including supposed Golden Dawn and Hermetic sources, one may doubt that the heroine Decima is going to copulate with a consubstantial unicorn in some aftermath of the farce, and then bear to that chaste beast a sacred child to commence another cycle of civilization.[3] As Peter Ure remarks, the unicorn is the property of the poet-hero Septimus, his imaginative talisman, and it leaves the play with him, since only his ravings give it life.[4] A reader of *The Player Queen,* as the play now stands, finds not an esoteric allegory but an odd farce, sometimes genuinely gay, sometimes grotesque, whose more profound meanings have to do with the peculiarities of Yeats's temperament, and not of his vision. This is not to deny the self-mockery of apocalyptic symbolism in the play. Here, as later in *The Herne's Egg,* Yeats seems to be attempting a cure for some of his obsessions by ridiculing them. Only tone-deaf scholars could read either play as serious testament to Yeats's esoteric preoccupations.

There is a greater danger of reading *The Player Queen* as an aesthetic allegory, in the manner of Mrs. Vendler, for such reading is not only more plausible but also more destructive of what the play's actual virtues are. Decima may be the muse of Septimus (or one of them) but she is hardly the Muse herself, and it seems unfair to call her personality "metallic" or to say that she feels no sorrow at her husband's infidelity.[5] If one raises her to the dignity of the Muse, then one courts the error of believing that Septimus's vision of the Unicorn has corporeal warrant, and that beyond the Prime Minister there is a more apocalyptic marriage looming for Decima. But that mistakes the poet's vision, which in this play is not of our world, and means we must assume that Septimus and the old beggar are accurate temporal prophets. As Mrs. Vendler says, "if we are to distrust Septimus' vision of the Unicorn as the supplanting beast, the whole play collapses." [6] We are to distrust it, indeed to disbelieve it as we disbelieve the old beggar, but as we are reading heroic farce, the play does not collapse, though it does keep buckling. The Unicorn is chaste because he does not exist, and will go on hesitating until he vanishes before some freshly unreal imagining. There may or may not be a divinity in *The Herne's Egg;* I demonstrate my skepticism in Chapter 23 of this book. But there is certainly no divinity in *The Player Queen,* and even no *daimonic* world whatsoever. If we are to believe the old beggar when he prophesies the Unicorn, why should we not believe him when he more quietly and urgently tells Decima "another secret." In the world of death there may be no one living except the old jackass who instructs the old beggar in his apocalyptic braying. "Who knows but he has the whole place to himself?" There are no revelations of substance to be made in this farce, only revelations of temperament, and of human weariness in Yeats at the strain of his own mythologies. The Prime Minister is quite effectual for the world of farce, and he and Decima are well-matched as opportunists, as players who have learned to assume a Mask. When we hear the poetic rant of Septimus (itself a parody of Yeatsian visionaries like Martin Hearne and Paul Rutledge) or the braying of the old beggar we are listening to posturing and true madness respectively, and both belong to the objective world, to those who cannot choose a Mask. Septimus is a Pistolian rhetorician and not a poet precisely because he lacks the *antithetical* discipline that would keep him faithful to Decima, and so make her an embodiment of the Muse, which she never has been.

What then is valuable about *The Player Queen?* How, if at all, does it show the Yeatsian exuberance, the *sprezzatura* that Septimus only feigns? I return to earlier questions; why did Yeats have to free himself to complete the play by turning it to farce?

And, more troublesome, what makes serious versions of the Mask doctrine possible in Yeats, when his fullest invention in illustration of the doctrine (barring *A Vision* itself) wavers through so many destructive ironies? I argued in Chapter 12, analyzing *Per Amica Silentia Lunae,* that Yeats's mature doctrine of the Mask is his own *clinamen* from Romantic tradition, his saving swerve away from his precursors. The Rose, though probably unattainable, was the object of desire, even desire itself; the Mask is desire taken up into the mind, or in Stevensian terms, the mind's attempt to find what will suffice. Ellmann, in his suggestive discussion of the Mask, gives us a useful clue by contrasting Browning and Yeats, Browning's "soul-sides, one to face the world with," and one to confront the beloved, as against Yeats's doctrine "that we face with a mask both the world and the beloved." [7] The contrast is more complex, and worth investigating, for reasons outlined in this study's introductory chapter. Browning and Yeats share the same prime precursor, Shelley, and the same problem in poetic influence, how to be true to the *antithetical* quest while avoiding the role of the Poet in *Alastor.* This book has no space for a detailed comparison of *Pauline, Paracelsus,* and *Sordello* with *The Wanderings of Oisin, The Shadowy Waters,* but such comparison should be made. Yeats, who was strongly affected by Browning's *Essay on Shelley* (*The Philosophy of Shelley's Poetry* should be compared closely to it), feared Browning's influence, and consciously avoided it, precisely because he recognized that the poet of *Dramatic Lyrics* and *Men and Women* had adopted a very different *clinamen* away from Shelley, than his own.[8] Browning's apparent rejection of Shelleyan "subjectivity" did not deceive Yeats, but he understood that his own internalization of quest-romance was contrary to Browning's. Browning's "fashioner" or "objective" poet finds a Mask, but not an anti-self:

> The auditory of such a poet will include, but only the intelligences which, save for such assistance, would have missed the deeper meaning and enjoyment of the original objects, but also the spirits of a like endowment with his own, who, by means of his abstract, can forthwith pass to the reality it was made from, and either corroborate their impressions of things known already, or supply themselves with new from whatever shows in the inexhausti-

ble variety of existence may have hitherto escaped their knowledge. Such a poet is properly the ποιήτης, the fashioner; and the thing fashioned, his poetry, will of necessity be substantive, projected from himself and distinct.[9]

Here are the two "soul-sides," located by Browning *in the poet's audience*. The poet faces both the world, who cannot understand without him, and spirits like his own, the potential beloved. What he projects from himself will seem totally distinct from him to the world, but something closer to related spirits. This "fashioner" thus wears a Mask that is not a Mask to fellow intellects. Yeats, as Ellmann observes, wears the Mask toward both sides.[10] This contrast between Browning and Yeats points to an aspect of the Yeatsian Mask that critics have neglected; a poet's Mask, or a player's, does not exist apart from the poet's audience. It is made, or found by him, but he strives to place it in their "deceived" possession. Mask, *A Vision* explains, is the Ought or that which should be, and our Mask is the Will or what Is of our anti-self, our opposite cone. All possible unity is from the Mask, and Yeats quoted the description of the *antithetical* Mask from his wife's automatic script as a "form created by passion to unite us to ourselves."[11] To complete the necessary definitions, before returning to Browning and Yeats, and then to *The Player Queen,* we need to recall the Mask of Phase 17, "Simplification through intensity" when true, "dispersal" when false. Browning, though he is quoted in *A Vision,* receives no phase assignment, but clearly he is a poet of Phase 17 with Yeats, their master Shelley, Landor (whom they both admired), and Dante, the supreme poet. The Mask of these poets represents intellectual or sexual passion, may seem "some Ahasuerus or Athanase," and finds its corresponding Image in a female divinity, or deified female.[12]

Browning found his Mask in the intellectual passion of being "God's spy," his corresponding Image in all the victimized women of his dramatic lyrics, culminating in the Pompilia of *The Ring and the Book*. Yeats observes, with great insight, that the poet's Will, "when true to phase, assumes, in assuming the Mask, an intensity which is never dramatic but always lyrical and personal."[13] Applied to Browning, this observation helps us see that *Childe Roland to the Dark Tower Came* or *Andrea Del Sarto,* to take examples from Browning's greatest poems, are not less self-revelatory than *Pauline* or *Paracelsus.* They are poems in which the artist or poet remains the *antithetical* quester, but fails by abandoning the quest. Browning too, like Yeats, must free himself from self-consciousness in order to explore his own consciousness of self. His dramatic monologues so frequently enter into the grotesque because such entrance is his own saving *clinamen* from his precursor Shelley. But Browning remained always another kind of poet also, one who wore no Mask when he wrote his love lyrics.

The Player Queen, as it now stands, has few overt connections to Yeats's love for Maud Gonne. Ellmann quotes from a draft of the play in which the Player Queen speaks of taking up her lover's thoughts:

> Let me become all your dreams. I will make them walk about the world in solid bone and flesh. People looking at them will become all fire themselves. They will change, there will be a Last Judgment in their souls, a burning and dissolving. . . .[14]

This is Yeats's deepest personal dream, of Maud Gonne as an apocalyptic Image of his own fulfilled desire. It is not present in the completed *Player Queen,* yet it affects that drama, and we come in time to realize that the play is an inversion of the dream. Septimus, dramatist and poet, worships the Unicorn as Yeats did his idealized Maud and the Rose, and Decima, like the actual Maud, is hardly an appropriate surrogate. Septimus is not a poet of the Tragic Generation, but a parody of Dowson and his fellows, and Decima is a parody of the Tragic Generation's dream of woman. But Septimus is only parody; Decima is more than that, and nearly makes the play something other than farce. Her symbolic meaning, for Yeats, is as the harlot-Helen of a new dispensation, but this scarcely appears in the play. Ure sensibly indicates that no audience "could penetrate so far," and one can affirm that this esoteric identification belongs to the critics and not to the work.[15] The result is that Decima, as a character, hovers uneasily between her old self, as the poet's wife, and the new self she takes on with the Mask of becoming the Queen. Neither we nor Yeats know at the play's close whether Decima has grown into her Mask or not, and our inability to know prevents the play from attaining coherence. Yet, and I find this odd, Yeats contrives to give us a character who survives the incoherence of her context. Something lives in Decima, more I think than in any other female character, even Deirdre, in Yeats's plays. She has an exuberance that moves us, and a pathos the critics, with the exception of Ure, have failed to credit. She belongs to something in Yeats's vision that failed to develop, or that could have developed only at the expense of qualities Yeats refused to yield. The paradox of *The Player Queen* is that Decima is too strong for the play, and yet her strength is the play's only clear virtue. Drama no more served Yeats's Mask than it did Browning's "soul-side," and *The Player Queen* demonstrated finally that Yeats's achievement as a dramatist had to center itself elsewhere, in passions more remote from the self and anti-self alike.

The Resurrection

We can find part of that achievement in *The Resurrection,* a more powerful play than *Calvary,* in every way an imaginative advance upon the 1921 dance-play that first presented Yeats's vision of Christianity in theatrical terms. *The Resurrection* was begun in 1925, and printed in 1927, but this is a very different play than the definitive one Yeats first printed in 1931, and the earlier version will be considered at some points in my discussion.

The Resurrection is best known for the two songs that respectively introduce and end it, included as *Two Songs from a Play* in *The Tower.* The opening song prophesies the play's most intense moment, when the Greek will pass his hand over the side of the figure of Christ, and scream out: "The heart of a phantom is beating!" Yeats's musicians, as they unfold the curtain, sing not of Christ but of "holy Dionysus," whose "beating heart" is borne away by a virgin, who has torn the heart from the dying god. In the Introduction to the play, Yeats cites an "experiment" of Sir William Crookes, who "touched a materialised form and found the heart beating." This violent shock brought "the sense of spiritual reality" and gives Yeats what he calls his play's "central situation." [16] We should brood on this "experimental" source, for it informs Yeats's notion of resurrection in the play, which has little to do either with traditional Christian ideas, or with Blake's sense of resurrection-to-unity, the reviving of Albion or Man. Yeats's Christ is resurrected as any phantom can be, so far as Yeats is concerned. That is, the play takes as context the world of A Vision, rather than the world as it is conceived either by a Christian or a naturalist, or by Blake. In A Vision's world, the astrological symbolism of The Resurrection's opening song is more than symbolism, for the world keeps returning upon itself, and always in determined patterns.

Ellmann's unraveling of the opening song's figures is a useful start.[17] Dionysus, child of Zeus and Persephone, victim of a Titanic sparagmos, lives on in his beating heart, carried by Athena ("a staring virgin") to Zeus, who swallows the heart, and re-begets Dionysus upon Semele. In Yeats's first stanza, "then" the Muses sing of the Great Year beginning again; their singing treats God's death as "but a play," which is not to deprecate, but to distance the event. With the second stanza, Yeats imparts an astrological analogue by way of Virgil's Fourth Eclogue. Virgil prophesies the return of Astraea and her Age of Gold, a prophesy long assimilated to Christian tradition as the great pagan foretelling of the Christ. At the time of divine death and rebirth, a full moon in March, the moon stands next to Virgo, who bears the star Spica. So Athena, Astraea, Virgo, and Mary form a series, with Dionysus and Christ, the beating heart or star, as another. Yeats's language is closer to Shelley's variation upon Virgil in the closing Chorus of Hellas, and Ellmann is mistaken in contrasting Yeats's sense of cyclical upheaval to Shelley's supposed prophecy of a great age.[18] I would surmise that Yeats's allusion to Virgil is deliberate, and his echo of Shelley not, but rather another instance of Shelley's inescapable influence upon him. He had read Shelley's own comment upon the final Chorus of Hellas:

The final chorus is indistinct and obscure, as the event of the living drama whose arrival it foretells. Prophecies of wars, and rumours of wars, etc., may safely be made by poet or prophet in any age, but to anticipate however darkly a period of regeneration and happiness is a more hazardous exercise of the faculty which bards possess or feign. It will remind the reader "magno *nec* proximus intervallo" of Isaiah and Virgil, whose ardent spirits overleaping the actual reign of evil which we endure and bewail, already saw the possible and perhaps approaching state of society in which the *"lion shall lie down with the lamb,"* and "omnis feret omnia tellus." Let these great names be my authority and my excuse.[19]

Shelley's language is skeptical, here and in the Chorus. He knows that the darker prophecy is safer, and that the vision of regeneration calls into question the faculty of the imagination that bards may only "feign." Directly after the stanza Yeats appears to parody comes the vision Yeats appropriates:

> Oh, write no more the tale of Troy,
>   If earth Death's scroll must be!
> Nor mix with Laian rage the joy
>   Which dawns upon the free:
> Although a subtler Sphinx renew
> Riddles of death Thebes never knew.[20]

The subtler Sphinx is the Egyptian one, Yeats's Second Birth as it was Lionel Johnson's Second Death, or Shelley's. Though Shelley goes on to sing of a regeneration greater than the Resurrection ("more bright and good/ Than all who fell, than One who rose"), he ends the Chorus, and *Hellas,* in despair at inevitable cyclic return. He sees what Yeats sees, but not in a spirit of acceptance, let alone Yeatsian exultation. The cycles of gold and blood, hate and death, must return, the prophecy he drained to its dregs, and the weary world can neither die nor rest, but must repeat the past. Shelley's despair is Yeats's delight, but they see the same phenomenon, the call of "Virgo and the Mystic Star" to the fabulous darkness, the formless form of Christian fabling.

Yeats's play is thoroughly consonant with the ferocity of its opening song. It is all dialogue between two minor disciples of the slain Messiah, one Greek (Egyptian in the first version), the other Hebrew, until a Syrian disciple enters to add a third voice.

The nationalities are not well chosen, if they are meant to indicate the three constituents of Christianity. While the Syrian does introduce the element of mystery-religion, the Hebrew does not embody the law or teaching nor the Greek embody reason. The Alexandrian Greek is closer to Yeats himself in the first version, where as the Egyptian he affirms that Jesus was "an appearance or a phantom," but never a living man. The Egyptian's God, like Yeats's, is a juggler, who manipulates appearances. The Hebrew, in both versions of the play, is not a Hebrew at all, but what Yeats would consider a sentimental rationalist, whose view of Christ, though personally courageous, is wholly naturalistic, even reductive. In the revised play, the Greek is a kind of humanist, for whom Christ was a phantom, but only as all the gods were phantoms. Though the Greek says that man "does not surrender his soul" to the gods, but "keeps his privacy," this ought not to be taken as Yeats's own position, for Yeats lacked the Greek's confidence in man's capacity not to surrender to influx. The Syrian is closer to the Gnostic Yeats than either Greek or Hebrew, humanist or naturalist, can be. It is the Syrian who proclaims the Yeatsian dispensation: "What if the irrational return? What if the circle begin again?" But, dramatically considered, the three young men are revealed best not by what they say before Christ's Resurrection, but by their response to Resurrection when it occurs. Here, Yeats is brilliant. After the figure of Christ enters, the Hebrew says nothing, but only kneels. There is nothing he can say, for the natural has been overcome. The Greek screams when his hand feels the heart of a phantom beating, and yields to Yeats's version of Heraclitus: "God and man die each other's life, live each other's death," the formula upon which *A Vision* is founded. The Syrian simply observes and describes, for this is a mystery to which he is attuned, as Yeats is. Whether it is a greater mystery, the play does not say, but clearly there is a profound contrast between the Resurrection that has taken place, and the Dionysiac cry of "God has arisen" that grows silent in front of the house the young men guard, the house where Christ has come again to be with his disciples. In some sense that Yeats would not altogether acknowledge, the play hesitates upon the threshold of becoming Christian drama.

What remains is the closing song, more powerful than the opening, indeed one of Yeats's greatest. The first stanza (the only one in the original version) does not make much advance upon the play's opening song, but the stanza added in the 1931 play joins itself to what is most powerful and central in Yeats's imagination, his sense of "vacillation" between self and soul. Several critics have noted Yeats's indebtedness in this last stanza to his own account of the Tragic Generation in *The Trembling of the Veil*. There Yeats quotes from Johnson's *The Dark Angel,* and comments that "our love-letters wear out our love . . . every stroke of the brush exhausts the impulse." [21] The Dark Angel turns the Muses to Furies, and tortures delight with unfulfillable desire. Dreams become fears, and the Paterian pure flame becomes an "evil ecstasy," Yeats accepts this; it is the toll we pay to cycle. As in Shelley's *The Triumph of Life,* love and love's pleasure, good and the means of good, cannot be reconciled. What remains is man's desperate glory; only his heart, however corrupt, feeds "whatever flames upon the night." *The Resurrection,* in this stanza, draws back from the threshold of belief to the aesthetic skepticism of Shelley and of Pater; Yeats has come very near to Lionel Johnson's anguished acceptance of remorse and miracle, but will not take the final step. In *The Resurrection,* he returns to the strength of his beginnings in *The Wanderings of Oisin*. Without the final stanza of 1931, the play would be incomplete. With it, Yeats has again chosen swordsman over saint, the lyrical personality of the Shelleyan poet over the passion-spent character that seeks final refuge from quest.

The King of the Great Clock Tower

Useful criticism of this play, and of its more satisfying sequel, *A Full Moon in March,* must begin with Helen Vendler's insight: these are plays that concern the relation of Poet to Muse, and more particularly of Yeats to his own Muse, the Shelleyan epipsyche he had confronted, or convinced himself he had beheld, in Maud Gonne.[22] We are wrong, in reading Yeats, ever to forget for long his characterization of himself as a young man who "had gathered from Shelley and the romantic poets an idea of perfect love," and who "was twenty-three years old when the trouble of my life began." [23] Yet these savage late plays, though they return again to that love and that trouble, are fearfully far in spirit from the young man's descriptions of his beloved's beauty. There is a magnificent juxtaposition between Yeats remembering "a complexion like the bloom of apples" and "stature so great that she seemed of a divine race" and the Stroller remarking: "She is not so tall as I had thought, not so white and red, but what does it matter. . . ." [24]

It does not matter. Only what the Stroller calls "the image in my head," to which he has never shown disrespect, matters. Unlike *The Player Queen* and *The Herne's Egg*, these plays are not overt parodies of the Yeatsian myth, but they might as well be. They are a just burden for Yeats's critics, who do not as yet recognize the burden. I refer not to the Orphic fantasies of the esoteric critics, but to the general respect with which the plays are read, though they are grotesque as drama and bad as poetry. The most impressive reading, as so often, is Whitaker's, whose description is rather more moving than the works he describes. [25] For in these plays the hard, symbolic bones are not under the skin, but obtrude, and we may feel at times that we are being offered only the bones themselves, as though Yeats's most outrageous convictions were value enough. But Yeats is not Nietzsche; his ideas do not radiate a vitality we are uneasy to reject. In these plays of 1934–35, he allowed himself to forget his rhetorical art, and the reader skeptical of Yeats's apocalypse will want the art badly, and be impatient with what takes its place.

The first *King of the Great Clock Tower* is in prose and verse, the second wholly in verse, as is *A Full Moon in March*. The difference between the *King* play and the *Full Moon* is the King himself, who is not present in the later play, where the poet-Stroller appears again as the Swineherd. I do not recall that any critic has had a kind word for the King, but he is certainly more sympathetic than either the Queen or the Stroller, not that the play has any patience for our sympathies. He is in the line of Wilde's Herod, which means that he is an irrelevance, as Yeats saw when re-working. But he helps the play, such as it is, by representing "the unimaginative, everyday intelligence," as Rajan says.[26] Of the Muse, his Queen, he knows nothing, though he has known her for a year. Her silence is unendurable to him, and invites the Stroller's entrance. One feels with the King when he protests: "But what have I to do with it?" He is no antagonist, to poet or Muse, who need no antagonist but one another. If everyday sense speaks in the play, it sounds out when the King says to the poet: "Go now that you have seen!" But the poet has come to die, then to watch a dance, and then to sing, in a characteristic Yeatsian ordering.

The world (or time, if one would read the King so) slays the poet out of exasperation and jealousy, as good motives as it could want for killing a man. When the King hears the stroller's prophecy, of dance, song, and kiss, he is half-right to cry out: "Extravagance and lies," for extravagance, as in the Crazy Jane poems, is the mood of the matter. Yet the King's motive for the execution is worth a closer glance; beneath the understandable exasperation and the plausible jealousy is the King's horror of his passive, silent moon of a Queen: "Do something, anything, I care not what/ So that you move." Her lips move at last (but only by proxy, in the Second Attendant's song) to sing a Thel-like Blakean song, of *The Sick Rose* variety, dreading the violation of her consciousness (which she calls her body). She dances before the severed head, and Yeats owes us the song to which his play has been building. What do we get? Both the song, and its alternative that Yeats provides, are bad poems, exhausted repetitions of Yeatsian patterns and figures. It would be kinder to call them self-parodies than poems, for they are formulaic rant. If they are the play's excuse, then it cannot be excused.

What then of the theme, of poet and Muse; has Yeats added anything, either to his own *daimonic* story, or to the relevant categories made by the Decadents? I read *The King of the Great Clock Tower,* and much else in late Yeats, and hear myself murmuring:

> It means the distaste we feel for this withered scene
> Is that it has not changed enough. It remains,
> It is a repetition.[27]

An unchanging fiction ceases to give pleasure, and it seems un-likely that *The King of the Great Clock Tower* can give pleasure to any but the specialist.

A Full Moon in March

Yeats himself was dubious enough about *The King of the Great Clock Tower* so that he debated retaining it, and chose to do so for the sake of its lyrics. His doubts, and perhaps a desire to re-duce the relation between poet and Muse to its gray particulars, prompted *A Full Moon in March,* to which a kind of nasty power cannot be denied. Here the imaginative self dies a masochistic death, supposedly in order to beget a stronger life upon that death. Though Whitaker finds a Blakean pattern in this, nothing could be further from Blake, who insisted upon just the opposite.[28] The Daughters of Beulah, Blake's Muses, must sacri-fice themselves, for creation to go forward; Blake's Muse exists to be transcended. What triumphs in *A Full Moon in March* is that sadistic Female Will or Sphinx against which Blake had fought all through his life. Precisely what Blake refused to learn is the Nietzschean acceptance Whitaker rightly assigns to Yeats: "Pain is also a joy, curse is also a blessing, night is also a sun." [29]

By reducing the play to essentials, to Queen and Swineherd, Yeats gained the greater intensity he sought, a final fable of the moon-like Muse and the self-sacrificing poet. These would have been Keats's terms, had he not progressed beyond his earlier vi-sion to the purgatorial humanism of *The Fall of Hyperion,* the proper poem to which *A Full Moon in March* should be com-pared. The parallels are startling, and suggest unconscious influ-encing, or else renewal of a fundamental poetic pattern, but there is at least one moment of apparent recall on Yeats's part. The Swineherd comes to the dangerous Queen, who awaits her singer, and has yet to be moved by any song. A full moon in March, time for death and cyclic re-birth has come, and the Swineherd looks round to observe: "but I am here alone." Keats stands at the altar of the Muse's ruined temple, and says: "I sure should see / Other men here; but I am here alone." The formula, "but I am here alone," means: "I am the poet." The Queen and Keats's Moneta are equally harsh, have the same terrible potential, but Keats, like Blake and Shelley, knows of a High Romantic dialectic that Yeats has forsaken. So Keats, courteously but firmly, educates his Muse, moves her to tears, and to the questioning of her own savage cross-categories, her animus against poetry. Yeats follows a different path, closer to Mallarmé and Wilde, choosing or being chosen by a Muse who cannot be educated. The Swineherd is a sacrifice, a priestly offering to the only divinity Yeats truly recognized, creative death.

Whitaker is justified in saying that the play "condenses the myth of *The Resurrection* and reverses its perspective." But why then is *The Resurrection* so much the better play or poem? [30] It may be that *The Resurrection* has the same illegitimate power as *The Second Coming,* a masquerade of Yeats's Gnosticism in Christian terms, whereas *A Full Moon in March* is the poem Yeats rightfully ought to have written, *The Second Birth* with all Christian implications omitted. Certainly *A Full Moon in March* has the great spiritual merit of being an honest presentation of Yeats's deepest poetic convictions. But is all of Yeats there, as his adepts insist? If so, we ought to see clearly what we are offered. The poet dies, and the Muse descends; that is the whole of it. Is this what will suffice, or is it "an old delusion, an old affair with the sun,/ An impossible aberration with the moon"? [31] Whitaker learnedly exhumes the dank Hermeticisms: Moon and Sun, Silver and Gold, Virgin Mercury and Virgin Sulphur, Shadow and Swan; I do not doubt that *A Full Moon in March* is superb spiritual alchemy, but is it mere art as well? [32] Is it, the final question, the "simplification through intensity" that is Yeats's version of the Romantic Imagination, or is it a parody thereof?

No single critic, or even body of critics, will decide, as our memory of Dr. Johnson's admonitions should remind us. I find *A Full Moon in March* only a hollow image of fulfilled desire, a gross aberration prompted by the quester's weariness, or pseudo-apocalypse caused through the aged impatience that wills what it despairs of imagining. Judgment lies, someday, with the Common Reader; will he be deeply moved by *A Full Moon in March?* The Queen is no longer passive; is it more profound that she be murderous? The Stroller is now the Swineherd; as he says: "What do I know of beauty?" He has courage, and knows he sings nonsense, whatever he sings. Yeats's joke, I am afraid, is on his adepts. As for love, "I picked a number on the roulette wheel," the Swineherd says. He is honest, and trusts the wheel (as Yeats did not). And he is, quite deliberately, a bad, a trivial poet. That too, Yeats is now saying, is part of the story. No one is going to anthologize his song of murderous Jill and hollow-hearted Jack, no matter how benighted the age becomes. All the better, he and Yeats would think, for the story has grown too old already; a satyric postlude is now required.

That leaves us with the Muse. "What can she lack whose emblem is the moon?" The play does not so much answer as complete what becomes a rhetorical question: "But desecration and the lover's night." This, Yeats tells us, is the burden of poetry, this alone must "delight my heart with sound." This is "all time's completed treasure," or as Blake's Mental Traveller concludes by saying: "And all is done as I have told." This did not suffice for Blake, or for Shelley, or for Keats; is it Yeats's triumph that for him this did suffice?

19: The Tower

Sailing to Byzantium

Sailing to Byzantium was written in August–September 1926, four years before the writing of *Byzantium*. F. L. Gwynn was the first, I believe, to indicate a crucial difference between the historical vision of the two poems.[1] The first Byzantium is that praised in *A Vision,* the city of Justinian, about A.D. 550, while the city of the second poem is as it was "towards the end of the first Christian millennium." The cities are both of the mind, but they are not quite the same city, the second being at a still further remove from nature than the first.

Melchiori, in an intricate study of the poem, showed that *Sailing to Byzantium* recalls Yeats's early story, *Rosa Alchemica,* and so there is no reason to doubt that the poem is a finished version of Yeats's kind of alchemical quest.[2] The highest claim yet made for *Sailing to Byzantium* is that of Whitaker, who says of this poem and *Among School Children* that "in them is created a new species of man who—unbeknownst to himself, as it were—*is* his contrary."[3] Yeats would have delighted in this claim, but that the poem justifies it is open to some question.

Yeats's first intention in *Sailing to Byzantium* was not to speak in his own proper person, but as "a poet of the Middle Ages." A medieval Irish poet, seeking to make his soul, sets sail for the center of European civilization. But, as Curtis Bradford demonstrates, this persona gradually is eliminated from successive drafts of the poem, and the speaker in the final version may be taken as Yeats himself, a Yeats seeking his *daimon* at the center of Unity of Being, a city where the spiritual life and the creation of art merge as one.[4]

The great example of such a visionary city in English poetry is of course Blake's version of the New Jerusalem, Golgonooza, the city of Los the artificer. There are Blakean elements in both Byzantium poems, but Yeats's city is emphatically not Blake's, and Blake would have disliked birds (however artificial) and dolphins as final emblems of imaginative salvation. The forms walking the streets of Yeats's city are images, but they are not the Divine Image or Human Form Divine that Blake insisted upon in his vision of last things. The vision of both Byzantium poems is more Shelleyan than Blakean, and the repudiation of nature in both poems has a Shelleyan rather than Blakean twist.

I would guess the ultimate literary source of Yeats's Byzantium to be in Shelley's longest poem, the allegorical epic, *The Revolt of Islam,* a poem that Yeats read early, and remembered often. It is not today among the more admired of Shelley's longer poems, and rightly stands below *Alastor,* which preceded it, and *Prometheus Unbound,* which came after. But it has considerable though uneven power, and it is a worthy companion to *Endymion,* having been composed in competition to Keats's longest poem. Most of the poem is an idealized account of left-wing revolution, not likely to move Yeats at any time in his life. But the first and final cantos are almost purely visionary, and they had considerable effect upon Yeats, who cites them in his major essay upon Shelley.

In Canto I of Shelley's poem, there is a voyage to an immortal Temple:

> . . . likest Heaven, ere yet day's purple stream
> Ebbs o'er the western forest, while the gleam

> Of the unrisen moon among the clouds
>   Is gathering. . . .

Shelley's starlit dome is surrounded by "marmoreal floods," and reveals itself to us only through the arts, and then only in part:

> Like what may be conceived of this vast dome,
>   When from the depths which thought can seldom pierce
> Genius beholds it rise, his native home,
>   Girt by the deserts of the Universe;
>   Yet, nor in painting's light, or mightier verse,
> Or sculpture's marble language, can invest
>   That shape to mortal sense— [5]

Within the Temple, which is lit by its own radiance, brighter than day's, are paintings wrought by Genii in a winged dance, and also the forms of departed sages, set against the background of fire. It seems only a step from this to Byzantium.

"I fly from nature to Byzantium," reads one canceled line of Yeats's poem, and another canceled phrase salutes the city as the place "where nothing changes." The poet is asking for transfiguration, though at the expense of being made "rigid, abstracted, and fanatical/ Unwavering, indifferent." For his need is great, his function as poet being done:

> All that men know, or think they know, being young
> Cry that my tale is told my story sung. . . .[6]

Yeats seeks the Condition of Fire, as Blake sought it in Golgonooza, or as Shelley's Adonais attained it, but his motive here is very different from Blake's or even Shelley's. Byzantium is not attained after:

> Mystery's tyrants are cut off & not one left on Earth,
> And when all Tyranny was cut off from the face of
>   Earth. . . .[7]

Nor does the soul of Yeats, after reaching the Holy City, serve as a beacon, "burning through the inmost veil of heaven," guiding others to the Eternal. Yeats's Condition of Fire is neither a criticism of life, as Blake's and Shelley's are, nor is it a manifestation of a freedom open to all who would find it, nor indeed is it a state of imaginative liberty at all. It is "extreme, fortuitous, personal," like the moments of visionary awakening in Wallace Stevens, though it does not present itself honestly as being such. It is also a state, ironically like the "sweet golden clime" sought by Blake's Sun-Flower, in which the human image must subside into the mechanical or merely repetitively natural, unless it is willing to start out upon its quest again. For Byzantium is no country for men, young *or* old, and the monuments it contains testify to aspects of the soul's magnificence that do not support humanistic claims of any kind whatsoever. Keats, standing in the shrine of Saturn, stands in Byzantium, and is told by the scornful Moneta that those to whom the miseries of the world *are* misery do not come into that shrine. Yeats would have found this irrelevant, for his Byzantium does not admit the "sentimentalist," the *primary* man, at all. We need not find this excessively relevant, but we might hold it in mind as we read *Sailing to Byzantium,* for the limitations of the poem's ideal ought to be our concern also.

"God's holy fire," in this poem, is not a state where the creator and his creation are one, as in Blake, but rather a state where the creator has been absorbed into his creation, where the art work or "artifice of eternity" draws all reality into itself. Yeats's too-palpable ironies in the last stanza of the poem are redundant and, as Sturge Moore remarked, the poet is unjustified in asserting that he is "out of nature." [8] He is where he always was, poised before his own artifact, and so less accurate than the Keats who contemplated the Grecian urn, knowing always his own separation from the world wrought upon it.

I am suggesting that *Sailing to Byzantium* belies its title, and is a rather static poem, and a peculiarly evasive one. The poem that did not get written is, in this case, more impressive than the final text. If Mrs. Yeats and Jon Stallworthy were right, then the poem began as a prose fragment exploring again that tragedy of sexual intercourse which is the perpetual virginity of the soul.[9] A man past sixty, in early autumn, broods on the loves of his lifetime, and decides that "now I will take off my body" even as "for many loves have I taken off my clothes." As once his loves "longed to see" but could not be enfolded by his soul, perhaps his soul now can cease to be virgin. The line of a later verse draft, "I fly from nature to Byzantium," would then be a wholly dualistic sentiment, abandoning sexual for spiritual love. That is hardly characteristic of Yeats, early or late, and shows only a mood, however powerful. The prose fragment says "I live on love," which is not very characteristic either. In the drafts of the opening stanza a significant change from the simplistic dualism, and the tense concern for love, is quickly manifested. The contrast presented is between the Christ child, smiling upon his mother's knee, and the old gods in the Irish hills, with whom the poet identifies. He is Oisin again, finding no place in the Ireland of St. Patrick, and so he sails to Byzantium.[10]

The flight then is not so much from nature as from a new dispensation of the young. The old poet of the old faith is doubly alienated, and this complex estrangement is the double root of the poem. As a poet, Yeats voyages to find a new faith; as a man, his quest is away—not from the body so much as from the decrepitude of the body. Byzantium is the state of being of "the thing become," as one of the drafts puts it, "and ageless beauty where age is living." In the final draft of the poem's first stanza, much of this richness of the quest-motive is gone, and age alone seems to impel the poet on his journey.[11]

Much else dropped out of the final poem, including both a prophetic and a purgatorial element. The final line—"Of what is past, or passing, or to come"—is severely qualified by the rest of the last stanza, but in the drafts it is presented without irony:

> And set in golden leaves to sing
> Of present past and future to come
> For the instruction of Byzantium. . . .[12]

There is an echo of Blake here, not of the voice of the Bard of Experience, but of the purged prophet Los in *Jerusalem,* crying out in triumph that he beholds all reality in a single imagining:

> I see the Past, Present & Future, existing all at once
> Before me; O Divine Spirit sustain me on thy wings!
> That I may awake Albion from his long & cold repose.[13]

Blake-Los affirms his mission in the context of experience, the "long & cold repose" of man, while Yeats seeks his function in the context of a reality beyond experience, but the affinity is clear nevertheless. So is the necessity of purgation, of being made free of the Spectre or Selfhood, if the prophetic role is to be assumed, evident both in Blake and the Yeats of the drafts, but not of the final text, where only the heart, natural passion, is to be consumed away. Yeats, in one draft attempts to mount the purgatorial stairs as Dante does, or Keats in *The Fall of Hyperion,* but fails:

> When prostrate on the marble step I fall
> And cry amid my tears—
> And cry aloud—"I sicken with desire
> Though/ and fastened to a dying animal
> Cannot endure my life—O gather me
> Into the artifice of eternity." [14]

This does not match the incisiveness gained when Yeats says of his heart: "It knows not what it is," in the final text, but something valuable is lost also, the consciousness that an experiential purgatory must still be borne if a humanizing prophecy is to be uttered. Yeats, as always, knew very well what he was doing as a reviser, and he finds intensity through simplification in the final text. What *Sailing to Byzantium* lacks is just the reverse, the simplification through intensity that sometimes does take Yeats into the Condition of Fire.

The Tower

This, as befits the title poem of its volume, is one of Yeats's best poems, and seems to me more impressive than *Sailing to Byzantium,* though it has less reputation at this time. Yeats aspires here also toward being "a new species of man," but in this poem's earlier moments he knows well enough that he belongs to an older species, the artists who long to be their own contraries, yet never attain to the condition of the *daimon.* Whitaker subtly presents the analogue of Tennyson's Ulysses, another old man who lusts after action, seeking a death that will be his own creation.[15] Other Victorian dramatic monologues suggest themselves also, including perhaps the greatest, Browning's visionary Pope brooding on the abyss of history, and on the necessity for accepting human responsibility, lest all action be wasted, and human death lose all significance.[16] Yeats's poem almost sustains such comparison without loss of dignity, which is a considerable tribute to it.

The Tower is primarily a poem about an excess of imagination, or perhaps an imagination in excess of its historical stimuli, and its Anglo-Irish excursiveness is hardly a poetic virtue, not being handled by Yeats with much saving irony. The poet is growing old, but his vision refuses to darken, and his ear and eye continue to expect an impossible sublimity. With Blake, he continues to know that less than all cannot satisfy man, yet his decrepit age threatens to make his desire merely grotesque. The minute particulars the Muse demands would make of the poet an object of derision, yet how can "imagination, ear and eye . . . be content with argument and deal/ In abstract things"? To this apparently insoluble dilemma the meditative second part of the poem provides no resolution, but it provides something better, a thorough rejection of all self-pity and all imagination-destroying remorse.

Out of the past, both from history and from his own creations, Yeats calls forth "images and memories," to ask them two questions: do all humans rage aginst growing old? and more complexly (because addressed more to himself), is it accomplishment or frustration, the woman won or the woman lost, that most engages the supposedly mature yet still fantastical imagination? The two questions may seem finally to be one, for Yeats's art as early as *The Wanderings of Oisin* was founded upon a rage against growing old, and upon the Shelleyan conviction that the most poetic images are necessarily those of unfulfilled and unfulfillable desire. Confronting his own Hanrahan, his reckless antithesis, Yeats asks ironically for all the knowledge that the mythical after-life can gain one of the labyrinth beings of other selves. The labyrinth image is from Blake, but Hanrahan is not a very Blakean figure, for he never explored the intricate, great labyrinth of an-

other self, any more than Yeats did. Self-annihilation, finally
learned by Blake's Los, was not possible for Hanrahan, or for his
creator, or for any man. What is immensely moving here is Yeats's
clear self-condemnation, for he implicitly states a failure of desire
on his part in his love for Maud Gonne. Like Hanrahan, he
turned aside, and could not give all to love. Far in the background, and yet relevant, is Shelley's similarly conscious failure in
his *Epipsychidion,* where the limitations of selfhood triumph over
the poet's intense love for Emilia Viviani. Hanrahan, in the story
Red Hanrahan's Curse, felt "a great anger against old age and all
it brought with it," but his struggle with self never proceeded far
enough for him to accept the four sacred emblems—cauldron of
pleasure, stone of power, spear of courage, sword of knowledge—
that could have been his.[17] Taken together, the four attributes
would have unified him in the image of a Blakean Divine Man,
or God. The implication in *The Tower* is that Yeats, like Hanrahan, has failed, but the failure is not less heroic than most simpler
fulfillments of desire.

In the third section of *The Tower,* Yeats turns to what is left,
as his dream-drunken Hanrahan could not. Like Hanrahan, the
poet has not attained Unity of Being, and so finds himself at the
impasse of knowing perfection neither in his life nor in his work.
But nothing in the first section, with its conflict of active imagination and fading nature, or in the second with its parallel conflict
of imagination and the unfading self, compels the poet to surrender his Blakean and Shelleyan pride in the continued autonomy
of the imagination. Whitaker boldly claims more for Yeats here,
and speaks of a pride "that is not the ego's apprehensive desire to
possess and dominate but the whole being's exultant sense of creative giving." [18] This is to grant Yeats more than he dared to assert for himself, and neglects his near-identity with Hanrahan in
the second part of the poem. There is, one needs to admit, much
Anglo-Irish posturing and drum-beating in Part III, and much
purely Yeatsian striking of attitudes as well. Here the poem is in
decline, and its celebration of "upstanding men" for their pre-
dawn fishing expeditions is rather inappropriate if not silly. A little irony would have helped, for once, but it does not come, and
the poem becomes very vulnerable to the charge of "excessive

dramatization" that Yvor Winters has urged so vigorously against Yeats's work. As Winters remarks of Yeats's ideal, "the gentlemen should be violent and bitter . . . and they should be fond of fishing." [19] Yeats's "upstanding men" are not to attach themselves to tyrants, but they are to show equal contempt for the historical victims of tyranny, and we begin to feel that the excited imagination the poet insists he still possesses is perhaps not the most mature of imaginations. A touch of the Wordsworthian "sober coloring," which Yeats despised, is needed to temper the "headlong light" of an old man's pride.

From this nadir of private prejudice, the poem does make an impressive recovery, setting aside its penultimate stanza, which irks with more dawn-fishery. A swan-song is reinforced by a fine conclusion celebrating an imaginative conception of death, in which a fading horizon is another testimony to the Blakean Prolific, moving the bound or outward circumference of energy further out into the realms of being. The "bird's sleepy cry" is as ambiguous as the undulations of Stevens's casual flocks of pigeons at the close of *Sunday Morning*. Among the deepening shades, as the poet too goes downward to darkness, the imaginative gesture remains an extended one, and the act of dying suggests only another fictive covering woven by the poet himself.

Meditations in Time of Civil War

This diverse poem, or series of poems, is a less satisfactory achievement than the earlier *Nineteen Hundred and Nineteen,* and is considered here before that poem only because it helps provide an introduction to it, this ordering also being Yeats's own in his arrangement of *The Tower* as a volume. Though both poems are acts of spiritual judgment brought by the self against the self, *Meditations* lacks the bitter urgency and hallucinated intensity of *Nineteen Hundred and Nineteen*. *Meditations* also suffers from the relative immaturity of Yeats's most mature historical views, since the poet allows himself an utter reliance upon them here. A man (and a poet) does not cease to be a sentimentalist and rhetorician merely by *declaring* himself to be the possessor of a vision of reality, and there is much self-deception in *Meditations*. One of Yeats's most remarkable powers is his ability to write a poetry of assertion or statement that yet convinces his critics he has considered and transcended all contrary assertions. *Meditations* is a triumph of romantic irony, but hardly a profound example of a reconciliation between experience and art, as some of its critics have claimed it to be.

Yeats begins with a meditation upon "Ancestral Houses," which is hard to accept on his own terms. There is a shock-value in employing bitterness and violence as eulogistic words, but there is also a mindlessness involved that is very different from the high intelligence always manifested by Blake and Nietzsche in their persuasive definitions and transvaluations. Yeats is afraid that "our greatness" may vanish with "our violence," and gives a sardonic picture of the degeneration of a tough, eighteenth-century *antithetical* elegance into "slippered Contemplation." From the effete "Great House" of the rich, Yeats turns to "My House," set in a Blakean landscape, and exhibiting the familiar Miltonic-Shelleyan emblem of the lonely tower of solitary meditation. Yet meditation is perhaps the wrong word here; the solitary imagines in a "daemonic rage," for Yeats is unwilling to give up the bitterness and violence out of which, he insists, the strength of artistic sweetness must come if it is to come at all.

"My Table," upon which the poem is being written, centers on "Sato's gift, a changeless sword," and through that sword on a better tradition of elegance than we met in "Ancestral Houses." Yeats was fascinated by living tradition, and nothing pleased him better than a continuous family line of achievement and craftsmanship. Because Eastern tradition, for all its continuities, may suggest a mode of existence disliked by Blake, in which a lack of contraries led to no progression, Yeats insists that the apparently unchanging look of Sato's house concealed the "aching heart" of perpetual seekers after perfection. This point is emphasized by one of Yeats's more mechanical ingenuities. The inheritor of Sato's house was wrought to so high an intensity of aspiration that "it seemed/ Juno's peacock screamed," the "irrational cry, revelation" of *A Vision*.[20] Opposed to this apocalyptic apprehensiveness is the inane indifference manifested toward the same peacock im-

agery in the eighteenth-century Anglo-Irish gardens of the penultimate stanza of "Ancestral Houses."

Part IV, "My Descendants," follows, and is devoted to Yeats's
eugenic fears for his children, lest they decline into "common
greenness." The stony consolation offered to the self comes here
out of an appropriate bitterness and violence, since a destructive
wish is all that now remains of the earlier antithetical pride that
began the poem. In "The Road at My Door" Yeats ironically contrasts himself as poetic brooder, opening the door of his house, to
"Falstaffian man," to laughing men of action who relieve *their*
bitterness in the joy of violence. From this contrast the poem rises
at last to some sustained power, after five sections in which marvelous rhetoric has served to set forth only a complex of prejudices. Section VI, "The Stare's Nest by My Window," is a moving
self-recognition on the poet's part. His dreams of ritual ordering,
he acknowledges for once, were fantasies, and brutalize the heart,
till there is "more substance in our enmities/ Than in our love."
The powerful refrain, "Come build in the empty house of the
stare," is an appeal, passionate despite its irony, that the honey-
bees, emblems of creativity, come again to the "closed in" poet
who cries now: "My wall is loosening."

The final meditation, "I see Phantoms of Hatred and of the
Heart's Fullness and of the Coming Emptiness," is one of Yeats's
apocalyptic chants, in which he never fails as a poet. In a mist
"like blown snow," the visionary stands upon his broken tower
and sees, under the light of an unnatural because unchangeable
moon, the image of "a glittering sword out of the east," portend-
ing all the senseless brutalities of civil war spreading throughout
the world, particularly evident as the murder of social classes by
one another. One of Yeats's visionary triumphs follows:

> Their legs long, delicate and slender, aquamarine
>   their eyes,
> Magical unicorns bear ladies on their backs.
> The ladies close their musing eyes. No prophecies,
> Remembered out of Babylonian almanacs,
> Have closed the ladies' eyes, their minds are but a pool
> Where even longing drowns under its own excess;
> Nothing but stillness can remain when hearts are full
> Of their own sweetness, bodies of their loveliness.

Though its coloring is out of Moreau, Pater, and the Decadents, this is essentially a Blakean vision of the Female Will, closely parallel to the narcissistic dreaming of Enitharmon, Queen of Heaven, in the prophecy, *Europe*. Enitharmon's teaching is: "Between two moments bliss is ripe," and is an admonition to Oothoon, who in *Visions of the Daughters of Albion* proclaims bliss to be in the glancing moment. Yeats's ladies on unicorns find their self-regarding bliss perpetually "between two moments," but like "the rage-driven . . . troop" give way to the actual inhabitants of a time of troubles preceding the end, "give place to an indifferent multitude, give place/ To brazen hawks," birds of prey who "symbolize the straight road of logic, and so of mechanism," and whose "innumerable clanging wings" have brought in the dark of the moon.[21]

The whole of *Meditations* turns upon the last stanza of its last poem, and the inextricable strengths and weaknesses of the sequence mingle to demonstrate Yeats's dilemma in having chosen to make himself the kind of poet who labors to clarify the content of his own vision, like Blake, as opposed to the one who sees his authentic labor as perpetually redefining his own relation to that vision. The inevitable text for allusion is the *Intimations* Ode, and Yeats turns to it here:

> I turn away and shut the door, and on the stair
> Wonder how many times I could have proved my worth
> In something that all others understand or share;
> But O! ambitious heart, had such a proof drawn forth
> A company of friends, a conscience set at ease,
> It had but made us pine the more. The abstract joy,
> The half-read wisdom of daemonic images,
> Suffice the ageing man as once the growing boy.

Poets from Ben Jonson to Samuel Johnson have murmured sadder versions of those first three lines, and presumably some sadder versions are to come. The "ambitious heart," not the dead, made the choice, and it does suffice. But the close, however it gestures toward Romantic irony, is bested by its own Wordsworthian allusion, for is there really a more appropriate motto for this whole sequence than the Wordsworthian "shades of the prison-house begin to close"? One remembers (whether or not one is meant to) the tortured preference in *Tintern Abbey* for Wordsworth's version of "the abstract joy" over the "aching joys" and "dizzy raptures" that are so hopelessly in the past, and one notes that even the fully-read wisdom of natural images did not suffice the ageing man, and that this final poverty was itself a tribute to the former strength of Wordsworth's imagination. And how much of Yeats's own poetry must be judged, finally, as "the half-read wisdom of daemonic images"?

Nineteen Hundred and Nineteen

This is one of Yeats's masterpieces, and is in some ways a triumphant return to *The Wind Among the Reeds,* twenty years after. Where Yeats's personal prejudices, and his theories of history, obscure his vision four years later in *Meditations in Time of Civil War,* Yeats is remarkably free here. The cause may lie in the very different disturbances from which the poems rise. The Civil War necessarily embittered Yeats and his contemporaries, no matter which side they took, in a way that went beyond the cleaner bitterness of the 1919 Black and Tan Terror. Where, in the *Meditations,* Yeats feels shut out of action, and retreats to his own obsessions, here he has a proper sense that the context renders all action mere murder, and he retreats into self-mockery, which in him is always a sure gate to poetic splendor. There are many poets who go wrong when they turn upon themselves, but Yeats always prospers by it. It is particularly true that his overtly apocalyptic poems are least effective when he does not also pass a Last Judgment upon himself. Though *Meditations* is a much more complex poem, it makes too much of the drama of history, and too little of the abyss in Yeats himself. In *Nineteen Hundred and Nineteen,* Yeats walks naked, and finds the dark grown luminous, understanding that he has nothing. The anguish and glory of the poem are epitomized at the conclusion of its first section:

> But is there any comfort to be found?
> Man is in love and loves what vanishes,
> What more is there to say?

As Yeats remarked, this is "not philosophical but simple and passionate," the description echoing Milton's distinction between poetry and philosophy. The comfort to be found is that man *is* in love, reminding one of the parallel persistence in Stevens:

> Like a rose rabbi, later, I pursued,
> And still pursue, the origin and course
> Of love, but until now I never knew
> That fluttering things have so distinct a shade.

To continue to love what vanishes is to know the distinctness of what Yeats here calls a "tumult of images," produced by the wind-driven dancing feet of the daughters of Herodias, emblems to Yeats of the apocalypse he had expected in 1899. As before, Yeats's source is in Pater, and in his fellow-disciple of Pater, Symons. Jeffares quotes the most relevant lines of Symons's *The Dance of the Daughters of Herodias:*

> And always when they dance, for their delight,
> Always a man's head falls because of them.[22]

The dancer with the severed head is the wrong emblem for this poem, for these daughters are blind, and have no purpose whatsoever. In the tumult of images, the most central is that describing the daughters' indirection: "Their purpose in the labyrinth of the wind." The labyrinth is Urizenic, product of the fallen mind's exploration of a "world of cumbrous wheels." [23] We are returned to the fundamental inverted image of *A Vision,* for the serpentine labyrinth is the fallen version of the mental gyre of vision. Thus Yeats controls his image of the labyrinthine winds almost too comprehensively; we go from "the circle of the moon" at the start, to "dragon-ridden" days, to the "shining web" or "dragon of air" of Loie Fuller's Chinese dancers, to the whirling path of the Platonic Year and the dance to which it compels all men. This modulates to the apocalyptic "winds that clamour of approaching night," and onward first to the meditative labyrinth of art or politics, and then to the "winds of winter" of Yeats's, and the world's old age. The "levelling wind" blows on in the poem, and shrieks at the vanished generations, to climax at last in the great wind of the poem's concluding section. But this is stuff for a mechanical kind of reader, and though it has been noted happily by a series of critics, it begins to seem a positive handicap to the poem. One can turn around against Yeats his unfair and inaccurate criticism of Shelley in *A Vision,* where the ancestor-poet of Phase 17 is said, "in moments of fatigue," to give himself up to "fantastic, constructed images." [24]

The more imaginative pattern of *Nineteen Hundred and Nineteen* is not in the continuity of its imagery, but in the dialectical relation between its images. This depends upon the argument of the poem, which shows Yeats forsaking his emerging system, and returning to the great Romantics, particularly to the teaching of Blake and Shelley as to how the poet's imagination needs to meet a time of political disillusionment. Loss of civilization, personal loss, cannot be converted into imaginative gain, as they are by Wordsworth, Coleridge, sometimes Keats, working through a compensatory and sympathetic imagination. Loss in Yeats, at his finest, as in *Nineteen Hundred and Nineteen,* is more than the Body of Fate of the poet of Phase 17; it must be accepted for its own sake, as Shelley accepts it in his *Ode to the West Wind.* It belongs to experience, and experience cannot by its nature be redeemed. Shelley, confronting Mont Blanc, struggles to protect himself against a violence from without, and answers with a violence from within, the imagination that learns its own freedom from the power of process that has no intentions toward it. The poet's soul learns its own solitude, and hears the voice of disjunctiveness and dangerous freedom:

> Thou hast a voice, great Mountain, to repeal
> Large codes of fraud and woe; not understood
> By all, but which the wise, and great, and good
> Interpret, or make felt, or deeply feel.

The fifth section of *Nineteen Hundred and Nineteen* mocks all these: the great, the wise, the good, and turns at last upon itself to mock mockers, as Blake mocked Voltaire and Rousseau.[25] Even as the passage in *Mont Blanc* prophesies the Speech of the last Fury in *Prometheus Unbound* and Shelley's dark speculations on the relation between good and the means of good in *The*

Triumph of Life, so *Nineteen Hundred and Nineteen* recalls *The Second Coming* and prophesies *Cuchulain Comforted.* Preceding the promised end is the time of troubles, and what marks the time, for Yeats as for Shelley, is that good and the means of good are irreconcilable. The best who lack all conviction are the wise, the great, the good; wherever Shelley placed himself among these, Yeats presumably saw himself caught in the antinomies of "the wise want love; and those who love want wisdom." *Nineteen Hundred and Nineteen* strives toward an insight that Yeats does not want to reach, as his interests are scarcely those of a reformer. Behind the poem's pungent self-castigations is the High Romantic vision that haunts Yeats's rhetoric, but hardly his deepest thoughts: "We want the creative faculty to imagine that which we know; we want the generous impulse to act that which we imagine; we want the poetry of life: our calculations have outrun conception; we have eaten more than we can digest." [26] The consequence is presented in the poem's most powerful lines:

> The night can sweat with terror as before
> We pieced our thoughts into philosophy,
> And planned to bring the world under a rule,
> Who are but weasels fighting in a hole.

This is the world without imagination, with the reductive depths of our being breaking upward into our conceptualized evasions. Few poems by Yeats are as grimly honest as this one; a desperate naturalism faces a Gnostic revelation, and ends in terror, with the image of "that insolent fiend Robert Artisson," a fourteenth-century incubus, lurching past us, "his great eyes without thought," like the Beast of *The Second Coming* slouching onward to its revelation. Only one of the poem's six sections attempts to explore the means by which a poet, as poet, can confront the time of troubles, but that section is the poem's glory. Section III opens with an apparent reference to Asia's song of transfiguration in *Prometheus Unbound:*

> Some moralist or mythological poet
> Compares the solitary soul to a swan. . . .

As the section continues, other echoes are heard, of *Alastor* and perhaps of a Spenserian swan or two. The swan is the poem's image of poetry, of the solitary reverie setting itself against the apocalypse:

> The wings half spread for flight,
> The breast thrust out in pride
> Whether to play, or to ride
> Those winds that clamour of approaching night.

But this is followed by a stanza of powerful qualification, founded upon a vital moment in Blake's brief epic, *Milton*. Yeats is exploring the problematics of poetic solitude. In the first section of the poem he affirms that the observer of the present state of the world

> Has but one comfort left: all triumph would
> But break upon his ghostly solitude.

Critics have remarked already on the rich strangeness of Yeats's word "break" in several of his poems, but particularly here and in *Byzantium*.[27] The word's use here hints at both "mar" and "create," as perhaps it does at the close of *Byzantium* also. When solitude is invoked again in Section III it is presented as a state of being lost:

> A man in his own secret meditation
> Is lost amid the labyrinth that he has made
> In art or politics;
> Some Platonist affirms that in the station
> Where we should cast off body and trade
> The ancient habit sticks,
> And that if our works could
> But vanish with our breath
> That were a lucky death,
> For triumph can but mar our solitude.

"Some Platonist" here, like "some moralist or mythological poet" earlier, conceals a definite indebtedness, to Blake here, as to Shelley earlier. In Blake's *Milton*, that great precursor, though in

heaven, cannot escape the labyrinth he had made in art and politics and in personal life:

Say first! what mov'd Milton, who walkd about in Eternity
One hundred years, pondring the intricate mazes of Providence
Unhappy tho in heav'n, he obey'd, he murmur'd not   he was silent
Viewing his Sixfold Emanation scatter'd thro' the deep
In torment! To go into the deep her to redeem & himself perish? [28]

The image of "the intricate mazes of Providence," parodies
Milton's own description of the labyrinthine philosophical confusions of the Fallen Angels in Hell. The Sixfold Emanation, in
Yeatsian terms, is the manifold *daimon* which determines our
choices in art and politics alike. Blake meant by it everything
Milton had created and loved. But, in Blake as in Yeats, one does
not die "a lucky death," and the solitude of the poet cannot be
maintained in any state of being. Yeats's reaction to the self-de-
feat of poetic solitude comes in one of his greatest passages:

> The swan has leaped into the desolate heaven:
> That image can bring wildness, bring a rage
> To end all things, to end
> What my laborious life imagined, even
> The half-imagined, the half-written page;

That image is precisely apocalyptic; it has the potential of
raising the poet's solitary self-consciousness to the pitch where imagination casts out all that is not itself, "a rage/ To end all
things." Yet Yeats lives his laborious life for the sake of a larger
imagining, and it is his strength as a poet to persist until the page
is fully imagined, fully written. His temptation here is the one
that Shelley's Poet yielded to in *Alastor,* in a passage as important
for Yeats as any poetry he had ever read, except perhaps for the
speeches of the sage Ahasuerus in *Hellas.* The Poet of *Alastor,* in
his self-destructive quest, pauses on a shore:

> . . . at length upon the lone Chorasmian shore
> He paused, a wide and melancholy waste
> Of putrid marshes. A strong impulse urged

His steps to the sea-shore. A swan was there,
Beside a sluggish stream among the reeds.
It rose as he approached, and with strong wings
Scaling the upward sky, bent its bright course
High over the immeasurable main. . . .

The Poet observes this emblem of his own imagination rise to
its home, and reflects on the necessity for rising to his own, the resolve that will soon take him to death:

And what am I that I should linger here,
With voice far sweeter than thy dying notes,
Spirit more vast than thine, frame more attuned
To beauty, wasting these surpassing powers
In the deaf air, to the blind earth, and heaven
That echoes not my thoughts? [29]

He too must leap into the desolate heaven, for the image of
the swan's ascent has brought him his freedom, which is wildness,
the rage to end all things. *Alastor* is a relentless quest-romance,
and concludes in wildness. The peculiar power of *Nineteen
Hundred and Nineteen* is that Yeats persuades us that he feels the
authentic strength of this temptation, this very personal and High
Romantic apocalypse of imagination, yet restrains himself from
yielding to such temptation, particularly in the time of troubles.
The temptation of imagination is resisted for the sake of imagination, as the creative force divides against itself. But the particular
strength of the poem, which makes it one of Yeats's triumphs, is
Yeats's moving doubt of the strength of his own subjective solitude. His own system does not save, cannot comfort, and returns
upon itself in the poem's closing emblems of annunciation, peacock and cock, whose cries will herald more violence than even
Yeats can bear to contemplate. The poet, no more than other
men, fears the history that no man can master, and curbs the
tendency in himself to hail the superhuman. *Nineteen Hundred
and Nineteen* is a powerful antidote to such poems as *The Second
Coming, Leda and the Swan,* and *The Statues,* poems in which
Yeats is a little too much at ease in his own system, a touch too se-

cure in a superhuman posture as he contemplates the terrible an-
nunciations made to men.

Leda and the Swan

Part of the argument of this study is that Yeats has been overpraised, frequently on grounds that are likely to seem dubious as
more time passes, and our perspectives are corrected by longer
views. Our critics of Yeats have been too ready to establish Yeats's
superiority by dangerous juxtaposition with his masters:

> This account of his rituals has necessarily called attention to the
> deliberate character of his art. Although he has powerful feelings
> to express, his poems are in no sense their "spontaneous overflow."
> The "lyric cry" of Shelley is not his way. He gathers his intensity
> and force, which have hardly been equalled in modern verse, by
> creating, with the aid of symbol, myth, and ritual, patterns where
> thoughts and feelings find unexampled voice. There is nothing un-
> planned in his art; its many surprises come from long preparation,
> like the discoveries of a great scientist.[30]

That is Richard Ellmann's introduction to a discussion of
Leda and the Swan, and though Shelley is invoked there as a customary example of the bad old way Yeats chose not to follow, I
propose to take the hint by juxtaposing Shelley and Yeats on the
adventures of God as rapist, the "lyric cry" against the Yeatsian
patterns, in the achievement and its limitations. In the first scene
of Prometheus Unbound, Act III, God is about to be overthrown,
as we know, but he is profoundly deceived, and expects immi-
nently the arrival of his Son by Thetis, who will have overthrown
Demogorgon, God of the abyss, and then will ascend to make permanent the tyranny of heaven. Shelley, that spontaneous outcrier
of lyrics, creates a speech and situation of extraordinarily subtle
and complex irony, replete with inverted allusions to Revelation
and Paradise Lost. For God has begotten no son upon his mortal
victim, and the fierce spirit rising up from the abyss to fill the vacuum of heaven is Demogorgon himself, demon of transformations,

master of the gyres. At the apex of his paean to his own supposed triumph, Jupiter addresses Thetis:

> And thou
> Ascend beside me, veiled in the light
> Of the desire which makes thee one with me,
> Thetis, bright image of eternity!
> When thou didst cry, "Insufferable might!
> God! Spare me! I sustain not the quick flames,
> The penetrating presence; all my being,
> Like him whom the Numidian seps did thaw
> Into a dew with poison, is dissolved,
> Sinking through its foundations:" even then
> Two mighty spirits, mingling, made a third
> Mightier than either, which, unbodied now,
> Between us floats, felt, although unbeheld,
> Waiting the incarnation, which ascends
> (Hear ye the thunder of the fiery wheels
> Griding the winds?) from Demogorgon's throne.
> Victory! victory! Feel'st thou not, O world,
> The earthquake of his chariot thundering up
> Olympus? [31]

She did not put on his power, let alone his knowledge, but then it is Shelley's magnificence to show us that Jupiter had no accurate knowledge anyway, and not much more power than he had true knowledge. Jupiter is suffering the anxiety that he himself is; his suffering, and his confusion, together come to the most of him. He is a rather poor version of God, but except for being unluckier, he is close enough to Milton's God to be something more than a parody. Like Yeats, after him, Shelley centers upon the human victim of God's rape but, unlike Yeats, Shelley is strongly humanistic, and the human involuntarily thwarts God's design merely by being human. God's might was insufferable indeed, and she sustained him not, but since he is as stupid as he is confused Jupiter did not and does not understand. Indeed, he failed to put on her knowledge, which was that she was not conceiving.

Leda and the Swan is a powerful piece of rhetoric, and I assume that few contemporary readers will be persuaded by me to prefer the Shelleyan passage to it. I wish though that the Yeats sonnet had just a touch of the Shelleyan skepticism about divine power and knowledge. As the poem stands, it is difficult to defend against the impressive strictures of the late Yvor Winters:

> The greatest difficulties reside in the remainder of the sestet. "Did she put on his knowledge with his power?" The question implies that she *did* put on his power, but in what sense? She was quite simply overpowered or raped. . . . That is, if we are to take the high rhetoric of the poem seriously, we must really believe that sexual union is a form of the mystical experience, that history proceeds in cycles of two thousand years each, and that the rape of Leda inaugurated a new cycle; or at least we must believe that many other people have believed these things and that such ideas have seriously affected human thinking and feeling. But no one except Yeats has ever believed these things, and we are not sure that Yeats really believed them. . . .[32]

A reader tempted to dismiss Winters too quickly here should ask himself: "What is there of value in the poem?" The subject of the poem, as is so frequent in Yeats and throughout Romantic tradition, is a single moment, Blake's "pulsation of the artery" or Pater's "privileged moment." This would be clearer except for Yeats's revisions, which were somewhat unfortunate, in a pattern repeated throughout Yeats's revisions; the sacrifice of clarity and fullness for the sake of dramatic shock. It is of course a heresy to decry Yeats's revisions in his later poetry (more critics are prepared to see a loss in his re-writing of earlier poems), but I find all too often that the later poems give more to the whole man in the reader in their draft forms. In this poem, Yeats originally wrote:

> > Being so caught up
> > Did nothing pass before her in the air?

This appeared, finally, as:

> > Being so caught up,
> > So mastered by the brute blood of the air,

which adds little in itself and takes away the crucial question: did she have a vision as she was being victimized? For that is all I could offer Winters as the point of the poem. Whitaker, who values the poem highly, as do Ellmann and the common reader of our time (if we may suppose that we have one) cites Blake as analogue, in what I take to be an implicit defence of the poem's significance.[33] But the citation is a dangerous one to make for Yeats's poem, if one restores it to its context. At the end of Book I of his poem *Milton,* Blake rises to a great chant celebrating the natural world (hardly his usual occasion for celebration) as being the continual re-creation of the Sons of Los. The provisional redemption of experience through vision is the theme, and I suppose that in some sense it is, or ought to be, a theme of *Leda and the Swan,* since Yeats also is attempting a saving vision of time:

> Every Time less than a pulsation of the artery
> Is equal in its period & value to Six Thousand Years.

> For in this Period the Poets Work is Done; and all the Great
> Events of Time start forth & are conceivd in such a Period
> Within a Moment; a Pulsation of the Artery.

Milton 28:62–29:3

Whitaker omits "the Poets Work is Done," which is to omit the damaging contrast between the poets, for I assume that we are not to conceive of Yeats's swooping Godhead as a poet? Ironically, the brute is a poet of history, writing in humans rather than words, but this is to be a poet as Iago was. Like Winters (and every man, or rather every ear) I admire the sonority of the poem, but suspect it to be power purchased by the loss of knowledge.

On a Picture of a Black Centaur
by Edmund Dulac

This powerful if confusing poem is one of Yeats's cries of exultation at having had the revelation that will let him write *A Vision.* The centaur has been identified as Irish culture (by Unterecker) and Yeats's muse (by Ellmann), but both identifications create as much difficulty as they resolve.[34] Evidently, the centaur is another idealized *antithetical* self, which Yeats has loved "better than my soul," another of his preferences for an assumed personality over actual character. But the poem distinguishes between a past use for this anti-self, and a present lack of need for it, because his new revelation now allows the poet's soul to seek Unity of Being strictly in historical terms. The theme of the poem appears to be the poet's awareness that he has escaped a Swiftian madness, and the dismissed centaur is analogous to the Houyhnhnms.

The centaur is a *persona* close to madness, for his hooves "have stamped at the black margin of the wood," probably identical with "Jonathan Swift's dark grove" in the later poem, *Parnell's Funeral*. In the wood are the horrible green parrots who had driven the poet half insane, but against whom he is now fit to keep a watch in the closing lines of this poem. To make sense of the poem, it is necessary to read its final lines with an inserted phrase: "And there is none so fit [as myself now] to keep a watch and keep/ Unwearied eyes upon those horrible green birds." The parrots are nightmare images representing the poetic powers apparently available in the world of madness, and the centaur or assumed self has stamped Yeats's earlier works down into the "sultry mud" that marks the "black margin" between ordinary reality and the greater intensity of demonic possession. This stamping by the *persona* is murderous to the soul, which requires the wholesome food of the natural world, and which Yeats has fed for too long on the "mummy wheat" of occultism, gathered in what Blake too would have called "the mad abstract dark" of quasi-imaginative systems. But now, Yeats insists, full revelation has come. Though natural bread is still not vouchsafed, the "full-flavoured wine" of an historically-grounded vision has been made available to him. The centaur can be dismissed, the assumed anti-self of *Per Amica Silentia Lunae* can be urged to join the seven sleepers of Ephesus in "a long Saturnian sleep," to wait for a revelation that Yeats himself does not need any longer, for he has his own. Despite all these words of dismissal, Yeats insists that he *has* loved the mask he assumed, but he alone is fit for the greater vigil to come. A soul that has mastered the history of all souls can stand against the demonic birds of poetic madness.

Among School Children

In Book V of *The Prelude,* following his beautiful account of the Boy of Winander, Wordsworth meditates upon his own childhood education, and prays for its continuation in children to come:

> Mad at their sports like withered leaves in winds;
> Though doing wrong and suffering, and full oft
> Bending beneath our life's mysterious weight
> Of pain, and doubt, and fear, yet yielding not
> In happiness to the happiest upon earth.
> Simplicity in habit, truth in speech,
> Be these the daily strengtheners of their minds;
> May books and Nature be their early joy!
> And knowledge, rightly honoured with that name—
> Knowledge not purchased by the loss of power! [35]

The last line is the theme also of Yeats when he goes among school children, but his concern for himself as opposed to the children is a little more naked than Wordsworth's, the Egotistical Sublime being compounded by the ardors of a poetical career more genuinely prolonged than Wordsworth's. If in *Leda and the Swan* we are confronted with power purchased by the loss of knowledge, and in the *Black Centaur* poem with a confident assumption that power and knowledge have been purchased together by the loss of the natural, here in *Among School Children* Yeats movingly returns to Wordsworth's concern. The knowledge is his, but the power is departing. What rises in the place of power is the darkened ecstasy of the famous last stanza, perhaps Yeats's most memorable protest against his own Gnostic dualism:

> Labour is blossoming or dancing where
> The body is not bruised to pleasure soul,
> Nor beauty born out of its own despair,
> Nor blear-eyed wisdom out of midnight oil.
> O chestnut-tree, great-rooted blossomer,
> Are you the leaf, the blossom or the bole?

> O body swayed to music, O brightening glance,
> How can we know the dancer from the dance?

Not without a loss of power, is part of the answer to the final question. But why does the poem end then in a kind of ecstasy? The best answer among the critics is Whitaker's, who couples this poem with *Sailing to Byzantium,* as the work of "a new species of man who . . . *is* his contrary. . . . Hence the piercing vigor, even exultation, in the conclusions of such poems, where expression of desire is at the same time ecstasy in the attainment of the true goal." [36] That is eloquent idolatry, and seems to evade the baffled irony of the conclusion to *Sailing to Byzantium,* and the genuine doubt implicit in the questions that conclude *Among School Children.* For Yeats, even unknowingly, has not become his own antithesis, joined himself to the *daimonic,* in either of these poems. He is neither out of nature, in the one poem, nor willing to be out of it, in the other. *Among School Children* may well be esteemed for the wrong reasons; it may even be over-esteemed (as I think it is), but it is a poem in which (as in so few others) Yeats knows his own limitations and the limitations of poetry, and of thought. Nature is the bounding outline here, the circumference that Yeats can no more expand than Plato, Aristotle, or Pythagoras could. The chestnut-tree is leaf, blossom, and bole, a thing and not a ghostly paradigm; the dance is man's enterprise, neither thing nor paradigm, to be apprehended but not to be known. Here also, man can incarnate the truth (momentarily) but he cannot know it. [37]

All Souls' Night

This is the "Epilogue" to *A Vision* but, like *The Second Coming* and *Leda and the Swan,* it appears a stronger work when isolated from its context. *Two Songs from a Play,* also printed in *The Tower* volume, seem to me best discussed in their context in *The Resurrection* (see p. 334). *All Souls' Night* is a formal triumph, a remarkably gracious poem that manages to take Yeats's system lightly but suggestively, and without the aid of merely self-defensive irony, of the kind that the introductory prose to *A Vision* clumsily employs. All the aid the poem needs it rightly finds in the rich tumult of three vivid personalities, occultists all, the painter W. T. Horton, the actress Florence Farr Emery, and the astonishing cabalist and adventurer, S. L. MacGregor Mathers. These are allied not only by their arcane obsessions, but as self-defeated questers, heroic failures of the peculiar variety epitomized by Browning's Childe Roland, archetype of the failed artist. *All Souls' Night* deprecates the sober ear and the outward eye, and celebrates the dead who in their lives were drunk with vision, as Yeats chooses (here) to see himself as being. In death the questers have found their element, and drink from the whole wine of their gnosis. Yeats, a living man, is blind and drinks his drop, but is half contented to be blind, whether to the faults of the dead or of the full vision awaiting him in the whole wine of his own death, when his glance and thought alike will be fulfilled.

All this, including the linking imagery of sight and blindness, is overt and effective in the poem. More effective is an implicit defence, not so much of *A Vision,* as of Yeats's own lack of *sprezzatura,* of the splendid spiritual recklessness of his occultist companions. Where they went out in self-ruining quests after the mysteries, Yeats has remembered his destiny as a poet, and settled into productive domesticity, writing *A Vision* as his pragmatic substitute for the quest. Horton, Florence Emery, and Mathers have the dignity of heroic failure, and the occultist's honorable death; Yeats's role is to hoard their recklessness, so as to make them into a poem. We cannot all fail; to be Childe Roland is not enough, one must also write his poem. *The Tower,* certainly Yeats's finest volume of verse up to the time of its publication, and surpassed, if at all, only by *The Winding Stair,* which followed, attains its rightful epilogue in *All Souls' Night,* an apologia for the poet's ambiguous role among *antithetical* questers. To celebrate, not his system, but his personal good fortune in having achieved a system, whatever its status, Yeats hymns the departed who came beyond their parallel systems to the dark tower, there to demonstrate their triumphal courage in the face of whatever mummy truth.

20: The Winding Stair

After *The Tower,* this is Yeats's finest single volume of lyrics, particularly if we include the sequence *Words for Music Perhaps,* which will be discussed, however, in the next chapter, it being a work in its own right. *The Winding Stair* contains two of Yeats's greatest poems, *A Dialogue of Self and Soul* and *Vacillation,* and one of his most central, *Byzantium,* which I think has been overpraised. More than *The Tower, The Winding Stair* exhibits Yeats's most complex legacy from Shelley, the conscious strife between heart and head, the awareness of division. The volume's motto might be from Yeats's true rival among twentieth-century poets writing in English:

> The trumpet supposes that
> A mind exists, aware of division, aware
> Of its cry as clarion, its diction's way
> As that of a personage in a multitude:
> Man's mind grown venerable in the unreal.[1]

That last line may be taken as warning against the hieratic element in *The Winding Stair,* particularly as shown in *Blood and the Moon* and *Byzantium*. The volume begins though with the flawless *In Memory of Eva Gore-Booth and Con Markiewicz,* a Romantic elegy for two "pictures of the mind" who could not learn that: "The innocent and the beautiful/ Have no enemy but time." [2] This is the innocence again of *The Second Coming* and *A Prayer for My Daughter,* but the poem is not vitiated by a ritualized ideal, and its second part triumphs by touching a universal plangency.

With *Death,* the next poem, a celebration of the assassinated Kevin O'Higgins, the universal is invoked again, but perhaps less justly. To say, out of context, that "Man has created death" seems more Blakean than the statement is within the context of the brief poem. Yeats cannot have the irony both ways; if the poem means that there is no death, as in *A Vision,* then the compliment to the courage of O'Higgins is lessened when the poet says of that "great man in his pride," who mocks dying: "He knows death to the bone," itself a more powerful line out of the poem's context. Yeats returns more movingly to this death after the reader encounters one of the volume's and the language's glories.

A Dialogue of Self and Soul

The Higher Criticism of Yeats, when it is more fully developed, will have to engage the radical issue of his subjectivity, particularly as it is expressed in his myth of the *antithetical* man. A beginning has been made, by Whitaker and Priscilla Shaw in particular, but the subject is immense and crucial, for in the end Yeats will stand or fall by it.[3] Before he was forty, Yeats had concluded that

> . . . in the end the creative energy of men depends upon their believing that they have, within themselves, something immortal and imperishable, and that all else is but as an image in a looking-glass. So long as that belief is not a formal thing, a man will create out of a joyful energy, seeking little for any external test of an impulse that may be sacred. . . .[4]

This is a pure and beautiful solipsism, with something of the Paterian splendor of Stevens's Hoon (who is himself not quite a solipsist, since he is in the act of *finding*, even if it be only of himself, more truly and more strange). Nothing in the Self's wonderful declaration at the close of the *Dialogue* goes beyond re-affirmation of this ecstatic and reductive solipsism, since the source to which every event in action or in thought is followed will turn out to be the self: "Measure the lot; forgive myself the lot!" We are moved by the reciprocal blessings that follow, and yet we might be a touch uneasy also, for the self happily is blessing the self. "Everything" is, after all, "'but as an image in a looking-glass," and so we but look upon ourselves.

Buber remarks, with too transcendentally bitter a wit, that the spirit withers *gloriously* in the air of monologue. His oxymoron is accurate, but his own emphasis is too much on the withering. Yeats's title might well have been *Two Monologues of Self and Soul*, for in fact where is there dialogue in this glorious poem? That is hardly a fault, as we are dealing with a poem *qua* poem. There are, for me, no faults to be discerned in this poem, for like *Vacillation* and *The Man and the Echo* it is a poem of total self-revelation, and Yeats is never stronger than when he is totally exposed.

The Soul takes the lead, despite the necessary priority of the Self in the title, and the triumph of the Self's solitary declaration in the poem's second part. For the poem's genetic impulse belongs to the Soul; Yeats has been very near the gates of death (having just experienced his first severe illness since childhood) and he turns to consider the Last Things in a very different spirit than that of *A Vision*. His moral character or *primary* half summons his dominant personality or *antithetical*, questing half, to a judgment. The "winding ancient stair" is Dantesque and Blakean, both purgatorial and a Jacob's ladder for a new struggle of naming. The time approaches dark of the moon:

> Fix every wandering thought upon
> That quarter where all thought is done:
> Who can distinguish darkness from the soul?

The Soul's difficult question is not in the poem's first published version. There is no answer in the poem, and the Soul expects none. Nor does the Self attempt an answer, but only muses upon a ceremonial sword, as Oisin might have done. If the Self will not regard the Soul, it is because the blade is emblematical not only of love and war, but of the joyful and solipsistic creative energy that reduces all else to an image in a looking-glass. Sato's sword is yet more solipsistic as an emblem:

> . . . still as it was,
> Still razor-keen, still like a looking glass
> Unspotted by the centuries.

The soul, still anxious for dialogue, rightly sees its antagonist now as the obsessed imagination, and appeals for both imagination and intellect to focus on "ancestral night," that the purgatorial cycles of death and birth may be ended. There is no reply, as the obsessed Self continues its sustained brooding. This reverie is purposeful, and the questing Self seeks and finds emblems of day to set against the purgatorial tower in order to claim justification for the "crime" of rebirth. Giving the Self up for lost, the Soul is permitted the blessing of monologue:

> Such fullness in that quarter overflows
> And falls into the basin of the mind
> That man is stricken deaf and dumb and blind,
> For intellect no longer knows
> *Is* from the *Ought,* or *Knower* from the *Known*—
> That is to say, ascends to Heaven;
> Only the dead can be forgiven;
> But when I think of that my tongue's a stone.

The Soul is describing a state of being perilously close to Phase 1 of the Great Wheel. The cost of complete objectivity is everything that makes us human, as we become absorbed by supernatural context. Ascending to Heaven is the same as yielding to "complete passivity, complete plasticity." The Soul (and this is the poem's necessary limitation) is a Yeatsian initiate, or at least has read *A Vision* carefully. Only the dead can be forgiven, for only the dead can undergo the complex Yeatsian purgatorial process. The Soul speaks for many readers of *A Vision* in flinching from the process. But the difference is that the Soul yields to the process; its language indeed is not drawn from Phase 1 but from *A Vision*'s general definition of the Four Faculties, where Creative Mind and Body of Fate are the Knower and the Known, and Will and Mask are the Is and the Ought.[5] The final speech of the Soul in the poem is thus reduced to the voice of anonymous process, and appropriately ends upon the image of a stone.

The most neglected of truths about the *Dialogue*'s famous declaration of autonomy by the Self, is that the Self ignores Yeats's account of the laws of process as completely as the Soul accepts them. The poem's largest irony is that the Soul is an esoteric Yeatsian, and the Self a natural man. Where Yeats, in the Epilogue to *A Vision,* insisted: "No living man can drink from the whole wine," the Self begins by observing: "A living man is blind and drinks his drop." Where the Soul insists upon a darkness, from which it cannot even distinguish itself, and worships a plenitude of supernatural influx so full "that man is stricken deaf and dumb and blind," the Self confesses its blindness but lives in vision, the vision of self-confrontation and self-forgiveness. What the Self fights free of is everything in Yeats that has mythologized at its expense.

What the Self offers instead is to divest itself of everything except the life it has lived, which it would live again, not in the purgatorial and supernatural way of *A Vision*'s dreamings-back, but naturally, with all the pain of Self necessarily entailed. This is a more openly autobiographical Yeats than the great shaper of the *Autobiographies:*

> Endure the toil of growing up;
> The ignominy of boyhood; the distress
> Of boyhood changing into man;
> The unfinished man and his pain
> Brought face to face with his own clumsiness.

Painful enough; more painful is what the next stanza describes, the involuntary acceptance by the finished man of the caricature of himself his enemies have provided. The *Last Poems* has an undistinguished and disgruntled piece called *Are You Content?* Like the "I am content" that so powerfully opens the *Dialogue*'s two final stanzas, this recalls a legend of the days just before Shelley's death. His double comes upon the poet and demands: "How long do you mean to be content?" Yeats too now confronts his double, his own Soul, and bitterly answers the same question with "Forever!":

> I am content to live it all again
> And yet again, if it be life to pitch
> Into the frog-spawn of a blind man's ditch,
> A blind man battering blind men.

Rhetorically, this is at a successful extreme, even for Yeats. Dialectically, it is a Gnostic rather than a naturalistic statement (though modified by "if it be life"). Yeats is too shrewd to keep his vision of life's bitterness so general, and pitches us with him "into that most fecund ditch of all," the self-maiming pride of a defeated Romantic love:

> The folly that man does
> Or must suffer, if he woos
> A proud woman not kindred of his soul.

This is part, though only part, of the High Romantic pride of the last stanza, the pride of being "such as I." The great original of the injunction to cast out remorse, and so Yeats's direct ancestress here is again the audacious Cyntha of Shelley's *The Revolt of Islam:*

> Reproach not thine own soul, but know thyself,
> Nor hate another's crime, nor loathe thine own.
> It is the dark idolatry of self,
>   Which, when our thoughts and actions once are gone
>   Demands that man shall weep, and bleed, and groan;
> O vacant expiation! Be at rest.—
> The past is Death's, the future is thine own.

Yeats does not take precisely this advice, since for him "our thoughts and actions once are gone"; and yet return, to be followed to their source in Self. Yeats has his own "dark idolatry of Self," to replace the Christian variety which he has joined Cyntha in casting out. The sweetness that flows into his breast is very close to the sublime variety the "eagle look" of Maud Gonne had induced in him ("So great a sweetness flows/ I shake from head to foot") and is a kind of triumph of the Self over its own capacity for loss, remembering what is fit for a man and poet of Phase 17, whose Body of Fate is "loss." The categories of *A Vision*, which oppressed and captured the Soul, re-enter the Self's realm of the *Dialogue* only as a reminder of how lonely the Yeatsian ecstasy must be. The blessing given and taken at the close is hardly a sanctification of the commonplace, as it might have been for Wordsworth, but rather a more intense and less humanly admirable late version of the Sublime mode. That does not make it less attractive, or less magnificent as a poem.

Blood and the Moon

Yeats, and some of his critics after him, made too much of his supposed eighteenth-century ancestry, the Anglo-Irish "group" (only Yeats could have found them that) of "Goldsmith and the Dean, Berkeley and Burke." In *The Seven Sages* (also in this volume) he wrote perhaps his worst poem ever upon the theme of these late-found precursors, while their presence is a burden for the otherwise grimly impressive *Blood and the Moon*. Of the four sections of this theatrical but splendid poem, only the second, with its pseudo-Swiftian rant, fails. To Whitaker, Yeats's most learned and devoted apologist, the poem's meaning is Dantesque and its admittedly powerful posturings are justified because Yeats is fully conscious of his hatred and its limitations:

> Despite a rather common critical assumption based upon our usual blindnesses, self-dramatization does not preclude self-knowledge.[6]

But whose self-knowledge? Is the self-knowledge of Yeats of a Wordsworthian or a Blakean order, or is it the knowledge of the actor, mocking wisdom in the name of a momentary power? More than a preference for particular poets depends upon an accurate answer to the question. *Blood and the Moon* prophesies, in Yeats, the poems and plays of the final years, work now admired all but universally, and rather out of proportion to its actual merits. Honesty is not in itself a poetic virtue; I gladly acknowledge that *Blood and the Moon* is a very honest poem. But its strength is not there. What Yeats means by "blessed" in the poem is not easy to understand, but it cannot be what is meant at the close of *A Dialogue of Self and Soul* and of *Vacillation*.

In the apocalyptic afterthought of *Prometheus Unbound*, Act IV, a chorus of rejoicing spirits comes from "Thought's crowned powers" to watch the dance of redeemed time. These skiey towers of joy are invoked ironically by Yeats, in further mockery of the emblematic tower he sets up as mockery of our "time/ Half dead at the top." Yeats himself (against his own intention, doubtless) can be thought of as "A bloody, arrogant power/ Rose out of the race/ Uttering, mastering it." His tower and his winding stair represent what Romantic tradition has found so many emblems for, the power of the mind, of the most terrible force in the world, over Milton's universe of death: "Everything that is not God consumed with intellectual fire." The problem with this luminous line is that, as I think Frye remarks somewhere, God occupies the place of death in the Yeatsian vision, and indeed we are being told that the mind's fire consumes all that is alive here. Intellectual power, in the poem, is knowledge but hardly wisdom:

> For wisdom is the property of the dead,
> A something incompatible with life; and power,
> Like everything that has the stain of blood,
> A property of the living.

That is not Dantesque, but Jacobean; one would not be surprised to hear it as part of the dying speech of one of Webster's or Tourneur's anti-heroes. We meet here, not the chastened, more human Yeats of the *Dialogue* or *Vacillation* but the Gnostic adept, inhabiting Kafka's universe without showing Kafka's compassion or his sense of shared guilt. Kafka, not Yeats, is Dant-esque, as perhaps Beckett is also, if that quality of creative temper is to be found in our time at all.

The last two sections of *Blood and the Moon* are difficult and compelling verse; to understand them is to grasp Yeats's meaning at its most authentic and dismaying intensity. These two twelve-line stanzas, better than any other passages in his work, offer a full justification for the mordant quality of his vision, his highly individual sense of the bitterness of his own life. O'Higgins has been slain: "Whether for daily pittance or in blind fear/ Or out of abstract hatred." Yeats, who so admired him, broods in his own lonely tower of murderous intellect, savoring the moon's mockery, its unstained purity, and unable to find a Stoic comfort in this bitter taste of a poet's ineffectual innocence:

> Odour of blood on the ancestral stair!
> And we that have shed none must gather there
> And clamour in drunken frenzy for the moon.

In the song from *The Resurrection* printed in *The Tower* as one of *Two Songs from a Play* the "odour of blood when Christ was slain" makes ineffectual all Greek wisdom and art, not a result in which Yeats can have rejoiced. This is a similar reduction to vanity, and a terror to a great poet who properly feels the immense pride of poetry (hardly felt in our contemporary Age of Auden, with its subversion of that saving pride). This strong section is followed by a stronger. Yeats mounts to the empty room at the top of his never-quite-restored tower. In his own Notes to *The Winding Stair* he gives us our starting point:

> Part of the symbolism of *Blood and the Moon* was suggested by the fact that Thoor Ballylee has a waste room at the top and butter-flies come in through the loopholes and die against the window-panes.[7]

One remembers Tom O'Roughly, in *The Wild Swans at Coole*, where Tom sings that "wisdom is a butterfly/ And not a gloomy bird of prey," and also Yeats's Note to *Meditations in*

Time of Civil War where he says that a hawk symbolizes, for him, the straight road of logic, and a butterfly the crooked road of intuition (the accent of Blake's *Proverbs of Hell* can be heard in this).[8] The butterflies of wisdom perish at the tower's top; "thought's crowned powers" have turned deathly. Yeats bitterly takes back his celebration of his Anglo-Irish precursors; "no matter what I said," no wisdom is to be found except in the spooky world of *A Vision*'s Instructors. After this, it is curious relief, if not indeed a final irony, for the poem to conclude in celebration of the stainless glory of the moon. Total nihilism is difficult matter for poetry, yet Yeats is a strong enough poet to have written *Blood and the Moon,* where the self-reduction to nihilism is too forceful to be halted, and too eloquent to be discarded. When the poem ends, the poet and the reader have nothing except the strength to accept the unstained and coldly unaffected moon.

The *Coole Park* Poems

Yeats clearly thought these poems profoundly representative of him; he included both in *The Oxford Book of Modern Verse,* where he placed *Sailing to Byzantium* and the last section of *Vacillation* also, but otherwise only minor or occasional lyrics, and those mostly elegiac or political (or both). The elegiac tone is found in the *Coole Park* poems, but essentially these poems are celebratory, with Coole an Irish Urbino, Lady Gregory as the Duchess-patroness, and Yeats as Castiglione. It can be a temptation to read these poems in the spirit of George Moore (particularly just after reading *Hail and Farewell,* Volume III) but the poems justify resisting such temptation.

Coole Park, 1929, the first and lesser of the two, described by Yvor Winters as "a typical meditation on the virtues of old families," is rather (as Yeats says) a meditation upon a swallow's flight.[9] Jeffares shows that this is, in turn, a meditation upon a Pythagorean emblem, the swallow being used "as an image of indolence and an interruption of time."[10] Yeats reverses the emblem; the swallow's flight is Yeats's own poetic flight under the

influence of Lady Gregory, who saved him from ill health and
acedia, both partly resulting from his astonishingly prolonged
courtship of and frustration by Maud Gonne. The poem's central
image is the reverse of the opening image in *The Second Coming*.
These poetical birds hear their keeper:

> And half a dozen in formation there,
> That seemed to whirl upon a compass-point,
> Found certainty upon the dreaming air. . . .

The poem's impressive meaning is that for these writers and
men of culture—Synge and Yeats himself among them—things did
not fall apart, because Lady Gregory maintained the ceremony of
innocence, or at least enough of it so that true work could be
done. The "certainty" Yeats found, thanks to his patroness, is very
like the uncertain but necessary and saving graciousness Pater's
Marius found first in one ritual, and then in another.

Coole Park and Ballylee, 1931, is a more ambitious poem,
both more memorable and less indisputable, since some characteristic faults enter into it. Though still celebratory, it celebrates in
high desperation. The poem's vision is now immensely wide, with
Lady Gregory (invoked in the fourth stanza) a compass-point
again, but no certainty of innocence found through her. She is
near death, toiling with stick from chair to chair, and Yeats himself is past sixty-five. Urbino wanes, and the courtier looks out
upon a world he rejects, a darkening flood or blood-dimmed tide
upon which the emblem of apparent inspiration drifts.

"Water is his great symbol of existence," Yeats had written of
Shelley more than thirty years before, "and he continually medi-
tates over its mysterious source." [11] Yeats remembered the Poet of
Alastor addressing the river as the image of his life, and perhaps
he remembered also Rossetti's *The Stream's Secret,* a poem in
Alastor's tradition and another of his own early favorites. *Coole
Park and Ballylee* is one of Yeats's series of revisionary swerves
away from *Alastor,* taking its emblems of water as "the generated
soul" and the swan's flight as now unattainable inspiration, from
Shelley's poem. The *clinamen* or personal swerve of Yeats from

his source here is that the later's poet's alienation from nature and society is presented as part of a historical process of decline, whereas in *Alastor* the poet's alienation is due only to the incompatibility of imagination and nature. Shelley's Poet asks nature to do what it cannot, sustain the force of a quest whose energy no context can confine, or fulfill. Yeats is more resigned, to imaginative entropy and to natural inadequacy alike. But he is not resigned to the present moment, to a world where the great glory of the house of Gregory is spent, and where fashion or mere fantasy decrees how we shift about. Shelley, who came from the world whose passage Yeats laments, was more than willing to see it pass.

Yeats's poem is greatly conceived, and intricately executed, and yet it is tendentious; it has too overt a design upon us. Denis Donoghue rightly sees the second stanza as being tainted by a tactlessness that seeks self-exalting emblems at the expense of what Yeats himself liked to call reality and justice.[12] The failure in imaginative tact is larger, later in the poem. All the poem's emblems are imposed, never discovered, to use Stevens's distinction. The force of life is felt, but only as the threat of impending death. What is missing is the detachment of magnificence, so that Yeats is capable of approving attitudes that hold ancestral spots "more dear than life." Famous as the last stanza is, one wonders at calling a generation "the last romantics" whose chosen theme was "traditional sanctity and loveliness." Is *that* "whatever most can bless/ The mind of man or elevate a rhyme"?

At Algeciras—A Meditation upon Death

This pungent lyric, one of his very finest, reacts to Yeats's serious illness of October 1928. It may be Yeats's most genuinely Blakean poem, in its magnificent setting-aside of a characteristic Newtonian attitude, and in the visionary affirmation that casts off what Blake called "the Idiot Questioner." This is "Newton's metaphor," referred to in the poem:

> I do not know how I may appear to the world; but to myself I seem to have been only like a boy, playing on the seashore, and

diverting myself, in now and then finding another pebble or pret-
tier shell than ordinary, while the great ocean of truth lay all un-
discovered before me.[13]

In the lyric the old poet meditates upon death, brooding on
the uncanny "heron-billed" birds who suggest, to him, influx, the
start of a new dispensation. They will rise at another dawn, to return across the straits, but now they provoke reverie:

> Often at evening when a boy
> Would I carry to a friend—
> Hoping more substantial joy
> Did an older mind commend—
> Not such as are in Newton's metaphor,
> But actual shells of Rosses' level shore.

With a subdued, almost a charming irony, Yeats opposes the
shells as Minute Particulars to Newton's conceit of the shells as
small natural truths distracting from the vision of an immense
natural truth. The particular complexity of Yeats's art is in the
middle two lines of the stanza quoted; they appear to mean the
boy Yeats's hope that a more substantial joy was entrusted for
safe-keeping to his own mind, to be realized when he was older.
The shell, in Wordsworth and Landor, and Shelley and Yeats after
them, is an emblem of the poetic power; so Yeats had employed it
in *The Song of the Happy Shepherd*, which he placed first among
his lyrics, when he arranged the section of early poems he called
Crossways. Where the shells kept Newton from the larger vision
they prophesied for Yeats the "more substantial joy" of his mature poethood. That is the meaning of the poet's powerful and in-
spiring confidence in the last stanza of this deeply satisfying meditation upon death:

> Greater glory in the sun,
> An evening chill upon the air,
> Bid imagination run
> Much on the Great Questioner;
> What He can question, what if questioned I
> Can with a fitting confidence reply.

The convalescent poet, in Algeciras for the sun, feels the chill of death even as he apprehends more than a natural glory. The Great Questioner is God, deathly as always in Yeats, but the reply, for once, is confidently in the power of the imagination.

Byzantium

This is the *Kubla Khan* or *Ode on a Grecian Urn* of Yeats's lyric accomplishment, provocative of remarkably varied readings, ranging from Helen Vendler's, that it "is a poem about the images in a poet's mind," to Cleanth Brooks's, this it is about the life after death, following *A Vision*.[14] Yeats is responsible for the poem's ambiguity, since his central image, the dome, is starlit *or* moonlit. The poem's phase therefore is 1 or 15, Phase 1 being the death before life, and Phase 15 the full perfection of images. The poem's sources are very varied, and mostly not very esoteric, despite attempts to show otherwise. *Byzantium* is one of the most Shelleyan of Yeats's poems, and two starting points for its vision are clearly present in *Adonais* and *The Witch of Atlas*. But there are many striking parallels to the poem elsewhere in Shelley, and throughout Blake, as is inevitable, for Yeats is working here in the area of greatest poetic concern to him, and to his interpretation of his direct precursors.

Byzantium is, among much else, an elegy for the poetic self, and appears to have been at least partly elegiac in its genesis. As Shelley's *Adonais* is more Shelley's elegy for himself than one for Keats, so *Byzantium* is a vision granted to Yeats to help warm him back into life after a loss of being, but consciously for a little time only. Like *Adonais*, *Byzantium* is a high song of poetic self-recognition in the shadow of mortality, and is deliberately purgatorial and Dantesque in its situation and imagery.

Whitaker insightfully remarks of both Byzantium poems that "in each poem the speaker moves on his winding path or whirlpool-turning toward the timeless, through the sea of generation toward the condition of fire, which descends to meet him by way of its own gyre or winding path." [15] Whitaker cites Henry More and Thomas Taylor as likely sources; I suspect that Yeats derived the pattern from closer to hand, in Shelley (whose sources tend also to be less esoteric than some recent scholarship, which lusts after the esoteric, cares to allow). Shelley's most elaborate mythological patterns are in *The Revolt of Islam,* a boyishly exuberant fantasy, rather than in the mature and chastened sequence of *Prometheus Unbound, The Witch of Atlas* and *Adonais,* or in the yet more severely purged *The Triumph of Life.* When Laon and Cyntha are sacrificed by tyranny in *The Revolt of Islam,* they move in death through a labyrinthine stream, a winding path or whirlpool-turning, toward the timeless "Temple of the Spirit," and their movement is from fire to fire, Eternity in some sense descending to meet them. In *Adonais,* Shelley exhausts the windings of generative existence, and approaches the timeless, only to find it descending to meet him by way of its own intricate web of approaches. Seeking an unknown, the poet is found by

> . . . that sustaining Love
> Which through the web of being blindly wove
> By man and beast and earth and air and sea,
> Burns bright or dim, as each are mirrors of
> The fire for which all thirst; now beams on me. . . .

This is the Condition of Fire, and life stands out against it as a dome *staining* the radiance of Eternity, a work of loss, and yet the staining means also the transformation of whiteness into all the colors of the arts. The relevance of this dome to *Byzantium*'s, where Yeats originally wrote that the dome "distains" (outshines) all that man is, is clear. But the immediate Shelleyan source of *Byzantium* is even more clearly *The Witch of Atlas,* which accounts for the Emperor's soldiery and the scene-setting at the opening of Yeats's lyric, and contributes something also to the ironic coloring of the golden bird of *Sailing to Byzantium* and the embittered scorner, "more miracle than bird or handiwork," of this poem:

> The king would dress an ape up in his crown,
> And robes, and seat him on his glorious seat,
> And on the right hand of the sunlike throne
> Would place a gaudy mock-bird. . . .

> The soldiers dreamed that they were blacksmiths, and
>   Walked out of quarters in somnambulism;
> Round the red anvils you might see them stand
>   Like Cyclopses in Vulcan's sooty abysm,
> Beating their swords to plowshares.

Yeats, haunted still by *The Witch of Atlas,* when he writes his "official" death poem, *Under Ben Bulben,* is so close to the poem that the baleful magic of Poetic Influence comes into play now when we read Shelley's poem, so that it seems as if Borges is right and Yeats somehow has created his precursor. The Witch goes on her Yeatsian voyage through the generative sea, moving upward on a labyrinthine winding path, with the elements resisting her:

> Beneath, the billows having vainly striven
> Indignant and impetuous, roared to feel
> The swift and steady motion of the keel.
>
> Or, when the weary moon was in the wane,
>   Or in the noon of interlunar night,
> The lady-witch in visions could not chain
>   Her spirit; but sailed forth under the light
> Of shooting stars. . . .

On her voyagings, she builds herself "a windless haven," a copy of Heaven paralleling the copy built as Pandemonium by Milton's fallen angels. The Witch's version is dominated by a dome, from which she descends for closer observation of the flux below of blood and mire:

> By Moeris and the Mareotid lakes,
>   Strewn with faint blooms like bridal chamber floors,
> Where naked boys bridling tame water-snakes,
>   Or charioteering ghastly alligators,
> Had left on the sweet waters mighty wakes
>   Of those huge forms—within the brazen doors
> Of the great Labyrinth slept both boy and beast,
> Tired with the pomp of their Osirian feast.

What *Byzantium* avoids is the polemical and antinomian aspect of Shelley's poem, yet even in Shelley the Witch is far from feeling our griefs, for she belongs to the interlocking worlds of art and the life-before-birth. Her perspective is the perspective of the gaze downward and outward from Byzantium to our world, rather than the gaze upward and inward of Yeats's poem, which moves out from the human. Our sorrows, to the Witch, are only "the strife/ Which stirs the liquid surface of man's life":

> And little did the sight disturb her soul—
>   We, the weak mariners of that wide lake
> Where'er its shores extend or billows roll,
>   Our course unpiloted and starless make
> O'er its wild surface to an unknown goal:—
>   But she in the calm depths her way could take,
> Where in bright bowers immortal forms abide
> Beneath the weltering of the restless tide.

The "bright bowers" are precisely those of Byzantium, where the golden smithies of the Emperor are the same red anvils at which the sleep-walking soldiers of Shelley's vision accomplish the prophecy of Isaiah. The Condition of Fire dominates in Byzantium, and the element of fire draws Yeats, Shelley, and Blake together here:

At midnight on the Emperor's pavement flit
Flames that no faggot feeds, nor steel has lit,
Nor storm disturbs, flames begotten of flame,
Where blood-begotten spirits come
And all complexities of fury leave,
Dying into a dance,
An agony of trance,
An agony of flame that cannot singe a sleeve.

Men scarcely know how beautiful fire is—
  Each flame of it is as a precious stone
Dissolved in ever-moving light, and this
  Belongs to each and all who gaze thereon.
The Witch beheld it not, for in her hand
She held a woof that dimmed the burning brand.

The flames rolling intense thro the wide Universe
Began to Enter the Holy City   Entring the dismal clouds

In furrowd lightnings break their way the wild flames whirring up
The Bloody Deluge living flames winged with intellect
And Reason round the Earth they march in order flame by flame
From the clotted gore & from the hollow den
Start forth the trembling millions into flames of mental fire
Bathing their Limbs in the bright visions of Eternity.

Like the fire of the Witch's weaving, the flame of *Byzantium* outshines ("distains") natural flame, and like the fire of Blake's apocalypse, the Byzantine flame cannot harm the nature it dims. For these are the flames of simplification through intensity, the condition and simplicity of fire deriving from the hearth of Shelley's Witch and from the Furnaces of Urthona the Smith at the conclusion of *The Four Zoas:*

> The hammer of Urthona sounds
> In the deep caves beneath his limbs renewd his Lions roar
> Around the Furnaces & in Evening sport upon the plains
> They raise their faces from the Earth conversing with the Man
>
> How is it we have walkd thro fires & yet are not consumd
> How is it that all things are changd even as in ancient times. . . .

But to see the similarities of Yeats's New Jerusalem and its refining fire to those of Blake and Shelley is to see less than half the relation between Yeats and his precursors here. Both Blake and Shelley would have quarreled bitterly with the following sentences, a definitive summary of Yeats's vision by Gordon and Fletcher:

> The whole city, with its great dome and its mosaics which defy nature and assert transcendence, and its theologically rooted and synthetic culture, can serve the poet as an image of the Heavenly City and the state of the soul when it is "out of nature." [16]

Shelley's intellect is too skeptical for him to assert transcendence, and Blake defies nature in a complexly dialectical way only, one in which the natural is not transcended but is superseded by "an improvement of sensual enjoyment." And both poets violently rejected all "theologically rooted and synthetic culture," being as much of the permanent Left as Yeats was of the Right. *Byzantium* derives from Blake and from Shelley but also, as critics have shown, from Plotinus and from Wilde, from the Order of the Golden Dawn and from early twentieth-century scholars and from a lifetime of profound interest in the visual arts.[17] What Blake and Shelley clearly provided for Yeats were examples of what he, Yeats, interpreted as being a close association between the realms of an *antithetical* or anti-naturalistic art, and of death or the life after death and before birth. It can be shown that Yeats's interpretations of Blake and Shelley in this regard were creative misinterpretations, as I think I show elsewhere in this study, but that appears to be a normal procedure in the working of poetic influence. What is important, I think, for the understanding of *Byzantium* is that Yeats consciously found models for his ambiguity of presentation, a holy city at once a place only of images, and the place of the life after death.

The drafts of *Byzantium,* as presented by Bradford and by Stallworthy, show a movement toward rather than away from this deliberate ambiguity, as they make clear how much Yeats excluded in the process of revision, while retaining the poem's essential doubleness.[18] The poem's motto, and a description of its ideal, can be found in the early, excluded lines: "I tread the emperor's town,/ All my intricacies grown clear and sweet." Among the excluded intricacies are a curious apparent reference to Blake's *London,* and a reference to "a certain square where tall flames wind and unwind/ And in the flames dance spirits," a square that recalls the public square in *The Revolt of Islam* where Laon and Cyntha are burned and rise as spirits from the flames, or the public square of apocalyptic transformations described by the Spirit of the Earth in *Prometheus Unbound,* Act III, Scene IV.[19]

Byzantium, in its definitive version, begins with a distinction between unpurged images of day receding, and the purged images of night, which will help to constitute the poem. As I have implied already, I do not believe that *Byzantium* can be read strictly as a poem about images in Yeats's mind, though I wish that it could be, since Yeats knew a great deal about images and no more about death than the rest of us, and most of his ideas about death in *A Vision* are not imaginatively very interesting. I agree with Mrs. Vendler's argument that a critic's business is to show the relevance of *Byzantium* to human experience, but I fear that *Byzantium* simply is not overwhelmingly relevant, unlike *Adonais* or *The Four Zoas* or, in *The Winding Stair*, sequences like *A Dialogue of Self and Soul* and *Vacillation*. This being the case, *Byzantium* does seem somewhat vulnerable to the strictures of Yvor Winters, who rejected the poem because "Yeats had, in fact, only a vague idea of what he was talking about," the poem's subject being "the poet looking out from eternity on those who are coming in." [20] Winters is too harsh; one can agree with him and still agree with Gordon and Fletcher that "what is asserted with clarity, unforgettably, is Byzantium itself; and the stylisation of nature's violence and disorder." [21] But this turns us to the central question that governs the poem's meaning and value; what, *in the poem,* is "Byzantium itself"?

Yeats thought that Shelley "believed inspiration a kind of death," and Byzantium is for Yeats a state of inspiration, a kind of death, and an actual historical city, all at once.[22] For this to be possible, phantasmagoria is necessary, and Yeats begins and ends his poem as a phantasmagoria. Indeed, the *given* of the poem is this phantasmagoria; either we grant it to Yeats, or the poem cannot be coherent. *Kubla Khan* is a precisely similar phantasmagoria, and the Byzantium of Yeats is thus analogous to Coleridge's Xanadu, another domed sacred city (an analogy first remarked by G. Wilson Knight). That is, to read *Kubla Khan* we must allow Coleridge his waking dream, and to read *Byzantium* we must accept the dialectic of waking dream also. Yeats has a vision of a quasi-historical *Byzantium;* he stands somehow in its streets as night comes on. He stands also in his own mind, observing a struggle of images to make a poem, and he stands finally in Eternity, beyond the generative sea, watching "the ghosts swimming, mounted upon dolphins, through the sensual seas, that they may dance upon its pavements." [23]

Yeats himself enters the poem with the first line of its second stanza. The first stanza is bare of man, day's image, and of night's images as well. Present only is the dome, image of Eternity, scorning and outshining the human, for it presides here over a phase of being that has no human incarnations, though we cannot know as yet whether it is the phase of complete beauty or of complete plasticity. Neither of these states can be described, and there is appropriately no description as such in the first stanza.

I think it evident from the remaining four stanzas that, in the phantasmagoria of this Eternity, Phases 1 and 15 of Yeats's system somehow exist simultaneously. Yeats, himself not a ghost but recently having come very near the gates of death, confronts a purged image, a Virgilian shade, at once an emblem of "death-in-life" or complete beauty, and "life-in-death" or complete plasticity. In hailing this superhuman image, Yeats in effect takes on the role of Dante, a Dante who has found his guide to the world of death and judgment.

The golden bird and bough next invoked undoubtedly do have some backward reference to the same properties in *Sailing to Byzantium*, as many critics have noted, but something of the irony of presentation in the earlier lyric has dropped out here. In the starlight of Phase 1, the golden bird hermetically shepherds the dead to their transformations, triumphing like the cocks in Hades; or in the moonlight of Phase 15, the artifact distains all that is natural, glorying in its perfect beauty, yet embittered by the light that betokens also a natural sexuality it cannot share. The function of this stanza has not yet been defined satisfactorily by any Yeats critic, in my judgment, and one can wonder how much the poem would suffer if the stanza were to be omitted, which is the ultimate functional test. Readers should be invited to the experiment of attempting the poem without it; does it contribute to the poem's argument, if there is a sustained argument?

If this is one of the problems of understanding and valuing *Byzantium*, another is presented by the sequence of the poem's two remaining stanzas. Winters rightly observed that "the fourth stanza deals with the purification of the entering spirits, and the fifth with their struggle to enter: as far as the mere logic of the discussion goes, these stanzas ought to be in reverse order." [24] Again, a reader could be invited to reverse the order; he would find the reversal brings about a dialectical gain, and a rhetorical loss. As the poem stands, the fourth stanza does describe the reduction of ghosts into the simplicity of the Condition of Fire, and the fifth deals with the shock of encounter between the incoming ghosts and what Blake would have called the Furnace of Urthona, the golden smithies of Yeats's Emperor (himself as much a surrogate for God as the Kubla Khan of Coleridge). Both stanzas are rhetorical triumphs, but the last is particularly powerful, in its juxtaposition of contending forces. The last five lines, one of Yeats's remarkable condensations, form an epitome of the entire poem:

> Marbles of the dancing floor
> Break bitter furies of complexity,
> Those images that yet
> Fresh images beget,
> That dolphin-torn, that gong-tormented sea.

Here the marbles break all three: furies, images, and sea, but Mrs. Vendler rightly points out that grammatical necessity and practical reading part, with the force of "break" spent before the end, so that "the last three lines stand syntactically as absolute." [25] The effect is very strong, particularly since the verb "break" is being used so individually. To break is to divide, but to divide is to make, whether the divisions be of human fury, images, or waves, so that in *Byzantium* "break" seems to mean both "mar" and "create." Whitaker notes the "strange richness" of the word "break" in *Nineteen Hundred and Nineteen* as "suggesting both temporal loss and a partial transcendence of that loss." [26] In terms of the apparent argument of *Byzantium*, the breaking accomplished by the marbles of the dancing floor is a transcendence, but the poem has inherent strength enough so that one feels the loss also.

If *Byzantium* primarily concerned the creation or enjoyment of a work of art, then the final lines would be a triumph of transcendence, and Ellmann would be justified in saying that the ghosts of the poem, the blood-begotten spirits, were being immortalized by the refining fire.[27] But there is far too much in the poem concerning the Last Things, and far too little necessarily depicting aesthetic process. The breaking of furies in the poem is a casting-away rather than a refining of the human, and the

poem's coherence finally does belong to the realm where Cleanth
Brooks assigns it, *A Vision*'s account of "the relation of the living
to the living dead." [28] Brooks finds the poem, like *A Vision*, to be
"imaginatively true," unlike Winters, who found both poem and
system to be replete with "easy emotion." [29] As I tried to indicate
in my chapters on *A Vision*, the system is not imaginatively coherent, but its emotion is impressively difficult, and the total effect is
equivocal. I think that *Byzantium* must stand or fall with *A Vision*, and cannot prophesy time's final judgment.

Vacillation

This poem, or sequence, is one of Yeats's great achievements, and
is allied to other works beyond dispute, *A Dialogue of Self and
Soul* and the death poem, *The Man and the Echo*, in particular.
Yeats is never finer as a poet than when he vacillates, when he suffers uncertainty, and severely doubts his own mythologies. In this
he is the heir of the agnostic and skeptical Shelley, rather than of
Blake, who hated all doubt and uncertainty as much as Shelley
hated remorse and self-contempt. Pity, Blake insists, divides the
soul because it is another experimental state of mind, and so disa-
bles the imagination, and indeed leaves the poet who feels it less
able to feel the urgency of his own vision. Yeats's soul was not
often divided by pity, of course, but the involuntary divisions in it
were as much inescapable as similar divisions in Shelley.

The crucial division in Shelley was between head and heart, a
good instance being the contrasting hymns of 1816, the skeptical
Mont Blanc and the visionary *Hymn to Intellectual Beauty*. The
Yeatsian antinomy of self and soul, personality against character,
has been discussed earlier in this chapter. *Vacillation* is subtler
work even than the *Dialogue*, possessed by real poetic difficulty
rather than the mere complications of much other Yeats.

To vacillate is not only to fluctuate in consciousness, but to
move from side to side, as in the movement of gyres. Yeats does
not use the word in the poem after the title, nor does it occur elsewhere in his poetry, but the state of mind it betokens seems as
characteristic of him as "mobility" is of Byron or "wildness" of

Emerson. It is useful to know that Yeats considered calling the poem *Wisdom*, for "vacillation" does become a kind of wisdom here. Speaking of the whole body of his poetry, Yeats could say: "The swordsman throughout repudiates the saint, but not without vacillation," thinking backward to Oisin's repudiation of St. Patrick, and *Vacillation*'s respectful farewell to the mystical Von Hugel.[30] Ellmann rightly cautions that this is over-simplification, though "vacillation" appears so rich a word for Yeats, so dialectical, that perhaps over-simplification is not the problem.[31] As with Stevens, Yeats's mode tends toward qualified assertion, rather than the asserted qualifications of Eliot and his followers. The personality asserts, and Yeats stands upon it; his character qualifies, without lessening the imaginative or indeed moral force of the declaration. The wisdom involved is hardly that of Blake, for the "extremities" of *Vacillation* are not the contraries, but are closer to Blake's "negations" which stifle progression. Rather, the wisdom is a skeptical humanism skeptical also of itself, and poised before the abyss of unknowing that Demogorgon inhabits. "The deep truth is imageless" is paralleled in an early draft of *Vacillation:* "No imagery can live in heaven's blue." [32]

Yeats remarked that he began *Vacillation* as an attempt to shake off the "Crazy Jane" mask, and this reaction against a defiant vitalism is the mood of the first section of the poem.[33] The body's death and the heart's remorse alike destroy the antinomies upon which Yeats has founded his thought. Man runs between extremities, negations, and so more than divinity lies beyond our antinomies; experience itself does. Many times Yeats has denied death, and cast out remorse, in the name of the "joy" or "genial spirits" that are so crucial to Romantic creativity. But if the denial and the casting-out vanish in the larger context of life's experience, then what is joy?

Vacillation, in asking and then attempting to answer this question, puts itself in the central line of the Greater Romantic Ode, with *Intimations, Dejection,* the *West Wind,* the *Nightingale,* and their series of later nineteenth-century descendants. *Le Monocle de Mon Oncle,* despite its immensely different, almost directly contrary tone, is an exactly parallel poem to *Vacillation,* being a descendant of the same tradition. All these are poems lamenting not the decline of creative power, but the loss of an instinctive joy in the exercise of such power. And all vacillate, in different ways, in their balancings of loss against compensatory imaginative gain. The occasions are very disparate, and Yeats's is the only one of these poems that hesitates toward a conventionally religious resolution of the balancing. *Dejection* concludes in the accents of Christian orthodoxy, but this is consolation for absolute loss, as Coleridge perhaps over-dramatically presents it. I find it very difficult to believe that Yeats the man was much tempted by Christianity, then, before, or later, despite the curious arguments advanced by several critics. But Yeats is subtler anyway; he vacillates here not toward belief, but toward a different kind of poetic subject matter, and then veers back toward his own individualized concerns.

Vacillation, in the six sections before its final chant, makes no direct answers to the question concluding its first section. The direct answer comes in the tone and gesture, the exuberance of break-through in the final section. But there are implied answers all the way through. The second section, a vision of a burning tree from the *Mabinogion,* presents a blind joy of self-immolating poetic absorption that, by implication, is no longer available to the mature Yeats. The Poet-hero of *Alastor,* and all his Yeatsian descendants, could choose this fury of creative conflagration, but not the experienced poet in his mid-sixties, who is condemned to know what he knows and that he knows.

The magnificent third section takes the other side of the division between poets suggested by the "Preface" to *Alastor,* those who burn to the socket. These, caught in Lethean foliage until middle age, are adjured then to learn a more appropriate philosophy:

> No longer in Lethean foliage caught
> Begin the preparation for your death
> And from the fortieth winter by that thought
> Test every work of intellect or faith,
> And everything that your own hands have wrought,
> And call those works extravagance of breath
> That are not suited for such men as come
> Proud, open-eyed and laughing to the tomb.

This powerful recovery is in part a reply to the first section, but its reply is heroic gesture, not argument. The antinomies have not been re-affirmed, and their existence is pre-condition for Yeatsian joy. In the fourth section, the Paterian privileged moment is invoked, as Yeats describes an epiphany past fifty, and something of the pattern of the poem begins to be clarified. Section I states the problem of lost joy as it confronts a poet past sixty-five. Each section in turn, after that, proceeds in a rough chronology, as the illusory though imaginative choice is made, of attitudes toward death and life. So, the self-consuming poet of Section II is a Shelleyan youth; the first stanza of Section III moves toward middle age, and the second arrives at meridian. The epiphany at fifty is a last blazing-up, and lasts "twenty minutes more or less," while in Sections V and VI an aging man yields first to remorse, and then to a surrender of poetic significance, before the bitter sense of triumphant mutability:

> From man's blood-sodden heart are sprung
> Those branches of the night and day
> Where the gaudy moon is hung.
> What's the meaning of all song?
> "Let all things pass away."

When the dialogue of Section VII begins, its force takes on extraordinary added reverberation from this sad downward curve of a lifetime's loss of joy. The Soul, taking precisely the stand maintained in *A Dialogue of Self and Soul,* urges the Heart to leave seeming for reality. Yeats chooses Heart rather than Self because the dialectic is not between character and personality here, but between a sanctified and unsanctified imagination. A particular effectiveness is felt in the heart's liberation from its earlier remorse. The heart knows that a born poet must write of "things that seem," of earthly complexity and not the simplicity of fire, which needs and nurtures no poet. When the Soul is reduced to the dogmatism of St. Patrick again ("Look on that fire, salvation walks within."), the Heart goes far beyond Oisin in choosing the "unchristened heart" of Homer as its ideal. Indeed, "having to choose" would be more accurate, for a poet's heart must choose as the greatest of poets chose. As Section VIII insists, Yeats must "play a predestined part," the poet's. In the first draft of Section VIII Yeats wrote: "I swear to god that I/ With fierce unchristened heart shall live in Homer's company," in which the direct accent of Yeats-as-Oisin is heard again.[34] We are in a deliberately climactic moment as Yeats respectfully renounces the faith of his own grandfather and accepts the Homeric faith of his own father, a belief in action and the poetry celebrating action. The answer to "What is joy?" the return of the revitalized antinomies, is implicit in the glancing reference to the parable of the lion and the honeycomb: "Out of the eater came forth meat, and out of the strong came forth sweetness." One strength both slays the lion, and then feasts upon its sweetness. Joy does not depart permanently from the Samsons of poetry, such as Homer, Shakespeare, Blake, in whose company Yeats desires to find himself. Vacillation is wisdom, or as much of wisdom as can be won through being a poet, because poetic realities, things that seem, are ceaselessly in flux. To cease to vacillate is to be struck dumb in the simplicity of fire, or as Yeats's only rival in modern poetry put it, never to know that fluttering things have so distinct a shade.

21: Words for Music Perhaps

Though some of these songs were written as late as 1932, the crucial ones stem from a burst of exuberance in the Spring of 1929, a return of life in which Yeats felt he shared again in "the uncontrollable energy and daring of the great creators." [1] In some sense these are Yeats's Mad Songs, with a tradition behind them that includes the incredible anonymous *Roaring Mad Tom,* a poem so powerful as to surpass Blake and Shakespeare in their mastery of this kind, let alone Scott, Wordsworth, Tennyson, Browning, and Yeats. The overt influence on Yeats, as so often, is Blake, whose dialectical attack upon all dualism is severely reduced in Yeats's series. One way to see both the achievement and the limitation of *Words for Music Perhaps* is to realize that Yeats is forgetting again, quite deliberately, his own systematic wisdom in regard to himself. He is a poet of Phase 17, *daimonic* man, not an exuberant *positive* man of Phase 16, like Blake and Rabelais. But, in the spring of 1929, he felt the humanizing fury of Blake and Rabelais in him, the apocalyptic vitalism he had described so well in *A Vision*'s account of Phase 16. He felt the element of frenzy, the delight in shining images of force, and chanted his being's triumph over its own incoherence. That he triumphs in many of these lyr-

398

ics must be allowed; none of them indeed is entirely a failure. Whether he is quite being himself is another matter, as he knew, and the shade of Blake hovers uneasily near some of the poems. Yet no one since Blake has done so well in this vein, unless it be the Browning of *Johannes Agricola* and related monologues, where a deeper intellectual energy than Yeats's swerves into a dramatic art of derangement and convolution.

The first poem in Yeats's series, *Crazy Jane and the Bishop*, turns upon the interplay between its two refrains, the parenthetical *"all find safety in the tomb"* and *"The solid man and the coxcomb,"* where 'coxcomb' is restored to something of its root meaning of he who wears the jester's cap, or simpleton, since it is hardly likely that the Bishop is denouncing Jack the Journeyman as a fop. If the Bishop and Crazy Jane's lover together find safety in death, the lyric's meaning is affected also by this use of "safety." Safety from what? The poem is a curse, but also a haunting, since her dead lover bids Crazy Jane to the blasted oak, but himself wanders out from it to stay in the night of his death. She finds shelter if solitude under the oak, a shelter that the tomb's safety cannot provide since the dead, being Yeats's dead, do not sleep but suffer purgation.

I am puzzled that a number of critics, beginning with Walter E. Houghton, have found *Words for Music Perhaps* to be a work of "heroic tragedy." [2] There is no tragedy for Crazy Jane, nor can she be tragic in herself. Even if she were only a crazy old witch, cursing a moralizing Bishop under a blasted oak at midnight, she might be regarded as anything from frightening to pathetic, depending upon your standpoint, but not as tragic. Yet her poems are not even dramatic lyrics; they are rigorously conventionalized mad songs, and their interest has nothing to do with their supposed singer. Nor can their meanings have much to do with simplistic dramatic reversals. *Crazy Jane and the Bishop* would not be much of a poem if its achievement were located where Ellmann and Unterecker find it, in our growing realization that birch-tree Jack is the solid man and the moralizing Bishop the coxcomb.[3] The Bishop's back is hunched like a heron, but that no more makes the Bishop the Hunchback of *A Vision*'s Phase 26, than it makes him an *antithetical* emblem, like the Heron.

The mad song's singer must present neither a tragic heroism nor an ironic reversal of orthodox values, but simply the wisdom of a more radical wholeness than reason, nature, and society combine to permit us. The unfortunate Bishop, within the context of the series, is hardly a menace or in any way a worthy opponent. He is a convention and thus a convenience, the Wedding Guest for Crazy Jane (and Yeats) to hold with a glittering eye. Mad songs depend upon extravagance, not in any current sense of that word, but in the root sense of roving beyond all limits, the sense still conveyed by Ludwig Binswanger's *Verstiegenheit,* the psychic state of the person who has climbed too high to be able to return.[4] Crazy Jane and the other *personae* of *Words for Music Perhaps* are extravagant; they are the Prolific of Blake's *The Marriage of Heaven and Hell* who cease to be Prolific when the Devourer as a sea no longer receives the excess of their delights. They insist that energy is the only life, without acknowledging at any time that there must be some bound or outward circumference of energy, some reason, no matter how far out it is placed. Decay and impending death, to the extravagant, do not bring any tragic sense; their apocalyptic world does not admit of tragedy. Yeats sees this when he says of the mood in which *Words for Music Perhaps* was begun, "it seemed to me that but for journalism and criticism, all that evasion and explanation, the world would be torn in pieces."[5] Energy and daring, the exuberance of the extravagant, define a universe where only entropy is the antagonist, and that is not a tragic universe. Somewhere Nietzsche observes that a few hours of mountain climbing make scoundrel and saint into the same man, and something like this is meant when Crazy Jane tells us that solid man and coxcomb find safety together in the tomb. This is safety from extravagance, from the experience of a height incommensurate with the breadth of being, to borrow Binswanger's formulation.

Crazy Jane Reproved, the next of the series, is a more delicate and intricate poem. Ellmann and Jeffares helpfully find the source passage in the *Autobiographies:*

> Is it not certain that the Creator yawns in earthquake and thunder and other popular displays, but toils in rounding the delicate spiral of a shell.[6]

But this need not suggest, as Ellmann and Jeffares say, that we are to take the song's title straightforwardly, and think that Crazy Jane is being reproved, whether by herself or by the poet, for her choice of lovers.[7] Rather, the point is that Jane scorns every manifestation of Heaven and Zeus, whether it be storm, Europa's bull, or the painstaking design of the Creator's toil. Her "fol de rol, fol de rol," is directed against every argument from design whatsoever, and her apparent warning against her own choice of love is another extravagant affirmation.

Deliberate limitation would seem to enter with *Crazy Jane on the Day of Judgment,* but for the poem's title, which conveys the singer's refusal to acknowledge the metaphysical inadequacy of sexual love. If she has found, from experience, how little union can be shown, how little knowing there is in sexual knowing, the finding has not altered her extravagance, which insists that in apocalypse, the passing away of time, all could be known and shown, and love finally satisfied by taking soul as well as body. In *Crazy Jane and Jack the Journeyman,* Yeats is much subtler, the poem being one of the most accomplished of his career. Parkinson provides a valuable account both of the poem's origin, and its early draft.[8] Starting in what Yeats took to be his own occult experience of "the black mass of Eden," the poem moved through a lover's quarrel as to love's endurance, and then past Crazy Jane's skepticism of that endurance into the ghostly intensity of Yeats's vision of the sexuality that still prevails among the dead. Love, Crazy Jane says, is only a coiled thread or "skein unwound/ Between the dark and dawn." This is the deliberate reversal of Blake's image of the golden string which the poet is to wind into a ball. For Crazy Jane, love unwinds the winding path, and leaves a choice of fates, either to be the lonely ghost that comes to God, or likelier for her:

> The skein so bound us ghost to ghost
> When he turned his head
> Passing on the road that night,
> Mine must walk when dead.

She is to be led, not to heaven's gate built in Jerusalem's wall, but out upon the lonely ghost's roads of sexual purgatory, the roads of *The Cold Heaven.* This is the accepted price of extravagance, part of a higher price paid in this life as well, which is the meaning of *Crazy Jane on God,* the much slighter lyric that follows. Here the background material in Yeats's prose is more memorable than the foreground of the poem. The refrain, *All things remain in God,* is peculiarly reduced by Yeats's critics when they gloss it by his prose obsessions, but they clearly follow Yeats's intentions in this. Late Yeats is haunted by the image of the uninhabited, ruinous house suddenly lit up, but the immense suggestiveness of the image invariably is spoiled by Yeats himself in his perpetual search for occult evidence. *Crazy Jane on God* hardly survives comparison with the Paterian eloquence of its operating principle as stated in *Per Amica Silentia Lunae:*

> We carry to *Anima Mundi* our memory, and that memory is for a time our external world; and all passionate moments recur again and again, for passion desires its own recurrence more than any event. . . .[9]

With the next poem, an immense vitalism returns, but if the terms are derived from Blake, the dialectic nevertheless is not his, and belongs to the Gnostics and occultists. *Crazy Jane Talks with the Bishop* is the central poem of *Words for Music Perhaps,* showing both the Yeatsian extravagance, and the characteristic *clinamen* of the way in which Yeats handles his own difficult case of Poetic Influence when Blake is the precursor. Critics have noted the Blakean source for the powerful last stanza, but not the movement in meaning, the change in emphasis, between Blake and Yeats. The Spectre of Urthona, element of nervous fear within the creative mind, exults over the divisions he has made between Los and Enitharmon:

> The Man who respects Woman shall be despised by Woman
> And deadly cunning & mean abjectness only, shall enjoy them
> For I will make their places of joy & love, excrementitious
> Continually building, continually destroying in Family feuds
> While you are under the dominion of a jealous Female
> Unpermanent for ever because of love & jealousy.
> You shall want all the Minute Particulars of Life.
>
> *Jerusalem* 88:37–43

But this is the voice of natural man, or rather of the natural man lodged within the poet's imagination. In the apocalypse of *Jerusalem,* the liberated imagination speaks:

South stood the Nerves of the Eye. East in Rivers of bliss
the Nerves of the
Expansive Nostrils West, flowd the Parent Sense the Tongue.
North stood
The labyrinthine Ear, Circumscribing & Circumcising the
excrementitious
Husk & Covering into Vacuum evaporating revealing the
lineaments of man. . . .

Jerusalem 98:16–19

Both passages emphasize that the excrementitious "Husk & Covering" is a creation of the blocked senses, and of the blocked mind controlling them. The Spectre of Urthona can make our places of joy and love excrementitious only through the wars of jealousy, the imagination's fear of its own freedom. Crazy Jane does not know Blake's difficult wisdom, but she knows and sings again the Gnostic wisdom of Yeats's extravagance:

"A woman can be proud and stiff
When on love intent;
But Love has pitched his mansion in
The place of excrement;
For nothing can be sole or whole
That has not been rent."

There is a Gnostic assumption here that the place is "of excrement," while Love has the audacity to pitch its mansion where it lacks priority. This is precisely opposite to Blake's emphasis, and is Yeats's Spectre of Urthona speaking. That the rending has happened Blake would not dispute with Yeats, but he would not believe rending in itself is the path to wholeness, or to being sole, a Minute Particular of vision. Still, Crazy Jane is never more impressive poetically than she is here, for her authentic extravagance would be difficult to match. She attracts Yeats, and his readers, because of the sublime and grotesque fury of what we might

call, wryly, her "anthropological disproportion," again following
Binswanger as the theoretician of extravagance.[10]

This disproportion is not the theme of the last Crazy Jane
poem in *Words for Music Perhaps*. In ridding himself of the *persona* (except for her reappearance in one lyric among the *Last
Poems*) Yeats assimilates her to his more general theme of "sexual love is founded on spiritual hate," which he credits to Blake,
without understanding what Blake meant by it. His source in
Blake must have been this:

> But Albion fell down a Rocky fragment from Eternity hurld
> By his own Spectre, who is the Reasoning Power in every Man
> Into his own Chaos which is the Memory between Man & Man
>
> The silent broodings of deadly revenge springing from the
> All powerful parental affection, fills Albion from head to foot
> Seeing his Sons assimilate with Luvah, bound in the bonds
> Of spiritual Hate, from which springs Sexual Love as iron chains: [11]

This "spiritual Hate," as Yeats fails to see, is *not* between men
and women, but between Albion and his Sons, or between what
man was before his fall, and the Zoas or warring faculties into
which he has broken up after his fall. On the level of Blake's
moral allegory, this has the psychological meaning of the Oedipal
revulsion from our own natural affections that exists in all men.
In Blake's historical allegory, this has the political meaning of the
hatred of British kingship for its subjects. On either level, Luvah
is the Zoa or faculty of the affective life, and Blake is saying both
that the other faculties assimilate to the affective life, thus un-
fairly blaming sexual love for their common bondage, and that
the sexual love of all men under the British royal tyranny becomes debased by the "iron chains" of law and custom. Yeats's
misinterpretation of this passage is one of his less creative swerv-
ings away from Blake, and critics in any case ought to stop following Yeats in attributing the decadent notion that sexual love is
founded on spiritual hate to what Yeats called "Blake's old
thought." [12] Blake did not father or share in Yeats's dialectics of
love, which belong more to the Romantic Agony than to the High
Romanticism of Blake and Shelley.

The Romantic Agony is certainly the context of *Crazy Jane*

Grown Old Looks at the Dancers, a marvelous lyric and one of the ornaments of *Words for Music Perhaps.* Too old for the dance of sexual love, Crazy Jane watches the sado-masochistic pairing of an "ivory image" and "her chosen youth." Whether one or the other or both die is left ambiguous, to Jane and to us, but Jane's desire for participation, whatever the cost, is revealed, in the poem's climax, and in its refrain, *Love is like the lion's tooth.* The poem culminates an obsessive theme that Yeats had broached in *Per Amica Silentia Lunae* and then developed fully in *A Vision*'s account of *daimonic* love.

Despite the passing of Crazy Jane, *Words for Music Perhaps* scarcely loses lyric momentum in the eighteen poems that follow. No other modern poet shows the verve and intensity of song that Yeats does in this late phase, though Auden has a larger range and virtuosity as a song writer. For the most part the argument of the songs in the middle of Yeats's series is in their movement, and needs commentary of a sort my limitations as a prosodist keep me from being able to contribute. But the closing group, XXI through XXV, brings back the vitalistic extravagance of Crazy Jane, with her *daimonic* possession. Yeats returns to the Cruachan of *The Hour Before Dawn,* the windy plain where he locates the Irish Hell Gate. On this purgatorial plain, a saint dances and sings a song that could as well belong to Yeats's version of Tom O'Bedlam, who does sing the three songs that follow. We hear of the profane perfection not only of mankind, but of birds and beasts as well. Yeats's passion here may owe much to his interpretation of Plotinus, as Wilson and Rajan say, but the poetic idea involved is much closer to Blake, whom Yeats read and re-wrote long before he knew Plotinus.[13] And, despite the school of critics who read Blake and Plotinus alike as adepts of the one Perennial Philosophy, Blake's vision of Minute Particulars is not identical with Plotinus's vision of timeless individualities. In his brilliant introduction to *The Words upon the Window-pane,* Yeats explains the timeless individuality or *daimon* of Plotinus as containing "archetypes of all possible existences whether of man or brute, and as it traverses its circle of allotted lives, now one, now another, prevails." [14] But the Minute Particulars of Blake are not archetypes, in any sense, and traverse no circles of allotment, and, though Yeats echoes his own phrases about Plotinus, he portrays, in these lyrics, individualities which are irreducible, imaginative kernels lodged within natural creatures, including men. The dancer at Cruachan proclaims the particulars that dance and sing aloud, and Tom the Lunatic takes his stand with whatever maintains "the vigour of its blood." In *Old Tom Again* he mocks the "fantastic men" who follow Plotinus in believing that things, the Minute Particulars, are other than self-begotten, and something close to Tom's voice is heard in the last poem of the series, where Plotinus himself swims "out of perfection" into the generative sea. There "salt blood blocks his eyes," and the timeless individuality of the sage does not prevail in its enterprise of clearly displaying the archetypes or "Golden Race" of Zeus to him. The Golden Race "looks dim," and something of the irony of the later *News for the Delphic Oracle* already is apparent.

Yeats's vitalism in *Words for Music Perhaps* is poetically more impressive and humanly more acceptable than the equally intense vitalism of *On the Boiler* and *Last Poems*. But why? The later vitalism is not more polemical, though certainly it is more tactless, intruding as it does into the spheres of social and political relations in the name of a suspect eugenics. However odd it seems to attribute tact to Crazy Jane and Tom the Lunatic, they do preserve a decorum of stance that makes their poems possible. They do not rant, unlike the chanter of many of the *Last Poems*. The difference is in their role as oracles of Yeats's own extravagance, the authentic *Verstiegenheit* of his difficult nature. We are rightly suspicious of Yeats's extravagance because we sense that at bottom he is more cunning and skeptical than we are, and we know he is not Nietzsche or Rimbaud, "acrobats straining at the extreme limits of themselves," as Cioran calls them. In the *Last Poems* Yeats indeed has a delirium to propose, but we resist this rage, on the principle suggested by Cioran: "The only minds which seduce us are the minds which have destroyed themselves trying to give their lives a meaning." [15] In *Words for Music Perhaps,* Yeats is more modest. He knows his limits there, we know ours, but he shows us also his extravagance, and the path it would take if his deepest nature did not save him from joining the world of Crazy Jane and Tom the Lunatic, acrobats of revolt.

22: *Supernatural Songs*

Oisin's quarrel with St. Patrick is taken up again, but by the more formidable Ribh, in this remarkable sequence of twelve poems or fragments. Ribh surmounts the impossible absurdity of the role Yeats assigns him, an early Irish Christian Hermit whose faith came out of hermetic Egypt, as compared to the "alien" Christianity brought in by St. Patrick. The extravagance of this *persona* does not matter, for it is the conscious extravagance of Yeats himself at his most daring, and after a few lines the reader rightly assumes that it is Yeats proper who speaks. This is Yeats in a cultivated mood of Blakean exuberance, celebrating the re-opening of the sexual gate, into an increased perceptiveness. One can also surmise that this is a Yeats influenced more directly and profoundly by D. H. Lawrence than he himself realized, but the influence is natural enough, stemming as it does from a common Blakean element in Yeats and Lawrence.

It is probably unwise to consider the *Supernatural Songs* without close reference to Yeats's life. Except for the final poem of the series, the great sonnet *Meru,* all of the songs stem from Yeats's post-operative state in the summer of 1934. The effect of the

Steinach operation on Yeats may have been largely psychological, but whatever it was there is a fresh exuberance in Yeats after 1934, though whether there was fresh creative energy only later readers, more detached than ourselves, can judge. Though there are marvelous poems written during Yeats's last five years, this final phase seems a descent from *The Tower* and *The Winding Stair*.

Ribh is Yeats's most complex *persona,* because through him the poet tries to grasp more than can be held, at once, by any man; a completeness that would be supernatural. For all the esoteric ambition involved, Ribh is a less extreme version of Browning's *Johannes Agricola in Meditation*. Johannes Agricola is quite mad, but his tumbling monologue convinces that nothing will stop his getting to God, though what God could do with him, God alone knows. Like Johannes, Ribh has the Emersonian freedom, wildness, insightfully compared by Whitaker to the Blakean "excess." [1] The salvation of which Johannes is so aggressively certain is like the impossible wholeness which Ribh strains to find possible.

The *Supernatural Songs* open with *Ribh at the Tomb of Baile and Aileen,* where the ninety-year-old hermit reads his unnamed book by the light of a ghostly lovers' reunion:

> . . . when such bodies join
> There is no touching here, nor touching there,
> Nor straining joy, but whole is joined to whole;
> For the intercourse of angels is a light
> Where for its moment both seem lost, consumed.

Yeats's source is presumably Swedenborg, but could as easily be Blake, or even Milton, in a passage that greatly affected Blake.[2] Ribh, his eyes made aquiline by his hermit's discipline, is open to the solar light of angelic intercourse, though the leaves of fallen nature somewhat break the light's circle. Rhetorically the poem is very impressive, but its careful ironies do not save it; Ribh asserts he reads by a supernatural light, however imperfect the circle. The lovers are long dead, their bone and sinew transfigured into alchemically pure substance, yet the occasion for their supra-sexual reunion is "the anniversary of their first embrace," as though the supernatural can only commemorate the natural. Ribh, like Yeats, has gotten the visionary point, but backwards. The vision of a more perfect sexual union (in Eternity) by Milton, Swedenborg, Blake, is a vision of sexuality redeemed from self-consciousness through being redeemed, not of the fallen body, but of the body's fall. Yeats is happy to mix sexuality and the spirit, only half in the belief that they are opposites yet finding them opposite enough, but Milton and Blake are monists, something the dualistic Yeats could never get clear about Blake. The resolution of opposites is *not* apocalyptic for Blake; it is, for Yeats-Ribh and all occultists. Ribh has not gone beyond the consciousness of opposites, and more than his sense of external nature breaks the perfection of his gyring light.

In Blake, the body is all of the soul that our fallen senses can perceive, but we would perceive more of the soul if our senses were enlarged and more numerous, as Blake's story holds once they were. Yet we would perceive more of the soul by changing our perception of and with the body. This is not the vision of Donne in *The Ecstasy,* or that of Ribh by the lovers' tomb. Donne's vision, for all its personal shading, remains orthodox. Ribh is viewing a purgatorial consequence of tragic love, and though he sees reunion where Dante saw separation, he sees as Dante saw, the human *and* the divine, not the human form divine of Milton and Blake. Still, this is not the whole story of what Ribh wants to see, and to be by seeing. In the next poem, *Ribh Denounces Patrick* (originally, *Ribh Prefers an Older Theology*) an attempt is made to naturalize the divine, which is of course rather different from the program of humanizing the Godhead: "Natural and supernatural with the self-same ring are wed." The older theology is natural theology, in which every Trinity must have man, woman, and child. If the Holy Ghost in Milton was reduced to a vacuum, as Blake ironically observed, in Yeats as in *Prometheus Unbound* it is incarnated in a child, or at least a parody of such an incarnation is displayed. Writing to Mrs. Shakespear, Yeats said the point of *Ribh Denounces Patrick* "is that we beget and bear because of the incompleteness of our love." [3] It is difficult to see this as part of the poem's meaning, and worth debating because it matters that Yeats misconceives his subject here.

Ribh's poem is a denunciation, and presumably as a dramatic lyric it must be allowed the particular vehemence of one theologian finding another to be crazed in the absurdity of his doctrine. But another kind of vehemence dominates the poem; if Patrick is crazed by Greek abstraction, then Ribh is crazed by what might be called Egyptian Druidism (Yeats's amalgam, not mine), or the worship of "juggling nature," the serpent formed of our embraces and whose scales reflect our multiplicity. Ribh is crazed enough to end in a horror that men seem to know no end; God is but three and yet we multiply incessantly. Ribh's point is presumably that we are not divine because our love is less perfect than God's; Yeats, to Mrs. Shakespear, calls this an incompleteness of love, damped by one of the opposing dualities, body or mind. But what would it mean if men "could beget or bear themselves"? Perhaps that they would undergo a second birth, and so become sons of God? The poem cites the Great Smaragdine Tablet, which in Blake's *Jerusalem* is employed by Los's Spectre in a desperate and unsuccessful attempt to draw Blake's Poetic Genius down into the abyss of the indefinite. Yeats looked the other way when he reached this passage, preferring to ignore Blake's most decisive rejection of occult tradition. We are compelled to copy copies, says Ribh, whereas presumably the Godhead originates an original, when it begets Godhead. This is nonsense, but good Hermeticism, and worthy of the double talk of the Smaragdine Tablet as unveiled by H. P. Blavatsky:

> What is below is like that which is above, and what is above is similar to that which is below, to accomplish the wonders of one thing.

As it stands, *Ribh Denounces Patrick* ends in a *non-sequitur*, since Yeats does not even hint what it is about the complete love of the Godhead that saves it from endlessly repeating the copying of itself. The next poem in the series, *Ribh in Ecstasy,* begins "What matter that you understood no word!," in which I take it that "you" might as well be any reader whatsoever. If Ribh's circle of light was broken, then "doubtless," as Yeats says, his song is sung "in broken sentences." This is Yeats's characteristic audacity, but here it means: "Am I incoherent? Very well then, I am incoherent. I am profound, I contain irrational truths." Does *Ribh in Ecstasy* contain them? The lyric is a declaration of having been caught up in the Godhead's sexual ecstasy, and then having fallen from it as that ecstasy's shadow. Whether the poem convincingly dramatizes the declaration I cannot judge, but *There,* the next in the series, is not reassuring:

> There all the barrel-hoops are knit,
> There all the serpent-tails are bit,
> There all the gyres converge in one,
> There all the planets drop in the Sun.

Bunyan does better than this in his little rhyme in which Eternity is seen as a ring, but this "There" is Yeats's Eternity, the Thirteenth Cone or Final Sphere, God, art's timeless moment, the ecstasy Ribh has shared. Still, the palpable irony does not save the quatrain from poetic triviality. Ribh is moved to the immense passion of *Ribh Considers Christian Love Insufficient,* one of Yeats's great poems and, with *Meru,* the crown and justification of this intense and uneven series. Ribh's excess of vehemence passes sometimes into incoherence, but here it attains to sublimity. The poem's source, as surmised by Ellmann, appears to be in one of Mrs. Yeats's spooky "communicators":

> He insisted on being questioned. I asked about further multiple influx. He said "hate God," we must hate all ideas concerning God that we possess, that if we did not absorption in God would be impossible . . . always he repeated "hatred, hatred" or "hatred of God" . . . said, "I think about hatred." That seems to me the growing hatred among men [which] has long been a problem with me.[4]

"Further multiple influx" is reminiscent of the baffled closing page of *A Vision,* with its unanswerable question: "How work out upon the phases the gradual coming and increase of the counter movement, the *antithetical* multiform influx." [5] There, as here, Yeats greedily looks for a new crop of mummy wheat, and Ribh shares in this savage expectation. Indeed, *Ribh Considers . . .*

may be counted as one of Yeats's apologias for his own hatreds. As such, it is not a more considerable poem, its immediate rhetorical shock being so great as to need no aids. But it may help in understanding the larger design of *Supernatural Songs*. Ribh, to Yeats, is his own possible Christianity, the sense in which Yeats's Irish Protestant heritage is still available to him. This sense is a difficult one, and no definitive view has developed in Yeats scholarship on the matter. Yeats's Christ is as individual as Blake's, and if Yeats was a Christian, then perhaps any man with a religious temperament could be called that. As this would not be very useful, it seems wiser to start with the eclectic difficulty, and to acknowledge that Yeats's religion was as private as Jung's or as Lawrence's, without having the Protestant patterning that is clear enough in Jung and Lawrence.

Yeats darkened the matter by his commentary on *Supernatural Songs:* "I would consider Ribh, were it not for his ideas about the Trinity, an orthodox man." If this is not a joke, then the orthodoxy is of the kind that could lead Yeats to say "that for the moment I associated early Christian Ireland with India." [6] Whitaker remarks of Ribh: "Like Emerson's Plato or Pater's Phidias, he balances West and East, lunar and solar, *Will* and *Creative Mind*. Yeats, of course, who balanced Balzac and Patanjali in his mind, offered ample opportunity for Ribh to speak through him." [7] The balance is the problem, and Ribh is perilously unbalanced, though Yeats (and Whitaker after him) think otherwise. It is not Christian love, the *caritas* that Blake attacked as the hypocritical "pity" of Urizen, that is insufficient for Ribh, but love of any sort.

Ribh begins his consideration by desiring hatred in order to clear his soul "of everything that is not mind or sense," so as to arrive at a fresh start for subjectivity. Why he (or Yeats) is free to choose whom to hate, but not to love, we are not told. The second stanza hardly shows hatred as "a passion in my own control." The soul is "jealous," which is not a freedom, and hatred of man, woman, or event scarcely liberates from terror and deception. Yet, from the last line of the second stanza on, the poem breaks free from its own compulsiveness and finds its way to the Romantic sources of Yeats's best imaginings. The soul is convincingly liberated, dubious as the means are, when it is shown how it "could walk before such things began," the things being all the impurities that followed the Creation-Fall. Once liberated, the soul can learn for herself, and Ribh ceases to speak for her. She is now the soul of Yeats's dialectic of self and soul, and she speaks for "character" as against "personality." It is a tribute to Yeats's art that the poem changes so abruptly when the self drops out. The "hatred" the soul learns is a genuine freedom, a freedom from outworn conceptualizations of the Divine, as of the self. If the soul truly turns "from every thought of God mankind has had," then it turns from the God not only of the theologians but of the theosophists also. The most Blakean lines in Yeats, the most Blakean lines I know outside of Blake, follow this freedom:

> Thought is a garment and the soul's a bride
> That cannot in that trash and tinsel hide.

Blake's Milton finds his bride, his emanation Ololon, and achieves his quest with a great declaration that informs Yeats's lines here:

> To bathe in the Waters of Life; to wash off the Not Human
> I come in Self-annihilation and the grandeur of Inspiration
> To cast off Rational Demonstration by Faith in the Saviour
> To cast off the rotten rags of Memory by Inspiration
> To cast off Bacon, Locke and Newton from Albions covering
> To take off his filthy garments, and clothe him with Imagination
> To cast aside from Poetry, all that is not Inspiration.[8]

It is in the spirit of this sublime speech that Ribh's soul declares: "Hatred of God may bring the soul to God." This is not the hatred of Ribh's self, not the hatred of man, woman, or event, but of the filthy garments and rotten rags, trash and tinsel, that conceal Blake's "Human Form Divine," the real man, the imagination. This is the light of the soul free from jealousy, by which we cease to quest for impurities. By this light the last stanza needs to be read, and I think has not been read. At the stroke of midnight, the time of *All Souls' Night,* of the epilogue to *A Vision,* and of the dance of spirits on the Emperor's pavement in *Byzan-*

tium, the time when "God shall win" in *The Four Ages of Man* in Ribh's song cycle, at this time, when we pass from the death-in-life of the generative world to the imagination's freedom, the soul ceases its tolerance entirely for what Ribh's self could still endure, mind or sense, a mental or bodily furniture. And, in that ecstasy, the poem ends with four violent exclamations, as violent as any effect in the older Yeats:

> What can she take until her Master give!
> Where can she look until He make the show!
> What can she know until He bid her know!
> How can she live till in her blood He live!

Is this defeat or victory, for Ribh's soul? Rhetorically, it is certainly victory, even exultation, but dialectically it may be a defeat. It is overtly a defeat for his self, but that came half-way through the poem. The soul can win only at its own expense, and Ribh-Yeats, after a Blakean epiphany, subsides into a desperate dualism again, at least until the difficult last line. The soul and the Godhead here are not united as one imagination, and it is the Gnostic in Ribh-Yeats that impedes the union. The poem looks for the uncanny, for the supernatural, or for the ring that will wed it to supernature. There is a line between the theosophists and Blake that Yeats declines to cross. Not that the poem as poem would be better if more imaginatively coherent; it might not be, as Yeats derives considerable urgency from his Gnosticism, particularly here.

After this intensity, Yeats wisely modulates in the next lyric, *He and She*. To Mrs. Shakespear, Yeats called this a poem "on the soul," expressing "my centric myth." [9] This interpretation wrecks a slight but bitterly charming lyric, on woman's fickleness and power of self-assertion, appropriate to Yeats's mixed (and fictionalized) memories of his relationship to Maud Gonne. What lives in the poem, the more strongly for coming just after Ribh's abnegation of self, is the song of the woman in flight, who exults "I am I, am I," with Ribh's answering comment: "All creation shivers / With that sweet cry" as though he recovers now from his self-darkening. The shivering of nature is its vibrant reaction to the return of personality, the reassertion of the serpent. This is amplified in the extraordinary *What Magic Drum?*, interpreted by Ellmann as the visit of a bestial father to see his offspring by a human mother, and read by Whitaker as an act of occult possession, in which Ribh opens himself to a transcendental force, the offspring thus being a revelation.[10] Ellmann's reading is grotesque, but that is Yeats's fault, not his critic's, while Whitaker abandons the horrible specificity of Ribh's vision:

Through light-obliterating garden foliage what magic drum?
Down limb and breast or down that glimmering belly move his
    mouth and sinewy tongue.
What from the forest came? What beast has licked its young?

To amplify Ellmann, and to explore the poem further, one needs to read the opening rather closely. There is a trinity in the poem, consisting of a male, Primordial Motherhood (not necessarily Eve), and the child, a Blakean kind of grouping, as in the various accounts of the birth and nursing of Orc. *What Magic Drum?* opens with a grotesque tenderness, the male being embraced by the mother while he holds the child, and straining not to desire her, lest the child be disquieted. But, in the three lines quoted above, he is startled into desire by the magic drum of nature's rhythm, the "light-obliterating garden foliage" referring us back to the closing lines of the first poem in this series. The supernatural light, only "somewhat broken" for Ribh, is totally obliterated by nature here, and as readers we are in the position of the "you" in the opening poem, the baffled natural man who confronts, "in the pitch-dark night," a hermit bearing an open book. In that darkness, another natural man (perhaps a beast only as the natural man is bestial) hears the drum-beat, and caresses either mother or serpentine ("that glimmering belly") child. The answer to the highly ironic last line, on this reading, is simply "man," natural man, who has come from the forest into a garden, there to lick his young. As a Blakean irony, the point of the poem is that it is a natural song, not a supernatural one, and if Ribh is its singer, he has gone too far now on the supernatural path to see this scene as we would see it. A good analogue is in the first two stanzas of *The Mental Traveller*, where the ordinary processes of human sexual intercourse and birth appear uncannily grotesque to the ballad's singer, who has descended from Eternity to view them.

Something of this sense of the uncanny is carried over into the next poem, *Whence Had They Come?*, characteristic of Yeats at this time both in its power and its cruelty, but here the incomprehension comes from the other, the natural side. Like the "beast" of *What Magic Drum?*, girl or boy experience what they take for Eternity at the onset of passion, but awake to a sense of apartness, of having been mediums through whom "Dramatis Personae spake." Possession in the mode of *Leda and the Swan* is again Yeats's theme, but now the approval of violence is stronger. Emotional as well as intellectual receptivity marks *Whence Had They Come?*, and the title is itself a cruel irony, the answer being that they, the Dramatis Personae who wield the lash and phallus, come from the victims of sadism and lust, the submissive and the frigid, in accordance with the dialectics of *A Vision*. But surely it is one divine annunciation too many, even for Yeats, to make the conception of Charlemagne yet another rape of Leda?

> What sacred drama through her body heaved
> When world-transforming Charlemagne was conceived?

Three gnomic poems following are conceptually more impressive, as Yeats moves us toward the massive sonnet, *Meru*, the twelfth and final poem of the series. *The Four Ages of Man* is really too minor a set of verses to sustain the elaborate commentary Yeats provided in his letters to Mrs. Shakespear. Its obvious point is man's defeat, successively by his own body, heart, mind, and at last, at midnight, by God. What is most interesting about the poem is how much has gone to produce so little, whether in man's final self-abnegation, or in Yeats's achievement here. This is still truer of *Conjunctions*, in its first couplet, founded on the horoscopes of Yeats's children, but less so in the second:

> The sword's a cross; thereon He died:
> On breast of Mars the goddess sighed.

The sentiment is ambiguous enough to be highly interesting, and the second line qualifies the first in a way that scholars who find Yeats to be Christian ought to ponder. *A Needle's Eye*, the last prelude to *Meru*, needs deeper pondering, as its image haunts such crucial poems as *Veronica's Napkin* and the marvelous death poem, *Cuchulain Comforted*. The stream here is all phenomena, the needle's eye the microcosmic and spatial analogue to the moment of moments, the pulsation of an artery:

> All the stream that's roaring by
> Came out of a needle's eye;
> Things unborn, things that are gone,
> From needle's eye still goad it on.

The quatrain is a declaration of faith, and the faith need not be an occult one. The stream is "manifold illusion," and human meditation can stop its roar. Yeats's finest tribute to the ravening mind, *Meru*, dismisses the rule and peace of civilization as a semblance, allied to that manifold illusion. The mind, the most terrible force in the world, cannot rest in the contemplation of a semblance:

> . . . but man's life is thought,
> And he, despite his terror, cannot cease
> Ravening through century after century,
> Ravening, raging, and uprooting that he may come
> Into the desolation of reality.

This is Yeats at his most definitive, the passage being linked to everything vital at the center of his vision. As in *The Second Coming* he is remembering, perhaps unconsciously, the confrontation between Prometheus and the final Fury in the first act of Shelley's lyrical drama, with its association of terror and ravin:

> In each human heart terror survives
> The ravin it has gorged: the loftiest fear
> All that they would disdain to think were true:
>
> The good want power, but to weep barren tears,
> The powerful goodness want: worse need for them.

> The wise want love; and those who love want wisdom;
> And all best things are thus confused to ill.

Yeats too, in *Meru,* places Promethean or Western man atop a holy mountain, and dismisses the whole of his enterprise: "Egypt and Greece, good-bye, and good-bye, Rome!" With Ribh, Yeats attempts to move to a very different mode of knowing. The Eastern hermits know the end of man's enterprise:

> That day brings round the night, that before dawn
> His glory and his monuments are gone.

To Ellmann, the poem is still Promethean: "Its principal emphasis is not on the illusory character of life, but on man's courage and obligation to strip illusion away, in spite of the terror of nothingness with which he will be left." [11] Ellmann cites an eloquent letter from Yeats to Sturge Moore: "We free ourselves from obsession that we may be nothing. The last kiss is given to the void." [12] This is certainly a Yeatsian (and Paterian) emphasis, but *Meru* has a very different stress. The poem emphasizes neither illusion nor man's reductive courage, since Ribh quests for ecstasy, indeed for being literally possessed. Whitaker rightly points to the strangely gay tone in which our civilization is dismissed, comparing it to the banter of the Norse gods facing the apocalypse.[13] Yet I find it difficult to agree to any reading of *Meru* which, like Whitaker's, finds that an acceptance of the total process of history yields Ribh, Yeats or any of us "the miracle of creative freedom." [14] The poem finds "the desolation of reality" even as Keats, in *Sleep and Poetry,* acknowledges that it is reality which, like a muddy stream, threatens his soul with destruction after his vision is dispelled. For each it *is* reality, and must be accepted, but it is a desolation, a ruin to the imagination, and so is not that final reality the imagination can make. *Meru* is a subtler poem than its best critics have found it to be. Day brings round the night, but dawn follows the departure of man's glory and his monuments. *Supernatural Songs* has gone the full cycle from our finding Ribh reading by an occult sexual glow in the pitch-dark night, to our awaiting a dawn neither natural nor supernatural, but re-imagined as a rebirth of what Wallace Stevens would call the first idea, man stripped of illusions by the ravenings of thought, the mind of winter:

> . . . under the drifted snow,
> Or where that snow and winter's dreadful blast
> Beat down upon their naked bodies. . . .

It is the central insight of Shelley's *Mont Blanc* again, which Yeats and Stevens share. The fictive covering is made by the mind, because reductive or wintry man is intolerable to the imagination, but the mind does not long tolerate its own fictions, including every historicism. Despite its Eastern colorings, *Meru* is esoteric only as the central Romantic visions of winter have been esoteric, and it could be absorbed at several points by *Prometheus Unbound.* The design of *Supernatural Songs* culminates in *Meru,* but it is not the design of *A Vision,* or of any related Gnostic quasi-determinism. Ribh asks us to "mark and digest my tale," and to carry his gospel to others. In Yeats's ancient quarrel between swordsman and saint, Ribh peculiarly speaks for the swordsman, for Oisin's choice of the dream, even for the nature-mocked madness of King Goll. But the dialectic of self and soul breaks in this sequence, and breaks I think because by 1934 Yeats's vision of history had failed him. I miss in Yeats's most devoted and learned exegetes any sense of this failure. Take as a representative sequence of letters by Yeats those he wrote to Dorothy Wellesley from May 1935 to December 1938 (he died two months later) and read through them in order.[15] Are they the letters of a poet who has found creative freedom through the acceptance of history as a total process? They show a poet who cannot stop studying the nostalgias, a defiant Romantic who does not begin to trust his own historicism, and has forgotten his own apocalypse. All this comes after the *Supernatural Songs* and needs to be studied in the last phase of poems and plays. The *Supernatural Songs* rise out of an abyss in Yeats's life, and though *Meru* was written before the others, and so before the Steinach operation (if the biographer Hone's dating of the poem is right), Yeats chose deliberately to place the poem as the conclusion to the series.[16] What *Meru* and the whole song sequence show is that Yeats was beginning to reject his own abstractions, not as an intellectual but when he wrote poems. The rage and lust that crowded upon him returned him to an earlier conflict in himself than his own involved rationalizations could accommodate, and perhaps this was poetically more gain than loss.

23: The Last Plays

The Herne's Egg

Yeats's plays of 1938–39, *The Herne's Egg, Purgatory,* and *The Death of Cuchulain,* all have the strength of their remorselessness, as they pursue the *antithetical* quest of a lifetime to its conclusion. They show us a poet who appears to have come full-circle, back to the apocalyptic passion of *The Shadowy Waters,* but who perhaps had never started around the circle, unlike the poet of *Alastor* and *Prince Athanase,* who certainly had made his effort to avoid the cyclic return that destroys vision in *The Triumph of Life.* Even more unlike is the poet of *Milton* and *Jerusalem,* who had known too well the cyclic irony of the Great Wheel or Circle of Destiny, and who had achieved a coherent vision of what it was in the human potential that yet might break the turnings of the Wheel.

   The Herne's Egg was begun in 1935, and carries on from *A Full Moon in March,* and its precursor, *The King of the Great Clock Tower,* but with the violent difference that now Yeats overtly chooses the grotesque as creative mode, producing what he himself called "the strangest wildest thing" he ever made. The play is a deliberate outrage, though Peter Ure insists it must be read quite seriously, and Whitaker finds depth in its "fol-de-rol." [1] Of the excesses of less balanced doctrinal exegetes, I will not speak. Rajan's sensible observation, that here the battle between self and soul grows progressively more sordid, approaches the dismal truth about this squalid play, which is a monument to the mounting confusion and systematic inhumanity of the last phase of Yeats.[2] Mrs. Vendler, with customary accuracy, calls it "rather arid and contrived." [3] But there is lasting power in it, the strength of a great imagination misused, and it raises again what so much of Yeats's last work perpetually raises, the question of why most of Yeats survives its own firm nonsense and spiritual squalor. There is a more unanswerable question to be asked about the last three plays in particular, including the universally praised *Purgatory*, which is: how can an incoherent work become an aesthetic satisfaction? In his bitterness and confusion, Yeats is less than coherent in all three of these plays, as I will show, and yet these plays do live. Even the confusion, an expression of what Blake would have called Yeats's Spectre, is not like the confusion of a lesser poet, but tends to be the parody of Yeatsian "vacillation," of this poet's refusal either to confirm or to deny his own myth of reality.

Congal, King of Connacht, is a travesty of the hero Cuchulain, but so is Cuchulain in *The Death of Cuchulain,* for in the bitter vision of Yeats in his last phase, even the *antithetical* defenders of Yeatsian values are necessarily fools. The best still lack all conviction, but all conviction is foolish anyway. The Great Herne, as Congal apparently learns, is indeed a god, as much as Zeus the swan was when he raped Leda. But Zeus engendered a cycle of civilization, while the Great Herne's complex sevenfold rape of Attracta, through the agency of Congal and six of his louts, engenders only a donkey. The reader may murmur, with the donkey-herd Corney at the play's end: "All that trouble and nothing to show for it,/ Nothing but just another donkey." Yeats presumably, despite his doctrinal exegetes, would not have resented the murmuring.

The play is less a parody of its sources, however Indian or Balzacian-Swedenborgian they may be, than it is a parody of Yeats's own mythology, a self-parody only in part intentional. It was written, Yeats said, "in the happier moments of a long illness that had so separated me from life that I felt irresponsible." [4] That catches the play's mood; its reality is purely *daimonic,* but this is the *daimonic* as seen by a poet in transit between the two realms of life and life-in-death, and so is irresponsible (justifiably) toward both. I have not tried to read it in the happier moments of a long illness, but I am willing to believe it is a golden book for such a time, and would move me then.

The Herne's Egg, perhaps not by design, is in the tradition of Blake's *The Book of Urizen;* it is a mockery of human foulness in envisioning the divine, though what is mocked in Yeats's play is Yeats's own *daimonic* "thought." The Great Herne or heron is the *antithetical* emblem of *Calvary,* the long-legged wader of some of the *Last Poems,* the magical bird of *Oisin* and *The Island of Statues.* As such he had been long in Yeats's head, too long for *The Herne's Egg* not to take his meaning for granted. All we are told about him by the play is that, in effect, he is a god like Blake's Urizen-Nobodaddy and Shelley's Jupiter, an irrational, arbitrary Devourer, not one of the Prolific, to employ the terms of Blake's dialectic. Does he exist at all, in his play? What happens if we read the play with a deliberate agnosticism, an experiment we conducted upon certain of the plays earlier? Can we read the Herne only as a delusion in the mind of his priestess Attracta (unfortunate name), a delusion communicated finally to the heroic (more or less) and skeptical Congal?

Unlike the swan, Zeus, the Great Herne is unable to manifest his own lust in action. His potency indeed is, for a god, remarkably limited, and does not extend much beyond thundering, in the grand Nobodaddy tradition. Every other instance of his efficacy in the play is naturalistically disputable, and so may be the thunder-epiphany itself. It cannot be ruled out (whatever Yeats's intentions, however contrary) that Attracta is both deluded and persuasive, ironically successful in at last converting even Congal to her murderous delusions, the irony being that at the close she may have been converted by him, as clearly the most attractive of the Great Herne's seven surrogates.

So unequivocally rancid a play is this, that the god's reality is not worth much dispute. Essentially *The Herne's Egg* has the same theme as the lyric *Leda and the Swan,* but the lyric's tone does not admit the possibility of delusion; there is a god there, however dreadful his manifestation may be. The tone of *The Herne's Egg* is, as noted above, like that of *The Book of Urizen* or Shelley's surprisingly squalid *Swellfoot the Tyrant;* it is a tone of the apocalyptic absurd, of which Blake is the English master, and Jarry the French. Yeats, in his youth, had attended the first performance of *Ubu Roi.* Aided by his ignorance of French, he attained a true 'Pataphysical understanding of what he saw, and rightly grew sad, "for comedy, objectivity, has displayed its growing power once more." He fulfilled his own prophecy, many decades later, in writing *The Herne's Egg,* for in brooding upon *Ubu Roi* he murmured: "after our own verse . . . what more is possible? After us the Savage God." [5] There may be a god in *The Herne's Egg,* and if there is, he is savage, but whether comedy displays any power in it is very doubtful. How funny is it? Yeats was capable of humor, but rarely where death or a god was concerned.

Even a rapid overview of *The Herne's Egg,* if accurate, will demonstrate its author's confusions (though whether some of these were deliberate, we cannot know). Congal and his rival, Aedh, have fought fifty ritual battles. Though these exercises are compared by at least one tone-deaf occultist exegete to Blake's Wars of Eden, they clearly have nothing visionary about them. As Aedh happily says, "all were perfect battles"; that is rather closer to the military mind, of all eras, than to the intellectual contests of Blake's Giant Forms, if one must be forced, by Idiot Questioners, into round statements of the obvious. Congal and Aedh, to Yeats, are any and all warring nations or parties, rich fleas on the "fat, square, lazy dog" of a *primary* culture nearing its cataclysm. Still, Yeats communicates a fondness for Congal, who is a good rhetorician, and a more impressive version of natural man than anyone else in his world. He is Cuchulain reduced to the hero of farce, "that wise, victorious, voluble, unlucky,/ Blasphemous, famous, infamous man." In search of herne's eggs for a victory feast, he has the misfortune (or fate) to encounter the crazed, bloody-minded Attracta, prophetess and self-promised bride to the Great Herne.

I am a little reluctant to add fresh items to the source study of *The Herne's Egg*, already so prodigiously enriched by the labors of Wilson and Melchiori, but an apocalyptic parody like this play has the uncanny attribute of satirizing all of Yeats's lifelong sources, so Spenser and Shelley must find their place also. Congal cites Ovid in diagnosing the virginity of Attracta to be the cause of her madness, but Yeats's language in describing the process of Attracta's god-making directly echoes Shelley's, when the Witch of Atlas creates her Hermaphrodite. Shelley himself would have welcomed the parody, since he himself (as Yeats must have known) was thus parodying the making of the False Florimell, herself a parody of certain Ovidian creations, which takes us back to Yeats's Congal and brings the dizzying wheel of influencings full circle. Attracta creates the Great Herne out of the "abominable snow" of her wintry virginity, even as Shelley's Witch, always to be virgin, kneads a "repugnant mass" of snow and fire to make the Hermaphrodite. If Congal is right, then Attracta is a mad poetess, and the Great Herne her dream of desire. Attracta believes in her vision: "There is no reality but the Great Herne." Whether Yeats believes this, or wants us to believe this, the play makes it impossible to know. Attracta thinks she burns "not in the flesh but in the mind," which ironically turns out to mean that she can be raped by seven men, and not have her overt faith disturbed. But her pragmatic nature is certainly disturbed by the sevenfold possession. As many critics observe, she is a different consciousness thereafter. The mystery, and Yeats's confusion, is why? Either she has taken on the Great Herne's power, with some of his knowledge, or else her relation to him is merely her delusion. The play's irony (and I take it to be indeliberate) is that Congal is convinced of the relation's reality, and dies of the conviction, but Attracta's later conduct tends to demonstrate just the opposite. She becomes a silly, all-too-human creature, and Yeats does not spare us her final debasement, when this Great Herne's bride urges a donkey-herd to beget Congal's new incarnation upon her. Doctrinaire Yeatsians evidently can accept this (some

as comedy, a few as seriousness), but the common reader rightly
rebels. *The Herne's Egg* is as bitter as it is confused, and every
kind of a failure. Yeats meant to purge himself of some of his own
obsessions by this play, but his poems written after it do not show
that the purgation was effective.

Purgatory

Yeats intended *Purgatory* to stand at the end of his last volume,
which he knew would be published posthumously. The play has
been much admired by eminent critics. Yeats himself insisted that
the play expressed his own conviction about this world and the
next. It is, then, the poet's deliberate testament, the work in
which, like Blake in *The Ghost of Abel,* Yeats passes a Last Judgment on himself. We turn to the play expecting to encounter the
wisdom and the human powers developed through a lifetime of
imaginative effort. What do we find?

We find if we read the play honestly and without precon-
ceived judgment, that it has its proper context where Yeats first
published it, in his tract *On the Boiler,* a remarkable essay in eugenics, rather of the "strength through joy" variety. In the play,
two wanderers, father and son, confront a ruined house and a
bare tree. The house has been ruined because its daughter followed lust and married basely; the tree is bare because a vengeful
thunderbolt has riven it. The older wanderer is the son of the degrading marriage; vengeance struck his mother at his birth, when
she died. Vengeance was more direct upon her base bridegroom,
stabbed by his son when that now aged wanderer was sixteen.
The younger wanderer is sixteen, and in the play's central action
he is stabbed to death by his father ("My father and my son on
the same jack-knife!"). This exercise in practical eugenics accomplished, the old wanderer is inspired to end the play with a
prayer: "Appease/ The misery of the living and the remorse of
the dead."

If the poet's conviction about this world is in the play, it
would seem that the old wanderer acts for Yeats in preventing
"the multiplication of the uneducatable masses," as *On the Boiler*

phrases it. That leaves the poet's conviction about the next world, if a reader is still minded to seek enlightenment from this testament. The somewhat more aesthetic purgation outlined in *A Vision* has little to do with the notion of purgation in the play, and apologists for the play have been driven to strained allegories to justify the play's apparent conviction as to the next world. The next world, toward the end, looked to Yeats like a cyclic repetition of this one, and so the lustful begetting of the murderous wanderer is doomed always to be re-enacted, despite the wanderer's violence and his anguished prayer. Whether or not Yeats fully intended it, the closing prayer is simply inaccurate and becomes an irony, for the actual repetition in the play is not one of remorse, but of fierce pleasure, of lust fulfilled and yet again fulfilled. The old wanderer anticipates the irony, saying of his parents' repeated sexual act: "If pleasure and remorse must both be there,/ Which is the greater?" but he cannot answer the question, and neither can Yeats, whose confusion is in the play as much as his conviction is.

Why is *Purgatory* so much admired? The question is important, not because Yeats thought the play was, but because so many of Yeats's less imaginative poems seem to be much admired for reasons akin to those underlying the high critical regard for *Purgatory*. Some merit *Purgatory* certainly has; Yeats shows remarkable skill in rendering the work's single action, so that the brutal and simple anecdote does become dramatic, if not quite a drama. And the metrical achievement, as Eliot granted, is original and considerable. Yet the play repels *on its own terms*. It can be argued that the repulsion is part of Yeats's design upon his readers, who are to be shocked into moral imagination, even as Sophocles or Euripides shocks us. Or it can be held that the play does not mean what it acts out, but collects its meaning on an esoteric level that finds only its emblematic pattern in the characters and their words and actions. This would be to treat Yeats as Cabala, and is an ill-service. Perhaps one's revulsion at the Yeatsian eugenics is merely picayune, whether in the context of what has now become the dramatic Age of Artaud, or in the more valid context of Sophoclean tragedy? A closer look at the play should at least clarify the difficulties into which Yeats's passionate (and perhaps, in this play, hysterical) convictions led him and his audience, or readers.

The easy way out of these difficulties, and many Yeatsians have taken it, is to insist that any parallels between Yeats's views and those of his murderous old man are merely misleading. So the play does not endorse such a eugenic vision, or its own final, desperate prayer, despite *On the Boiler,* which does *seem* to have been written by the same murderous old man. My argument is merely genetic, and I am glad to argue instead from the play's text. What is there in it that can justify a comment like Whitaker's: ". . . in *Purgatory,* the release is implicit in the consciousness which can accept in contemplation the terrible vision of the play," or does the play not imply a consciousness that merely shares such vision? Does Yeats's fury differ from the old man's? How far is the play from a consciousness that delighted in violence, and insisted that violence must be "embodied in our institutions."? [6]

The play's kernel is in its old man's contrast between two trees, the bare one stripped of what he revealingly calls "fat, greasy life" and the same tree seen after he has stabbed his boy to death, a tree "all cold, sweet, glistening light." The contrast does not work; it is the same tree, and therefore the same man, incapable of release. If it was dry before, it is as dry now. Is this a triumph of Yeats's dramatic irony, or an irony not altogether of Yeats's apprehension? What, in terms of the Yeatsian vision, is the old man's crime, or even his error? Whitaker says that the old man errs because he seeks by violence to annihilate history, unlike Yeats.[7] But what else did Yeats seek? Either that alone, or else a phantasmagoria to compensate for the inability to achieve that annihilation. The old man is Yeats's phantasmagoria, or at least a significant late part of it. I grant that the old man's own phantasmagoria is more limited, but did not Yeats share as well as make it? The true case against *Purgatory* is not Eliot's, who could not grant the play its title's validity, but belongs to the Blakean and Shelleyan ethic that Yeats had always been revising. "The remorse of the dead" cannot be appeased unless the living will cast out remorse, for remorse could not be if we freed ourselves from the opacity of Selfhood. *Purgatory,* unlike *The*

Herne's Egg, survives the squalor and grotesqueness of its own argument, but this is largely a rhetorical survival, based upon our deception. Yeats is not separate enough from the old man's rage to render the play's conclusion coherent. That hardly makes the play less powerful, but perhaps we ought to resent a work that has so palpable a design upon us. Eugenic tendentiousness is not a formula for great art, even in Yeats.

The Death of Cuchulain

Yeats's last play is not a fully finished work, and probably would have been improved had Yeats lived to revise it. Even as it is, I prefer it to *The Herne's Egg* and *Purgatory,* though it shares and even intensifies their moods and obsessions. Something of the late Yeats's dreadful and unpredictable greatness survives the palpable tendentiousness of *The Death of Cuchulain,* for the play's deliberate design is subverted by the poet's involuntary imagination. Yeats intends a final destruction of any myth of the hero, his own included. Cuchulain must die badly, and for no purpose and no result, die as evidence of the end coming to no end. The play is written by the same "very old man looking like something out of mythology" who spits out its prologue, and clearly it regards most of those who will read or see it as "people who are educating themselves out of the Book Societies and the like, sciolists all, pickpockets and opinionated bitches." It deserved to be as bad as such a prologue would prophesy, but imagination intervened, as did Yeats's affection for the hero he meant to level down to so bad a time as ours. Part of the mystery is dispelled when we realize that Yeats found freedom as a playwright whenever he wrote of Cuchulain. The best of his older verse dramas is certainly *On Baile's Strand,* a great work by any just standards, and *At the Hawk's Well* and *The Only Jealousy of Emer* are more satisfying poetry than all the other plays of the major phase. Even the least of the Cuchulain plays, *The Green Helmet,* is distinguished by the fine invention of the Red Man. Yeats as lunar poet never ceases to feel the force of his solar hero, who wins all the lunar ladies the poet never attained, and unlike Fergus never yields his glory to quest for a realm of dreams. But Yeats in 1939 was not minded to celebrate any hero, and wished to yield the hero's dignity to the tides of destruction. The immensely moving short poem, *Cuchulain Comforted,* that rose out of the play's composition, shows more overtly than the play does that Yeats could not bear his own design of degradation. But the play shows it also. Cuchulain, just before his death, is made to say: "Twelve pennies! What better reason for killing a man?" This bitterness demeans the hero, but only momentarily. When he has a vision of the bird-like shape he will take on in the after-life, he allows himself a quizzical question as to the shape's appropriateness "for the soul/ Of a great fighting-man," but he goes on to end magnificently, considering the dreadful circumstances Yeats imposes upon him. He is wounded, but fastens himself to a pillar-stone (with help from Aoife, murderous mother of his son), that he may die upon his feet. The Blind Man of *On Baile's Strand* fumbles at the hero's throat with a knife, to collect twelve pennies for the head. This is Yeats's brutal and sordid triumph over the enchantment of heroism, but a deeper imagination wells out of Yeats at the climax. When the blind man, about to strike, cries: "Are you ready, Cuchulain!" the hero disregards him, and beholding only the vision of last things, the shape his soul must take, quietly remarks: "I say it is about to sing." The moment is worth the play, and many plays besides.

At a better time, in 1917, just starting upon his major phase in *Per Amica Silentia Lunae,* Yeats wrote that "The poet finds and makes his mask in disappointment, the hero in defeat." But Cuchulain, unconquerable hero, though he is found here by Aoife, in some sense the mask he had made, does not know defeat. Not that this is, at all, "a play of rejoicing," of the hero's "transfiguration," as Wilson oddly says. Helen Vendler precisely renders the play's tone when she says that weariness and indifference, rather than tragic joy, come nearer its note.[8] Cuchulain, at the end, passes from quiet disgust through exhaustion to a state of simply not caring. He cannot understand his death, and he does not want to understand it. But even we, and Yeats, cannot understand it, for the hero's splendor is as beyond us as it is beyond the entire context of his play.

The Death of Cuchulain, though all in one scene, falls into three dialogues, between Cuchulain and successively Eithne, Aoife, and the Blind Man, and then one summary speech by the Morrigu, Goddess of War, a dance by Emer, and a final song by a Street-Singer. There is a progressive withdrawal from the theme of heroism as we pass through these six divisions, until we come to Yeats's personal dismissal of Cuchulain: "But an old man looking on life/ Imagines it in scorn." This is part of a song, the singer says, that "the harlot sang to the beggar-man," part of the song that Blake said would weave England's winding-sheet. Yeats means the death of heroic virtue as his theme, by which he means further not that the hero dies among us, but that he outlives his virtue, as we have. Things thought too long can be no longer thought, and worth dies of worth, as the gyres whirl on. That is Yeats's design in the play, what he wants it to mean, but is that what it means?

The largest irony of *The Death of Cuchulain* is that only the hero has grown indifferent; every other personage in the drama is moved intensely by love or hatred for him, or at least by a sense of gain or loss in his death. His heart has grown old, but not the hearts of the women who have loved and hated him—his wife Emer, his mistress Eithne Inguba, the Amazonian Aoife upon whom he begot the son he unknowingly fought and killed, the Morrigu or war goddess, and Maeve the queen, with whom he slept when he was a boy. These five are really too many, and some blend together, but as a group they share an enormous passion, of which Cuchulain is the unique object, and whether they intend love or revenge toward him is a matter of indifference, to him and to us. He is weary alike of love and hatred, and no more attached to one of his past women than any other. But he can still be moved by his heroic function: "I am for the fight,/ I and my handful are set upon the fight." He knows too much to abide wholly in the old code; he misunderstands and finds treachery where there is none, but forgives it anyway. If he lacks now "the passion necessary to life," it is not so much because he wants to die, as because he senses that his age is over. Either he must change, or see himself as monstrous, and he chooses to do neither. In his impatience with all passions directed toward him, he chooses not to undergo the great weariness of ascertaining the truth of the degree of love or hatred in such passions. "I make the truth!" which is to say both that the truth does not matter, and that only the heroic self does.

Yet, very movingly, the self's imaginings still matter, and beauty has not died of beauty, but can still be thought, and seen. Cuchulain, with six mortal wounds, remains a Last Romantic, saying to Aoife, when she binds him with what Blake would have called her veil of Vala: "But do not spoil your veil./ Your veils are beautiful, some with threads of gold." He is, after all, surrogate for the poet, confronted in a death duel by his *daimonic* beloved, but a very late version of the poet, who no longer knows or cares what the meaning of the *antithetical* quest is. Aoife, who would not have him die without knowledge, begins to recapitulate his saga, but he interrupts, simply and finally: "I cannot understand." And, in accordance with Yeats's system, he is not to be slain by the Muse in any case. The Blind Man, representative of the last crescents of the waning cycle, is the appropriate killer. When the Morrigu, after Cuchulain is slain, implicitly claims the hero as her victim, it is unclear whether or not we are to believe her, but we do not anyway. He is self-slain as he was self-conceived, a sun in setting as he was in rising. We believe the Morrigu when she says: "I arranged the dance," if this narrowly means Emer's dance of rage and mourning, which ends with the few faint bird notes of Cuchulain's comfort, his transformation in the death-between-lives. The Morrigu can provide context for Cuchulain, but not the wildness or unconditioned freedom even of his exhausted will.

I find all of this imaginatively moving, despite the abruptness with which Yeats conveys it. But the final song, one of Yeats's last testaments, mars all this, and is as unsatisfactory as *Under Ben Bulben*. The harlot's cry is that she would embrace the heroic ones, like Cuchulain, "but can get/ No grip upon their thighs," as they are no longer living men. Evidently, the harlot is the Muse, who gives herself, perforce, to some still among the living, but loathes as well as adores them. Her question is whether these living are the sole reality, whether for herself or for men, and Yeats's clear answer is "No," for the archetypes or heroic forms live also, as Cuchulain lived in Pearse and the other rebels who as wildly chose, with their handful, for the fight. Yet this is hardly the play's meaning, and gives the hero's death a significance that the play itself moves to reject. Cuchulain is not the Superman, accepting Eternal Recurrence and affirming an exultant self amidst it, nor does he fight for even the fight's sake, here at the end. All weary him equally, and he is weary of himself. He cannot be used, either as archetype to emulate in rebellion, or as imaginative image outlasting the ruin of civilization, an image the Muse as harlot pauses to remember in her whorings. Like *The Herne's Egg* and *Purgatory*, *The Death of Cuchulain* has a central confusion in it, because the Yeats of the last phase did. He cannot either reject or affirm the heroic, even as image, though he wants to reject the heroic as virtue or knowledge, and yet affirm it as image, lest he be left bare of all images. There is considerable fascination, even greatness, in *The Death of Cuchulain,* but the play is not wholly coherent. Cuchulain, Yeatsian man, cannot know the truth, and Yeats cannot quite bear for him to embody it, or to be completely free of it either.

24: The Last Poems

The Gyres

Dorothy Wellesley remembered the aged Yeats as crying aloud: "Why cant you English poets keep flowers out of your poetry?" [1] Pater, stung by the odor of meadowlark, complained that "nature in England runs too much to excess" or, in Fuseli's words, "nature puts me out." The grand statement of this tradition is Blake's fury against Wordsworth: "Natural Objects always did & now do Weaken deaden & obliterate Imagination in Me Wordsworth must know that what he Writes Valuable is Not to be found in Nature." [2] Yeats's posthumous volume, *Last Poems and Plays,* is one of the final monuments of the Romantic imagination's quarrel with nature, probably the last major one but for Stevens's *The Auroras of Autumn.*

The volume begins with *The Gyres,* whose tone presents the central problem of Yeats's last phase:

> Conduct and work grow coarse, and coarse the
> > soul,
> What matter?

This mood has been much admired by those Yeats critics who admire everything in Yeats. The poem is extraordinarily expressive, particularly in giving us Yeats's disgust, though less so when the saving remnant who are to disinter the *antithetical* civilization are described as "lovers of horses and of women" rather than, say, of dogs and of children. How seriously can the poem, or many of its companions, be read anyway, or is "seriously" simply an irrelevant adverb for any reading here? "Tragic joy" has been a much praised oxymoron among critics; presumably it must have an experiential meaning which is extra-aesthetic, unless it means that one feels only an aesthetic reaction when "irrational streams of blood are staining earth," which is only possible in the abstract. There is much abstract fury in the *Last Poems,* the triad of *The Gyres, Lapis Lazuli,* and *Under Ben Bulben* showing most of it. Yeats is a subtle self-satirist; as a disciple of Blake he knew how to make a poem mock its own dramatic speaker, and it is sometimes as dangerous to confuse Yeats with the speaker or singer of one of his poems, as it is to take Blake himself as the chanter of *The Tyger* or any of the other lyrics that belong to the Bard of Experience. But I think that the speaker of *The Gyres* is Yeats, even as Blake the man cries out in *To Tirzah* or *London,* and I find this makes me uncomfortable, though not as uncomfortable as I am made by the poem's reception among its critics. Jeffares is the saving exception; he accurately suggests that the Rocky Face of the poem is Shelley's Wandering Jew of *Hellas,* and he sanely observes that "there is an inhuman remoteness from ordinary life in the poem." [3] More disturbing, to me, is the quality of the poem's joy, which is coarser than the tragic joy of *The King's Threshold,* to which it has been compared by several critics.

The poem begins with a startled outcry, perhaps an exultant one, "The gyres! the gyres!" reminiscent of Blake's "Tyger! Tyger!" Old Rocky Face, not so much the sage Ahasuerus as the mask of the sage that Yeats now wears, looks forth from his cavern to see, not only the fall of an age, but an age in which the form of the good destroys itself. The vision, like those of *The Second Coming* and the songs from *The Resurrection,* goes back again to the speech of the last Fury in *Prometheus Unbound,* and to the despairing quietism of *The Triumph of Life,* and recalls also Yeats's own *Nineteen Hundred and Nineteen* and *Byzantium*. But the tone is very different from earlier Yeats, though the verbal formula is so familiar:

> What matter though numb nightmare ride on top,
> And blood and mire the sensitive body stain?

Ribh could have said this, without offence, but can Yeats-Ahasuerus? Ribh is in ecstasy, and so is oblivious of historical torment. Yeats, writing probably in the second half of 1936, may have the Spanish Civil War in mind, but his laughter, whatever its stimulus, is founded on a less elevated exclusion of knowledge. In the dark between cycles—and the nature of the dark is insignificant, whether it be the Resurrection, or the area between predatory polecat and owl of wisdom (delightfully arbitrary one supposes, but why the polecat?), or, very characteristically, "any rich, dark nothing'—in that time of the exchange of tinctures, the better social order of "workman, noble and saint" will return (presumably on the Fascist model, as in *On the Boiler*) "and all things run/ On that unfashionable gyre again." Aside from the social play in "unfashionable," the word recalls the "could frame" of *The Tyger*. Man cannot fashion the gyres or frame the Tyger's symmetry, in the views anyway of Yeats and of the Bard of Experience, who have in common an awe of the "composite God" of historical process, and both of whom tend, in odd ways, to argue from design. The Bard of *The Tyger* is of course not particularly joyous, since he is so very frightened, and never comes to see that he is frightening himself. Rationally and humanely, Yeats ought to be appalled (his poem would have little point otherwise) but he repeats "What matter?" because of his faith in his own myth as an explanation of the blood-dimmed tide. Whatever this gesture is, it is not artistic freedom, as Yeats's critics have held it to be, but the darkest of bondages to the idols of determinism.

The problem of *The Gyres* is finally one of seriousness and not of belief. If I face a fire that devastates, I need to know what another man means if he sees that fire only as light (or says he does), and if it moves him to delight of any kind, rather than anxiety for what is human that is being consumed. If he is an apocalyptic, of a Gnostic variety, he is justified in rejoicing that "Conduct and work grow coarse, and coarse the soul,/ What matter?" But then perhaps more of us shall ask now, amid the fires, how much light can a Gnostic apocalyptic give us, let alone a poet playing at such desperation? *The Gyres* is too energetic a poem to be dismissed as work grown coarse, and no matter, but I doubt that it always will be admired as so many among us have admired it.

Lapis Lazuli

Lapis Lazuli, except for its marvelous last movement, is a very similar poem. Its argument, like that of *The Gyres,* is against both nature and the social order, and perhaps against reason also. So Blake argued, against a Triple Accuser or three-headed whore that masqueraded as reason, nature and society, but Yeats has the problem of confronting a yet more depraved and plausible Accuser, in a worse time even than Blake's. Meditating upon a gift of lapis lazuli, Yeats stated the intended argument of his poem:

> . . . a great piece carved by some Chinese sculptor into the semblance of a mountain with temple, trees, paths and an ascetic and pupil about to climb the mountain. Ascetic, pupil, hard stone, eternal theme of the sensual east. The heroic cry in the midst of despair. But no, I am wrong, the east has its solutions always and therefore knows nothing of tragedy. It is we, not the east, that must raise the heroic cry.[4]

Yeats greatly admired *Lapis Lazuli,* and his critics have followed him in this admiration. Ellmann is representative in judging that "the lapis lazuli is made to yield the message of affirmation which he must have."[5] Not to find admirable Yeats's notion of "tragic joy," not to be among those who "know that Hamlet and Lear are gay," is to risk being classed with those "hysterical women" who open *Lapis Lazuli* by fearing the possibility of aerial bombardment. Perhaps we ought to remember that Yeats greatly preferred, among many others, say Oliver St. John Gogarty's poetry to that of Wilfred Owen because

. . . passive suffering is not a theme for poetry. In all the great tragedies, tragedy is a joy to the man who dies. . . . If war is necessary in our time and place, it is best to forget its suffering as we do the discomfort of fever. . . .[6]

To this we can juxtapose, quite fairly:

And of my weeping something had been left,
Which must die now. I mean the truth untold,
The pity of war, the pity war distilled.
Now men will go content with what we spoiled,
Or, discontent, boil bloody, and be spilled.
They will be swift with swiftness of the tigress.
None will break ranks, though nations trek from progress. . . .[7]

This is, of course, genuine prophetic poetry, very possibly the finest such in our time. Yeats, in the name of "tragic joy" and "Gaiety transfiguring all that dread," felt compelled to judge Owen "unworthy of the poets' corner of a country newspaper" because "he is all blood, dirt & sucked sugar stick." This critical judgment goes side-by-side (in the same letter) with a judgment upon the poetry of Dorothy Wellesley: "—your lines have the magnificent swing of your boyish body." [8] *Lapis Lazuli* is written by the man capable of these opinions, and its notion of tragedy derives from them. Inhumane nonsense is not always the best foundation for aesthetic judgment, and perhaps we might be a little wary of "the message of affirmation" Yeats is bringing to us.

Partly *Lapis Lazuli, The Gyres,* and *Under Ben Bulben* present us with a problem in rhetorical and spiritual authority. With the *antithetical* wisdom of Nietzsche as Zarathustra, one feels no inclination to quarrel. But is *this* wisdom?

All things fall and are built again,
And those that build them again are gay.

To this one can juxtapose, quite fairly, as texts for meditation:

Then said I unto them, Ye see the distress that we are in, how Jerusalem lieth waste, and the gates thereof are burned with fire: come, and let us build up the wall of Jerusalem, that we be no more a reproach.

(Nehemiah 2:17)

They which builded on the wall, and they that bare burdens, with those that laded, every one with one of his hands wrought in the work, and with the other hand held a weapon.

(Nehemiah 4:17)

This is not to reject "a gay, stoical . . . heroic song" fit for "swashbucklers, horsemen, swift indifferent men," but to question whether *Lapis Lazuli* is such song. The poem, to me, fails absurdly when it attempts to raise the West's "heroic cry," but its Eastern recovery compels a just admiration. The ascetic, his pupil, and his musical servitor are wonderfully rendered:

> There, on the mountain and the sky,
> On all the tragic scene they stare.
> One asks for mournful melodies;
> Accomplished fingers begin to play.
> Their eyes mid many wrinkles, their eyes,
> Their ancient, glittering eyes, are gay.

The gaiety of Lear is of course non-existent; whether one chooses to believe in the gaiety of the aging Yeats is an individual act of faith. In these gay eyes one believes; Yeats has made and not asserted them, or if he has asserted them, the assertion is not at the expense of what Owen called "pity." [9]

To Dorothy Wellesley

No critic can deny to Yeats an absolute pre-eminence as a writer of love lyrics. Faced by his constant power in this kind, one can wonder if any poet of our century enters into competition here with him. What Yeats combines is a marvelous formalism, indeed a high sense of the ceremonial, with an extraordinary sense of the fragility that belongs to the subject, a sense clearly derived from Shelley. The Shelleyan strain, here as elsewhere, is modified by the eloquent wryness of the later Yeats, as in the second line that follows a Shelleyan declaration of the limits of man's passion:

> Man is in love and loves what vanishes
> What more is there to say?

What enters into this strain in Yeats is a terrifying aesthetic pride, a profound dignity at war with the limitations the poet acknowledges in his subject. For, yet again, Yeats finds himself as a love poet in the Romantic tradition that sets imaginative expectation against natural experience, and that sees no hope for reconciling these contraries.

Yeats's love for Dorothy Wellesley shines forth in the very remarkable published correspondence between the two, and is as difficult to characterize as any human love whatsoever. The most moving letter from the old poet to his aristocratic disciple speaks of her boy-like beauty, her litheness at a particular moment, and responds to this kind of radiance by the poet's wishing that he might be a young woman, so as to be taken into his beloved's arms.[10] There is nothing here requiring psychoanalytic reduction; instead there is the noble pathos of the real man, the imagination, reaching out for a last full range of experience, and finding again that it is experience, and not desire, that shall fail.

The poem, *To Dorothy Wellesley,* is an enduring monument to the relationship, a poem of marmoreal beauty, and an astonishing demonstration of the aged Yeats's rhetorical resources. It begins, in the five lines of its first verse paragraph, with an assertion of the imagination's power over the world of sense and outer things. The hand of the poetess dominates these lines, and implied throughout the poem is her mastery of her art, a mastery that, alas, the merely historical Dorothy Wellesley never possessed. The "midnight of the trees" is moonless, and the dark of the moon is implied again in the poem's tenth line. Deliberately, Yeats sets his love tribute at Phase 1 of his system, and the poem's eighth line adjures the poetess to wait before she begins the act of composition, and to wait "Rammed full/ Of that most sensuous silence of the night." In that midnight, in the dark of the moon, a cycle of creations and destructions is to begin again, and the whole tone of Yeats's poem is to suggest the poetess's almost savage capability not to begin her creation prematurely. A stretch of her hand can reach supernaturally across space, and the trees themselves are but "famous old upholsteries," humanized by generations of touch. The great rhetorical question that is the second half of line eleven, "What climbs the stair?" is answered in the poem's last line. The poetess, like Yeats, has climbed a tower of consciousness in which a torch burns high, as in the natural tower of consciousness at the beautiful close of Keats's *Ode to Psyche*. But the characteristic shock of the late Yeats's mode is given to us at the close. The true poetess is one of the Proud Furies, not natural but *daimonic*, a creature who can share, somehow, in the *ur*-realm of Phase 1, where there is no human incarnation. The lady is worth Yeats's hope, as he says, but only by being removed utterly from our world, the world of "common women." The power of love, the pride of that power, is wonderfully conveyed, but with it we receive also another chilling touch of the great Yeats who is neither humane nor humanistic.

The Statues

Yeats dated this poem 9 April 1938, in the spring of his last year, and clearly intended it to be one of his testaments. It is a cluttered, arrogant poem, much praised by a series of intelligent exegetes, culminating in Whitaker, who sums up its complex relation to its principal sources in Pater, Nietzsche, Spengler, Sturge Moore, and perhaps even Hegel, and observes justifiably that "almost every phrase emerges from a lifelong meditation upon the meaning of history." [11] A poet of enormous gifts can meditate endlessly upon a vital matter, and still compose less than a great poem, if his own prejudices, fashionable and unfashionable, prevent his full humanity from entering into the meditation. In *The Statues*, Yeats's real man, the imagination, sleeps within him, and the necromancer awakens instead, grinding more mummy wheat in the abstract dark of his vision of man and history.

Yeats writes *The Statues* as a defence of Greek form against Asiatic formlessness, thus exalting what Blake had denounced, the Mathematic Form of the Reasoning Memory. Blake's Living Form, Gothic, praised as humanized form also by the major Victorian sages, is missing from Yeats's poem, probably because the poem assimilates Christianity itself to the seething "Asiatic" tide of modern democracy and humanitarianism, "this filthy modern tide" that Yeats sees "we Irish" as fiercely rejecting.

The spirit of *The Statues* is more Spengler's than Pater's, for Pater would have been moved to subtly deprecatory laughter by Yeats's social Pythagoreanism in this poem, though the fundamental rejection of "character" here is based on a Paterian observation. To Pater, the portrait-sculpture of Greece was "characterless, so far as *character* involves subjection to the accidental influences of life." For the Greeks possessed Unity of Being, and so unlike the Romantics they did not need to cultivate an ecstasy *against* the accidental influences of life; they had no cause to seek out the supreme moments of sensation celebrated in Pater's "Conclusion" to his *Renaissance*. Romantic art moves to heal the double division of man, between his consciousness and the outward world, and in his consciousness of himself. But this division is found to be largely inescapable, except in privileged moments, or in the continuous exertion of artistic creation. Yeats, though a Paterian Last Romantic, longs here for what Pater knew could not be. The prose draft of the poem, as cited by Jeffares, praises the victors at Salamis as beating down more than Asia: "Only they could beat down Nature with their certainty." [12] In *On the Boiler,* Yeats actually distinguished "the sexual instinct of Europe" from that of Asia, insisting that Doric sculpture had given a particular "goal, its fixed type" to the European sexual instinct.[13] This is the burden of the first stanza of *The Statues,* and is, at the least, grotesque. Perhaps the first stanza is worse than grotesque when a reader follows out the allusion it makes to a great passage in Blake's *Visions of the Daughters* of *Albion,* for Yeats does not compete very well with Blake at celebrating "the moment of desire."

The poem's second stanza is a recapitulation of *A Vision*'s description of the movement of Greek civilization to and beyond its point of culmination, the Age of Phidias or Phase 15. But the concern for the unique sexual instinct of Europe begins to be a little troublesome, as Yeats writes like a mixture of Kipling and Alfred Rosenberg. An Asiatic sexual tide seems to have been repulsed at Salamis, a "many-headed foam" whose "Asiatic vague immensities" uncomfortably betoken a grosser sexuality than the post-Phidian ideal:

> Europe put off that foam when Phidias
> Gave women dreams and dreams their looking-glass.

It is a little painful to read *The Statues* against the universal background of praise for it by its exegetes, who serve Yeats and us badly by finding high poetic value in the third stanza. Is the crankiness of the following redeemed by its profundity or eloquence?

> One image crossed the many-headed, sat
> Under the tropic shade, grew round and slow,
> No Hamlet thin from eating flies, a fat
> Dreamer of the Middle Ages. Empty eyeballs knew
> That knowledge increases unreality, that
> Mirror on mirror mirrored is all the show.
> When gong and conch declare the hour to bless
> Grimalkin crawls to Buddha's emptiness.

This has been deciphered by the critics, following Yeats, who obligingly began to decipher it in a letter:

> In reading the third stanza remember the influence on modern sculpture and on the great seated Buddha of the sculptors who followed Alexander.[14]

In the *Autobiographies* Yeats associated the portrait of Morris by Watts with "Buddha's motionless meditation," and critics have noted that he remembers that association in this stanza.[15] An image of meditation, associated with both Phidias and Morris, crosses to India in the wake of Alexander. Yeats's Hamlet is a man of action, and *not* the Pre-Raphaelite dreamer who is associated by Yeats with the West's true triumph in setting the archetype for Eastern meditation. Yeats's Hamlet does not know "that knowledge increases unreality," cannot know the Pythagorean metaphysic that defeated the Persians and then flowered more greatly first in Phidias, and then in the Alexandrine synthesis of

East and West. The thin, fly-eating Hamlet of Yeats is a kind of starved cat, a Grimalkin subjected to the massive sensible emptiness of the Buddha. I am not very happy about this reading of stanza three, but the fault is Yeats's, and not his exegetes. There are elaborate readings of stanza three, by Ellmann and Engelberg in particular (Engelberg's receives the palm) but they do not justify the grotesqueness of the stanza any more than my simplistic reductiveness does.[16] It is a bad, crabbed stanza, in a bad poem, and the learned ingenuities of criticism cannot rescue it, or us, from its ugliness. The fourth and final stanza is more lucid, but here the plain nastiness of *On the Boiler* becomes the problem. Is this more tolerable for having been versified?

> When Pearse summoned Cuchulain to his side,
> What stalked through the Post Office? What intellect,
> What calculation, number, measurement, replied?
> We Irish, born into that ancient sect
> But thrown upon this filthy modern tide
> And by its formless spawning fury wrecked,
> Climb to our proper dark, that we may trace
> The lineaments of a plummet-measured face.

If lines four through six of this stanza began with "We Germans" rather than "We Irish," perhaps the critics would see the stanza more clearly for what it is, a disfigured and disfiguring emanation from hatred. Rajan is nobly alone among the critics in seeing, or at least in clearly saying what he sees.[17] But what are the values, aesthetic or otherwise, of this stanza? Pythagorean Fascism is a rather visionary variety of that blight, but is Fascism nevertheless. I find it difficult, as a lover of Blake's poetry, to forgive Yeats the association of his nightmare ideal with Blake's humanism in the carefully placed use of "lineaments" in the last line of the poem. Describing his painting, "The Ancient Britons," Blake wrote:

> The Beauty proper for sublime art, is lineaments, or forms and features that are capable of being the receptacles of intellect; accordingly the Painter has given in his beautiful man, his own idea of intellectual Beauty.[18]

Like Shelley, Blake uses "intellectual Beauty" in the dominant eighteenth-century sense of "intellectual," meaning "spiritual" or "beyond the senses." Yeats's ideal of "We Irish," whether in *The Statues* or *Under Ben Bulben* or *On the Boiler,* has rather more in common with what Blake, in the same passage, calls the Ugly rather than the Beautiful Man. Which of these is closer to the Yeatsian "ancient sect" who must battle "this filthy modern tide" and "its formless spawning fury"?

> The Beautiful Man acts from duty, and anxious solicitude for the fates of those for whom he combats. The Ugly Man acts from love of carnage, and delight in the savage barbarities of war, rushing with sportive precipitation into the very teeth of the affrighted enemy.[19]

I do not know whether its parody is deliberate, but an early scene in Beckett's wonderful novel, *Murphy,* is the best comment I know on Yeats's *The Statues.* Neary, a Pythagorean adept, unhappy in love, seeks to obliterate his lineaments by battering them out against the noble buttocks of Cuchulain that stand as monument to Pearse in the Dublin General Post Office, but is prevented from doing so by the untimely intervention of a policeman, representative of the "calculation, number, measurement" of the Irish State.

News for the Delphic Oracle

It is a relief to turn to this fine lyric after reading *The Statues.* As with the brief lyric, *The Delphic Oracle upon Plotinus,* Yeats closely follows MacKenna's translation of Porphyry's rendition of the Delphic oracle's vision concerning Plotinus in the after-life. Writing on Berkeley, Yeats named his favorite quotations as of July, 1931:

> . . . I forget that gregarious episcopal mask and remember a Berkeley that asked the Red Indian for his drugs, an angry, unscrupulous solitary that I can test by my favourite quotations and find neither temporal nor trivial—"An old hunter talking with

gods, or a high-crested chief, sailing with troops of friends to Tenedos," and the last great oracle of Delphi commemorating the dead Plotinus, "That wave-washed shore . . . the golden race of mighty Zeus . . . the just Aeacus, Plato, stately Pythagoras, and all the choir of immortal love." [20]

Berkeley here is being transformed into the aged Yeats's vision of himself as wild old wicked man, but the favorite quotations have their own reverberations, backward and forward, in Yeats's work, and are akin to those few other touchstones he kept to throughout his life—Shelley's Ahasuerus and Athanase, and Morris's Homeric Heracles moving at once on two levels, among the shades and at the feast of the gods. The quotation from Browning's *Alastor*-like *Pauline* is also cited in *A Vision* to describe Phase 4, whose Will is "Desire for Exterior World" but whose Body of Fate sadly is only "Search." [21] Like the Oracle's vision of Plotinus, the passage of Browning affords insight not only for the lyric under discussion but for many of the *Last Poems:*

> They came to me in my first dawn of life,
> Which passed alone with wisest ancient books,
> All halo-girt with fancies of my own,
> And I myself went with the tale—a god,
> Wandering after beauty—or a giant,
> Standing vast in the sunset—an old hunter,
> Talking with gods—or a high-crested chief,
> Sailing with troops of friends to Tenedos;—
> I tell you, nought has ever been so clear
> As the place, the time, the fashion of those lives.

This is essentially Shelleyan quest—"wandering after beauty" —but in the youthful, Promethean Browning it is also a defiant assertion of what Pater and Yeats would proclaim as the true goal of Romantic quest, the profane perfection of mankind or self-deified men. Yeats finds the same profane perfection in the reception of Plotinus by "the sons of God . . . not however to hold him to judgment but as welcoming him to their consort to which are bidden spirits pleasing to the Gods." [22]

News for the Delphic Oracle is a genuinely playful poem,

wonderfully modulated in tone and rhythm. Its formal ancestors are Shelley's playful mythological lyrics of 1820, particularly *Arethusa* and the *Hymn of Pan,* and once again the peculiar humor of *The Witch of Atlas* where the Witch's beauty draws into sexual worship not only the attractive but also

> Pigmies, and Polyphemes, by many a name,
>   Centaurs, and Satyrs, and such shapes as haunt
> Wet clefts,—and lumps neither alive nor dead,
> Dog-headed, bosom-eyed, and bird-footed.

Nothing more esoteric than Shelley, aside from some phrasing out of Porphyry upon Plotinus, gets into Yeats's poem, much to its advantage. The dew, referred by Wilson to the nectar of Porphyry, the cavern, and Pan are all together in Shelley's high-spirited but plangent *Hymn of Pan,* which will no doubt be vouchsafed esoteric Platonic commentary also, in time.[23] The strength of Yeats's lyric, like its ancestors in Shelley, is a power of robust, urbane, loving mockery of the mythic material employed. The notables in Yeats's poem are not so stately any more, but "golden codgers" and the faery beloved, Niamh, of early Yeats is coldly called "Man-picker," nor is the entry of great Plotinus very hieratic:

> Plotinus came and looked about,
> The salt-flakes on his breast,
> And having stretched and yawned awhile
> Lay sighing like the rest.

It is evidently possible, with enough occult lumber on the mind, to be tone-deaf enough so as to hear these lines as "essentially a moving tribute to Plotinus." [24] But no tribute is paid to any figures of tradition or mythology in this poem; its strength is that it celebrates the flux of sexuality as the exuberance of mankind's imperfect perfection. This is exactly contrary to *Byzantium,* with its systematic disdain for the fury and the mire:

> Straddling each a dolphin's back
> And steadied by a fin,

> Those Innocents re-live their death,
> Their wounds open again.
> The ecstatic waters laugh because
> Their cries are sweet and strange. . . .

Even though Yeats is describing a particular picture he had seen, it is clear enough that he is parodying his own *Byzantium*. Not the purified but the waters of the merely generative sea are ecstatic, and the stanza ends with a rude pitching of the Innocents into the wading choir of love. The final stanza, with its deliberately brutal juxtaposition of a tender Poussin with intolerable music played in Pan's cavern drives home the poem's parodistic lesson:

> Foul goat-head, brutal arm appear,
> Belly, shoulder, bum,
> Flash fishlike; nymphs and satyrs
> Copulate in the foam.

The splendid relish of the poet is hardly to be mistaken. This is not a scorning aloud of mere complexities. The news for the Delphic oracle is that the foam of Aphrodite retains all its properties even "in the stainless place, far from the wrong that mocks at law," and that Plotinus in the after-life has not attained to a Byzantium, nor risen "above the bitter waves of this blood-drenched life, above the sickening whirl, toiling in the mid-most of the rushing flood and the unimaginable turmoil." [25] Nor need we believe that the "angry, unscrupulous" man who wrote this poem found Pan's music "intolerable" or that foam "bitter."

Long-legged Fly

This uncanny lyric is one of Yeats's subtlest triumphs, a miraculous attuning of diction, rhythm, and profound satisfaction in the creative moment, Blake's "pulsation of an artery." Blake is behind the poem, but Pater more directly so, for the movement of the mind upon silence is the Paterian movement of sensations and impressions that must speed up so as to produce the hard flame, burning like a diamond, that aesthetic apprehension demands. The Stevens of *An Ordinary Evening in New Haven XII,* provides a direct analogue to the Yeats of *Long-legged Fly,* with Pater as the likely link, being as he is a direct ancestor of both poets. Stevens seeks to speak "the poem as it is/ Not as it was," and tries to center the poem "in the area between is and was," by means of "a casual litter" in which the self, the town, and the weather came together and "said words of the world are the life of the world." *Long-legged Fly,* to me anyway, is not as satisfying as this; Yeats too has only "a casual litter" to offer, but he is more hieratic even than Pater and cannot accept an aesthetic reality of shifting surfaces. *Long-legged Fly* would be still more persuasive if it were more casual, its greatest image being its most casual, that of Helen practising "a tinker shuffle/ Picked up on a street." But Yeats is pressing hard though subtly in this lyric, seeking to justify the extravagant claim that art alone engenders and preserves the sexual cycles in civilizations. *The Statues* founders on that claim, and on much else besides; *Long-legged Fly* survives the extravagance.

Partly this is because Yeats is too cunning to give us an image of the artist at work until the close of the poem. The poem's refrain is an answer to the powerful question that ends Shelley's *Mont Blanc,* addressed by poet to mountain:

> Winds contend
> Silently there, and heap the snow with breath
> Rapid and strong, but silently! Its home
> The voiceless lightning in these solitudes
> Keeps innocently, and like vapour broods
> Over the snow. The secret Strength of things
> Which governs thought, and to the infinite dome
> Of Heaven is as a law, inhabits thee!
> And what were thou, and earth, and stars, and sea,
> If to the human mind's imaginings
> Silence and solitude were vacancy?

Shelley here displaces the Spirit that first moved over the silence of the abyss. Its brooding and secret Strength inhabits Mont Blanc, but what would even that mountain be if the human mind moving upon silence did not find what would suffice? The mountain and its attendant phenomena are part of the war of the sky against the mind, and the mind moves to oppose its own imaginings, a violence from within, against this violence from without. Shelley scarcely needs assimilation to Stevens's language here, or to Yeats's. *Long-legged Fly* records three privileged moments of the creative trance, as *Mont Blanc* records one such moment. Shelley's moment is awesome, but concerns only a confrontation between nature and a solitary poet. Yeats's moments trace a wider pattern; historical power, the power of beauty, the power of art over fecund nature. I hear only one speaker in Yeats's poem, the poet himself, who intercedes magically as a keeper of solitude for Caesar, Helen, Michael Angelo:

> Quiet the dog, tether the pony
> To a distant post;
>
> Move most gently if move you must
> In this lonely place.
>
> Shut the door of the Pope's chapel,
> Keep those children out.

What is unique to Yeats is his sense of the precariousness of this moment of reverie before action. So he masterfully re-wrote the middle injunction, against disturbing Helen, from:

> Show much politeness, gentleness,
> Ceremony in this place.

Caesar prepares for the great battle to save civilization not by studying his war maps, but by aimless reverie, "his eyes fixed upon nothing." Helen (or Yeats's Helen, Maud Gonne) shows the secret of her fascination for poets:

> She thinks, part woman, three parts a child,
> That nobody looks; her feet
> Practice a tinker shuffle
> Picked up on a street.

In movement, this is as skilled as anything in Yeats. She prepares her power as Caesar prepared his, by that sheer inadvertence in which the arrow goes more surely to its mark. Neither labors as Michael Angelo does, in the final stanza, where his absorption is the completeness of the working artist's, all his being gathered into his moving hand. There is no inadvertence here, and the relation between the stanza and the unchanging refrain is therefore different the third time round:

> Like a long-legged fly upon the stream
> His mind moves upon silence.

The greatest artist, through labor out of Unity of Being, does what the geniuses of action and love do effortlessly through abandoning their minds to the stream's movement. All the artist's discipline takes him only where nature brings a man of action or a great beauty. The balance is redressed because the effect is more basic. Caesar's battle may save one civilization, and Helen's love start a whole new cycle of culture, but the claim for art is more audacious, as it was in *The Statues*.

A Bronze Head

The materials of *A Bronze Head* are unpromising; the obsession with re-birth, the eugenic rage of *On the Boiler*, the former lover's distaste for his ideal's long-played *persona* of "dark tomb-haunter," swathed in mourning, and visiting prominent burial-grounds as a political protest. The poem easily could have joined a score of fustian pieces in the *Last Poems*, outbursts of the *Why should not Old Men be Mad* variety:

> A girl that knew all Dante once
> Live to bear children to a dunce;
> A Helen of social welfare dream,
> Climb on a wagonette to scream.

Presumably these are Iseult and Maud Gonne, to both of whom Yeats had proposed marriage, in vain. However little a reader cares for the *Last Poems* (I speak only prophetically, as I seem to be the only reader made very unhappy by them so far), he will be startled by sudden and extraordinary imaginative recoveries among them. *A Bronze Head* is an exalted poem, transfiguring its materials. It opens with the poet visiting a museum, and reacting there in the manner of Pater, who had remarked that "a museum . . . oftenest induces the feeling that nothing could ever have been young." Staring there at a head of Maud Gonne, he is afflicted by a sense of what he takes to be her death-in-life (she was to outlive him by many years). Of his former vision he sees only "human, superhuman, a bird's round eye," fit for a mythic beauty. Awesomely, there follows a vision of Maud as she is, searching the sky for a non-existent sign, to redeem her life's defeat:

> What great tomb-haunter sweeps the distant sky,
> (Something may linger there though all else die;)
> And finds there nothing to make its terror less
> *Hysterica passio* of its own emptiness?

Lear's *hysterica passio* haunted Yeats. To hold down the mad violence rising from within is here more difficult because the madness is a terror of an inner abyss. Maud Gonne has become a figure rather like Blake's Enion at the close of "Night I" of *The Four Zoas,* living at the verge of non-entity, redeemable only by a distant apocalypse. Yeats's mood will grow apocalyptic at the poem's end, but a complex tenderness fortunately intervenes. The lover in the poet remembers the dark tomb-haunter as once she was, or seemed to be:

> . . . her form all full
> As though with magnanimity of light,
> Yet a most gentle woman; who can tell
> Which of her forms has shown her substance right?

There are four forms here, not just two: the Shelleyan epipsyche, effluent with glory; an actual woman, as in *Adam's Curse;* the tomb-haunter of the present; the superhuman *antithetical* incarnation, whose hawk-like eye will be invoked again in the final stanza. To the genuinely open question he has asked, Yeats has no answer, unless the extreme idealism of the philosopher McTaggart be right, and all four forms be true at once. This is a Spenserian answer to the dilemma of substance and form, and is consonant with the complex myth of the Gardens of Adonis. But Yeats is too troubled here to stand so securely at one of the sources of his poetic tradition, and does not affirm the composite-ness of substance. Of the four forms, the vision of light is no longer possible, and the "most gentle woman" and the "dark tomb-haunter" realistically are seen as one:

> But even at the starting-post, all sleek and new,
> I saw the wildness in her and I thought
> A vision of terror that it must live through
> Had shattered her soul.

Both Maud and her poet were involuntary prophets; the wild-ness of the filly's freedom is at one with the crone's emptiness. What follows this mutual realization is Yeats at his greatest, bringing together clairvoyance and a pathos of immense nobility:

> Propinquity had brought
> Imagination to that pitch where it casts out
> All that is not itself: I had grown wild
> And wandered murmuring everywhere, "My child, my child!"

Imagination that casts out all that is not itself is definitive of poetic apocalypse. Yeats himself, apprehending his beloved's doom, acquired her wildness, which was no way to protect her (or to win her). And for the victim of such consciousness of self, raised to an absolute pitch, there was no way to go but the way down and out that led to the tomb-haunter. There remains the fourth form, the supernatural, to which Yeats gives the last stanza, completing a sweep back to the opening lines. Unfortunately, the last stanza is a descent from the magnificence of the third. If the apocalyptic "sterner eye" did look through Maud Gonne's eye, as in the statue, it saw only as Yeats's eye at its most prejudiced saw. The decline and fall of a "foul world" needs better evidence than the spirit of *On the Boiler* provides:

> . . . gangling stocks grown great, great stocks run dry,
> Ancestral pearls all pitched into a sty. . . .

This means that the young ladies of the poet's acquaintance are marrying badly, in his opinion, scarcely a conclusion of apocalyptic import, and less than this poem deserved of Yeats.

The Apparitions

> Then I went to luncheon with Virginia, who gave me an imitation of Yeats telling her why he was occult. He has been confirmed in this theory because he saw a coat-hanger emerge from his cupboard and travel across the foot of his bed; next night, it emerged again, clothed in one of his jackets; the third night, a hand emerged from one of the cuffs; the fourth night—"Ah! Mrs. Woolf, that would be a long story; enough to say, I finally recovered my potency."

> Harold Nicolson, *Diaries,* 9 November 1934 [26]

Though this has not been one of the more admired of the last poems, it is one of the more admirable, and refreshingly honest. Yeats's best poems of self-revelation tend to be involuntary, rather like the confessional intensities of Browning that make their way into his dramatic monologues despite all his efforts contrariwise. Only when he intimates his own skepticism as to after-life or rebirth is Yeats very interesting on the Last Things. *The Apparitions* is based on a group of death dreams, and ends in the spirit of *The Man and the Echo,* but its true subject is Yeats's rather subtle skepticism, toward natural and supernatural alike. "Because there is safety in derision," he begins, and we fear we are in for rant, as at the disfiguring close of *A Bronze Head,* with its "heroic reverie mocked by clown and knave," but Yeats has better judgment here. Not even *Long-legged Fly* is as skilled in the use of a refrain as *The Apparitions.* He sought safety, he tells us, from the popular eye, and so chose to talk about an apparition, rather than be plausible, but

> *Fifteen apparitions have I seen;*
> *The worst a coat upon a coat-hanger.*

The dream is real enough, and its prophecy terrible to any man. In the second stanza, he goes on to the social joy of "half solitude," and the entertainer's freedom to yield to phantasmagoria with an indulgent friend as listener, and again the refrain enters its insistent counter-song. Until the music deepens, and a declaration almost as moving as the one concluding *A Dialogue of Self and Soul* comes forth:

> When a man grows old his joy
> Grows more deep day after day,
> His empty heart is full at length,
> But he has need of all that strength
> Because of the increasing Night
> That opens her mystery and fright.
> *Fifteen apparitions have I seen;*
> *The worst a coat upon a coat-hanger.*

This is the true answer to *A Bronze Head;* it is Yeats's own heroic humanism, free of rancor, bitterness, eugenic claptrap, and occult mummery. He will not turn into a dark tomb-haunter, nor climb his boiler to rant upon it. *Hysterica passio* comes of the heart's emptiness, and Yeats knows better than his hostile critics (such as myself) how much *hysterica passio* there is in his *Last Poems.* But there is also a joy, not a tragic joy (which is nothing but *hysterica passio* disguised), but a growing natural joy, filling the depths of the empty heart. It is a joy of natural knowledge, purchased at the cost of power, unlike *antithetical* joy, but purchased at a good price. The knowledge is a finding of limited good, of a strength allowing mystery to be faced without mystification, and fright without mythology. As knowledge, it is skeptical even of skepticism; the apparitions do come, even though in dreams of the night, and they do prophesy accurately (they gave him five more years, which is what he had). And, if the account he gave Virginia Woolf was accurate, they gave him more than that.

The Circus Animals' Desertion

This poem, in manuscript, first was called *Despair* and then *On the Lack of a Theme,* before Yeats was found by the inevitable title. Parkinson gives the text of a rejected last stanza:

> O hour of triumph come and make me gay!
> If burnished chariots are put to flight
> Why brood upon old triumph, prepare to die;
> Even at the approach of the un-imaged night
> Man has the refuge of his gaiety;
> A dab of black enhances every white,
> Tension is but the vigour of the mind,
> Cannon the god and father of mankind.[27]

Parkinson rightly says that the stanza was well rejected, as it "shows a superficiality of perception that could come only from weariness and neglect," but I do not agree that it "was not close to Yeats's heart." [28] Yeats, at the end, returned to the insight of Shelley's Demogorgon: "The deep truth is imageless," but he awaited the "un-imaged night" with the convictions he had been strengthening for a lifetime, and one of these was definitively phrased by him in that last couplet, little as we like it. *The Circus Animals' Desertion* is a distinguished poem, probably a permanent one, but it is not made any more humane by substituting the present last stanza for the one above. The poem gained by being made less explicit, but its nature was not radically altered. I think Yeats's critics tend to misread the famous revised conclusion:

> Now that my ladder's gone,
> I must lie down where all the ladders start,
> In the foul rag-and-bone shop of the heart.

This is not at all an affirmation, and hardly a tribute to the holiness of the heart's affections. Nor is it the kind of assault upon nature that Blake makes when he speaks so bitterly of the selfish virtues of the natural heart. Yeats is being true both to his Gnosticism and to his Romanticism, and Gnostic Romanticism, whether in Kafka or Yeats, finds its sublime in the grotesque, here the heart seen as grotesque.

More than the four death poems, *The Circus Animals' Desertion* shows us what Yeats's difficulties as a poet would have been had he lived for a few more years, though the two superb death poems, *The Man and the Echo* and *Cuchulain Comforted*, intimate something of these difficulties. The *Last Poems* are both a fulfillment and a devastation of the Yeatsian myth, much as *The Triumph of Life* was for Shelley's. The poet is in despair for the lack of a theme, but he has gone beyond the possibility of finding a fresh one. Yeats's last letters and last poems show again the almost superhuman vitality of his imagination, so that these difficulties would have been overcome, but Yeats would have passed into yet another phase of his art in doing so. The change might have been as radical as that between *The Wind Among the Reeds* and *In the Seven Woods*. But further surmise must wait upon an account of *The Circus Animals' Desertion*, and the death poems.

In *Vacillation* Yeats allows the Heart the poetic honor of taking up the Self's struggle against the Soul, of making the claim for personality against character. *The Circus Animals' Desertion* is something of a palinode in relation to *Vacillation*, in that Yeats chooses the heart again, but without affection or respect for it. To be satisfied with one's heart as poetic theme is to acknowledge what it pained Yeats to recognize, that his concern was not with the content of the poetic vision, as Blake's was, but with his relation as poet to his own vision, as Wordsworth's was, and Shelley's and Keats's also. There are very few poets in English whose subject is the content of poetic vision, but Blake is certainly among them. Browning and Stevens are poets who developed from one concern to the other, and ended with the content of the poetic vision as their subject. This is hardly a question of greater or lesser fortune among poets; to choose between the two kinds is a choice of greatnesses, as in a reader's ultimate preference between Blake and Wordsworth. But it is a misfortune for a poet to mistake his natural kind. In *The Circus Animals' Desertion*, Yeats discovers his kind with considerable bitterness, but this is a bitterness that possesses aesthetic dignity.

His circus seasons are over, and the properties of his mythologies are on the dump:

> I sought a theme and sought for it in vain,
> I sought it daily for six weeks or so.
> Maybe at last, being but a broken man,
> I must be satisfied with my heart. . . .

The triple use of "sought" emphasizes the abandonment of quest, and the "must" the deep reluctance of the poet to deal only with his own affective life, after a career of powerful phantasmagoria, and of the seeking of many masks. The poem's central section, perhaps the three most remarkably controlled stanzas in the *Last Poems,* form a miniature history of that career. Critics of Yeats can learn from the poet's choice of his three crucial works: *The Wanderings of Oisin, The Countess Cathleen,* and *On Baile's Strand.* Here the three books of *Oisin* are characterized as "vain gaiety, vain battle, vain repose," all "themes of the embittered heart," starved for Maud Gonne. *The Countess Cathleen* is seen strictly as the culpability of its heroine, crazed by the pity that Blake denounced as dividing the soul. Though the fanatic heart of Maud Gonne is being condemned, one of Yeats's subtlest swerves of meaning takes place, as the enchantment of the poetic vision itself replaces the genetic circumstance. When *On Baile's Strand* is reached, the fight of Cuchulain with the tide intimates the genesis of thwarted passion again, but the enchantment of art is now thoroughly dominant. The poet's phantasmagoria, complete and masterful images grown in pure mind, rises above all genesis, until age brings the poet down. Though fallen upon the reductive, Yeats does not accept it, any more than Stevens does in his *Man on the Dump.* This is not praise of the dump:

> A mound of refuse or the sweepings of a street,
> Old kettles, old bottles, and a broken can,
> Old iron, old bones, old rags, that raving slut
> Who keeps the till.

We are so delighted by this exuberance of particulars that we forget the delight is gone. Yeats regrets all his ladders, Platonic and otherwise. To know where all the ladders start is not to prefer the start to the higher rungs. Yeats is not Stevens's Mrs. Alfred Uruguay; his errors are those of the expansionists, not the reductionists. He *must* lie down, he says, but he has not *chosen* "the foul rag-and-bone shop of the heart."

25: The Death Poems

The Man and the Echo

The triumph of *The Circus Animals' Desertion,* Yeats's equivalent of Stevens's *Man on the Dump,* is the prelude to Yeats's four "death poems," which carry on from the poet's desperate resolve to begin again in the heart. Of these four poems—*The Man and the Echo, Cuchulain Comforted, The Black Tower,* and *Under Ben Bulben*—one can remark that they allow a last view both at Yeats's characteristic achievements and his failures. The first two are among the very best of his poems, the third is given to posturing, and the fourth, though famous, is for the most part a poor poem, with some remarkable passages but much bluster as well. Here again, a comparison of Yeats to Stevens is revealing. Stevens's parallel death poems, poised before a nothingness since Stevens accepted no beliefs, are *As You Leave the Room* and *Of Mere Being,* more open than the Yeats poems, and more of a farewell tribute to the dignity of human life. Stevens's poems touch outward reality, the persistence of the world that will survive the poet, but here the advantage is not necessarily his. He is in the

line, here as elsewhere, of Wordsworth and Keats even as Yeats is
again in that of Blake and Shelley, refusing to recognize any reality that can triumph over the human.

The Man and the Echo, in the draft version given by Dorothy
Wellesley, is even more a poem of personal remorse than Yeats allowed it to be in the final version.[1] Addressing the oracular cleft
of Alt on Ben Bulben as though it were another Delphi, Yeats
shouts his secret to the stone:

> All that I have said or done
> Now that I am old and ill
> Seems to have done but harm, until
> I lie awake night after night
> I never get the answer right.

The third line in this outcry became "Turns into a question
till," when Yeats, in revision, was warier of passing a Last Judgment upon himself. As question, it better suits the profound and
noble skepticism of this poem, which ends in the two greatest of
Yeats's genuinely open questions:

> O Rocky Voice,
> Shall we in that great night rejoice?
> What do we know but that we face
> One another in this place?

If the first question is addressed to Shelley's Ahasuerus, the
second might be directed to his Demogorgon, and with as little
hope of a reply. Unlike *The Black Tower* and *Under Ben Bulben,* this poem has something better to do than affirm again the
myth of a "composite God" of historical process. Yeats, like us,
does not know, knows that he does not know, and is willing to tell
the truth. The dialogues between character and personality are
ended; the stony answer of the Echo is either "Lie down and die"
or "Into the night." Yet Yeats is not in the despair of what Blake
called Ulro, the solipsistic self-absorption of obsessive doubt. He is
where Shelley was, at "the verge where words abandon us, and
what wonder if we grow dizzy to look down the dark abyss of how
little we know." And though he must die soon, he is not ready to

take Echo's advice to lie down and die. The Man of this poem has the Heracles of *A Vision* in him, and knows also that he will work to the end in the spirit of Blake's Milton:

> To cleanse the Face of my Spirit by Self-examination
> To bathe in the Waters of Life; to wash off the Not Human
> I come in Self-annihilation & the grandeur of Inspiration
>
> To cast off the idiot Questioner who is always questioning
> But never capable of answering. . . .[2]

Even so Yeats speaks of the great work of cleaning man's dirty slate, and standing at last in judgment on his own soul.

Cuchulain Comforted

Dorothy Wellesley, in her account of Yeats's last days, gives "the prose theme" of *Cuchulain Comforted,* as Yeats read it aloud to her. In it, one of the shades says:

> . . . you will like to know who we are. We are the people who run away from the battles. Some of us have been put to death as cowards, but others have hidden, and some even died without people knowing they were cowards. . . .[3]

That final group is not in Yeats's poem. The great puzzle of this very authoritative poem, one of the most inevitable that Yeats wrote, is why Cuchulain the hero finds himself among the cowards in the after-life. Part of the clue may be in the omitted group of "the prose theme." Is Yeats not, in this poem, facing his own, his human death, thinking that he will die, with some personal cowardice unknown? Yet this is the poet who stirringly asked the massive rhetorical question: "Why should we honor those that die upon the field of battle?" and added the magnificent explanation: "A man may show as reckless a courage in entering into the abyss of himself." [4] *Cuchulain Comforted* will always have the authority of mystery about it; Yeats chose to write it in his hieratic mode, and he found for it a tone of revelation imperfectly apprehended, a half-light that darkens into religion.

What compels many readers of the poem is a sense of Yeats's own involvement here in the Last Things. Now, they seem to say, he enters into the abyss of himself.

Helen Vendler, in her fine analysis of the poem, illuminates it by its Dantesque overtones. Yeats, at the end, is still Blake's disciple, and as the old Blake worked to correct Dante's vision by the eternally apocalyptic light of his own, so Yeats, neither a Christian believer nor yet a disbeliever in *any* revelation whatsoever, including the Christian, appears to work here to modify Dante's vision into his own. "They had changed their throats and had the throats of birds," Yeats chants at the close, echoing subtly, as Mrs. Vendler shows, Dante's vision of Brunetto Latini as one who somehow seemed victorious and not defeated, though condemned to the Inferno.[5] There is no sense at the close of *Cuchulain Comforted* that the cowards have been defeated, either in this life or in the after-world. We are given instead an obscure sense of appropriateness, and we do not feel the hero dishonored when he ends surrounded by a choir of his contraries, and presumably becomes identical with them. The appropriateness is presented as an enigma, the formal equivalent in the poem of Yeats's own doubts about the hero, and perhaps also about his own potential for heroism.

Cuchulain, in the poem, exchanges an individual meditation on wounds and blood for a sharing in a communal activity of stitching, and of singing a communal song. The quick of Yeats's invention is in this, in a movement against his own deepest convictions, as in *The Man and the Echo*. Perhaps this is in part what Conor Cruise O'Brien means, in his helpful essay on Yeats's politics, when he ends with a note on *Cuchulain Comforted,* saying that the poem "may contain the fall of Fascism." [6] Cuchulain, according to "a Shroud that seemed to have authority," involuntarily frightens the shrouds by the rattle of his arms, "mainly because of what we only know." The mystery of the poem centers in that unique knowledge of the shrouds, which may be the burden of their song when they begin to sing. They have neither human tunes nor words, which means, in the terms of *A Vision,* that they are not in any stage of the *Meditation* (as Mrs. Vendler thinks) for they have cast off all of their lives except their cowardice. But they certainly are not "pure souls who have escaped from the round of birth and death," as Wilson thinks, for they do remain cowards.[7] Evidently they are at the end of the state Yeats calls the Shiftings, but still in it until the very last line of the poem, when they enter the state of Beatitude. Cuchulain is just behind them, and is in the act of passing out of the Phantas-magoria or third phase of the state of Meditation into the Shift-ings in the course of this poem (see pp. 270–271 of my discussion of *A Vision*). Yeats's systematic account of the life-after-death or death-between-lives is relevant here, and it works in the poem, provided that we get it right, but I do not think it strictly neces-sary for apprehending this poem. The Shrouds are more advanced in the purgatorial process than Cuchulain is, but do not reach the climax of it themselves until "They had changed their throats and had the throats of birds," a change in which Cuchulain must and will follow them. In this restricted sense only is *Cuchulain Comforted* what Yeats himself called it, a sequel to *The Death of Cuchulain*. In that play Cuchulain, just before his death, has a vi-sion of the after-life:

> There floats out there
> The shape that I shall take when I am dead,
> My soul's first shape, a soft feathery shape,
> And is not that a strange shape for the soul
> Of a great fighting-man?

And, to the Blind Man who is groping at his neck and asking if he is ready, he affirms:

> I say it is about to sing.

That line, and the last of *Cuchulain Comforted,* have a triumph in them, which must be a guide to the mystery of the lyric. The Shrouds, poor things that they are, serve as Virgils to Cuchulain's Dante, or perhaps as a composite Brunetto Latini. The hero lingers in the Meditation (sixth line of the poem), but they instruct him how his life can grow much sweeter if he will emulate them in undergoing the Shiftings. At the end of the Shift-ings, the completeness which to Yeats means justice has been brought about, and cowards and the hero are blended in one company. But the mystery abides; what is it that they know which makes them still afraid? The systematic answer, out of *A Vision*, is too simplistic to be adequate to the poem's majesty. Being further on in purgation, they know what the hero cannot yet know, that all must live again, and being not yet in the Beatitude, they are still cowardly enough to fear arms. There is a deeper possibility, worthier of the poem's splendor, and more fitting for Yeats's augmenting obsession with his own final isolation. They know what Yeats knows, that the communal experience is as momentary in death as it is in life. What they truly fear is what Cuchulain the hero will never fear, despite all systems and their gradings. They fear the solitude of the soul's rebirth, and experience a proleptic fear when they encounter the hero. Despite the promise of *A Vision*, and the apparent degradation of the hero, they too stand in a Last Judgment upon themselves.

The Black Tower

While both *The Man and the Echo* and *Cuchulain Comforted* are among Yeats's double handful of central poems, and *Under Ben Bulben*, for all its flaws, has the prestige of being Yeats's "official" death poem, *The Black Tower*'s only distinction is that it is Yeats's very last poem, being dated 21 January 1939, just a week before he died. The drafts of the poem (as transcribed by Stallworthy) show that it started as an apocalyptic defiance by the men of "this high lonely place" who wait for the wind to blow "from the black pig's dike," that place where the Yeats of the early poem, *The Valley of the Black Pig*, and of *The Celtic Twilight*, had expected "an Armageddon which shall quench all things in the Ancestral Darkness again." *The Black Tower*, even in its final version, has this apocalyptic urgency, but too little is done in the poem's actual text to show that the urgency is justified.

It has been suggested, by W. J. Keith, that *The Black Tower* is an Arthurian poem, deriving from the legend of the Castle of Sewingshields.[8] Arthur and his court sleep there until the king's great horn be blown again. Though this detail gets into the poem it is not developed, nor are the associations of the tower with towers in Shelley and Browning, as noted by some critics, very convincing. Whoever the men of the old black tower are, they have Yeats's approval, as they wait hopelessly for the cycles of civilization to turn over. But do they merit our interest? The poem, dated 21 January 1939, is Yeats's final effort; must we take it, with *Under Ben Bulben,* for his testament?

Without enthusiasm, we evidently must. The prose draft, as given by Stallworthy, is almost a manifesto: "I speak for the gyres of the black tower," and Mrs. Yeats is the authority for the scholarly tradition that the poem's subject is political propaganda.[9] The soldiers of Yeats's army are destitute, "their money spent, their wine gone sour," but they stand fast, like the heroic dead in their tombs, against the banners of the modern world, which Yeats dies hating. The poem's only grace, rather less than a saving one, is "the tower's old cook," a grotesque catcher of small birds in the morning, while the obdurate and stronger warriors "lie stretched in slumber." Whether the bird-catcher has heard what he claims to hear, Arthur's horn blown again, the poem does not tell us. It matters only that the soldiers do not believe him. If there is irony here, we can hope it is Yeats's own, turned against his own obduracy, as he waits and does not wait for a horn he does not expect ever to hear. As for the cook, one can honor Ellmann's wry suggestion that he represents the poetic imagination, and still feel that this had better not be the case.[10] The sublime may have fallen into the grotesque in our time, but hopefully not so far.

Under Ben Bulben

Johnson thought Gray's two fine Pindaric odes a pair of cucumbers. *Under Ben Bulben* (first entitled by Yeats *His Convictions*) seems to me to merit that particular vegetal comparison more than Gray's poems do. It also merits Winters's description of it as giving "a clear summary" of Yeats's "ideas and attitudes" as a "final statement." I do not recall, in my reading of available criticism of Yeats, anyone stating what is perhaps too palpable to be worth the stating, how bad and distressing the poem is. In Section V of the poem, Irish poets are admonished to learn their trade, a crucial lesson being to scorn "base-born products of base beds." By ignoring the squalid present, the Irish bards will preserve their nation:

> Cast your mind on other days
> That we in coming days may be
> Still the indomitable Irishry.

One grants that nothing else in the poem is that bad, but readers might wonder about some of the convictions which they are being bequeathed. The moral center of the poem is Section III, which quotes and approves "Send war in our time, O Lord!" from the *Jail Journal* of the nineteenth-century Irish revolutionary, John Mitchel. Yeats's prayer was to be answered soon enough after his death, though the war's outcome was not what he would have wished. That is of small consequence. What matters a great deal, to me but surely to others as well, is the critical reception that Yeats's prayer has received. Whitaker is representative of many other Yeats critics when he says that Section III of *Under Ben Bulben* "reminds us of a *wisdom* known by us as individuals" (italics mine). This wisdom tells us "that any individual may attain proximately—through that doubling of the intellect, that unification of conscious and unconscious, which completes his partial mind—the state of vision." [11] What Section III says clearly is that violence is, in itself, a positive good and indeed a necessity for man. Only when a man is "fighting mad" does he complete his partial mind, only then is his blindness dispelled and his heart at peace. Very simply, if you would become a visionary, or find your work, or choose your mate, engage first in "some sort of violence," a war if at all possible. That Yeats, as a good Gnostic, was being true to himself here, we need not doubt, but perhaps his vision should begin to be recognized as what it was.

There is nothing new in *Under Ben Bulben;* it summarizes the ideas and images of many of the *Last Poems*. But something should be said of its conscious summoning of Romantic tradition, and abuse of that tradition.

Yeats begins this formal presentation or grand testament of his convictions by invoking his authorities, poetic and supernatural, Shelley and the Sidhe. The chosen image from Shelley is the "choice sport" of the enigmatic Muse of myth-making, the Witch of Atlas, her voyage by the Mareotic Lake, to learn the wisdom that, Yeats says, "set the cocks a-crow," even as the cocks of Hades in their crowing are elected for analogue in *Byzantium*. What wisdom? Presumably that,

> Though grave-diggers' toil is long,
> Sharp their spades, their muscles strong,
> They but thrust their buried men
> Back in the human mind again.

But the Witch of Atlas, pragmatically speaking, is a more drastic humanist:

> For on the night when they were buried, she
>   Restored the embalmers' ruining, and shook
> The light out of the funeral lamps, to be
>   A mimic day within that deathy nook;
> And she unwound the woven imagery
>   Of second childhood's swaddling bands, and took
> The coffin, its last cradle, from its niche,
> And threw it with contempt into a ditch.

Here are two dramatically conceived but essentially lyric gestures, with Yeats's clearly being derived from Shelley's. They are not otherwise related though, for Yeats means his to be read all but literally. Shelley's Witch is unwinding imagery; Shelley is attacking those who make too much of death. Yeats is making a great deal of it, for his "human mind" is located within what Shelley deprecates as "a mimic day within that deathy nook."

The gist of what Yeats means is in his charge to poet, sculptor, and painter when he bids them "Bring the soul of man to God/ Make him fill the cradles right," for these cradles are also coffins, and most certainly are what Shelley means when he calls the coffin the last cradle of second childhood. Yeats invokes Blake and the two finest of Blake's disciples in his old age—Palmer and Calvert—but he is not to be judged as being any more in their spirit here than in Shelley's. It will always be salutary to ask readers of *Under Ben Bulben* to juxtapose Yeats and Blake in letters each writes as he knowingly approaches his death, for here the final issue of Yeats's romanticism can be seen and judged:

> To-day I am full of life and not too disturbed by the enemies I must make. This is the proposition on which I write: "There is now overwhelming evidence that man stands between two eternities, that of his family and that of his soul." I apply those beliefs to literature and politics, and show the change they must make.[12]

> I have been very near the Gates of Death & have returned very weak & an Old Man feeble & tottering, but not in Spirit & Life not in The Real Man The Imagination which Liveth for Ever. In that I am stronger and stronger as this Foolish Body decays.[13]

Yeats's vitalism is its own overwhelming evidence, and much more impressive than anything in *Under Ben Bulben*. His application of that vitalism is something else again, whether in literature or politics. His vision is of Man standing between two eternities, but hardly representing an eternity in himself. Blake's vitalism is unabated; the body decays, but its growing weakness is only a foolishness, and not a Gnostic evidence against its eternity. The Imagination of Man, in Blake's vision, does not stand between eternities, for the Real Man the Imagination never dies. Life is the Imagination, and needs no evidence of survival. Much in even the *Last Poems* knows this, but Yeats wanted to know more. Whether his imaginative legacy will prove to be in poems like *The Man and the Echo* and *Cuchulain Comforted,* or in poems like *The Black Tower* and *Under Ben Bulben,* will be for generations of his readers to decide.

Conclusion:

The Composite God

> Poetry is a purging of the world's poverty and change and evil and death. It is a present perfecting, a satisfaction in the irremediable poverty of life.
>
> Wallace Stevens

The late Martin Buber had a convincing distaste for all gnosis, and expressed it pungently with regard to Jung's doctrines of the self. Yeats was not Jung, but Buber's criticisms apply equally well to him, despite the disclaimer of one excellent Yeats scholar.[1] One need not believe in a transcendent God, as Buber certainly did, to feel the force of an essentially humanist attack on all those who believe in the contemporary "composite God" of "possession by process, that is by unlimited causality." The desperate freedom Yeats imported into *A Vision* as the Thirteenth Sphere is born of a Swiftian passion absolutely central to the poet in his final days, but it does not alter the irony that *A Vision* remains only another example of what Buber called "the dogma of gradual process," by which the quasi-historical thought of our time has worked "to establish a more tenacious and oppressive belief in fate than has ever before existed."

Yeats knew himself to be the heir of a great tradition in poetry, of the visionaries who have sought to make a more human man, to resolve all the sunderings of consciousness through the agency of the imagination. When Blake claimed his imagination's freedom, he cried out: "my Path became a solid fire, as bright/ As the clear Sun; & Milton, silent, came down on my Path." Blake was one of the Instructors who came down on Yeats's path, but he failed to do for Yeats what Milton had done for him. Shelley called our minds "mirrors of the fire for which all thirst," and Yeats is most moving when he asks "What or who has cracked the mirror?" His answer is "to study the only self that I can know, myself, and to wind the thread upon the pern again." [2] But his desire remained to speak with more than the voice of a solitary ego, and a lifetime of pursuing communal voices in gnosis mastered him, and made him a minion of the "composite God" that his best imaginings scorned. Against *A Vision,* and the poems written out of it, the voice that is great within us rises up, and asks a freedom that Yeats did not allow. One longs for Yeats's comment on the following critique, while feeling for him nevertheless the reverence due to the last of the High Romantics, the last of those poets who asserted imaginative values without the armor of continuous irony. That so great and unique a poet abdicated the idea of man to a conception of destiny, however Homeric, is not less than tragic, for

He misuses the name of destiny: destiny is not a dome pressed tightly down on the world of men; no one meets it but he who went out from freedom. But the dogma of process leaves no room for freedom, none for its most real revelation of all, whose calm strength changes the face of the earth—reversal. This dogma does not know the man who through reversal surmounts the universal struggle, tears to pieces the web of habitual instincts, raises the class ban, and stirs, rejuvenates, and transforms the stable structures of history. This dogma allows you in its game only the choice to observe the rules or to retire: but the man who is realizing reversal overthrows the pieces. The dogma is always willing to allow you to fulfill its limitation with your life and "to remain free" in your soul; but the man who is realising reversal looks on this freedom as the most ignominious bondage.[3]

Notes

Chapter 1. Introduction

1. Jorge Luis Borges, "Kafka and His Precursors," *Labyrinths* (New York, 1964), 201.

2. *The Poetry and Prose of William Blake,* ed. David V. Erdman (New York, 1965), 137.

3. Geoffrey H. Hartman, "False Themes and Gentle Minds," *Philological Quarterly,* vol. xlvii, No. 1 (January 1968), 59.

4. G. H. Hartman, *Wordsworth's Poetry, 1787–1814* (New Haven, 1964) 296–7.

5. A. C. Bradley, *Oxford Lectures on Poetry* (Bloomington, 1961), 240–44.

6. For a full study of Wordsworth's influence on *Alastor,* see H. L. Hoffman, *An Odyssey of the Soul* (New York, 1933), *passim.*

7. Lady Augusta Gregory, *Cuchulain of Muirthemme* (London, 1903), 352–3.

8. Frederick A. Pottle, *Shelley and Browning* (Chicago, 1923), 36.

9. Blake, 189, 320.

10. *Shelley, Poetical Works,* ed. Thomas Hutchinson (London, 1943), 15.

11. Hoffman, 44, compares Shelley's Poet to Ovid's Narcissus.

12. Shelley, 160–61.

13. There is no general study of the influence of Shelley's poetry. Roland A. Duerksen, *Shelleyan Ideas in Victorian Literature* (The Hague, 1966) confines itself to the effect of Shelley's reformist and socialist views, citing (p. 14) the famous judgment of Marx: "Those who understand them and love them rejoice that Byron died at thirty-six, because if he had lived he would have become a reactionary *bourgeois;* they grieve that Shelley died at twenty-nine, because he was essentially a revolutionist and he would always have been one of the advanced guard of socialism."

14. A crucial text here is the "Dedication" to *The Revolt of Islam.* These fourteen stanzas (Hutchinson, 37–40) comprise the fullest account of poetic incarnation in English until Whitman's *Out of the Cradle Endlessly Rocking,* and may have been Shelley's most influential lines.

15. Yeats, *Essays and Introductions* (New York, 1961), 192.

16. Yeats, *Letters to the New Island,* ed. Horace Reynolds (Cambridge, Mass., 1934, 97.

17. *The Letters of W. B. Yeats,* ed. Allan Wade (New York, 1955), 46.

18. In 1929, Yeats writes Mrs. Shakespear (*Letters,* 759) that "I have turned from Browning—to me a dangerous influence—".

19. *Letters,* 781.

20. "Essay on Shelley," *Browning, Poetry and Prose,* ed. S. Nowell-Smith (London, 1950), 677.

21. Betty Miller, *Robert Browning: A Portrait* (London, 1952), 9.

22. Ibid., 168.

23. *Essays and Introductions,* 70.

Chapter 2. Late Victorian Poetry and Pater

1. Yeats, *Autobiographies* (London, 1955), 302–3.

2. Yeats, *The Oxford Book of Modern Verse* (New York, 1936), ix.

3. *Autobiographies,* 302.

4. *Oxford Book, ix.*

5. Wallace Stevens, *Opus Posthumous* (New York, 1957), 213.

Chapter 3. The Tragic Generation

1. *Oxford Book, xi.*

2. *Autobiographies,* 311.

3. Yeats, *A Vision* (New York, 1961), 130. Hereafter, *Vision* B.

4. *Autobiographies,* 305.

5. Thomas Whitaker, *Swan and Shadow: Yeats's Dialogue with History* (Chapel Hill, 1964), 260–62.

6. *The Complete Poems of Lionel Johnson*, ed. Ian Fletcher (London, 1953), 346.

7. Ibid., 346–7.

8. *Autobiographies*, 312.

9. Ibid., 313–14.

10. Ibid., 313

11. *Complete Poems of Johnson*, xiv.

12. Ibid., 347. Fletcher is quoting Taylor's translation of Plotinus, *Enneads* VI. ix. For a more sustained reading of *The Dark Angel* than my own, see the excellent essay by Fletcher in *Interpretations*, ed. John Wain (London, 1955), 155–78. Fletcher emphasizes Johnson's transcendence of the self, which the critic finds "altogether at variance with the poem's inward situation." (173)

13. *Autobiographies*, 315.

14. *Vision B*, 130.

Chapter 4. Shelley and Yeats

1. *Autobiographies*, 62–4.

2. Richard Ellmann, *Yeats, The Man and the Masks* (New York, 1948) 48–9.

3. *Autobiographies*, 64.

4. Ibid., 171–3.

5. Shelley, 456.

6. *Essays and Introductions*, 65.

7. Ibid., 424–5.

8. *Autobiographies*, 65.

Chapter 5. Blake and Yeats

1. *Essays and Introductions*, 509.

2. Blake, 37.

3. *Essays and Introductions*, 510.

4. Ibid., 405.

5. Ibid., 518.

6. Blake, 707.

7. Ibid., 318.

8. Quoted by Ellmann, *The Man and the Masks*, 6.

9. *The Collected Poems of Wallace Stevens*, 374.

10. Blake, 394.

11. J. B. Yeats, *Letters to His Son W. B. Yeats and Others 1869–1922*, ed. with a memoir by Joseph Hone (New York, 1946), 93.

12. *Autobiographies*, 114.

13. Ibid., 161.

14. The previous studies are: Hazard Adams, *Blake and Yeats: The Contrary Vision* (Ithaca, 1955), 44–56, and Deborah Dorfman, *Blake in the Nineteenth Century* (New Haven, 1969), 190–226.

15. Dorfman, 216.

16. *The Works of William Blake, Poetic, Symbolic, and Critical,* ed. E. J. Ellis and W. B. Yeats, three vols. (London, 1893), I, 238.

17. Ibid., 239–40.

18. Printed in Adams, *Blake and Yeats,* 287.

19. Ellis-Yeats, 241.

20. *Essays and Introductions,* 195.

21. See Ellmann's discussion, *The Man and the Masks,* 20.

22. A. N. Jeffares, *A Commentary on the Collected Poems of W. B. Yeats* (Stanford, 1968), 54.

23. Yeats, *Mythologies* (New York, 1959), 356–7.

24. Ellis-Yeats, 239.

25. Ibid., 240.

26. Ibid., 242–3.

27. Ibid., 243.

28. Whitaker, 6–7.

29. Ellis-Yeats, 249.

30. Ibid., 259–60.

31. Ibid., 288.

32. Ibid., 289.

33. Ibid., 290.

34. Ibid., 294.

35. Ibid., 331.

36. *Essays and Introductions,* 112.

37. *Vision* B, 137.

38. *Essays and Introductions,* 112.

39. Ibid., 114.

40. Ibid., 117.

41. Blake, 38.

42. *Essays and Introductions,* 119.

Chapter 6. Anglo-Irish Poetry and *The Wanderings of Oisin*

1. *Letters,* 447.
2. *Letters,* 446.
3. *Essays and Introductions,* 94–5.
4. Browning, 673.
5. Whitaker, 315 n. 87.
6. *Essays and Introductions,* 61.
7. Ibid., 112.
8. Ibid., 113.
9. Browning, 687.
10. *Letters,* 798.
11. Yeats, *Explorations* (New York, 1962), 392–3.
12. Whitaker, 22–8; Ellmann, *The Man and the Masks,* 51–2.

Chapter 7. Early Lyrics and Plays

1. *Vision* B, 140.
2. Ibid., 109.
3. Northrop Frye, *Fables of Identity* (New York, 1963), 222.
4. *Essays and Introductions,* 53, 64.
5. Louis MacNeice, *The Poetry of W. B. Yeats,* with a foreword by Richard Ellmann (New York, 1969), 11.
6. Ibid., 61.
7. Thomas Parkinson, *W. B. Yeats, Self-Critic* (Berkeley, 1951), 32.
8. Ibid., 137.
9. *The Variorum Edition of the Poems of W. B. Yeats,* ed. Peter Allt and Russell K. Alspach (New York, 1957), 846, 842.
10. Ellmann, *The Man and the Masks,* 187.
11. Parkinson, 157 ff.
12. Yvor Winters, *The Poetry of W. B. Yeats* (Denver, 1960), 3.
13. Parkinson, 13–14; Frank Kermode, *Romantic Image* (London, 1961), 96–102.
14. Balachandra Rajan, *W. B. Yeats* (London, 1965), 24–7.

Chapter 8. The Wind Among the Reeds

1. *Autobiographies,* 321.
2. Ellmann, *The Man and the Masks,* 159. See *Variorum Poems,* 800.
3. *Last Poems and Plays* is exactly contrary to this, in theme.
4. A. N. Jeffares, *W. B. Yeats, Man and Poet* (New Haven, 1949), 100–103.
5. Ian Fletcher, "Rhythm and Pattern in Autobiographies," in *An Honoured Guest,* ed. D. Donoghue and J. R. Mulryne (New York, 1966), 177.
6. *Variorum Poems,* 800.
7. *Essays and Introductions,* 8.
8. Richard Ellmann, *The Identity of Yeats* (New York, 1954), 313–14.
9. Ibid., 251.
10. Blake, 391.

Chapter 9. The Shadowy Waters

1. David R. Clark, *Half the Characters Had Eagles' Faces: W. B. Yeats' Unpublished "Shadowy Waters," The Massachusetts Review,* Autumn-Winter 1964–5, 151–80.
2. Ibid., 154.
3. Ibid., 171–2.
4. *Letters to the New Island,* xii.
5. *Letters,* 454.
6. Parkinson, *Yeats, Self-Critic,* 59–75, S. B. Bushrui, *Yeats's Verse-Plays: The Revisions, 1900–1910* (Oxford, 1965), 16–33.
7. Ellmann, *Identity,* 84.
8. *Letters to the New Island,* ix.
9. Clark, 165.
10. Ibid., 152–3.
11. *Essays and Introductions,* 90.
12. Ellmann, *Identity,* 80–81.
13. *Essays and Introductions,* 71–2.
14. Maud Gonne, *Yeats and Ireland,* in *W. B. Yeats, Essays in Tribute,* ed. Stephen Gwynn (Port Washington, N. Y., 1965), 32.

Chapter 10. The Middle Plays

1. Peter Ure, *Yeats the Playwright* (London, 1963), 133–4.
2. *The Variorum Edition of the Plays of W. B. Yeats,* ed. Russell K. Alspach (New York, 1966), 712.
3. Ibid., 1167.
4. Giorgio Melchiori, *The Whole Mystery of Art* (London, 1960), 38–51.
5. Ibid., 53.
6. *Variorum Plays,* 713.
7. Ibid., 713.
8. Ibid., 713. For "a Shelley and a Dickens in the one body," see *Essays and Introductions,* 296.
9. *Variorum Plays,* 316.
10. Bushrui, 117–19.
11. *Autobiographies,* 511.
12. *Variorum Plays,* 315.
13. Blake, 159. See also *Essays and Introductions,* 47.
14. Ellmann, *The Man and the Masks,* 166–7.
15. Bushrui, 68.
16. For a directly contrary view, see Ellmann, *The Man and the Masks,* 167.
17. *Letters,* 425.
18. Ellmann, *The Man and the Masks,* 19.
19. J .B. Yeats, *Letters,* 125.
20. *Letters,* 548–9; *Autobiographies,* 470–71.
21. J. B. Yeats, *Letters,* 62–3.
22. *Letters,* 549.
23. *Autobiographies,* 123.
24. *Variorum Plays,* 480.
25. *Explorations,* 415–16; *Variorum Plays,* 397.
26. *Variorum Plays,* 391, 389.
27. *Vision B,* 131, 137, 148, 169.

Chapter 11. The Middle Poems

1. Corinna Salvadori, *Yeats and Castiglione* (Dublin, 1965), 3, 40, 83.
2. Maud Gonne MacBride, *A Servant of the Queen* (London, 1938), 328–30.

3. Winters, 6.
4. Rajan, 69.
5. Blake, 37.
6. George Moore, *Hail and Farewell; Vale* (London, 1947), 113.
7. *Variorum Poems*, 820.
8. Whitaker, 158; Ellmann, *Identity*, 114.
9. Moore, 115.

Chapter *12*. Toward *A Vision: Per Amica Silentia Lunae*

1. *Letters*, 624.
2. *Essays and Introductions*, 509–10.
3. *Autobiographies*, 274 n.
4. *Mythologies*, 332. See the epigraphs to my book for a possible source.
5. Blake, 254.
6. *Explorations*, 60.
7. Shelley, "Notes on *Queen Mab*."

Chapter *13*. *The Wild Swans at Coole*

1. See Graham Martin's essay on the volume, in *An Honoured Guest*, ed. Donoghue and Mulryne, 55.
2. *Jeffares, Commentary*, 154.
3. For a different view of the contrast with Shelley, see Melchiori, 106–7.
4. Ellmann, *Identity*, 253.
5. Kermode, 30.
6. Winters, 15.
7. D. J. Gordon, *W. B. Yeats, Images of a Poet* (Manchester, 1961), 32.
8. Kermode, 40.
9. Gordon, 33–4.
10. Ibid., 34.
11. Ibid., 36.
12. *Autobiographies*, 23.
13. Letter to J. B. Yeats, quoted in: Joseph Hone, *W. B. Yeats, 1865–1939* (New York, 1962), 295.
14. *Essays and Introductions*, 78.
15. Quoted in Adams's *Blake and Yeats*, 287.
16. Whitaker, 69.

Chapter 14. A Vision: The Great Wheel

1. Helen Hennessey Vendler, *Yeats's Vision and the Later Plays* (Cambridge, Mass., 1963), 1–5.

2. Whitaker, 3–8.

3. Ellmann, *The Man and the Masks,* 30.

4. *Vision* B, 135–6.

5. *Limbo,* in *Coleridge, Poetical Works,* ed. E. H. Coleridge (London, 1912), 430.

6. Philip Rieff, *Freud: The Mind of the Moralist* (New York, 1967), 382.

7. Ellis-Yeats, I, 242.

8. Ibid., 288.

9. Northrop Frye, "The Rising of the Moon: A Study of 'A Vision'," in *An Honoured Guest,* ed. Donoghue and Mulryne, 10–12.

10. Ellmann, *The Man and the Masks,* 96.

11. Philip Rieff, *The Triumph of the Therapeutic* (New York, 1966), 130–31.

12. The definitive essay in this regard remains Conor Cruise O'Brien's "Passion and Cunning: An Essay on the Politics of W. B. Yeats," *In Excited Reverie,* ed. A. N. Jeffares and K. G. W. Cross (New York, 1965), 207–78.

13. *Letters,* 917.

14. Shelley, 15.

15. Frye, "The Rising of the Moon," 32–3; Whitaker, 134, 281.

16. *A Vision* (London, 1925), xi. Hereafter, *Vision* A.

17 Ibid., 14–15.

18. Ibid., 14 n.

19. *Vision* B, 82.

20. *Vision* B, 73. The preceding definitions are from *Vision* A, 15.

21. *Mythologies,* 337; on the source of the term, *antithetical,* see *Vision* B, 72.

22. *Vision* A, 17–18.

23. *Essays and Introductions,* 356. The "double contemplation" just previous is from *Vision* B, 94.

24. *Vision* B, 83.

25. *Mythologies,* 335 n.

26. He also misinterpreted, partly through ignoring the context, *Jerusalem* 54:12.

27. *Mythologies,* 336–7.

28. *Vision* A, 27.

29. *Vision* B, 136–7.

30. Ibid., 27.

31. Ibid., 28.

32. Whitaker, 302 n. 22, quotes H. W. Nevinson noting in a 1916 diary that Yeats "talked of Freud and Jung and the Subconscious Self, applying the doctrine to art."

33. Ellmann, *The Man and the Masks,* 7–20.

34. *Vision* B, 136.

35. Ibid., 105.

36. Ibid., 105.

37. Ibid., 108.

38. Ibid., 140.

39. Ibid., 141.

40. Ibid., 142.

41. Ibid., 143.

42. Ibid., 138–9.

43. Ibid., 138.

44. Ibid., 138–40.

45. Ibid., 132.

46. *Variorum Plays,* 566.

47. *Among School Children,* l. 34; in a note, *Variorum Poems,* 828, Yeats gave Porphyry's commentary on Homer's Cave of the Nymphs as his source for the phrase. For Stevens see *Collected Poems,* 315–16: "It seems/ As if the health of the world might be enough./ It seems as if the honey of common summer/ Might be enough. . . ."

48. *Vision* B, 131.

49. Ibid., 107.

50. Ibid., 134.

51. Ibid., 134.

52. Ibid., 140.

53. Ibid., 140.

54. Ibid., 140.

55. Ibid., 131–2.

56. Ibid., 147.

57. Ibid., 151.

58. Ibid., 154.

59. Ibid., 163. See *Oxford Book of Modern Verse,* xxxiv–xxxv.

60. Ibid., 165.

61. Ibid., 167.

62. Blake, 254.

63. *Vision* B, 179.

64. Ibid., 182.

65. Ibid., 182.

66. Blake, 62.

Chapter 15. *A Vision:* The Dead and History

1. Emerson, *Journals,* entry June 1852. Most readily available in *Selections from Emerson,* ed. S. E. Whicher (Boston, 1960), 327. For Emerson on history and the Sphinx, see Whicher's note, 501. Yeats may have been affected by Emerson's use of the Sphinx as the image of the "relation between the mind and matter," for which see Emerson's *Nature* IV, 3 (Whicher, 36).

2. *Vision* B, 187.

3. Ibid., 187–8.

4. Blake, 387.

5. *Vision* B, 184.

6. Ibid., 190.

7. Wallace Stevens, *The Necessary Angel* (New York, 1951), 76–7.

8. *Letters on Poetry from W. B. Yeats to Dorothy Wellesley* (London, 1964), 177.

9. *Vision* B, 226.

10. Ibid., 226.

11. Ibid., 233.

12. Ibid., 233.

13. Blake, 193.

14. *Vision* B, 234, as is the next passage quoted, which follows it directly.

15. Ibid., 193.

16. Ibid., 202.

17. Ibid., 210.

18. Ibid., 210–11.

19. Ibid., 193.

20. Ibid., 211; Blake, 222.

21. Ibid., 235.

22. Ibid., 236.

23. Ibid., 238.

24. Ibid., 239.

25. Ibid., 239.

26. Ibid., 239.

27. Ibid., 240.

28. Ibid., 263.

29. Whitaker, 95.

30. Whitaker, 93.

31. *Vision B*, 268.

32. Ibid., 269.

33. D. J. Gordon, *Images of a Poet*, 84.

34. Richard Ellmann, *Eminent Domain* (New York, 1967), 14–22.

35. *Vision B*, 270–71.

36. Ibid., 275.

37. Ibid., 161.

38. Ibid., 275.

39. Shelley, *Hellas*, 692–703, in *Poetical Works*, 468.

40. *Vision B*, 279.

41. Whitaker, 89.

42. *Vision B*, 279–80.

43. Ibid., 292–3.

44. Ibid., 294.

45. Ibid., 295.

46. Ibid., 296.

47. Ibid., 297–8.

48. *Vision A*, 212–13.

49. Ibid., 215.

50. *Vision B*, 302.

Chapter 16. Four Plays for Dancers

1. *Essays and Introductions,* 226.

2. Ibid., 222.

3. Ibid., 235.

4. *Explorations,* 64; Yeats gives an account of Noh, 64–68. It should be noted that the close of the essay on p. 70 prophesies the close of *A Vision,* employing the same Homeric vision of Heracles among the shades.

5. *Essays and Introductions,* 54.

6. Blake, 34.

7. Peter Faulkner, *William Morris and W. B. Yeats* (Dublin, 1962), 12.

8. *The Collected Works of William Morris* (London, 1913), Vol. XVIII, I, 109.

9. F. A. C. Wilson, *Yeats's Iconography* (New York, 1960) 59–69; Rajan, 97; Vendler, 206.

10. Ure, 70.

11. *Vision* B, 126 ff.

12. Ibid., 128.

13. *Mythologies*, 337.

14. *Variorum Plays*, 378.

15. Wilson, *Iconography*, 126–7.

16. Whitaker, 266.

17. Vendler, 220.

18. Ibid., 224–5.

19. Ibid., 226.

20. Ibid., 226.

21. Wilson, *Iconography*, 227–30.

22. David R. Clark, *W. B. Yeats and the Theatre of Desolate Reality* (Dublin, 1965), 43–59.

23. *Variorum Plays*, 777.

24. *Variorum Poems*, 601.

25. Blake, 359.

26. *The Revolt of Islam*, 1. 3394.

27. *Variorum Plays*, 789.

28. *Autobiographies*, 171; Vendler, 172–3; Wilson, *Iconography* 174–7; Ellmann, *Eminent Domain*, 22–23.

29. Vendler, 173–4.

30. *Variorum Plays*, 790.

Chapter 17. Michael Robartes and the Dancer

1. On the biographical conetxt, see: John Unterecker, *A Reader's Guide to William Butler Yeats* (New York, 1959), 163–4; Jeffares, *Commentary*, 234–5.

2. See Peter Ure, "Yeats's *Demon and Beast*," *Irish Writing*, 31 (1955).

3. Priority here seems to rest with G. Wilson Knight's great book, *The Starlit Dome* (London, 1941) 219, 225. See the discussions by Donald Weeks, "Image and Idea In Yeats's *The Second Coming*," *PMLA*, 53 (1948), 281 ff., and in my *Shelley's Mythmaking* (New Haven 1959, Ithaca, 1969), 93–5.

4. Jon Stallworthy, *Between the Lines, Yeats's Poetry in the Making* (Oxford, 1963), 16–25.

5. Ellmann, *Identity*, 290.

6. Stallworthy, 20.

7. Donald Davie, *"Michael Robartes and the Dancer,"* in *An Honoured Guest,* ed. Donoghue and Mulryne, 78.

8. Stallworthy, 20, 22.

9. Ibid., 22.

10. In the drafts, Yeats begins with a hawk, not a falcon. The falcon may have been suggested by the Egyptian Sphinx in the Temple of Abu Simbel, particularly if Yeats read Petrie's *History of Egypt* (we know that he had read Petrie's *Revolutions of Civilization*). Abu Simbel's Sphinx is the falcon-headed Harmachis the Sun-god, but the falcon is found also in sculptures showing the Pharaoh as Horus the War-god; Yeats's Sphinx has both associations, sun and war. There may be also some deep level of association for Yeats between the literal meaning of Sphinx, based on a verb for drawing tight or squeezing, and the drawing-tight of the *primary* gyre in Yeats's own time. The blank gaze suggests not only the Egyptian Sun-god, but the Late Romantic Sphinx of the Decadent poets and painters, who emphasized the Sphinx as a central image of woman's solipsistic self-absorption, or what Blake had called the Female Will. For Blakean analogues, see Northrop Frye, *Fearful Symmetry* (Princeton, 1947), 140, 302.

11. Blake, 72–3.

12. Shelley's *Poetical Works*, 222.

13. Ibid., 377.

14. Conor Cruise O'Brien, "Passion and Cunning: Politics of Yeats," in *Excited Reverie,* ed. Jeffares and Cross, 276.

15. For a contrary view, see the excellent reading in Vendler, 99.

16. Jeffares, *Commentary*, 242.

17. I find support now for my view of the meaning of "ceremony" in Anne Butler Yeats's remark that this "sense of ceremony" sees "ceremony as an approach to things." The remark is in Marilyn G. Rose, "A Visit With Anne Yeats," *Modern Drama,* 7 (December 1964), 303. My source however is Joseph Ronsley, *Yeats's Autobiography, Life as Symbolic Pattern* (Cambridge, Mass., 1968), 132.

18. Winters, 10.

19. *Essays and Introductions*, 420.

20. *Shelley's Poetical Works*, 268.

21. Blake, 551.

22. Blake, 763. Erdman notes that this is not part of the text of *The Four Zoas* "but aphoristic comment upon it":

> Unorganized Innocence, an Impossibility
> Innocence dwells with Wisdom but never with Ignorance

Yeats had transcribed *The Four Zoas* from manuscript, and so presumably had encountered this Blakean distinction as early as 1889 or thereabouts.

23. John Sparrow recorded a conversation with Yeats that took place at Oxford in May 1931. Yeats cited the description of sexual intercourse in Lucretius as being the finest ever written: "The tragedy of sexual intercourse is the perpetual virginity of the soul." See Jeffares, *Yeats, Man and Poet*, 267.

Chapter 18. Later Plays

1. Ellmann, *The Man and the Masks*, 212.
2. *Variorum Plays*, 1306.
3. F. A. C. Wilson, *W. B. Yeats and Tradition* (New York, 1958), 180–85.
4. Ure, 144.
5. Vendler, 127, 135.
6. Ibid., 135–6.
7. Ellmann, *The Man and the Masks*, 172.
8. Browning's influence was dangerous because when Yeats yielded to it at all, he tended to yield altogether. Thus the early *How Ferencz Renyi Kept Silent* (1887), *Variorum Poems*, 709–15, recalls Browning in nearly every line, and subsequent narratives, *Baile and Aillinn* (1901), *The Two Kings* (1912) and *The Gift of Harun Al-Rashid* (1923) show the continuity of the influence. Yeats never learned to write verse narrative, because he could not find a direction away from Browning's kind of narrative.
9. Browning, 671.
10. Ellmann, *The Man and the Masks*, 172.
11. *Vision* B, 82.
12. Ibid., 141.
13. Ibid., 141.
14. Ellmann, *The Man and the Masks*, 173.
15. Ure, 140.
16. *Variorum Plays*, 935.
17. Ellmann, *Identity*, 260–62.
18. Ibid., 261.
19. Shelley, 479–80.
20. Shelley, 477.
21. *Autobiographies*, 315.
22. Vendler, 145.

23. Unpublished material, cited by Jeffares, *Man and Poet*, 58, 59.

24. Ibid., 59; *Variorum Plays*, 997.

25. Whitaker, 284–90.

26. Rajan, 159.

27. Stevens, *Collected Poems*, 390.

28. Whitaker, 285.

29. Ibid., 286.

30. Ibid., 288.

31. Stevens, *Collected Poems*, 239.

32. Whitaker, 289.

Chapter 19. The Tower

1. F. L. Gwynn, "Yeats's *Byzantium* and Its Sources," *Philological Quarterly*, XXXII, I, Jan. 1953, 9–21.

2. Melchiori, 218–25.

3. Whitaker, 274.

4. Curtis Bradford, "Yeats's Byzantium Poems: A Study of Their Development," in *Yeats*, ed. John Unterecker (Englewood Cliffs, N.J., 1963), 93–130.

5. Shelley, 51.

6. Bradford, 98.

7. Blake, 373.

8. *W. B. Yeats and T. Sturge Moore, Their Correspondence, 1901–1937*, ed. Ursula Bridge (New York, 1953), 162.

9. Stallworthy, 89–90.

10. A fuller study than this book can be, of Yeats's place in the tradition of displaced or internalized quest-romance, would relate the "sailing" of this lyric not only only to *The Wanderings of Oisin* and *The Shadowy Waters*, and their source in *Alastor*, but to the many versions of sea-quest in later nineteenth-century poetry. Yeats had read many more minor poets of the generation just before his own than most of his scholars have.

11. Bradford, 111.

12. Ibid., 102.

13. Blake, 157.

14. Bradford, 101.

15. Whitaker, 198, 201.

16. See the tribute to "the great reverie of the Pope in *The Ring and the Book*, with all its serenity and quietism," in *Letters to the New Island*, 97.

17. *Mythologies,* 241.

18. Whitaker, 198.

19. Winters, 5.

20. *Vision* B, 268.

21. *Variorum Poems,* 827.

22. Jeffares, *Man and Poet,* 225.

23. Blake, 342.

24. *Vision* B, 144.

25. Jeffares, *Man and Poet,* 224.

26. Shelley, *A Defense of Poetry.*

27. Whitaker, 225; Vendler, 118.

28. Blake, 95.

29. Shelley, 21.

30. Ellmann, *Identity,* 176.

31. Shelley, 243.

32. Winters, 7.

33. Whitaker, 108.

34. Unterecker, 189–90; Ellmann, *Identity,* 264.

35. *The Prelude,* V, 416–25.

36. Whitaker, 274–5.

37. *Letters,* 722.

Chapter 20. The Winding Stair

1. Stevens, *Collected Poems,* 377.

2. I offer little comment on this elegy, because of my admiration for Ian Fletcher's "Yeats and Lissadell," in *W. B. Yeats 1865–1939,* ed. D. E. S. Maxwell and S. B. Bushrui (London, 1965).

3. Besides Whitaker, consult the lucid discussion in Priscilla Shaw, *Rilke, Valéry, and Yeats: The Domain of the Self* (New Brunswick, 1964).

4. *Explorations,* 151.

5. *Vision* B, 73.

6. Whitaker, 215.

7. *Variorum Poems,* 831.

8. Ibid., 827.

9. Winters, 17.

10. Jeffares, *Commentary,* 344.

11. *Essays and Introductions,* 85.

12. Denis Donoghue, "On *The Winding Stair*," *An Honoured Guest*, ed. Donoghue and Mulryne (New York, 1966), 120–21.

13. Jeffares, *Commentary*, 350.

14. Vendler, 114; Cleanth Brooks, Jr., "Yeats: The Poet as Myth-Maker," *The Permanence of Yeats*, ed. Hall and Steinmann (New York, 1961), 76–81.

15. Whitaker, 112.

16. D. J. Gordon, *Images of a Poet*, 86.

17. Ibid., 81–9; Melchiori, 200–34; Gwynn, "Yeats's *Byzantium* and Its Sources."

18. Bradford, "Yeats's Byzantium Poems," 116–30; Stallworthy, 115–36.

19. Stallworthy, 117, 123.

20. Winters, 12.

21. Gordon, 89.

22. *Essays and Introductions*, 80.

23. Unpublished prose by Yeats, quoted in Jeffares, *Commentary*, 353.

24. Winters, 12.

25. Vendler, 117–18.

26. Whitaker, 225.

27. Ellmann, *Identity*, 221–2.

28. Brooks, 76.

29. Brooks, 84; Winters, 12.

30. Ellmann, *The Man and the Masks*, 272.

31. Ellmann, *Identity*, 268–9.

32. Ibid., 270.

33. *Letters*, 788, where *Vacillation* is called *Wisdom*.

34. Curtis B. Bradford, *Yeats at Work* (Carbondale, 1965), 129.

Chapter 21. Words for Music Perhaps

1. *Variorum Poems*, 831.

2. Walter E. Houghton, "Yeats and Crazy Jane: The Hero in Old Age," *The Permanence of Yeats*, ed. Hall and Steinmann, 330.

3. Ellmann, *Identity*, 275; Unterecker, 226.

4. Jacob Needleman, *Being in the World, Selected Papers of Ludwig Binswanger* (New York, 1967), 342–49.

5. *Variorum Poems*, 831.

6. *Autobiographies*, 249.

7. Ellmann, *Identity*, 276; Jeffares, *Commentary*, 372.
8. Thomas Parkinson, *W. B. Yeats, The Later Poetry* (Berkeley, 1964) 77, 211–13.
9. *Mythologies*, 354.
10. Needleman, 343.
11. *Mythologies*, 336–7; *Jerusalem* 54:6–12.
12. *Letters*, 758.
13. Wilson, *Tradition*, 211–16; Rajan, 150–51.
14. *Explorations*, 368.
15. E. M. Cioran, *The Temptation to Exist*, trans. Richard Howard (Chicago, 1968), 45.

Chapter 22. Supernatural Songs

1. Whitaker, 112–13, 115.
2. *Letters*, 805; Blake, *Jerusalem* 69:43–4; Milton, *Paradise Lost*, VIII, 620–29.
3. *Letters*, 824.
4. Ellmann, *Identity*, 283.
5. *Vision B*, 302.
6. *Variorum Poems*, 837–8.
7. Whitaker, 112.
8. *Milton* 41:1–7.
9. *Letters*, 828–9.
10. Ellmann, *Identity*, 283; Whitaker, 119.
11. Ellmann, *Identity*, 233–4.
12. *Yeats and Sturge Moore: Correspondence*, 154.
13. Whitaker, 117.
14. Ibid., 118.
15. *Letters on Poetry;* see particularly the letter of May 4, 1937, pp. 135–6, upon which so much of Whitaker's argument relies. But what is the tone of "You must feel plunged as I do into the madness of vision," if there is not desperation in it as well as extravagant exultation?
16. Hone, 436.

Chapter 23. The Last Plays

1. Ure, 156; Whitaker, 292.
2. Rajan, 164.

3. Vendler, 160.

4. *Variorum Plays*, 1311.

5. *Autobiographies*, 348–9.

6. *Explorations*, 441.

7. Whitaker, 272.

8. Vendler, 240.

Chapter 24. The Last Poems

1. *Letters on Poetry*, 173.

2. Blake, 655.

3. Jeffares, *Man and Poet*, 289–90.

4. *Letters on Poetry*, 8.

5. Ellmann, *Identity*, 187. For Yeats on the poem, *Letters on Poetry*, 83.

6. *Oxford Book of Modern Verse*, xxxv.

7. Wilfred Owen, *Strange Meeting*.

8. *Letters on Poetry*, 113.

9. Yeats probably confused Owen's "pity" with the Urizenic "pity" that Blake condemned. Owen's "pity" is rather of the same imaginative kind as Blake's "that which pitieth" in *Europe*, which in the Creation-Fall is changed "to a devouring flame." Yeats could not conceive of a "pity" that would belong to the Blakean Prolific rather than the Devouring, but Blake and Owen could.

10. *Letters on Poetry*, 108. See also, 113.

11. Whitaker, 235.

12. Jeffares, *Commentary*, 490.

13. *Explorations*, 451.

14. Letters, 911.

15. *Autobiographies*, 87.

16. Ellmann, *Identity*, 189; Edward Engelberg, *The Vast Design; Patterns in W. B. Yeats's Aesthetic* (Toronto, 1964), 202–3.

17. Rajan, 184.

18. Blake, 535.

19. Ibid.

20. *Essays and Introductions*, 408–9.

21. *Vision* B, 110.

22. From MacKenna's version of Porphyry's *Life of Plotinus*, as quoted in Jeffares, *Commentary*, 390.

23. Wilson, *Tradition*, 219.

24. Ibid., 220.
25. MacKenna's version of Porphyry on Plotinus; Jeffares, *Commentary*, 388.
26. Harold Nicolson, *Diaries and Letters, 1930–39*, ed. Nigel Nicolson (London, 1966), 188.
27. Parkinson, *The Later Poetry*, 174.
28. Ibid., 175.

Chapter 25. The Death Poems

1. *Letters on Poetry*, 179–81.
2. Blake, 141.
3. *Letters on Poetry*, 193.
4. Unpublished material, quoted by Ellmann, *The Man and the Masks*, 6.
5. Vendler, 248.
6. O'Brien, "Passion and Cunning: Politics of Yeats," 278.
7. Wilson, *Tradition*, 248.
8. W. J. Keith, "Yeats's Arthurian Black Tower," *Modern Language Notes*, 75 (Feb. 1960). I owe this reference to Jeffares, *Commentary*, 514.
9. Stallworthy, 223, 227.
10. Ellmann, *Identity*, 209.
11. Whitaker, 264.
12. *Letters*, 910.
13. Blake, 707.

Conclusion: The Composite God

1. Whitaker, 50.
2. *Mythologies*, 364.
3. Martin Buber, *I and Thou*, 2nd edition (New York, 1958), 57.

Index